Social Policy in the United Sta

PRINCETON STUDIES IN AMERICAN POLITICS: HISTORICAL,
INTERNATIONAL, AND COMPARATIVE PERSPECTIVES

SERIES EDITORS
IRA KATZNELSON, MARTIN SHEFTER, THEDA SKOCPOL

Social Policy in the United States

FUTURE POSSIBILITIES IN HISTORICAL PERSPECTIVE

Theda Skocpol

PRINCETON UNIVERSITY PRESS

PRINCETON, NEW JERSEY

Selection, Introduction, and conclusion copyright © 1995 by Princeton
University Press
Published by Princeton University Press, 41 William Street,
Princeton, New Jersey 08540
In the United Kingdom: Princeton University Press,
Chichester, West Sussex

Library of Congress Cataloging-in-Publication Data

Skocpol, Theda.
Social policy in the United States : Future possibilities in historical
perspective / Theda Skocpol.
p. cm. — (Princeton studies in American politics)
Includes bibliographical references.
ISBN 0-691-03786-8
ISBN 0-691-03785-x (pbk.)
1. United States—Social Policy. 2. Welfare state. I.Title. II. Series.
HN57.S525   1994   94-13215
361.6'1'0973-dc20   CIP

This book has been composed in Sabon

Princeton University Press books are printed on acid-free paper and meet
the guidelines for permanence and durability of the Committee on
Production Guidelines for Book Longevity of the Council on Library
Resources

Printed in the United States of America

Third printing, and first paperback printing, 1995

10 9 8 7 6

Contents

Acknowledgments

I AM GRATEFUL to Steven Mintz for suggesting that this selected collection of my essays on American social policy be pulled together and published. Walter Lippincott, Jr., the Director of Princeton University Press, is a longtime friend and professional associate, and I am very glad to have worked with him on this book. My thanks to Bill Laznovsky, Jennifer Matthews, and others at Princeton University Press who did such a fine job on the production and advertising. I also greatly appreciate Margie Towery's work on the Index. Many others contributed to parts of this collection, and I have tried to thank them in the notes to the individual chapters.

Social Policy in the United States

American Social Policies:
Future Possibilities in Historical Perspective

DEBATES about fundamental reworkings of national social policy are at the center of U.S. politics—and are likely to remain there for the foreseeable future. Some debates are hardy perennials that keep recurring. "Welfare reform," for example, has come up at least once a decade since the 1950s, and President Bill Clinton's boldly declared intention to "end welfare as we know it" is only the most recent version of a long-standing aspiration to substitute wage-earning jobs for dependency on public aid by the poor.

The idea that Social Security for the American elderly may be "too expensive" is another debate that keeps coming up. Back in the early 1980s, the administration of conservative President Ronald Reagan had to beat a hasty retreat from hopes to cut Social Security, when it discovered the widespread, bipartisan popularity of this program and had to face the political clout of organized elderly constituencies. But conservative plans fundamentally to revamp Social Security have never gone away, and recently the bipartisan Concord Coalition, led by former Senators Paul Tsongas and Warren Rudman, has renewed the call to save America from public bankruptcy through cuts in "middle-class entitlements" including Social Security. Even some liberals are willing to contemplate sharp cuts in programs for the elderly, out of desperation to free up tax resources to pay for new social programs to aid children and working-aged families.

Somewhat more surprising, perhaps, has been the return of debates about the federal government's role in ensuring health care for all Americans. This is an issue that had all but disappeared from the national agenda after the late 1970s. But in the fall of 1991 an obscure Democratic candidate, Harris Wofford, overcame a forty-point deficit in the opinion polls to win a special senatorial election in Pennsylvania. Mr. Wofford ran television commercials promising that he would work for health insurance covering every American; and his surprise victory over a well-established Republican opponent was widely attributed to this emphasis on universal insurance. Suddenly electoral politicians awoke to the worries about health coverage that were spreading among middle-class citizens, who no longer feel secure about their jobs and employment-based benefits.

During his campaign for the presidency in 1992, Democratic candidate Bill Clinton picked up on the theme of comprehensive health care reform, even as he highlighted the need for new national policies to promote jobs and training for employment. After President Clinton assumed office in January 1993, officials in his administration and task forces assembled around its edges set to work devising bold new plans for reworking America's social and economic policies. Some steps were taken quickly and quietly, such as the summer 1993 expansion of the Earned Income Tax Credit to boost the incomes of low-wage working families. In other areas, such as job training and welfare reform, elaborate plans have been worked out, only to run up against draconian budgetary constraints that will probably prevent their full implementation. Democratic candidate Bill Clinton had, after all, not only promised to reinvigorate national economic and social policies; he had also promised to cut the national budget deficit and reduce taxes for the broad American middle class.

Even in the face of powerful budgetary and political constraints, Clinton chose to stake much of his presidential prestige on a comprehensive "Health Security plan" unveiled in the fall of 1993. Echoing themes of universal protection reminiscent of former President Franklin Roosevelt's legislation for Social Security during the New Deal, President Clinton unabashedly hopes to make the 1990s a watershed for U.S. public social provision comparable to that of the 1930s. As the President declared in his September 22, 1993, speech to the Congress and the nation:

> It's hard to believe that once there was a time—even in this century—when retirement was nearly synonymous with poverty, and older Americans died in our streets. That is unthinkable today because over half a century ago Americans had the courage to change—to create a Social Security system that ensures that no Americans will be forgotten in their later years.
>
> I believe that forty years from now our grandchildren will also find it unthinkable that there was a time in our country when hard-working families lost their homes and savings simply because their child fell ill, or lost their health coverage when they changed jobs. Yet our grandchildren will only find such things unthinkable tomorrow if we have the courage to change today.
>
> This is our change. This is our journey. And when our work is done, we will have answered the call of history and met the challenge of our times.

Stirring presidential rhetoric aside, the specific proposals of the Clinton administration are certain to be fundamentally reworked, even mangled, by Congress before anything becomes law. This is true not only for health care reform, but also for proposed changes in welfare, employment programs, and programs dealing with the needs of working families. Still, no matter how much—or how little—actually happens during the (one-or two-term) presidency of Bill Clinton, fundamental issues are not going to go away. Financing health care, caring for an aging population, retraining displaced employees, putting welfare mothers to work, and making employment sustainable along with parenthood for all American families—all of these matters and more will require repeated attention from presidents, congressional representatives, state and local governments, and citizens. Well into the early twenty-first century, the United States seems certain to be reconsidering and revising its public social policies.

So how are we to make sense of the making and remaking of social policies in the United States? Many people would answer this query timelessly—in moral-ideological terms, or else in supposedly value-neutral technical terms. For moralists, battles over U.S. social policy may be seen as clashes between advocates of "big government" versus "the market," or as combat between those who want to economically aid the needy versus those who want to control and reform their behavior. Meanwhile, for many professional experts, social policymaking is understood as a matter of doing "objective" research on the extent of societal problems, in order to devise optimal cost-efficient "solutions" for politicians to enact.

Moralists and technocrats thus look at social policymaking in very different ways. But they have in common an almost total lack of historical and political sensibility. Both moralists and technocrats tend to look at policy formation outside of the context of America's historically changing governmental institutions, and without reference to broader political tendencies and alliances. Consequently, moralists are unable to understand why their version of "good" triumphs or fails to triumph over "evil" at any given moment. And technically oriented policy experts feel no responsibility to consider matters of governmental feasibility, or to take responsibility when the "efficient" solutions they propose either are not accepted, or else lead to unintended and unwanted outcomes.

The lack of historical and political sensibility is, in a way, quite comfortable for moralists and technocrats alike. In the face of political failures, moralists can simply redouble their shrill, absolutist cries for good versus evil. And technocrats can retreat to academia or think tanks and continue working out perfect solutions for unnamed future politicians to adopt—with unforseen consequences, for which the experts need take no responsibility. What moralists and technocrats both fail to achieve, however, are reliable insights into the political constraints and possibilities for making and remaking American public policies at any given historical juncture, including the present.

This collection of essays reveals how much we can learn about limits and possibilities in the *politics* of U.S. social policymaking by taking a long historical view. The American social policies discussed in these essays stretch from such nineteenth-century programs as pensions for Union veterans of the Civil War and workhouses for the poor, to such early twentieth-century measures as "mothers' pensions" and health programs for babies and pregnant women, to more currently prevalent and familiar policies or proposals about Social Security, employment training, Aid to Families With Dependent Children, and health care reform. The reader of this volume may well learn facts about the past that he or she did not previously know—such as the fact that massive federal government spending for the elderly started, not in 1935 with Social Security, but in the late nineteenth century with generous pensions for former Union soldiers of the Civil War and their family dependents. The reader will also notice important continuities and shifts across U.S. political debates about such familiar matters as health care, welfare, and Social Security for the elderly.

But this collection is not just a recounting of past and present U.S. social policies. More than that, it features arguments about *how* changing governmental institutions, social conflicts, and political alliances prompted and allowed certain kinds of social policies to be publicly debated in each major period of modern American history. And this collection offers explanations about *why* some kinds of proposed policies were successfully enacted, or expanded, in each period of modern U.S. history—while others fell by the wayside in political defeat, or else could not be successfully implemented or sustained after an initial legislative enactment.

Lessons about the past are not merely of antiquarian interest. They speak to issues that continue to animate U.S. social policy debates today.

It is often claimed, for example, that Americans are a people inherently opposed to taking "handouts" from government. Social Security programs created during the Great Depression of the 1930s are seen as something of an exception to the normal "hardy individualism" of U.S. citizens. But a full historical purview leads to a very different conclusion. Since the nineteenth century, large numbers of mainstream American citizens have been delighted to accept—and politically support—certain generous, federally funded social benefits. While middle-class and working-class Americans are typically reluctant to see public monies spent for the poor through welfare programs, they have repeatedly been willing to support politically and pay taxes for social benefits that are considered to be "earned" by worthy citizens such as themselves. Aid to the poor has also been acceptable to broad groups of American citizens, whenever such aid has been part of broader policies that express shared values and also benefit middle-class citizens.

Social security benefits for the retired elderly are the best contemporary example of support by Americans for universal social policies. People "earn" pensions linked to their records of employment and the levels of their wages. And Social Security encompasses almost all employed Americans and their families. In recent decades, Social Security has thus enjoyed broad, political bipartisan support across lines of class and race.

Conservatives who are opposed to large governmental programs of social provision understand well that Social Security is hard to cut back as long as it has middle-class support. It is therefore not incidental that contemporary conservative tactics for shrinking Social Security take the form of efforts, first, to convince young middle-class employees that Social Security is a "bad deal" for them economically, that they would be better off to turn to private investments for retirement. Another tactic is to attempt to undermine the confidence of all Americans that Social Security will be there in the future, by suggesting that the system is "bound to go bankrupt" as the aging post–World War II "baby boom" generation ages. Conservatives propose to "save" Social Security by trimming it back into a program targeted especially on the most needy elderly, and taking better-off middle-class people out of the system. Some of them may honestly believe this is just a matter of "fiscal responsibility," but many surely have learned a lesson from political history: Social Security has expanded and survived *because* it has middle-class participation and support. If middle-class Americans can be removed from the system, it would soon turn into one more welfare program for the poor, and could easily be cut back even further in the future.

Analyses in this collection show that arguments over particular social policies at given moments of U.S. history have been closely linked to perspectives on what the U.S. government should do, and to beliefs about what it apparently *can* do effectively. Policy debates are also influenced by the reactions of governmental officials, citizens, and politically active social groups to previous public policies. Prior policies may be seen as models to be extended or imitated; or they may be seen as "bad" examples to be avoided in the future.

Back in the early twentieth century, for example, some politicians and trade unionists wanted to imitate Civil War pensions, extending them into pensions for most elderly working Americans. But most politically active middle-class groups in that era viewed Civil War pensions as a negative precedent, because they were trying to reduce the power of the kinds of elected legislators and party politicians who had worked to expand Civil War pensions in the first place. Similarly, today, some politicians and groups want to build upon existing parts of U.S. social policy—for example, moving from universal Social Security for the elderly to universal "health security" for all Americans. Simultaneously, however, there are groups arguing that the U.S. federal government invariably "messes up" any program it touches. They point to problems with the postal service, or with earlier federal regulatory programs, in order to argue that the quality of American health care will inevitably be undermined if the national government takes a stronger role in the system.

Indeed, a historical perspective on today's debates over health care reform helps us to understand why the comprehensive health security plan introduced by President Bill Clinton in September 1993, apparently to great acclaim, so quickly became the target of rhetorically devastating attacks against "government bureaucracy." To be sure, President Clinton and his advisors tried to use lessons from U.S. political history in devising and arguing for their version of comprehensive health care reform. We have already noticed the President's attempt to link up with favorable attitudes toward Social Security by emphasizing universal health coverage that "can never be taken away" from any American. In addition, the President and his advisors tried to be clever about the issue of state power. They took it for granted that Americans are wary of giving "the state" a stronger role than "competitive market forces." Consequently, they proposed a version of health reform—called managed competition—that supposedly did not rely on taxes, and that allegedly would preserve and enhance market competition in the offering of health insurance "choices" to all Americans.

Still, the President and the health care experts who advised him may have failed to notice a quite important—historically noticeable—nuance about American reactions to governmental power. Especially since the 1980s, conservatives have proclaimed that Americans invariably hate taxes. But history shows that middle-class Americans have been quite willing to pay taxes when they were sure that these monies would go for worthy purposes from which they along with other citizens benefit. At the same time, history also reveals that many sorts of proposed social policy reforms—including proposals for publicly guaranteed health coverage in the 1910s, 1930s, 1940s, and 1970s—have been highly vulnerable to ideological counterattacks against government "bureaucracy." Arguably, Americans resent government regulations even more than they may dislike taxes.

Of course, the Clinton health care reform plan of 1993 was very susceptible to the "bureaucracy" criticism. It tried to achieve universal coverage and cost control in health care by overlaying multiple existing private bureaucracies—hospitals, insurance companies, medical associations, state and local governments—with still more layers of federal bureaucratic regulation. Conservative critics have been able to ridicule the proposed Clinton reforms for their regulatory complexity.

Although the U.S. government has always been in many ways much *less* bureaucratic than the governments of other advanced-industrial nations, nevertheless there are understandable reasons why Americans fear public regulation. Precisely because the federal government in the United States lacks strong administrative bureaucracies that can reach directly into localities or the economy, national-level politicians tend to enact programs that rely on a combination of financial incentives and legal rules to get things done. The federal government partly bribes and partly bosses around state and local governments and nongovernmental groups—getting them to help the federal government do what it cannot do alone. Ironically, however, this sort of situation often gives rise to louder outcries against "federal bureaucratic meddling" than might exist if the national government were able to act directly. Such outcries are especially likely to occur if the federal government proposes to regulate more than to subsidize.

Thus, in the debates over the Clinton health care plan, lots of groups—including insurance companies, but also hospitals and state governments—fear that federal regulations might financially squeeze and forcibly remodel their operations over time—and without giving them offsetting benefits in the form of generous federal subsidies to pay for currently uninsured groups of citizens. This worry about the "bureaucracy" of the Clinton health care plan is obviously enhanced by the fact that the President's declared objectives include "controlling costs" in the national health care system, as well as extending coverage to all Americans. The President promised to do all of this without raising new general tax revenues. Ironically, by trying to quell worries about taxation, the President and his allies heightened even more deep-seated—and historically very predictable—worries about "governmental bureaucracy" in the United States.

I have mentioned only a few of the insights about the contemporary politics of U.S. social policymaking that might be gleaned from the essays collected in this volume. Understandings of past politics can also help to illuminate today's debates over welfare reform, or family policies, or the feasibility of federally sponsored employment programs. There is little need for me to go over all the connections between historical analysis and contemporary policy choices, because many of the chapters to come speak explicitly about them. In the Conclusion, moreover, I draw upon historical understanding from my own value-standpoint to talk about how U.S. social policies might be remade for the dawn of the twenty-first century.

Working from their own value premises, many readers will make connections between past patterns and future possibilities other than the ones I have highlighted. That is fine. This little book will have achieved its objective if it convinces people of varying persuasions that historical analysis is highly relevant to understanding the limits and possibilities of social policymaking today. The future of U.S. social policy is not determined; it depends on political debates and developments happening now and in the years to come. As future possibilities take shape, the protagonists in contemporary debates can learn much from the past. Historical understanding, centered on governmental institutions and shifting political alliances, can help politicians, experts, and citizens alike to make wise choices about what should—and can—come next in American social policy.

CHAPTER ONE

State Formation and Social Policy in the United States

"AMERICANS may be defined as that part of the English-speaking world which instinctively revolted against the doctrine of the sovereignty of the State and has . . . striven to maintain that attitude from the time of the Pilgrim Fathers to the present day" (Pollard, 1925, 31). Citizens of the United States view themselves as fortunate not to be subject to any overbearing "state." And observers rightly have trouble identifying elements of concentrated sovereignty in the American political system—except, perhaps, when the USA acts aggressively on the world stage. There are, of course, excellent historical reasons why Americans lack a strong or positive sense of the state. Nevertheless, we can learn a surprising amount about American politics by treating state-society relationships in strictly analytical terms.

To imagine that the United States has been a dynamic society and capitalist economy unencumbered by any state would be an ethnocentric illusion. Instead, the specific organizational forms that state activities have taken in America have profoundly affected the social cleavages that have gained political expression and helped to determine the sorts of public policies that U.S. governments have—and have not—pursued from the nineteenth century to the present day. Drawing on my own current research, I can illustrate this argument by exploring why the historically evolved patterns and phases of U.S. public social provision have differed from those characteristic of European welfare states.

SOCIAL POLICIES IN THE UNITED STATES

Modern "welfare states," as they eventually came to be called, had their start between the 1880s and the 1920s in pension and social insurance programs established for industrial workers and needy citizens in Europe and Australasia. Later, from the 1930s through the 1950s, such programmatic beginnings were elaborated into comprehensive systems of income support and social insurance encompassing entire national

Adapted from *American Behavioral Scientist* 35(4/5), (March/June 1992). © 1992 Sage Publications, Inc.

populations. In the aftermath of World War II, Great Britain rationalized a whole array of social services and social insurances around an
explicit vision of "the welfare state," which would universally ensure a
"national minimum" of protection for all citizens against old age, disability and ill health, unemployment, and other causes of insufficient
income. During the same period, other nations—especially the Scandinavian democracies—established "full employment welfare states" by
deliberately coordinating social policies, first with Keynesian strategies
of macroeconomic management and then with targeted interventions in
labor markets.

Comparative research on the origins of modern welfare states typically
measures the United States against foreign patterns of "welfare state development." America is considered a "welfare state laggard" and an "incomplete welfare state" because it did not establish nationwide social insurance until 1935 and because it never has established fully national or
comprehensive social programs along European lines. But this approach
overlooks important social policies that were distinctive to the United
States in the nineteenth and early twentieth centuries. It also distracts us
from analyzing why U.S. social policies since 1935 have been characterized by sharp bifurcations between "social security" and "welfare,"
as well as by persisting federal diversity in certain policy areas.

Early American "social policy" included state and local support for
the most inclusive system of primary and secondary public education in
the industrializing world (Heidenheimer 1981; Rubinson 1986). It also
included generous local, state, and federal benefits for elderly Civil War
veterans and their dependents. By 1910, the U.S. federal government
was giving old-age and disability pensions to over a third of all elderly
men living in the North and to many widows and orphans (and some
elderly men in the South) as well (Skocpol 1992, chap. 2). In terms of
the large share of the federal budget spent, the hefty proportion of citizens affected, and the relative generosity of the benefits by contemporary international standards, the United States had become a precocious
social spending state!

In the early 1900s, a number of U.S. trade union officials and reformers hoped to transform Civil War pensions into more universal
publicly funded benefits for all working men and their families. But this
was not to be. Many social reforms were enacted into law during the
progressive era, but not measures calling for new public social spending
on old-age pensions or other kinds of working men's social insurance.
The United States thus refused to follow other Western nations on the
road toward a paternalist welfare state, in which male bureaucrats
would administer regulations and social insurance "for the good" of
breadwinning industrial workers and their dependents.

Instead, America came close to creating a pioneering maternalist welfare state, with female-dominated public agencies implementing regulations and benefits for the good of women and their children. From 1900 through the 1920s, a broad array of protective labor regulations and social benefits were enacted by state legislatures and the national Congress to help adult American women as mothers or as potential mothers (for full details, see Skocpol 1992, Part 3). The most important of these "maternalist" social policies were mothers' pensions enacted by forty-four states to authorize regular benefits for impoverished widowed mothers, laws enacted by all but two states to limit the hours that women wage earners could work, laws enacted by fifteen states authorizing minimum wages for women workers, and the federal Sheppard-Towner Infancy and Maternity Protection Act of 1921, which authorized the U.S. Children's Bureau to supervise federal matching payments subsidizing local and state programs for maternal health education. Overall, a remarkable number of policies for women and children were enacted in the United States during a period when proposed regulations and benefits for male industrial workers were defeated.

The Great Depression and the New Deal of the 1930s subsequently opened possibilities for old-age pensions and social insurance. In what has been called a "big bang" of national legislation (Leman 1977), the Social Security Act of 1935 created a basic framework for U.S. public social provision that is still in place. Public health insurance was omitted from the Social Security Act, and later schemes for universal national health benefits also failed. Yet three major kinds of nation-spanning social provision were included in the 1935 legislation: federally required, state-run unemployment insurance, federally subsidized public assistance, and national contributory old-age insurance.

Unemployment insurance was instituted in 1935 as a federal-state system. All states were induced to establish programs, but each individual state was left free to decide terms of eligibility and benefits for unemployed workers, as well as the taxes to be collected from employers or workers or both. Unemployment benefits and taxation became quite uneven across the states, and it remained difficult to pool risks of economic downturns on a national basis or to coordinate unemployment benefits with Keynesian demand management. Despite efforts in the 1930s and 1940s to nationalize unemployment insurance and join its operations to various measures of public economic planning, no such explicit joining of "social" and "economic" policy developed in the postwar United States.

Public assistance under the Social Security Act was administered through a set of programs already existing in certain states by the early 1930s, for which the federal government would henceforth share costs. Assistance for the elderly poor and for dependent children (previously "mothers' pensions") were the most important programs to receive new federal subsidies. Free to decide whether they would even have particular programs, the states were also accorded great discretion to decide matters of eligibility and benefits and, in practice, methods of administration. Over time, as old-age insurance expanded to cover virtually all retired employees in the United States, federal old-age assistance became proportionately less important than it was originally. Meanwhile, by the 1960s, the Aid to Dependent Children program (now Aid to Families with Dependent Children [AFDC] providing benefits to caretakers as well as the children themselves) expanded enormously with a predominantly female adult clientele. Labeled "welfare," AFDC has very uneven standards of eligibility, coverage, and benefits across the states, generally providing the least to the poorest people in the poorest states and leaving many impoverished men and husband-wife families without any coverage at all.

Since 1935, the one program originally established on a purely national basis, contributory old-age insurance, has usurped the favorable label "social security" that once connoted the whole and has become the centerpiece of U.S. public social provision. Payroll taxes are collected from workers and their employers across the country. Ultimately, retired workers collect benefits roughly gauged to their employment incomes, with some redistribution toward the low-wage contributors to the system. After 1935, additional programs were added under this contributory insurance rubric: for surviving dependents in 1939; for disabled workers in 1956; and for retirees in need of medical care in 1965. Equally important, "social security" grew in coverage and benefits, as more and more employees and categories of employees were incorporated during the 1950s and benefit levels were repeatedly raised by Congress. By the 1970s, the United States, uneven and often inadequate in the help provided to unemployed and dependent people, had nevertheless become reasonably generous in the benefits offered to retired people of the working and middle classes.

"Welfare" became an explicit area of U.S. political controversy and policy innovation only during the 1960s, when the War on Poverty and the effort to create a "Great Society" were declared. For the first time since 1935, major new programs of needs-tested public assistance were established in the form of in-kind aid through Food Stamps and Medicaid. In 1972, moreover, old-age and other assistance programs (originally established as federal programs under Social Security) were nationalized, ensuring more standardized benefits. Still, the much larger AFDC program remained federally decentralized—and standards for other benefits, such as medical care, are often tied to this uneven standard bearer of the American welfare system. In turn, U.S. welfare remains, as always, both institutionally and symbolically separate from national economic management, on one hand, and from non-means-tested programs benefiting regularly employed citizens, on the other.

Existing Theories and Their Shortcomings

Among those seeking to understand the development of social policies in the United States, several approaches currently hold sway. Each offers insights but falls short of offering fully satisfactory explanations of the historical phases and policy patterns just reviewed.

One school of thought can be dubbed the *logic of industrialism* approach (e.g., Cutright 1965; Wilensky and Lebeaux 1965; Wilensky 1975, chap. 2) because it posits that all nation-states respond to the growth of cities and industries by creating public measures to help citizens cope with attendant social and economic dislocations. Once families are off the land and dependent on wages and salaries, the argument goes, they cannot easily cope with disabling accidents at work or with major episodes of illness, unemployment, or dependent elderly relatives unable to earn their keep. Social demand for public help grows, and all modern nations must create policies to address these basic issues of social security without forcing respectable citizens to accept aid under the demeaning and disenfranchising rules of traditional poor laws.

Plausible as this sounds, recent cross-national studies on the origins of modern social insurance policies have demonstrated that urbanization and industrialization (whether considered separately or in combination) cannot explain the relative timing of national social insurance legislation from the late nineteenth century to the present (see Flora and Alber 1981; Collier and Messick 1975). The United States in particular does not fit well into the logic of industrialism schema. Not incidentally, proponents of this perspective have tended to include data for "the U.S. case" only when doing cross-national analyses of social insurance for the period after 1935. Before the 1930s, the United States is an awkward outlier: This country was one of the world's industrial leaders, yet "lagged" far behind other nations (even much less urban and industrial ones) when it came to instituting public pensions and social insurance. Nor does this perspective help us to understand why the United States prior to 1935 emphasized public social provision first for veteran soldiers and then for mothers but not for working men.

Another school of thought—let us call it the *national values* approach—accepts many underlying dynamics posited by the logic of industrialism argument but introduces a major modification to explain why some nations, such as Bismarck's Imperial Germany in the 1880s, initiated modern social policies at relatively early stages of urbanization and industrialization, whereas others, most notably the United States, delayed behind the pace of policy innovation that would be expected from the tempos of urbanization and industrialization alone. The answer, say proponents of this approach (e.g., Grønbjerg, Street, and Suttles 1978; Kaim-Caudle 1973; King 1973; Rimlinger 1971), lies in the values and ideologies to which each nation's people adhered as urbanization and industrialization gathered force. Cultural conditions could either facilitate or delay action by a nation-state to promote social security, and cultural factors also influenced the shape and goals of new policies when they emerged. Thus Gaston Rimlinger (1971), one of the ablest proponents of the national values approach, argues that early German social insurance policies were facilitated by the weakness of liberalism and the strength of "the patriarchal social ideal" and "the Christian social ethic" in nineteenth-century Germany (p. 91). In the United States, however, laissez-faire liberal values were extremely strong and a "commitment to individual achievement and self-help" led to a "tenacious" "resistance to social protection" (Rimlinger 1971, 62).

Like the logic of industrialism approach, the national values school fails to notice, let alone explain, U.S. Civil War benefits or social policies for mothers and children. These approaches focus solely on modern social insurance and old-age pensions. Yet even here, general deductions from national values simply cannot give us adequate answers to many crucial questions about timing and programmatic structure.

Laissez-faire liberal values were in many respects more hegemonic and popular in nineteenth-century Britain than they were in the nineteenth-century United States, yet in the years before World War I, Britain enacted a full range of social protective measures, including workers' compensation (1906), old-age pensions (1908), and unemployment and health insurance (1911). These innovations came under the auspices of the British Liberal Party, and they were intellectually and politically justified by appeals to "new liberal" values of the sort that were also making progress among educated Americans around the turn of the century. Under modern urban-industrial conditions, the "new liberals" argued, positive governmental means must be used to support individual security, and this could be accomplished without undermining individuals' dignity or making them dependent on the state. If British liberals could use such ideas to justify both state-funded pensions and contributory social insurance this way in the second decade of the twentieth century, why couldn't American progressives do the same? In both Britain and the United States, sufficient cultural transformation within liberalism had occurred to legitimate fledgling welfare states without resort to either conservative-paternalist or socialist justifications (see Orloff and Skocpol 1984 for further elaboration of this argument).

Then, too, when American "New Dealers" of the 1930s at last successfully instituted nationwide social protections justified in "new liberal" terms, why did they end up with the specific array of policies embodied in the Social Security Act? Why was health insurance left aside, despite the availability of liberal rationales for it just as good as those put forward for unemployment and old-age insurance? And why did the public assistance programs subsidized under Social Security actually cement the dependence of many individuals on the arbitrary discretion of state and local authorities, rather than furthering individual dignity and the predictable delivery of citizen benefits as a matter of "rights"? A final query is perhaps the most telling: Given the clear value priority that Americans have always placed on individuals getting ahead through work, why did the New Deal as a whole fail to achieve proposed measures to guarantee jobs for everyone willing to work? Arguably, the social security measures that were achieved were less in accord with long-standing American values than governmental commitments to full employment would have been.

Arguments stressing the impact of either industrialism or national values on social policy development tend to downplay political struggles and debates. During the past fifteen years, however, many historians and social scientists have analyzed the political contributions of capitalists and industrial workers in shaping patterns of social policy since the 1930s in the capitalist democracies. As part of this trend, two sorts of class politics perspectives have been applied to American social politics: One highlights what is called "welfare capitalism," and the other stresses "political class struggle" between workers and capitalists.

Proponents of the *welfare capitalism* approach (e.g., Berkowitz and McQuaid 1980; Domhoff 1970; Ferguson 1984; Quadagno 1984) take for granted that corporate capitalists have dominated the U.S. political process in the twentieth century, and they look (in various ways) for economically grounded splits between conservative and progressive capitalists as the way to explain social policy innovations. Early in this century, the argument goes, certain American businesses preceded the public sector in evolving principles of modern organizational management, including policies for stabilizing and planning employment and protecting the social welfare of loyal employees. Prominent "welfare capitalists" then pressed their ideas upon policy intellectuals and public officials, so that public social insurance measures in key states and at the federal level were supposedly designed to meet the needs of progressively managed business corporations.

This perspective has served as a good lens through which to view the complementarities that have sometimes developed between public social policies once enacted—and the labor-management practices of American corporations. For example, many American corporations accommodated nicely to Social Security's contributory old-age insurance program, meshing it with their own retirement benefits systems, especially after World War II. But business groups originally opposed the passage of the Social Security Act as well as the passage of most earlier and later federal or state-level social and regulatory measures applicable to men or women workers. However adaptable American capitalists have proven to be after the fact, the historical evidence is overwhelming that they have regularly fiercely opposed the establishment of public social policies. Political processes other than the initiatives of capitalists have nearly always been the causes of U.S. social policy innovations.

The other class politics perspective takes for granted that capitalists everywhere tend to oppose the emergence and expansion of the welfare state. This "social democratic" or *political class struggle* approach has predominated in recent cross-national research on the development of social policies in Europe and the United States (see Bjørn 1979; Castles 1978, 1982; Esping-Andersen 1985; Korpi 1983; Myles 1984; Shalev 1983; Stephens 1979). No attention is paid by these theorists to early U.S. social provision for Civil War veterans, and their worker-centered definitions of modern social provision prevent them from analyzing pioneering U.S. social spending and regulations for mothers and women workers. To explain why American public social provision for working men commenced later and has not become as generous as European public social provision, this approach underlines the relative weakness of U.S. industrial unions and points to the complete absence of any labor-based political party in U.S democracy. Given these weaknesses of working-class organization, proponents of this approach argue that U.S. capitalists have been unusually able to use direct and indirect pressures to prevent governments at all levels from undertaking social welfare efforts that would reshape labor markets or interfere with the prerogatives or profits of private business. Only occasionally—most notably during the New Deal and afterwards through the liberal wing of the Democratic Party—have American workers or unions been able to muster sufficient strength to facilitate some innovations or expansions of public social provision.

Certainly, this emphasis on political class struggle between workers and capitalists helps to explain why the United States has not developed a comprehensive full-employment welfare state along postwar Scandinavian lines. Nevertheless, if our intention is not merely to contrast the United States to Europe since World War II but to explain the phases and specific patterns of U.S. social policies since the nineteenth century, then the political class struggle approach is insufficient in several ways. Strict attention to political conflicts of interest between capitalists and industrial workers deflects our attention from other socio-economic forces that have intersected with the U.S. federal state and with decentralized American political parties to shape social policy making. Until very recently, agricultural interests in the South and the West were crucial arbiters of congressional policy making. Associations of middle-class women were crucial—and often successful—proponents of social provision for women and children during the early twentieth century. And struggles over social welfare or labor market interventions have often involved regional, ethnic, and racial divisions. We need a mode of analysis that will help us understand why social identities and conflicts grounded in gender, ethnicity, and race have been equally or more telling than industrial class conflicts in the shaping of social provision in the United States.

Political class struggle theories have been argued with certain state and party structures in mind, namely, centralized and bureaucratized states with parliamentary parties dedicated to pursuing policy programs in the name of entire classes or other broad, nation-spanning collectivities. For much of Europe, the existence of such features of political organization has given substance to the presumption that the industrial working class may translate its interests into social policies, whenever "its" party holds the reins of national power over a sustained period. But of course the United States has never had a centralized bureaucratic state or programmatic parliamentary parties. Thus the American case highlights the importance of bringing much more explicitly into our explanations of social policy making the historical formation of each national state—as well as the effects of that state's institutional structure on the goals, capacities, and alliances of politically active social groups.

U.S. STATE FORMATION AND PATTERNS OF SOCIAL PROVISION

"State formation" includes constitution making, involvements in wars, electoral democratization, and bureaucratization—large scale historical processes, in short, whose forms and timing have varied significantly across capitalist industrializing countries. In sharp contrast to many European nations, the United States did not have a premodern polity characterized by monarchical absolutism, a locally entrenched standing army and bureaucracy, or recurrent mobilization for land warfare against equal competitors. Instead, the American colonies forged a federalist constitutional republic and (after some years of continued sparring with Britain) the fledgling nation found itself relatively geopolitically sheltered and facing toward a huge continent available for conquest from militarily unformidable opponents. Wars have never had the same centralizing effects for the U.S. state as they have had for many European states, in part because America's greatest war was about itself and also because mobilization for the two world wars of the twentieth century relied heavily on the organizational capacities of large business corporations and trade associations (Cuff 1973; Vatter 1985). Only after World War II, when the United States took on global imperial functions, did a federal "military-industrial complex" emerge, nourished by the first persistence into peacetime of substantial direct federal taxation.

The American Revolution was a revolt not only against the British Empire but against any European-style notion of concentrated political sovereignty—whether focused in a supreme parliament, as in Britain after the English Revolution, or in an official bureaucracy built up under absolute monarchy, as in much of Continental Europe. After years of political skirmishes between colonists and royal governors, a confederation of thirteen colonies separated Americans from Britain; then the founding fathers sought to cement a precarious national unity by designing a new federal government. Under the Constitution adopted in 1788, the powers of the states and the central government were carefully divided and balanced against one another in a "compound" arrangement (Scheiber 1978) that left many ambiguities for the future, while the new rules for the federal government spread cross-cutting responsibilities among Congress, the president, and a system of courts. In the words of Samuel P. Huntington (1968), "America perpetuated a fusion of functions and a division of power, while Europe developed a differentiation of functions and a centralization of power" (p. 110).

Americans looked to "the Constitution" and "the rule of law," as the loci of fundamental sovereignty. Especially in pre-Civil War America, these functioned as a "roof without walls" in the apt words of John Murrin (1987), as "a substitute for any deeper kind of national identity" because "people knew that without the Constitution there would be no America" (pp. 346-47). Although never-ending rounds of legislation in Congress and the states expressed shifting sets of special interests, the sovereign ideals of constitutionalism and the rule of law could reign impersonally above an economically expansionist and socially diverse country. Only during the Civil War did a Republican-run crusade to save a Northern-dominated nation temporarily transfer the locus of sovereignty to an activist federal government. But even the Civil War did not generate an autonomous federal bureaucracy: The forces of localism, divisions of powers, and distrust of government activism never disappeared, even in the North. The U.S. "Tudor polity" (Huntington 1968) reemerged in full force after the Southern states rejoined the union in the 1870s.

It will not do, however, to leave the matter here, stipulating that Europeans had concentrated sovereignties and a sense of "stateness" while Americans had neither. Stephen Skowronek (1982) places the totality of early American political arrangements in a framework that helps to highlight their distinctive features. Skowronek points out (1982, pp. 19, 24) that America certainly did have a state, both in the sense of "an organization of coercive power" (p. 19) and in the sense of "stable, valued, and recurring modes of behavior within and among institutions" (p. 24):

> The early American state maintained an integrated legal order on a continental scale; it fought wars, expropriated Indians, secured new territories, carried on relations with other states, and aided economic development. Despite the absence of a sense of the state, the state was essential to social order and social development in nineteenth-century America. (p. 19)

To be sure, this early American state was not a set of locality-penetrating bureaucracies headed by a monarch or a parliament. Rather, in Skowronek's telling phrase it was a "state of courts and parties" (p. 24). Operating across state and federal levels, courts and parties were the key organizations—and judges and party politicians the crucial "officials in action"—that made up the American state in the nineteenth century: "Party procedures lent operational coherence to the disjointed institutions of the governmental apparatus, [and] court proceedings determined the meaning and the effect of the law itself" (p. 27).

Courts were not very prominent in the original debates over constitutional design, yet as the nineteenth-century progressed they carved out a more authoritative role than the Founders had envisaged or than British courts enjoyed. "There is hardly a political question in the United States," observed Alexis de Tocqueville ([1850] 1969, p. 270) "which does not sooner or later turn into a judicial one." To be sure, early American judges and lawyers needed to adjust English common law precedents to U.S. circumstances, and they had to fend off various movements to codify the laws and reduce judicial discretion. Yet these elites and the courts through which they operated also enjoyed important advantages. They could take advantage of their countrymen's regard for the Constitution and legal procedures as common points of reference in a polity wracked with jurisdictional disputes, where fundamental issues regularly required adjudication. And there was no national civil bureaucracy that could compete with the courts by promoting "the national interest" in a more substantive fashion.

Along with courts, political parties and vocationally specialized partisan politicians became the pivots of the nineteenth-century American polity. Ironically, this happened even though the Constitution made no mention of them, given that the Founders disapproved "the baneful effects of the spirit of party" (George Washington, as quoted in Wallace 1968, 473). Foreign observers of the actual workings of American government noticed the increasing centrality and distinctiveness of U.S. parties. James Bryce (1895) observed in the 1880s that in "America the great moving forces are the parties. The government counts for less than in Europe, the parties count for more" (p. 5). A description of them is therefore a necessary complement to an account of the Constitution and government since "their ingenuity, stimulated by incessant rivalry, has turned many provisions of the Constitution to unforeseen uses" (p. 3). "The party organizations in fact form a second body of political machinery existing side by side with that of the legally constituted government" such that "the whole machinery, both of national and of state governments, is worked by the political parties" (Bryce 1893, 6). American parties, Bryce (1893) noted, "have been organized far more elaborately than anywhere else in the world, and have passed more completely under the control of a professional class" (p. 6).

The regular American parties of the nineteenth century managed the complex, never-ending processes of nominations and elections for local, state, and national offices. Party conventions became the typical means for nominating candidates, and the nineteenth century's frequent elections required that party supporters be kept in a high state of enthusiasm and readiness through canvasses and rallies. Crucially, from the Jackson era through the end of the century, parties also controlled the staffing and functioning of public administration in the United States (Shefter 1978). Administrative staffing through patronage was complementary to the intensified electoral activities of the new political parties. The opportunity to control the allocation of public offices inspired party cadres and allowed national and state party brokers to offer local loyalists influence over appointments allocated from their levels of government. In turn, public officeholders were highly motivated to contribute portions of their salaries and their time to foster the popularity of their party, for only if their party won the next election would their jobs be safe. Otherwise, the opposite party and all of its appointees would claim the "spoils of office."

Once in place by the 1840s, the parties and their managers proved remarkably resilient, dominating U.S. politics and knitting together the branches and levels of the "Tudor polity" throughout the nineteenth century (Keller 1977; McCormick 1986). The local roots of the parties sunk deep into particular neighborhoods; yet party efforts simultaneously spanned localities within states and, to a remarkable degree, reached across the nation as a whole. Certainly, the party organizations were not top down hierarchies; rather, they were ramified networks fueled by complex and shifting exchanges of favors for organizational loyalty. As such, however, they successfully linked local to state politicians and kept state politicians in touch with one another and with whatever national officeholders their party might have.

Not until the twentieth century—decades after electoral democratization and well after capitalist industrialization had created private corporate giants operating on a national scale—did the U.S. federal, state, and local governments make much headway in the bureaucratization and professionalization of their administrative functions (Shefter 1978; Skowronek 1982). With the greatest changes coming first at municipal and state levels, bureaucratic-professional transformations happened piecemeal through reform movements spearheaded by the new middle classes. As the various levels of government were thus partially reorganized, the fragmentation of political sovereignty built into U.S. federalism and into the divisions of decision-making authority among executives, legislatures, and courts was reproduced in new ways throughout the twentieth century. American political parties have remained uncoordinated in their basic operations, and in many localities and states, the major parties uneasily combine patronage-oriented and interest-group-oriented modes of operation (Mayhew 1986). Within the federal government, Congress, with its strong roots in state and local political establishments, has remained pivotal in national domestic policy making—even during periods of strong executive initiative such as the New Deal, the two world wars, and the Cold War (Amenta and Skocpol 1988; Fiorina 1977; Grodzins 1960, Huntington 1973; Patterson 1967).

The patterns of U.S. state formation just summarized have conditioned social policy making from the nineteenth century to the present. We can briefly survey some of the most important ways in which this has happened.

Early democratization of the U.S. white male electorate ensured that masses of ordinary Americans could support public schooling as a right of democratic citizenship rather than warily opposing educational institutions imposed from above by officials and upper classes, as happened in Europe (Katznelson and Weir 1985, chap. 2). In the United States, moreover, no national bureaucracy existed to regulate, finance, or serve as a central magnet for educational development, and no single dominant church served as a prop of a counterweight to the state. Thus local and voluntary forces, including Catholic parishes and a multiplicity of Protestant and Jewish sects, took more initiatives than they did in other nations. In a democratic political context, "participatory localism" encouraged many such groups to support free public schools, while others built and defended private schools. Decentralized federalism allowed local, state-level and private initiatives to compete with one another—and often to imitate one another as well, in waves of analogous institution building. The result was the world's first system of mass primary and secondary schooling.

In addition, nineteenth-century America's nonbureaucratic and party-centered patronage democracy had a strong proclivity for legislative enactments that would distribute material benefits to many individuals and local communities within the major party coalitions (McCormick 1979). In the context of close electoral competition between the Republicans and the Democrats between 1877 and 1896, patronage democracy fueled the expansion of de facto disability and old-age benefits for those who could credibly claim to have served the Union forces during the Civil War. The Republican Party, especially, enjoyed advantages from expanding access to Civil War pensions (McMurry 1922; Sanders 1980: Bensel 1984, chap. 3). That party could simultaneously promote high tariffs, with benefits finely tuned to reach groups of businesses and workers in various Republican areas of the country, and generous pensions, which spent the "surplus" revenues raised by the tariffs disproportionately on townsmen, farmers, and skilled workers who were also concentrated in Republican-leaning areas of the North. Moreover, during crucial, close-fought elections, the Republicans manipulated the processing of pension applications through the federal Bureau of Pensions in attempts to influence the Republican vote in such tightly competitive states as New York, Ohio, and Indiana.

Once American government began to bureaucratize and professionalize, the surviving structures of patronage democracy and elite perceptions of "corruption" in the Civil War pension system discouraged U.S. progressive liberals from supporting the generalization of veterans' benefits into more universal old-age pensions or working men's social insurance. The absence of strong civil service bureaucracies made it impossible for U.S. advocates of contributory social insurance to imitate the strategies of contemporary British social insurance advocates, who devised plans within national ministries and then persuaded parliamentary politicians to enact them. What is more, progressive reformers were preoccupied with building bureaucratic regulatory agencies that could circumvent the control of patronage-oriented political parties, and they feared that any new forms of public social spending directed at masses of voters would only reinforce party patronage (Orloff and Skocpol 1984; Skocpol 1992, chap. 5). The only way that social welfare reforms could be enacted in the United States during the early twentieth century was through waves of similar legislation across many of the state legislatures. But policies that would have entailed new public spending for male voters could not get enthusiastic support from nation-spanning groups active in reformist politics during this period.

Finally, the U.S. state and federal courts also discouraged regulations for working men. Prior to the 1930s, most U.S. courts invoked constitutional principles of "free contract" and "due process" for private property holders to overrule protective labor laws covering adult male workers. Frustrated reformers responded by channeling most of their efforts for regulatory reforms toward protective labor laws covering women workers alone (Skocpol and Ritter, 1991, 56-62). From the time of the 1908 "Lochner" decision, American courts allowed many such laws regulating female labor to stand. Judges accepted the arguments put forward by reformers and women's groups that governments possessed legitimate "police power" to protect future "mothers of the race" from overwork.

During the New Deal and in its aftermath, the United States finally launched nationwide public assistance and social insurance measures, including policies for working men and the elderly. Nevertheless, the Social Security Act was rooted in prior state-level laws or legislative proposals under active debate in the 1930s; and congressional mediation of contradictory regional interests ensured that national standards could not be established in most programs (Skocpol and Amenta 1985). Subsequently, American national mobilization for World War II—a mobilization less total and centrally coordinated by the state than the British mobilization for the same war—did not overcome congressional and local resistance against initiatives that might have pushed the United States toward a nationalized full-employment welfare state. Instead, this pivotal war enhanced federal fiscal capacities and created new possibilities for congressionally mediated subsidies and tax expenditures but did not permanently enhance public instrumentalities for labor market intervention or executive capacities for coordinating social spending with macroeconomic management (Amenta and Skocpol 1988).

Basic structural features of the U.S. state have thus powerfully set overall institutional limits for social provision in the United States. Yet fundamental patterns of state formation are only the starting point for analysis. In addition, political struggles and their policy outcomes have been conditioned by the institutional leverage that various social groups have gained, or failed to gain, within the U.S. polity. By analyzing ways in which America's distinctive state structure has influenced possibilities for collective action and for political alliances among social groups, we can go even further toward explaining the phases and patterns of U.S. public social provision from the nineteenth century to the present.

U.S. Institutions and Social Groups in Politics

America's precociously democratized federal polity has always made it difficult for either capitalists or industrial workers to operate as a unified political force in pursuit of class projects on a national scale. Ira Katznelson (1981, 1985) and Martin Shefter (1986) have spelled out the situation for workers in a series of important publications. Because in the United States white manhood suffrage and competing patronage parties were in place at the very start of capitalist industrialization, American workers learned to separate their political participation as citizens living in ethnically defined localities from their workplace struggles for better wages and employment conditions. No encompassing "working class politics" emerged; and American trade unions developed no stable ties to a labor-based political party during the period around the turn of the century when European social democratic movements were forged. Nationally, American workers were left without the organizational capacities to push for a social democratic program, including generous and comprehensive social policies. In localities where they did have considerable political clout, American workers tended to gain advantages on ethnic rather than class lines. Only during and after the New Deal was this situation modified, as alliances developed in many places between urban liberal Democrats and industrial unions. Yet the Democrats and the unions never went beyond flexible and ad hoc partnerships. Particular Democratic politicians put together unique constellations of supporters, sometimes including certain unions and sometimes not, while unions retained the option of supporting friendly Republicans as well as Democrats.

Whereas political forces claiming to represent the industrial working class had (in cross-national perspective) relatively little presence in U.S. social politics, national and local groups claiming to speak for the collective interests of women as homemakers were able around the turn of the twentieth century to mount ideologically inspired efforts on behalf of maternalist social policies. Patterns of exclusion from—and tempos of incorporation into—electoral politics shaped the possibilities for women's political consciousness just as they influenced possibilities for working-class consciousness. But the results for women were quite different.

In major European countries during the nineteenth and early twentieth centuries, either no one except monarchs, bureaucrats, and aristocrats had the right to participate in national politics, or else property ownership, education and other class-based criteria were used to limit electoral participation by categories of men. Thus European women were not the only ones excluded from the suffrage, and, at least at first, economically privileged women did not have to watch lower-class men exercise electoral rights denied to them. Class-defined political cleavages tended to proliferate and persist in Europe, and even politically active women's organizations oriented themselves to class issues. In the United

States by contrast, for almost a century the rights and routines of electoral democracy were open to all men (even to the black ex-slaves for some decades after the Civil War), but were denied to all women (Baker 1984).

By virtually universal cultural consensus, woman's "separate sphere" in the nineteenth century was the home, the place where she sustained the highest moral values in her roles as wife and (especially) mother. Yet this did not mean that American women stayed out of public life. Through reformist and public-regarding voluntary associations, American upper- and middle-class women, joined by some wives of skilled workers, claimed a mission that they felt only their gender could uniquely perform: extending the moral values and social caring of the home into the larger community. In the process, women's groups took a special interest in social policy issues that they felt touched the well-being of other women. By the progressive era, indeed, women's associations had concluded that women should act as "housekeepers for the nation." Promoting such ideas were huge, nation-spanning federations of women's clubs organized at local, state, and national levels. These included the Women's Christian Temperance Union, the National Congress of Mothers, and the General Federation of Women's Clubs—the last of which had by 1911 over one million members in thousands of clubs spread across all states. These women's federations were well-placed to press upon legislators and public opinion across the land the "moral necessity" for new social policies designed to protect women workers and mothers and children (for full details, see Skocpol 1992, Part 3).

Although such "maternalist" ideas about social welfare spread across the industrializing world in the late nineteenth and early twentieth centuries, they loomed largest in the United States for both social and political reasons. Socially, American women gained more and better higher education sooner than any other women in the world. This prepared a crucial minority of them for voluntary or irregularly recompensed public leadership, especially since regular elite career opportunities were limited. Widespread education also set the stage for strong alliances between higher-educated professional women and married housewives scattered across the nation, many of whom were relatively well educated and some of whom in every locality had been to college and worked as schoolteachers before marriage.

Politically, meanwhile, American women reacted sharply against their exclusion from a fully democratized male democracy. Throughout the nineteenth century, no major industrializing country differentiated worlds of politics—understood in the broadest sense as patterns of participation in public affairs—so sharply *on strictly gender lines* as did the

United States. Given the absence in the United States of bureaucratic and organized working-class initiatives to build a pioneering paternalist welfare state for industrial workers and their families, there was more space left for maternalism in the shaping of fledgling modern social policies. Thus the policies and new public agencies especially for women and children sponsored by American women's associations loomed especially large on the overall agenda of issues that progressive era legislators took seriously.

Using the same perspective that was just applied to understand the possibilities for working-class and women's political consciousness, we can also gain insights about the political outlooks and capacities of U.S. capitalists. To a greater degree than business people in many other capitalist nations, U.S. capitalists (in the apt phrase of David Vogel 1978) "distrust their state." This is, of course, somewhat ironic, given that American capitalists have not had to contend with a highly mobilized, nationally politically conscious working class and often get their way in governmental affairs. Yet U.S. business owners have had to operate in a long-democratized polity prone to throw up periodic moralistic "reform" movements, including farmers' movements and women's movements inclined to challenge business prerogatives. What is more, the distrust that U.S. capitalists feel toward government reflects the frustrations that they have recurrently experienced in their dealings with a decentralized and fragmented federal state—a state that gives full play to divisions within business along industrial and geographical lines.

Conflicts within the ranks of U.S. business are readily politicized because losers can always "go to court"—or back to the legislatures or to another level in the federal system or to a new bureaucratic agency—for another round of battle in the interminable struggles that never seem to settle most public policy questions. For U.S. capitalists, the state has seemed neither coherent nor reliable. Indeed, the uneven and inconstant effects of U.S. political structures help to explain why—contrary to the expectations of the "welfare capitalism" school—"progressive" corporate leaders have always found it difficult to inspire broad business support for national social policy initiatives, even those that might benefit the economy as a whole on terms favorable to the dominant sectors of business. With a few individual exceptions, American capitalists have never seen government as a positive means to achieve classwide purposes. For the most part, various industries and smaller as well as larger businesses have concentrated on fighting one another through politics. Different sectors of business have come together only episodically and then usually in efforts to block reformers or popularly appealing social movements that want to extend government regulation or taxation and spending for social welfare purposes.

The U.S. federal state with its single-member-district legislatures and its nonprogrammatic political parties allows considerable leverage to interests that can coordinate a policy stance across many legislative districts. What we may call "widespread federated interests" include women's associations such as the General Federation of Women's Clubs, organizations of farmers from the Grange to the American Farm Bureau Federation, business groups such as the Chamber of Commerce, and professional associations such as the National Education Association and the American Medical Association. Such widespread federations of local and state member units are ideal coalition partners for national policy advocacy groups that want to promote, obstruct, or rework social policies—especially as proposals have had to make their way through dozens of state legislatures or through the House of Representatives in Congress.

Occasionally, social groups organized as widespread federations have spurred the enactment of social policies in the United States. Examples of this include support by Union veterans in the Grand Army of the Republic for Civil War benefits during the 1880s and 1890s, support by the General Federation of Women's Clubs and the National Congress of Mothers for mothers' pensions, protective legislation, and Sheppard-Towner programs during the 1910s and 1920s; and support by Townsend Movement, an association of old people's clubs, for old-age benefits during the 1930s and 1940s. Equally or more often, however, widespread federations of commercial farmers and small businessmen have obstructed or gutted proposed social policies. For example, during the early New Deal from 1933 to 1935, federal agricultural policies had not the fully intended effect of strengthening interest group association among commercial farmers across the disparate crop areas of the South and the Midwest (Finegold and Skocpol 1984). In turn, this meant that the American Farm Bureau Federation was better able to ally with business organizations, including the Chamber of Commerce, to pressure congressional representatives against one liberal New Deal social welfare proposal after another from 1936 onward.

Pinpointing institutional leverage through Congress also helps us to make sense of the special role of "the South" in modern American social policy making, a role that certainly rivals that of either capitalists or the industrial working class. To be sure, the South's role cannot be understood without underlining the class structure of Southern cotton agriculture as a landlord dominated sharecropper system from the late nineteenth century through the 1930s (Alston and Ferrie 1985). Nor could we possibly ignore the explicit racism that ensured minority white dominance over black majorities in all sectors of economic and social life. Yet the South was militarily defeated in the Civil War, and by the

1930s, this region was not very weighty in the national economy as a whole, nor were its social mores typical of the nation. Thus socioeconomic factors and generalized references to racism will not alone tell us why Southern politicians had so much leverage during and after the New Deal that they could take a leading role in congressional alliances opposed to national welfare standards and any strong federal presence in economic planning.

The influence of Southern agricultural interests in the New Deal depended on the insertion of their class power as landlords and their social power as white racial oligarchs into federal political arrangements that from the 1890s to the 1960s allowed an undemocratized single-party South to coexist with competitive two-party democracy in the rest of the national polity (Key 1949) . Above all, Southern leverage was registered through a congressionally centered legislative process in Washington that allowed key committee chairmen from "safe" districts to arbitrate precise legislative details and outcomes. From the New Deal onward, the "national" Democratic Party used congressional committees to broker the internal divisions between its Southern and urban liberal Northern wings (Bensel 1984, chap. 7). This prevented the often contradictory orientations of the two wings from tearing the national party apart but at the price of allowing the enactment of only those social policies that did not bring the national state into direct confrontation with the South's nondemocratic politics and racially embedded systems of repressive labor control.

The U.S. state structure as it had been formed by the 1930s and 1940s, along with the operations of the New Deal party system, magnified the capacities of Southern economic and social elites to affect national policies at the same time that the capacities of other interests, including those sections of organized industrial labor allied with urban Democrats in the North were simultaneously enhanced by the same U.S. state structure and party patterns. Many features of the New Deal Social Security system—and indeed of the entire disjointed configuration of social and economic policies with which the United States emerged from the political watersheds of the New Deal and World War II—can be understood by pinpointing the social interests and the political alliances that were able to gain or retain enhanced leverage through the long-standing federal and congressional institutions of the U.S. state. The New Deal certainly brought social policy innovators to the fore through the newly active federal executive. It also energized urban liberal forces and created new possibilities for political alliances through the electorally strengthened and partially realigned Democratic Party. Nevertheless, in the end, America's federal state and regionally uneven democracy placed severe limits on the political alliances and policies that could prevail as the original foundations were laid for nationwide public social provision in the United States.

Finally, to understand major developments in social policies since the New Deal, it is crucial to remember that the United States was—paradoxically—both the "first" and the "last" to democratize its electorate among the long-standing capitalist democracies. It was the first for white males, who were irreversibly enfranchised by the 1830s, and it became the last for *all* citizens because, except briefly during Reconstruction and its immediate aftermath, most blacks in the United States could not vote until after the migrations from the South after the 1930s and the civil rights upheavals of the 1960s. For all of the twentieth century until the 1960s, the United States was a regionally bifurcated federal polity: a mass two-party democracy in the East, North, and West, coexisting within the same national state with a single-party racial oligarchy in the South. Only since the 1960s, through major transformations that are far from completed, have American blacks been mobilized into national democracy and has two-party electoral competition made headway in the deep South.

The civil rights revolution of the 1960s began the process of mobilizing blacks into the Southern electorate and on new terms into the national electorate and the Democratic Party. These are processes whose effects have been tumultuous both on agendas of debate over social policy and on political alliances concerned with policy alternatives from the Great Society to the present. Yet the incorporation of blacks into the national polity has not been happening in a social policy vacuum; it is taking place in the context of the configuration of social policies inherited from the New Deal. Within this configuration of policies, "social security" for the stably employed majority of citizens had become by the 1960s institutionally and symbolically bifurcated from "welfare" for the barely deserving poor (Skocpol 1988). For socioeconomic and political reasons alike, working-age blacks were disproportionately clients of the vulnerable welfare components of U.S. social provision.

During the social policy reforms of the 1960s and early 1970s, welfare clients temporarily benefited from the widespread recognition that the New Deal system of social policies had not adequately addressed issues of poverty or responded to the needs of blacks, who could now vote in greater numbers. Liberal Democrats tried to use welfare extensions and new "antipoverty" programs to incorporate blacks into their—otherwise undisturbed—national political coalition. But many social policy reforms of the 1960s and 1970s soon backfired to disturb rather than reinforce Democratic coalitions. National politics underwent a sea change, and since the 1970s conservative forces hostile to enhanced public social provision have found renewed sources of strength within and beyond the Democratic Party. This has left impoverished people, including many blacks, increasingly isolated in national politics. And it has left welfare programs more susceptible than ever to attacks by those who question the U.S. federal government's role in providing support for vulnerable citizens.

CONTINUING AMBIVALENCE ABOUT THE ROLE OF THE STATE

Presently, Americans remain as ambivalent about concentrated political authority as they were two centuries ago when the Constitution was framed. They are quick to see the ills that government can inflict and slow to perceive the good things that a responsible national state can do for all citizens. But it would be wrong to suggest that Americans have ever been a people "without a state" either in fact or in fancy. As long as we are prepared to specify the peculiar sets of institutions that have added up to America's distinctive versions of the modern state in different historical periods, we can identify the ways in which political officials have shaped policies and analyze the ways in which state structures have patterned the conflicts and alliances of major social groups.

The nineteenth-century American "state of courts and parties" presided over the widespread distribution of economic and social benefits. including the Civil War pensions that served as de facto disability and old-age pensions for many around the turn of the new century. Women who were excluded from America's early fraternal democracy created federations of voluntary associations to counter and reform the male-dominated system, and during the 1910s and early 1920s, these women's associations found themselves in a strong position to promote maternalist social policies across all states and in Congress. During the mid-twentieth century, America's unevenly bureaucratized and democratized federal state hampered social democratic class politics and placed severe limits on comprehensive provision for the poor and unemployed. Yet this same national state has allowed the elaboration of many public benefits for the broad working and middle strata—benefits that these groups have eagerly accepted and politically supported, even when it means paying visible federal taxes as in the case of social security's contributory retirement insurance. Americans are happy enough to take benefits from government when they are widely distributed and mesh well with private pursuits.

The poor in America have benefited the most from public social provision when they have been included in relatively universal programs along with the middle and working classes (see Skocpol 1991). When left to themselves, however, impoverished minorities have suffered the most from the divisions encouraged by America's fragmented political institutions and by the continuing ambivalence of most citizens about the proper—or possible—role of concentrated governmental authority in national life. No doubt, the poor and the marginal would have done better in a European-style full-employment welfare state. But U.S. political institutions have never allowed the possibility for any such comprehensive regime of public social provision to emerge here. And the weight of history being what it is, it seems unlikely that they ever will. In the future as in the past, the fate of the American poor will remain tied to possibilities for their inclusion in political coalitions that transcend class and race. Recurrently, U.S. political structures have encouraged and responded to such broad alliances on behalf of inclusive social policies. And there is every reason to hope that this might happen again in the future, even if Americans continue to be ambivalent about "the state."

REFERENCES

Alston, Lee J. and Joseph P. Ferrie. 1985. Labor costs, paternalism, and loyalty in southern agriculture: A constraint on the growth of the welfare state, *Journal of Economic History* 65:95–117.

Amenta, Edwin and Theda Skocpol. 1988. Redefining the New Deal: World War II and the development of social provision in the United States. In *The politics of social policy in the United States*, edited by Margaret Weir, Ann Shola Orloff, and Theda Skocpol. Princeton, NJ: Princeton University Press.

Baker, Paula. 1984. The domestication of politics: Women and American political society, 1780–1920. *American Historical Review* 89:620–47.

Bensel, Richard Franklin. 1984. Sectionalism and American political development, 1880–1980. Madison: University of Wisconsin Press.

Berkowitz, Edward and Kim McQuaid. 1980. *Creating the welfare state*. New York: Praeger.

Bjørn, Lars. 1979. Labor parties, economic growth, and redistribution in five capitalist democracies. *Comparative Social Research* 2:93–128.

Bryce, James. 1893. *The American commonwealth*, Vol. 1, 3rd ed., rev. New York: Macmillan.

———. 1895. *The American commonwealth*. Vol. 2, 3rd ed., rev. New York: Macmillan.

Castles, Frank. 1978. *The social democratic image of society*. London: Routledge & Kegan Paul.

———. 1982. The impact of parties on public expenditures. In Frank Castles (ed.), *The Impact of Parties*. Beverly Hills, CA: Sage Publications, 21–96.

Collier, David and Richard Messick. 1975. Prerequisites versus diffusion: testing alternative explanations of social security adoption, *American Political Science Review* 69: 1299–1315.

Cuff, Robert D. 1973. *The War Industries Board: Business-government relations during World War I*. Baltimore, MD: Johns Hopkins University Press.

Cutright, Phillips. 1965. Political structure, economic development, and national social security programs, *American Journal of Sociology* 70: 537–50.

Domhoff, William. 1970. *The higher the circles*. New York: Random House.

Esping-Andersen, Gösta. 1985. *Politics against markets: The social democratic road to power*. Princeton, NJ: Princeton University Press.

Ferguson, Thomas. 1984. From normalcy to New Deal: industrial structure, party competition, and American public policy in the great depression, *International Organization* 38, 41–93.

Finegold, Kenneth and Theda Skocpol. 1984. State, party, and industry: from business recovery to the Wagner Act in America's New Deal. In Charles Bright and Susan F. Harding (eds.) *Statemaking and social movements: Essays in history and theory* (pp. 159–92). Ann Arbor, MI: University of Michigan Press.

Fiorina, Morris P. 1977. *Congress: Keystone of the Washington establishment*. New Haven, CT: Yale University Press.

Flora, Peter and Jens Alber. 1981. Modernization, democratization, and the development of welfare states in Western Europe. In Peter J. Flora and Arnold Heidenheimer (eds.), *The development of welfare states in Europe and America* (pp. 37–80). New Brunswick, NJ: Transaction Books.

Grodzins, Morton. 1960. American political parties and the American System, *Western Political Quarterly* 13: 974–98.

Grønbjerg, Kristen, David Street, and Gerald D. Suttles. 1978. *Poverty and Social Change*. Chicago, IL: University of Chicago Press.

Heidenheimer, Arnold J. 1981. Education and social security entitlements in Europe and America. In Peter J. Flora and Arnold Heidenheimer (eds.), *The Development of Welfare States in Europe and America*. (pp. 269–304). New Brunswick, NJ: Transaction Books.

Huntington, Samuel P. 1968. *Political Order in Changing Societies*. New Haven, CT: Yale University Press.

———. 1973. Congressional responses to the twentieth century. In *Congress and the American Future*, 2nd edition, The American Assembly, Columbia University. (pp.6–38). Englewood Cliffs, NJ: Prentice-Hall.

Kaim-Caudle, P. 1973. *Comparative Social Policy and Social Security*. London: Martin Robertson.

Katznelson, Ira. 1981. *City Trenches: Urban Politics and the Patterning of Class in the United States*. New York: Pantheon.

———. 1985. Working-class formation and the state: nineteenth-century England in American perspective. In Peter B. Evans, Dietrich Rueschemeyer, and Theda Skocpol (eds.), *Bringing the State Back In*. (pp. 257–84). Cambridge and New York: Cambridge University Press.

Katznelson, Ira and Margaret Weir. 1985. *Schooling for All: Class, Race, and the Decline of the Democratic Ideal*. New York: Basic Books.

Keller, Morton. 1977. *Affairs of the State: Public Life in Late Nineteenth Century America*. Cambridge, MA: Harvard University Press.

Key, V. O. 1949. *Southern Politics in State and Nation.* New York: Alfred A. Knopf.

King, Anthony. 1973. Ideas, institutions and the policies of governments: A comparative analysis, parts I and II, *British Journal of Political Science* 3, 291–313, 409–423.

Korpi, Walter. 1983. *The Democratic Class Struggle*. Boston, MA: Routledge and Kegan Paul.

Leman, Christopher. 1977. Patterns of policy development: Social security in the United States and Canada, *Public Policy* 25, 26–291.

Mayhew, David R. 1986. *Placing Parties in American Politics*. Princeton, NJ: Princeton University Press.

McCormick, Richard L. 1979. The party period and public policy: An exploratory hypothesis, *Journal of American History* 66, 279–98.

————. 1986. *The Party Period and Public Policy*. New York: Oxford University Press.

McMurry, Donald, 1922. The political significance of the pension Question, 1885–1897. *Mississippi Valley Historical Review* 9, 19–36.

Myles, John. 1984. *Old Age in the Welfare State*. Boston, MA: Little Brown.

Murrin, John M. 1987. A roof without walls: the dilemmas of American national identity. In Richard Beeman, Stephen Botein, and Edward C. Carter II (eds.), *Beyond Confederation: Origins of the Constitution and the American National Identity*. (pp. 333–48). Chapel Hill, NC: University of North Carolina Press.

Orloff, Ann Shola and Theda Skocpol. 1984. Why not equal protection? Explaining the politics of public social spending in Britain, 1900–1911, and the United States, 1800s–1920, *American Sociological Review* 49, 6, 726–50.

Patterson, James T. 1967. *Congressional Conservatism and the New Deal*. Lexington, KY: University of Kentucky Press.

Pollard, A. F. 1925. *Factors in American History*. New York: Macmillan.

Quadagno, Jill. 1984. Welfare capitalism and the Social Security Act of 1935, *American Sociological Review* 49, 632–47.

Rimlinger, Gaston. 1971. *Welfare Policy and Industrialization in Europe and America*. New York: Wiley.

Rubinson, Richard. 1986. Class formation, politics, and institutions: schooling in the United States. *American Journal of Sociology* 92, 519–48.

Sanders, Heywood T. 1980. Paying for the 'bloody shirt': The politics of Civil War Pensions. In Barry Rundquist (ed.), *Political Benefits*. (pp. 137–60). Lexington, MA: Lexington Books, D.C. Health.

Scheiber, Harry N. 1978. Federalism and the constitution: The original understanding. In Lawrence M. Frieman and Harry M. Scheiber (eds.), *American Law and the Constitutional Order: Historical Perspectives*. (pp. 85–98). Cambridge, MA: Harvard University Press.

Shalev, Michael. 1983. The social democratic model and beyond: Two generations of comparative research on the welfare state, *Comparative Social Research* 6, 315–51.

Shefter, Martin. 1978. Party, bureaucracy, and political change in the United States. In Louis Maisel and Joseph Cooper (eds.), *Political Parties: Development and Decay*. (pp. 211–65) Beverly Hills, CA: Sage Publications.

Shefter, Martin. 1986. Trade unions and political machines: the organization and disorganization of the American working class in the late nineteenth century. In Ira Katznelson and Aristide Zolberg (eds.), *Working-class Formation: Nineteenth Century Patterns in Europe and the United States*. (pp. 197–276). Princeton, NJ: Princeton University Press.

Skocpol, Theda. 1988. The limits of the New Deal system and the roots of contemporary welfare dilemmas. In Margaret Weir, Ann Shola Orloff, and Theda Skocpol (eds.), *The Politics of Social Policy in the United States*. (pp. 293–311). Princeton, NJ: Princeton University Press.

———. 1991. Targeting within universalism: politically viable policies to combat poverty in the United States. In Christopher Jencks and Paul E. Peterson (eds.), *The Urban Underclass*. (pp. 411–36). Washington, D.C.: The Brookings Institution.

———. 1992. *Protecting Soldiers and Mothers: The Political Origins of Social Policy in the United States*. Cambridge, MA: The Belknap Press of Harvard University Press.

Skocpol, Theda and Edwin Amenta. 1985. Did capitalists shape Social Security? *American Sociological Review* 50, 4, 572–75.

Skocpol, Theda and Gretchen Ritter. 1991. Gender and the origins of modern social policies in Britain and the United States. *Studies in American Political Development* 5, 36–93.

Skowronek, Stephen. 1982. *Building a New American State: The Expansion of National Administrative Capacities, 1877–1920*. Cambridge and New York: Cambridge University Press.

Stephens, John. 1979. *The Transition from Capitalism to Socialism*. London: Macmillan.

Tocqueville, Alexis de. 1969; originally 1850. *Democracy in America*, 13th edition, translated by George Lawrence and edited by J. P. Mayer. Garden City, NY: Anchor Books.

Vatter, Harold G. 1985. *The U.S. Economy in World War II*. New York: Columbia University Press.

Vogel, David. 1978. Why businessmen distrust their state: the political consciousness of American corporate executives, *British Journal of Political Science* 8, 45–78.

Wallace, Michael. 1968. Changing concepts of party in the United States: New York, 1815–1828, *American Historical Review* 74, 453–91.

Wilensky, Harold. 1975. *The Welfare State and Equality*. Berkeley: University of California Press.

Wilensky, Harold and Charles Lebeaux. 1965. *Industrial Society and Social Welfare*. New York: Free Press.

CHAPTER TWO

America's First Social Security System: The Expansion of Benefits for Civil War Veterans

MOST OF US hold to a nostalgic image of a smaller-scale and less complicated American past, believing that federal and state governments in the United States did not become significant providers of social welfare until the middle of the twentieth century. This received portrait of yesteryear contains much truth, yet it hardly prepares us for some startling facts. Between 1880 and 1910, the U.S. federal government devoted over a quarter of its expenditures to pensions distributed among the populace. Aside from interest payments on the national debt in the early 1880s, such expenditures exceeded or nearly equaled other major categories of federal spending.[1] By 1910, about 28 percent of all American men aged 65 or more, more than half a million of them, received federal benefits averaging $189 a year.[2] Over three-hundred thousand widows, orphans, and other dependents were also receiving payments from the federal treasury.[3] During the same period, thousands of elderly men and a few hundred women were also residents of special homes maintained by the federal government or their respective states.[4]

This article analyzes the political forces behind the growth of federal Civil War pensions, by far the most extensive and expensive of all the

Political Science Quarterly 108(1) (1993).

[1] Richard Franklin Bensel, *Sectionalism and American Political Development, 1880–1980* (Madison: University of Wisconsin Press, 1984), 67. Bensel computed his percentages from the *1936 Annual Report of the Secretary of the Treasury on the State of the Finances* (Washington DC: Government Printing Office, 1937), table 5, 362–63.

[2] In 1910 there were 562,615 invalid Civil War pensioners on the rolls, receiving $106,433,-465, and the national population of males 65 years and over was 1,985,976. The sources for these figures are *Report of the Commissioner of Pensions*, included in *Reports of the Department of the Interior for the Fiscal Year Ended June 30, 1910*, vol. 1 (Washington DC: Government Printing Office, 1911), 146, 149; and U.S. Bureau of the Census, *Historical Statistics of the United States*, Bicentennial ed., pt. 1 (Washington DC: Government Printing Office, 1975), 15, series A 133.

[3] *Report of the Commissioner of Pensions* (1910), 272.

[4] Judith Gladys Cetina, "A History of Veterans' Homes in the United States, 1811–1930" (Unpublished Ph.D. dissertation, Department of History, Case Western Reserve University, 1977), chaps. 3–7. Veterans' homes, as well as state and local benefits for Union and Confederate veterans and survivors, are discussed in chap. 2 of my *Protecting Soldiers and Mothers* (Cambridge, MA: Belknap Press, Harvard University Press, 1992).

benefits that went to veterans and survivors of the war. The pattern and timing of pension expansion reveal that this was not merely a military program and not simply a mopping-up operation in the direct aftermath of the 1860s conflict. The human aftereffects of the Civil War interacted with intense political party competition between the 1870s and the 1890s to fuel public generosity toward a fortunate generation of aging men and their family dependents. As a result, the United States during the late ninteenth century became for many of its citizens a kind of precocious social spending state: precocious in terms of the usual presumption of an absence of federal involvement in social welfare before the New Deal, and precocious in terms of how the United States around 1900 compared to other western nations.

THE THEORETICAL CONTEXT OF THIS CASE

Not only popular and scholarly conceptions of U.S. welfare history but also most existing social scientific writings on the growth of western welfare states leave us ill prepared to understand the expansion of Civil War pensions. This is not the place to do an extensive review of the scholarly literature on the origins and growth of social policies in modern national states.[5] But it is pertinent to underline that all of the contending perspectives within that literature have heretofore focused on policies targeted on wage-earners, employees, and their dependents, or else on socioeconomically and demographically defined broad categories of people such as the elderly poor.

"Logic of industrialism" theorists have focused principally on social insurance and old-age pensions, arguing that they grew up historically in tandem with industrialization and urbanization.[6] The idea is that workers and families needed public income supplements once they were removed from the land and became vulnerable to the vagaries of wage-labor markets. Culturally oriented scholars have argued that "national values" influenced how quickly various industrializing nations instituted social insurance programs for wage-earners. These scholars stress that the industrializing United States was an extreme "laggard" in the

---

[5] For an overview of the literature, see Theda Skocpol and Edwin Amenta, "States and Social Policies," *Annual Review of Sociology* 12 (1986): 131–57. I critically discuss the applicability to the U.S. case of various explanations of social policy development in the Introduction to Skocpol, *Protecting Soldiers and Mothers*.

[6] For examples of "logic of industrialism" arguments, see Philips Cutright, "Political Structure, Economic Development, and National Social Security Programs," *American Journal of Sociology* 70 (March 1965): 537–50; Harold Wilensky, *The Welfare State and Equality* (Berkeley: University of California Press, 1975); and Robert W. Jackman, *Politics and Social Equality: A Comparative Analysis* (New York: Wiley, 1975).

creation of any national social policies, because its reigning liberal values—individualism, voluntarism, economic laissez faire, and distrust of government—discouraged any federal initiatives in social policy until the Great Depression spurred the extraordinary initiatives of the New Deal.[7] Finally, scholars oriented to class analysis—above all those who have advocated what has been called the social democratic model of welfare state development—have looked more broadly at the industrial labor regulations as well as social insurance measures instituted by industrial capitalist democracies. Proponents of the social democratic model have emphasized causal variables referring to the organizational capacities of industrial wage earners, arguing that organizationally strong working classes have at times been able to overcome political resistance from capitalists to spur the early creation and full development of welfare states designed to buffer workers and unions from the full force of market capitalism.[8]

Despite the many important disagreements among proponents of these various schools of thought, all of them have tended to see modern welfare states growing up along with and in response to industrialization and expansion of wage and salaried groups in national economies. Not surprisingly, debates in these terms about the growth of modern welfare states have altogether ignored the expansion of Civil War benefits in the late-nineteenth and early-twentieth-century United States. These benefits, after all, belie the notion that the U.S. federal government was uninvolved in social provision prior to the New Deal. And Civil War benefits were neither demanded by nor primarily extended to industrial wage earners. Many farmers and townspeople, often denizens of America's least industrial northern states (such as Maine), were among those who received the most generously funded pensions soonest and in the greatest numbers within total state populations.[9] Indeed, because they were disproportionately likely to have immigrated into the

[7] For examples of culturally oriented arguments, see Gaston Rimlinger, *Welfare Policy and Industrialization in Europe, America, and Russia* (New York: Wiley, 1971); Anthony King, "Ideas, Institutions, and the Policies of Governments: A Comparative Analysis," 2 parts, *British Journal of Political Science* 3 (July 1973): 291–313 and 3 (October 1973): 409–23; and Daniel Levine, *Poverty and Society: The Growth of the American Welfare State in International Comparison* (New Brunswick, NJ: Rutgers University Press, 1988).

[8] Major works by proponents of the social democratic model of welfare state development include John Stephens, *The Transition from Capitalism to Socialism* (London: Macmillan, 1979); and Walter Korpi, *The Democratic Class Struggle* (Boston, MA: Routledge and Kegan Paul, 1983). The entire school is ably reviewed in Michael Shalev, "The Social Democratic Model and Beyond: Two Generations of Comparative Research on the Welfare State," *Comparative Social Research* 6 (1983): 315–51.

[9] Heywood Sanders, "Paying for the 'Bloody Shirt': The Politics of Civil War Pensions" in Barry Rundquist, ed., *Political Benefits* (Lexington, MA: D.C. Heath, 1980), 150–54; and Skocpol, *Protecting Soldiers and Mothers*, 135–38, app. 1.

United States after the Civil War, the unskilled wage-earners of America's greatest industrial centers in the late nineteenth century were often not eligible at all for the disability or old-age pensions that went to Union Civil War veterans and their dependents.

Elsewhere I have argued at length that social scientists can best understand the rhythms and patterns of public social provision in modern national states by moving away from socioeconomically determinist theories toward what I call a "polity-centered" approach.[10] A nation's historically shaped governmental institutions and political parties have much to do with the kinds of public social-welfare benefits that are instituted, when, and by, and for whom. This is true in part because governmental officials and party politicians do not just respond to socioeconomic transformations in general; instead, officials and politicians pursue policies that reinforce the interests (and use the capacities) of the organizations within which their careers are embedded. The nineteenth-century United States had what Stephen Skowronek has aptly called a "state of courts and parties," in which party politicians were particularly well situated to shape governmental expenditures to the ends of partisan patronage.[11] The Republican party of the late nineteenth century was especially fortunate within U.S. patronage democracy, for it was able to knit together crossclass coalitions using complementary "distributive" public policies:[12] on the one hand, the Republicans devised finely adjusted tariffs to protect key industrial and agricultural interests while raising generous public revenues; on the other hand, they used Civil War pensions to distribute public largesse to additional groups in the North who were not so directly favored by the high tariffs. The administration of Civil War pensions, as we shall see, could also be managed to foster Republican electoral fortunes at watershed moments in the highly competitive politics of the late nineteenth century.

Governmental institutions and political parties also matter, because they afford special leverage to some social groups and ideas in politics, while making it more difficult for other groups and ideas to influence policy outcomes. In the late nineteenth-century United States, locally rooted and geographically widespread voluntary associations of Union veterans were ideologically well positioned to make claims as "saviors of the Republic"; and these groups enjoyed considerable access and le-

---

[10] See the full discussion in Skocpol, *Protecting Soldiers and Mothers*, 39–60.

[11] Stephen Skowronek, *Building a New American State: The Expansion of National Administrative Capacities, 1877–1920* (New York: Cambridge University Press, 1982), part 1.

[12] Richard L. McCormick, *The Party Period and Public Policy: American Politics from the Age of Jackson to the Progressive Era* (New York: Oxford University Press, 1986), chap. 5.

verage through congressional districts and intensively competitive party politics in the world's first mass democracy for white males. Meanwhile, the industrial wage-earners and trade-unionists, who have been identified as decisive to social policy making by many theorists of modern welfare states, were simply in a much weaker ideological and political position in the United States than they were in other industrializing capitalist countries of the day in Europe and Australia.[13] Not surprisingly, the first widespread program of honorable public social provision to develop in U.S. democracy was *not* workingmen's insurance or pensions for the poor alone, as in the fledgling foreign welfare states of the day. Rather, America's first national system of public social provision benefited a socioeconomically, ethnically, and, even racially diverse category of Union veterans and their dependents—people who happened to be especially well situated in the American political system in the decades following the northern victory in the Civil War.

Why do we need to pay attention to the structure and operation of the U.S. government and political parties to account for the expansion of federal Civil War pensions? Weren't these, after all, simply benefits for veterans that expanded automatically on account of the occurrence of the Civil War as a military conflict? Let me begin by dealing with this perfectly reasonable query. Then I shall recount the ways in which electoral competition, political party patronage, and crossclass political coalitions influenced the growth of generous federal social provision for many of America's elderly in the decades between the 1880s and the 1920s.

THE CIVIL WAR: NECESSARY BUT NOT SUFFICIENT FOR GENEROUS SOCIAL BENEFITS

The basic precondition for the later widespread disbursement of military pensions to military veterans and the survivors of deceased soldiers was the duration, intensity, and mass-mobilizing quality of the Civil War itself. "With the national economies on both sides fully integrated into their respective war efforts, the American Civil War was truly . . . the first 'total' war in the modern sense."[14] The conflict not only joined

---

[13] See Ira Katznelson and Aristide R. Zolberg, eds., *Working-Class Formation: Nineteenth-Century Patterns in Western Europe and the United States* (Princeton, NJ: Princeton University Press, 1986); Richard Oestreicher, "Urban Working-Class Political Behavior and Theories of American Electoral Politics, 1870–1940," *Journal of American History* 9 (June 1976): 466–80; and Francis G. Castles, *The Working Class and Welfare: Reflections on the Political Development of the Welfare State in Australia and New Zealand, 1880–1980* (Boston: Allen and Unwin, 1985).

[14] R. Ernest Dupuy and Trevor N. Dupuy, *The Encyclopedia of Military History from 3500 B.C. to the Present*, 2nd rev. ed (New York: Harper and Row, 1986), 820.

industrial with human mobilization; the pattern of warfare, especially once Union forces drove deeply into the South, was relatively unlimited in that it was directed against civilians and economic targets as well as military formations. What is more, the American Civil War, like the earlier French revolutionary wars and the later World Wars of the twentieth century, was "democratic," because the entire adult male citizenry was subject to calls to military service. At first, the calls in the North were voluntary; but in March 1863 conscription was instituted for men 20 to 45 years old who could not pay commutation or arrange for substitutes.[15]

The Civil War was also by far the most devastating war the United States has ever experienced. Some statistical facts about the North's experience of the Civil War can help to convey how traumatic it was. (White southerners suffered an even greater human impact.) About 2,213,000 men served in the Union army and navy.[16] This included about 37 percent of the northern men between the ages of 15 and 44 in 1860[17]—fully comparable to the massive one-third of British men who served in World War 1, a quintessential "total modern" war.[18] Overall, the Union side in the Civil War suffered 364,511 mortal casualities (including 140,414 battle deaths and 224,097 other deaths, mostly from disease).[19] These numbers translate into a ratio of about 18 northerners killed per thousand in the population, whereas only 1.31 Americans per thousand were to die in World War 1, and 3.14 per thousand would become mortal casualties in World War II.[20] As for the Union military's

[15] Eugene C. Murdock, *One Million Men: The Civil War Draft in the North* (Madison: The State Historical Society of Wisconsin, 1971), chap. 1; and James W. Geary, *We Need Men: The Union Draft in the Civil War* (DeKalb: Northern Illinois University Press, 1991).

[16] *Historical Statistics of the United States, Colonial Times to 1970*, Bicentennial ed., Bureau of the Census, Department of Commerce (Washington, DC: U.S. Government Printing Office, 1975), part 2, 1140, series Y.

[17] The 37 percent figure was estimated as follows, from *Historical Statistics*, part 1, 22–23, series 172–194: I added the 1860 population in 15–24 and 25–44 for the Northeast, North Central, and West regions; then I multiplied by the proportion of males (51.36 percent) in the total populations of these regions in 1860. Then I divided the 2,213,000 who served on the Union side of the Civil War by the estimated 5,903,832 men, 15–44, who lived in the nonsouthern regions in 1860.

[18] Arthur Marwick, *War and Society in the Twentieth Century* (London: Macmillan, 1974), 61.

[19] *Historical Statistics*, Part 2, 1140, series Y, 856–903.

[20] I divided the northern mortal casualties by a total population figure of 20,310,000 outside the South obtained from *Historical Statistics*, part 1, 22, series A 172–194. Battle deaths in proportion to population for World Wars I and II come from J. David Singer and Melvin Small, *The Wages of War, 1816–1965: A Statistical Handbook* (New York: John Wiley, 1972), 260.

wounded who survived, they numbered some 281,881, or about 14 per thousand in the northern population.[21]

The sheer dimensions of the Civil War as a martial event made possible the subsequent expansion of a generous pension system. This war created a large number of survivors of dead soldiers, along with many wounded and other veterans who might later claim rewards for latent disabilities or for their service alone. Nevertheless, no examination of the demographics of the war outside of the context of the nineteenth-century U.S. polity can account for the development of the pension system, as a contrast with the other major nation that experienced democratic military mobilization in early modern times.

From 1792 through 1815, revolutionary and Napoléonic France experienced mass-mobilizing wars. "Over two and a half million recruits passed through France's armies," most of whom died in combat or (especially) from disease, but some 150,000 of whom survived to be pensioned (along with an unknown number in the thousands who survived without pensions).[22] Benefits for French soldiers commenced in generous terms at the democratic height of the revolution, much as still more generous U.S. veterans' benefits were later to commence in the democratic North in the midst of the Civil War. Laws passed in France in 1793 reflected an historically unprecedented concern to pension not just officers but also disabled and needy common soldiers and the widows of soldiers who died in service.[23] The subsequent historical trajectory of French veterans' benefits was, however, conditioned by fiscal constraints and even more by the revival of bureaucratic controls and elite patronage under Napoléon.

In France after 1803, a large backlog of pension applications was efficiently processed by the bureaucracy, but the rates of pensions were sharply lowered, and the eligibility of common soldiers and their widows to receive help was restricted, even as French officers received proportionately more under the 1803 laws and through special grants to favorites from Napoléon himself.[24] Despite the benefit cutbacks, as backlogs of earlier-wounded veterans moved through the system, overall French pension costs attributable to the revolutionary and Napoleonic wars continued to rise modestly through the 1810s.[25] France continued during subsequent decades to do more for veteran

[21] *Historical Statistics*, part 2, 1140, series Y.
[22] Isser Woloch, *The French Veteran from the Revolution to the Restoration* (Chapel Hill: University of North Carolina Press, 1979), 206, 209–10, 308, and chap. 7 generally.
[23] Ibid.; and also Isser Woloch, "War-Widows Pensions: Social Policy in Revolutionary and Napoleonic France," *Societas* 6 (Autumn 1976): 235–54.
[24] Woloch, *French Veteran*, 101–109; and Woloch, "War-Widows Pensions," 244–51.
[25] Woloch, *French Veteran*, 206–207.

common soldiers than did other European nations.[26] But its veterans' benefits did not for many years become as generous (in levels or coverage) as they had been at the height of the revolution. And they would never become anywhere near as legally liberalized, socially far-reaching, or costly as those of the late nineteenth-century United States. The contrast, I maintain, was between a mass mobilizing French revolution that gave way to centralized bureaucracy and only episodically re-democratized postrevolutionary regimes, and a U.S. Civil War that entailed democratic mass mobilization without centralized bureaucratic controls and subsequently gave way to a restoration of full-fledged federal patronage democracy.

A glance backward in U.S. history also suggests the importance of democratic politics for the long-term expansion of veterans' benefits.[27] At the time of the American Revolution, the only pensions seriously debated by the Continental Congress were disability pensions for wounded soldiers and lifetime service pensions (at half-pay) for officers. In 1818, pensions were extended more generally to veterans of the U.S. War of Independence—but only to those who could prove the most dire poverty. Significantly, open-ended service pensions for all surviving Revolutionary warriors and widows—as opposed to the stricter disability and need-based pensions—did not emerge until after the advent of universal suffrage rights for all American white males. In 1832, service pensions were legislated for all veterans, benefitting some 33,425 men whose average age by then was 74.5 years. And in 1836, the widows of rank-and-file soldiers who had served during the War of Independence also starting receiving pensions. In contrast to postrevolutionary France, therefore, the postrevolutionary United States can be said to have further liberalized the terms of its military pensions, particularly after the advent of universal white manhood suffrage in its nonbureaucratic polity. But, of course, the expansions of U.S. military pensions prior to the 1860s were minimal compared to what was to come with the mass-mobilizing Civil War and its political aftermath.

[26] See the report prepared for the U.S. Sanitary Commission during the Civil War: Stephen H. Perkins, *Report on the Pension Systems and Invalid Hospitals of France, Prussia, Austria, Russia and Italy, with Some Suggestions upon the Best Means of Disposing of Our Disabled Soldiers*, Sanitary Commission no. 67 (New York: William C. Bryant and Co., Printers, 1863).

[27] This paragraph is based on William H. Glasson, *Federal Military Pensions in the United States* (New York: Oxford University Press, 1918), chaps. 2 and 3 (specifically 94–95); and John P. Resch, "Federal Welfare for Revolutionary War Veterans," *Social Service Review* 56 (June 1982): 171–95.

RAISING MASSIVE ARMIES IN A DEMOCRACY

Generous responses by the Union side to the needs of the soldiers and sailors fighting for its cause commenced within the first year of the Civil War, well before anyone imagined that the conflict would drag on so long and become so costly. The United States was a full democracy for white males, and the Republican party had risen to power in the name of "free land, free labor, and free men."[28] Generous treatment for soldiers was in accord with the outpouring of nationalist sentiment in the democratic North. It was also a practical necessity for a nonbureaucratic state, especially once the first rush of patriotic volunteering was over and prior to the institution of conscription in 1863. As John William Oliver, an early historian of Civil War pensions, put it, "our democratic nation was put to a test, the like of which few nations have had to meet. Without a creditable standing army, and lacking the power to compel men to enter upon military service, our Government had to resort to the policy of persuasion" to raise over a million volunteers in 1861 and 1862.[29]

During 1861, preexisting regular army benefits were granted to the first volunteers for the Civil War, yet this was understood to be only a stopgap approach. In February 1862, a new law specifically addressing the needs of Union soldiers and their dependents was enthusiastically enacted by the Republican-dominated Congress.[30] Secretary of the Interior J. P. Ushur proudly declared it "the wisest and most munificent enactment of the kind ever adopted by any nation."[31] Subsequently, the 1862 law was rendered more generous and systematic by a steady stream of legislative tinkering; but it was destined to remain the baseline of the Civil War pension system until 1890. Under the 1862 law, the award of pension benefits was directly linked to disabilities "incurred as a direct consequence of . . . military duty" or, after the close of combat, "from causes which can be directly traced to injuries received or disease contracted while in military service."[32]

Despite "a feeling, shared by several members of Congress, that in an army made up of citizen soldiers rather than mercenaries, it would be unjust discrimination to pension an officer at a higher rate than a pri-

[28] Eric Foner, *Free Soil, Free Labor, Free Men: The Ideology of the Republican Party before the Civil War* (New York: Oxford University Press, 1970).

[29] John William Oliver, "History of Civil War Military Pensions, 1861–1885," *Bulletin of the University of Wisconsin*, no. 844, History Series, no. 1 (1917): 5–6.

[30] Glasson, *Federal Military Pensions*, 124–25.

[31] As quoted in Oliver, "History of Civil War Military Pensions," 9–10, from House Exec. Documents, 38th Congress, 2nd sess. 1864–65, vol. 5, 11.

[32] As quoted in Glasson, *Federal Military Pensions*, 125.

vate,"[33] disability pensions under the 1862 law were graded according to rank. A lieutenant colonel or above totally disabled for manual labor originally received thirty dollars per month, while at the other end of the gradation of ranks, a private similarly disabled got eight dollars; and "proportionate pensions were to be given in each rank for partial disability."[34] Soon things became much more complicated, however. From 1864 on, new laws mandated special benefits (higher than those for total disability) for particular kinds of severe mishaps or for disabled veterans who required special attendants. In 1864, for example, the loss of both hands or eyes entitled a soldier to a pension of twenty-five dollars a month, and within a decade this was raised to fifty dollars. The system soon became rather baroque; for example, by 1872 there were two grades of disability for manual labor; the loss of one arm at the shoulder joint was worth $18.00, while the loss of an arm above the elbow joint was worth $15.00 a month; and "the loss of sight in one eye, the sight of the other having been lost before enlistment" was compensated at $31.25 a month![35] Much room for initiative and interpretation was introduced into the system, for veterans and doctors had to make the case for conditions such as "disability equivalent to the loss of a hand or a foot," and the Pension Bureau had to decide which claims or combinations of claims to allow. In later years, such extremely difficult to interpret conditions as "chronic diarrhea" and "nervous prostration" came to be covered by special pension rates.[36]

Under the 1862 law, widows, orphans, and other dependents of those who died for causes traceable to their Union military service also received pensions at the rates their relatives would have gotten for total disabilities.[37] The rates for dependents were very generous by preexisting historical standards in the United States and beyond; and the range of potential beneficiaries also became remarkably broad. According to the 1862 law, for example, dependent mothers and sisters of dead or injured solidiers could under certain circumstances receive pensions, and in due course dependent brothers and fathers were also made eligible. Normally, only one dependent relative was eligible at a time (for example, a mother if there was no widow, and so forth). In 1873, however, extra amounts were added to widows' benefits for each dependent child.

---

[33] Oliver, "History of Civil War Military Pensions," 9.

[34] Glasson, *Federal Military Pensions*, 126.

[35] Ibid., 129–38, esp. the table on 133.

[36] Ibid., 138.

[37] This paragraph draws upon ibid., 126–28, 138–42; and Oliver, "A History of Civil War Military Pensions," 10, 21–22.

PATTERNS OF PENSION GROWTH AFTER THE CIVIL WAR

Given the generosity of the basic Civil War pension law, as well as the magnitude of the needs immediately generated by the war, it is hardly suprising that each year thousands of former soldiers and survivors of soldiers who had died applied for military-disability pensions. Before pensioners from the Civil War started to be added to the rolls in 1862, the United States was paying benefits to 10,700 veterans and widows at a total cost of about $1 million per year; and beneficiaries and expenditures were declining each year.[38] By 1866, however, the Civil War enrollments had suddenly swelled the pension list to 126,722, with total disbursements mounting to about $15.5 million.[39] From 1866 through 1873 and 1874, the numbers of pensioners and the cost grew steadily as the human costs to the northern side of America's massive internal bloodletting registered in the public fisc.

The pension costs of the Civil War seemed to peak in the years after 1870, just as one might expect for a benefit system tied directly to disabilities incurred in wartime service. "We have reached the apex of the mountain," declared Commissioner of Pensions James H. Baker in 1872.[40] The numbers of new applications declined after 1870; the total number of pensioners stopped growing in 1873; and the total expenditures reached an apparent upper limit in 1874.[41] Although there were complaints about fraudulent pension claims even in this early period, the political impact of this concern was undercut when the system seemed to stop expanding.

Part of the reason for the mid-1870s pause in the expansion of the Civil War pension system must have been that the subjectively most pressing needs of the (then-youthful) veterans and survivors had already been addressed. True, the Pension Bureau refused to accept about 28 percent of the applications it received between 1862 and 1875.[42] Yet it is important to realize that large numbers of potential pensioners did not apply at all. Although the requirement to demonstrate service-con-

---

[38] Glasson, *Federal Military Pensions*, 124.

[39] Ibid., 273.

[40] As quoted in Oliver, "History of Civil War Military Pensions," 39.

[41] Glasson, *Federal Military Pensions*, 148–49.

[42] I calculated an acceptance rate of 72 percent (and a rejection rate of 28 percent) from figures presented for the years 1861 and after in the *Annual Report of the Commissioner of Pensions for 1888* (Washington DC: Government Printing Office, 1888), 35, table 6. The number of applications filed is calculated for the years 1861 through 1875, and the number accepted is calculated for 1861 through 1876, in the conviction that many applications filed in 1875 may have been processed during 1876. Interestingly, the 28 percent rejection rate for 1861 to 1875 was considerably lower than the rejection rate of about 38 percent for the entire period from 1861 to 1888. Presumably, applications in the period during and right after the Civil War were more likely to be corroborated by hard evidence of death or disability.

nected disabilities obviously limited applications from veterans, many potentially eligible veterans and survivors failed to apply for pensions during the decade after the war's end. A desire to forget the war and get on with life, an absence of financial need, unfamiliarity with the possibilities or the application procedures, and a reluctance on the part of some to take handouts from the government—all of these factors may have been involved in the initially low take-up rate for Civil War disability pensions. And that rate truly was rather low. Among the survivors of the Union soldiers who were killed during the war, plus the survivors of the veterans who died by 1870, only about 25 percent were receiving dependents' pensions in 1875.[43] We know that about 15 percent of the surviving ex-soldiers in 1865 had been wounded during the war.[44] Presumably most of them, if motivated, would have been in a very good position to claim some sort of disability benefits, and this does not include many others who could make the case for later disabilities that had remained latent during the war. Yet Table 1 reveals that only 6.5 percent of all veterans, or about 43 percent of the formerly wounded men who might have been especially eligible, had signed up for disability pensions by 1875.

Despite the initial reluctance of many veterans and surviving relatives to claim pension benefits, the "apex of the mountain" for Civil War pensions came not in the mid-1870s as Commissioner Baker declared, but two decades later. Along with Table 1, Figure 1 helps to show what happened to the Civil War pension system as it evolved from a generous, partially utilized program of compensation for combat injuries and deaths into an even more generous system of disability and old-age benefits, which were ultimately taken up by over 90 percent of the Union veterans surviving in 1910. In contrast to what happened in France after the revolution, the terms of eligibility for U.S. veterans' pensions became steadily more liberal in the decades after the Civil War. Accordingly, after the mid-1870s, the numbers of pensioners and the costs resumed upward trajectories and continued to grow until the

[43] For the war's mortal casualities of 364,511 see footnote 20; for the 106, 669 recipients of pensions for widows and dependents in 1875, see Glasson, *Federal Military Pensions*, 144. I divided the latter number by the former, to get a take-up rate of 29.3 percent. But actually, this percentage must be low, because about 100,000 more men died between 1864 and 1870, most presumably due to causes traceable to the war; and their relatives would have had time to apply for pensions before 1875. If these are included, the take-up rate for dependents' pensions in 1875 becomes 23 percent.

[44] I arrived at a percentage of 15.4 by dividing the number of wounded survivors of the Civil War (for which see footnote 16) by the number of union veterans in civil life in 1865 given in Table 1. Of course, this only a rough estimate, because some of the wounded surely died during 1864–1865, and others of the originally wounded who later recovered may have remained in the regular military after the end of the war.

TABLE 1
Take-Up Rates for Civil War Pensions

	Union Veterans in Civil Life	Disabled Military Pensioners	Percent of Veterans Enrolled as Pensioners
1865	1,830,000	35,880	1.96
1870	1,744,000	87,521	5.02
1875	1,654,000	107,114	6.48
1880	1,557,000	135,272	8.69
1885	1,449,000	244,201	16.85
1890	1,322,000	—	—
1891	—	520,158	39.34
1895	1,170,000	735,338	62.85
1900	1,000,000	741,259	74.13
1905	821,000	684,608	83.39
1910	624,000	562,615	90.16
1915	424,000	396,370	93.48

Sources: Historical Statistics of the United States, Colonial Times to 1970, Bicentennial Edition, Bureau of the Census, Department of Commerce (Washington, D.C.: U.S. Government Printing Office, 1975), part 2, series 957–970, 1145; and William H. Glasson, Federal Military Pensions in the United States (New York: Oxford University Press, 1918), 144, 271, 272.

facts of generational mortality overtook the ingenuity of politicians at channeling ever higher benefits to ever more people.

There were several notable legal watersheds along the way. The 1879 Arrears Act allowed soldiers with newly discovered Civil War-related disabilities to sign up and receive in one lump sum all of the pension payments they would have been eligible to receive since the 1860s. A decade later, the 1890 Dependent Pension Act severed the link between pensions and service-related injuries. Any veteran who had honorably served ninety days in the Union military, whether or not he had seen combat or been in any way hurt during the war, could apply for a pension if at some point in time he became disabled for manual labor. In practice, old age alone soon became a sufficient disability, and in 1906 the law was amended to state this explicitly.[45] After the turn of the century, moreover, Congress several times significantly raised the general benefit levels for both veterans and surviving dependents.

What happened after the mid-1870s to the Civil War pension system? Clearly, pensions became caught up in politics. But how, exactly? Cer-

[45] U.S. Bureau of Pensions, Laws of the United States Governing the Granting of Army and Navy Pensions (Washington DC: Government Printing Office, 1925), 43.

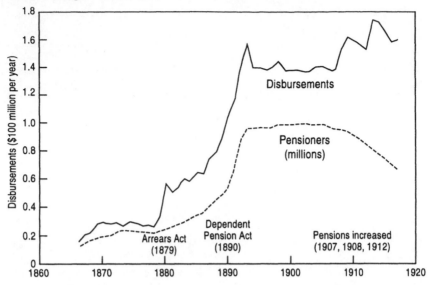

Fig. 1. The Expansion of Civil War Pensions, 1866–1917. *Source:* William H. Glasson, *Federal Military Pensions in the United States* (New York: Oxford University Press, 1918), 273.

tain political mechanisms that might have fueled expansion have been suggested by the small number of social scientists who have examined the matter. Let me comment briefly on their ideas before I develop my own arguments.

One argument about the liberalization of Civil War pensions is a pressure group thesis.[46] After the Civil War, hundreds of thousands of former Union soldiers organized themselves into veterans' associations, which in turn repeatedly lobbied Congress to improve benefits. Indeed, this social demand argument gains plausibility from the highly visible role that the most important northern veterans' organization, the Grand Army of the Republic (GAR), played in lobbying for legal liberalization in the years prior to the Dependent Pension Act of 1890, and the glee with which the organization greeted this law when it passed.[47] Other facts militate against simple reliance on the GAR pressure group thesis, however. During the 1870s, when the Arrears Act was urged through

[46] James Q. Wilson, "The Rise of the Bureaucratic State," *The Public Interest* 41 (Fall 1975): 88–89.

[47] Mary Dearing, *Veterans in Politics: The Story of the G.A.R.* (Baton Rouge: Louisiana State University Press, 1952), 397–401.

Congress, the Grand Army of the Republic was at best limping along, with many of its state-level departments in severe disarray and others avoiding political entanglements by concentrating on local fellowship and charity.[48] The national Grand Army of the Republic did not officially endorse or lobby for the Arrears Act, which actually seems to have affected the GAR more than vice-versa.[49] The new law stimulated thousands of applications for membership in veterans' associations (of which the GAR was the strongest) and also intensified the interest of Grand Army leaders in pension legislation and administration. In 1881–1882, the GAR set up a Washington, DC-based Pensions Committee to lobby Congress and the Pensions Bureau. The most rapid expansion of the GAR came during the 1880s—"immediately after the society . . . began its aggressive campaign for government aid to veterans." The organization reached the peak of its membership in 1890, when it enrolled 39 percent of all surviving Union veterans.[50] After 1890, as during the decade before, the GAR continued to pressure Congress on behalf of ever-more liberalized pension laws. Yet the GAR never did get all that it asked Congress to give; and even the Dependent Pension Act of 1890 fell a little short of the straight service pension (that is, for all veterans aged 62 and above, with no disability clause) that many within the GAR were demanding.[51]

[48] On the situation of the Grand Army in the 1870s, see Robert B. Beath, *History of the Grand Army of the Republic* (New York: Bryan, Taylor, and Co., 1888); Dearing, *Veterans in Politics*, chap. 6; Frank H. Heck, *The Civil War Veteran in Minnesota Life and Politics* (Oxford, OH: Mississippi Valley Press, 1941), 11–12, and chapter 2 generally; Edward Noyes, "The Ohio G.A.R. and Politics from 1866 to 1900," *The Ohio State Archaeological and Historical Quarterly* 55 (1946): 80–81; and George J. Lankevich, "The Grand Army of the Republic in New York State, 1865–1898" (Unpublished Ph.D. thesis, Columbia University, 1967), chaps. 4–6.

[49] Stuart Charles McConnell, "A Social History of the Grand Army of the Republic, 1867–1900" (Unpublished Ph.D. dissertation, Johns Hopkins University, 1987), 368–79; Elmer Edward Noyes, "A History of the Grand Army of the Republic in Ohio from 1866 to 1900" (Unpublished Ph.D. dissertation, Ohio State University, 1945), 79–89; and Lankevich, "Grand Army in New York State," 142–56.

[50] Wallace Evan Davies, *Patriotism on Parade: The Story of Veterans' and Hereditary Organizations in America, 1783–1900* (Cambridge, MA: Harvard University Press, 1955), 36, 160; and Stuart McConnell, "Who Joined the Grand Army? Three Case Studies in the Construction of Union Veteranhood, 1866–1900" in Maris A. Vinovskis, ed., *Toward a Social History of the American Civil War: Exploratory Essays*, (New York: Cambridge University Press, 1990), 141. McConnell reports a slightly higher GAR membership figure for 1890 (427, 981) than does Heck, *Civil War Veteran in Minnesota*, 257 (409, 489). I adjusted the percentage from McConnell, because Heck's figure crosschecks with the number officially given in *Journal of the Twenty-fifth National Encampment, Grand Army of the Republic* (Rutland, VT: Tuttle Company, 1891), 66.

[51] Although advocates of straight service pensions managed to get the National Encamp-

Another argument stresses the link between protective tariffs and the expansion of pension expenditures. Generous Civil War pensions become in this view a way to siphon off the embarrassing fiscal surpluses that high tariffs incidentally produced. Those supposedly pulling the political strings were protection-minded businesses in the northeastern "core" region of the country. The Republican party is pictured as controlled by such protectionist business interests, while the Democratic party opposed both high tariffs and generous pensions because both worked to the fiscal disadvantage of the South and other places (including New York City) with a stake in free commerce.[52] Midwestern agricultural areas that might otherwise have had an interest in free trade are considered to have been bought off by the disproportionate flow of pensions funded by tariff revenues to veterans and survivors in those areas. In current scholarship, this argument is most clearly put forward by the political scientist Richard Bensel.[53]

The historical sociologist Jill Quadagno adopts basically the same perspective, but also stresses that the 1890 pension liberalization was not as complete as it might have been, because provisions for a straight service/old-age pension were not incorporated into the legislation the Congress finally adopted. She attributes what she calls the "defeat of a national old-age pension proposal" in 1890 to the growing strength of free-trade proponents within the ranks of northern big business.[54] In my view, the evidence Quadagno offers for such free-trade business input to the 1890 legislative process is very skimpy. But it may not matter, because Quadagno makes too much of the slight concessions to fiscal responsibility built into the 1890 Dependent Pension Act. This law can hardly be called a defeat for old-age coverage, because it soon became, through administrative rulings and later legislative tinkering, a pension for all elderly Union veterans who had served ninety days or more.

What was the relationship between pensions and tariff revenues? Fig-

---

ments of the GAR to endorse that option in 1888 and 1890, key national GAR leaders preferred the more moderate disability-service pension that was actually enacted in 1890. Thus during 1889, the GAR's national Pension Committee supported the introduction of both types of bills in the respective houses of Congress. See McConnell, "Social History of the Grand Army of the Republic," 377; and Lankevich, "Grand Army in New York State," 235–37.

[52] See William H. Glasson, "The South and Service Pension Laws," *South Atlantic Quarterly* 1 (October 1902): 351–60.

[53] Richard Franklin Bensel, *Sectionalism and American Political Development, 1880–1980* (Madison: University of Wisconsin Press, 1984): chap. 3.

[54] Jill S. Quadagno, *The Transformation of Old Age Security: Class and Politics in the American Welfare State* (Chicago: University of Chicago Press, 1988), 36–47.

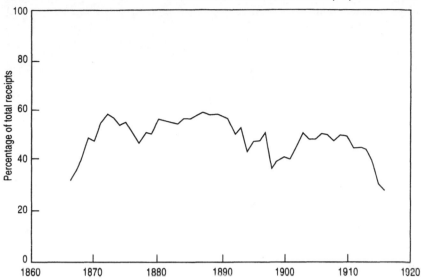

Fig. 2. Customs Receipts as Percentage of Total Federal Receipts, 1866–1916. *Source: Historical Statistics of the United States: Colonial Times to 1970*, Bicentennial ed., pt. 2 (Washington, D.C.: Bureau of the Census, 1975), 1106, series Y352, Y353.

ure 2 shows that customs receipts constituted between 30 percent and 58 percent of federal revenues during the entire period between the Civil War and World War I. Figure 3 shows that there was, indeed, a federal budget surplus—that is, an excess of total receipts over current expenditures—from 1866 to 1893. Clearly, the Dependent Pension Act of 1890, designed to make many more veterans eligible for pensions than under any previous laws, passed after a decade of spectacular federal surpluses. Curiously, however, the Arrears Act of 1879 passed at a time when there was practically no surplus—that is, when the customs receipts of the day were actually being spent on other items, especially on retiring the debt. Supported by both Republicans and northern Democrats, this critical piece of pensions legislation passed without a close connection to the spending of surplus revenues, and indeed there were many worries about how to cover its anticipated cost.[55] One suggestion at that time for paying the pension bill, which surely did not appeal to

[55] Glasson, *Federal Military Pensions*, 163, 166–73. In fact, because of the worries over costs, when the appropriations for the act were made, some new provisions were added to limit somewhat the amounts of arrears paid to successful applicants (see 172–73).

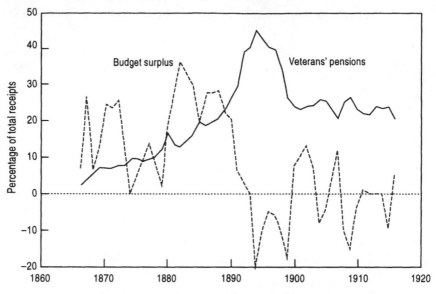

Fig. 3. Federal Surplus (Deficit) and Veterans' Pensions as Percentage of Total Receipts, 1866–1916. *Source: Historical Statistics of the United States: Colonial Times to 1970,* Bicentennial ed., pt. 2 (Washington, D.C.: Bureau of the Census, 1975), 1106, series Y352, and 1104, series Y337; and William H. Glasson, *Federal Military Pensions in the United States* (New York: Oxford University Press, 1918), 273.

eastern business interests, was to expand the money supply by printing Greenbacks. This notion came from George Lemon, a prominent Washington pension attorney (who would later become a vocal advocate of linking tariffs and pensions).[56] Apparently Lemon always put pensions first, which makes sense given that pension attorneys reaped a fee from every pension application they could drum up, and Lemon handled tens of thousands of cases.

Arguments pointing to organized veterans or tariff advocacy by protectionist northeastern industrialists are not so much wrong as incomplete and underspecified. Such groups were part of the Republican-orchestrated coalition behind the 1890 Dependent Pension Act. But there were other instruments in the band; and the party leaders who set the tune had their own organizational interests above and beyond those of the GAR and business groups.[57] The expansion of Civil War pensions

[56] Lemon's suggestion appeared in his newspaper, the *National Tribune,* February 1879. Subsequent issues show his advocacy of tariffs and the use of customs revenues to pay for ever-more generous pensions.

[57] For a political dispute in which the preferences of party politicians differed from those of

must be understood in relation to the structure of the nineteenth-century U.S. state and situated in terms of the dynamics of political party competition after the Civil War. The expansion of Civil War pensions reflected the proclivity of the nineteenth-century U.S. political parties to enact distributive policies, which allowed the spread of sometimes carefully timed and targeted benefits to key supporters in their geographically widespread crossclass constituencies.[58] The important legal watersheds also reflected the changing competitive strategies of the major political parties; and the forms of new legislation maximized possibilities for using pensions to recruit voters.

After the end of Reconstruction, the Republicans became locked in tight national-level competition with a revived Democratic party for control of the presidency and the Congress. This competition lasted until after the realignment of 1896, when the Republicans again became nationally dominant. The initial major liberalization of Civil War pensions through the Arrears Act was spurred by the revival of tight party competition. Yet the ensuing expansion of pensioners and pension costs soon worked differentially to the advantage of the Republican party, which learned the uses of the Pension Bureau in managing the application backlog spurred by the Arrears Act. After the mid-1880s, the national Democrats emphasized tariff reductions and backed off from pension liberalization, while the Republicans became the champions of a politically as well as fiscally complementary set of generous distributive policies, including pensions along with tariffs. The Dependent Pension Act of 1890 was very much a Republican-sponsored measure, an intraparty compromise; and later slight changes in this law also came under Republican auspices.

THE ARREARS ACT AND THE COMPETITIVE POLITICIZATION OF THE PENSION QUESTION

The Arrears of Pension Act passed the House on 19 June 1878, went through the Senate on 16 January 1879, and was signed into law by President Rutherford B. Hayes on 25 January. According to this law (as later amended in the appropriations process), whenever applicants for pensions had been awarded benefits starting some years after the war,

---

business groups advocating tariff reform, see S. Walter Poulshock, "Pennsylvania and the Politics of the Tariff, 1880–1888," *Pennsylvania History* 29 (July 1962).

[58] See Richard L. McCormick, *The Party Period and Public Policy: American Politics from the Age of Jackson to the Progressive Era* (New York: Oxford University Press, 1986), esp. chap. 5. For a discussion of how nineteenth-century U.S. political arrangements furthered distributive social policies, see Skocpol, *Protecting Soldiers and Mothers*, chap. 1.

their cases should be reopened and payments made back to the date of their discharge from the military or the death of the family breadwinner. What is more, anyone who applied for a new pension (up until July 1880) would, assuming it was eventually granted, automatically receive as part of the first payment all of the "arrears," or previous pension payments, to which he or she would have been entitled from the time of discharge or death. "The average first payment in 1881 to army invalids was $953.62; [and] to army widows, minor children, and dependent relatives, $1,021.51."[59] At a time in U.S. history when the average annual money earnings of nonfarm employees totaled about $400, these were considerable windfalls that could be put to excellent use.[60] As Hayes would later write in defense of signing this legislation: "Look at the good done. In every county of the North are small but comfortable homes built by the soldier out of his arrearage pay."[61]

The Arrears Act originated partly from a genuine desire to rationalize and reform preexisting laws, and partly from a politically well timed lobbying campaign organized by a few prosperous pension attorneys. For one thing, many members of Congress and officials were perturbed by inequities among veterans traceable simply to the date at which they applied for pensions; and in the current session House members had introduced more than eighteen-hundred private bills attempting to address such problems for individuals.[62] New laws often originate in this way, as officials and politicians themselves become dissatisfied with the operation of earlier policies and create revised measures, typically more expensive or interventionist, to correct the situation.

In addition, the leveling off of new applications in the 1870s was a problem for pension attorneys, and some major attorneys saw arrears legislation as an excellent way to stimulate renewed business. Because pension attorneys collected fees limited by statute to $10 apiece for each application they helped assemble and shepherd through the Pension Bureau, they had a strong interest in generating as many applications as possible. "By means of subagents and a very thorough system of advertising they were 'drumming' the country from one end to the other in search of pension claims. . . . Claims agents and attorneys were building up an enormous practice. Those most skilled in the system were gradually drifting to the nation's Capital. There they divided their energy between handling claims and lobbying for more favorable pension legis-

[59] Glasson, *Federal Military Pensions*, 175.
[60] *Historical Statistics of the United States, Colonial Times to 1970*, part 1, 165, series D 735–738.
[61] From Rutherford B. Hayes's 14 December 1881 letter to William Henry Smith, as quoted in Glasson, *Federal Military Pensions*, 164.
[62] Oliver, "History of Civil War Military Pensions," 51–52.

lation."[63] In October 1877, leading pension attorney George E. Lemon launched the *National Tribune*, a periodical news sheet distributed to Union veterans across the country, in order to agitate for arrears legislation and advertise his own firm's services. Another pension attorney, N. W. Fitzgerald, used the competing news sheet, *Citizen Soldier*, to the same end. And Captain R. A. Dimmick set up a lobbying group, the Soldiers' Association, to generate petitions advocating arrears legislation to be sent to Congress and state legislatures.[64]

Pension attorneys did not always get their way, however.[65] Therefore, it was very important that northern elected politicians from both parties were highly susceptible at this juncture to arguments on behalf of the Union soldiers and survivors. From the mid-1870s, with Reconstruction at an end and the Democratic South back in the national electorate, the two major parties became closely competitive both in national elections and in state elections throughout much of the East and Midwest. The Democrats regained control of the House in 1875 and were clearly savoring their renewed prospects for national power. For a time, the Democrats saw the pensioners' cause as a way to prove their nationalist credentials in the North, neutralizing the Republicans' "bloody shirt" tactics.[66] Neither party wanted to appear ungenerous to the widows and disabled soldiers.

The Democratic-controlled House was the first to pass the Arrears bill, with only four nonsouthern Democrats dissenting and no Republicans opposed.[67] While the bill was pending before the Senate, twenty-five senators faced reelection in their state legislatures, which chose senators in those days. Pressure orchestrated by the pension agents was directed to the state legislatures in order to influence their choices or to encourage incumbent senators to support the Arrears bill. In the end, the Arrears Act passed the Republican-controlled Senate with virtually unanimous support from northern Democrats as well as Republicans. After the passage of the Arrears Act and related appropriations legislation, moreover, Democratic spokesmen competed with Republicans to claim credit. In the words of an Illinois Democratic representative, "This side of the House deserves commendation for the liberality and zeal with which it has supported legislation in the interest of soldiers engaged in all wars waged in behalf of our government, thereby refuting

[63] Ibid., 53.
[64] These facts come from Glasson, *Federal Military Pensions*, 156–57.
[65] For example, the attorneys had been forced to accept statutory limits on their fees for handling pension applications.
[66] On this point, see Dearing, *Veterans in Politics*, 243–47.
[67] This paragraph is based on Oliver, "History of Civil War Military Pensions," 53–56.

every accusation against the [D]emocratic party of want of regard for the interest of the soldier."[68]

With the passage of the Arrears legislation, veterans and survivors had new motives to apply for both monthly pensions and the hefty initial lump-sum payments. As a contemporary critic wrote, the "effect of this law was to stir up a multitude of people to apply for pensions who had never thought of the matter before. In one year 141,466 men who had not realized that they were disabled until the Government offered a premium of a thousand dollars or more for the discovery of aches and disabilities, made application."[69] "Before 1879, new claims had been filed at the rate of 1,600 a month; after the new act took effect, new claims rose to over 10,000 a month."[70]

DEFEAT FOR AN ATTEMPT TO CENTRALIZE THE APPLICATION PROCESS

The avalanche of new applications stimulated by the Arrears Act was to be processed by a U.S. Pension Bureau that had few means at its disposal to detect fraudulent claims by pension applicants. Although the bureau was consistently staffed by old soldiers who were favorably disposed toward applicants, few contemporary observers doubted that the details of the application process were relatively honestly managed inside the agency itself. When pension claims arrived by mail in Washington, they were carefully filed and scrutinized for proper execution; then the Adjutant General's Office and the Surgeon General's Office of the War Department were asked to report from their records (which were "beyond change or alteration") all available data on a soldier's military service and wartime medical treatments.[71] Yet the processing of applications was also dependent upon thousands of doctors scattered in communities across the North, along with local witnesses, notaries, and lawyers.[72] From the time of the war, pension applicants were allowed to

---

[68] As quoted in ibid., 67.

[69] Eugene V. Smalley, "The United States Pension Office," *Century Magazine* 28 (new series, vol. 6 1884): 428.

[70] Robert McElroy, *Grover Cleveland: The Man and the Statesman* (New York: Harper and Brothers, 1923), 190.

[71] The quoted phrase is from "The Course of a Claim Through the Bureau" in *Report of the Secretary of the Interior for the Fiscal Year Ending June 30, 1891* (Washington, DC: Government Printing Office, 1891), 70. See also the accounts of the application process in Smalley, "The United States Pension Office," 430; the 15 December 1883 letter of instructions to local examining surgeons from the Pension Office—Medical Division, Department of the Interior (a pamphlet in the holdings of the Harvard College Library); and *A Treatise on the Practice of the Pension Bureau Governing the Adjudication of Army and Navy Pensions* (Washington, DC: Government Printing Office, 1898).

[72] Leonard D. White, *The Republican Era: 1869–1901. A Study in Administrative History* (New York: Macmillan, 1958), 211–14; and Smalley, "United States Pension Office."

testify for themselves or find their own witnesses in support of their applications; for example, neighbors might testify to a woman's marriage to a dead soldier and to her persistent widowed status and proper sexual conduct after his death. To certify the war-related disabilities on which pension awards to veterans depended before 1890, applicants also submitted affidavits obtained from local physicians. These doctors were situated far outside of Washington and perhaps enmeshed in the same social networks as the pension applicants they examined; they were not subject to any effective bureaucratic supervision by the bureau. As time passed after 1865, it became increasingly difficult for either the physicians or the central Pension Bureau officials to tell whether a wound or disease actually had originated in the war. Besides, without being able to cross-examine witnesses, Pension Bureau officials had to depend upon the honesty of supportive affidavits in the application. There were Special Examiners from the bureau detailed to look into certain applications, but these were only a minority of instances in which there were either special problems of documentation or glaring reasons to suspect irregularities.[73] The 1879 Arrears Act itself repealed a previous rule that had limited the use of parole evidence (for example, the supportive testimony of kinspeople, neighbors, and former comrades-in-arms) rather than the records of the War and Navy Departments to settle long-pending claims. This "change opened the way for the renewal of many longstanding claims of doubtful character."[74]

More important, during the period when the Arrears Act was passed, Congress refused to enact a major proposal for reforming the administrative system by which pension applications were processed. This was the "Sixty Surgeon Pension Bill," embodying a plan that had been pressed for several years by J. A. Bentley, the commissioner of pensions from 1876 to June 1881. In place of the existing system that "permitted claims to be established upon affidavits prepared in secret by the claimants and their friends, and upon the certificate of the neighborhood physician,"[75] Commissioner Bentley proposed the following arrangement:

The whole country was to be divided into pension districts of such a size . . . that one surgeon devoting his entire time to the duties assigned him could make all required medical examinations in that district. A highly qualified [and generously paid] surgeon was to be appointed for each district, and was

[73] The mission and early procedures of this division of the Bureau can be glimpsed in *General Instructions to Special Examiners of the United States Pension Office* (Washington, DC: Government Printing Office, 1882).

[74] Glasson, *Federal Military Pensions*, 165.

[75] Oliver, "History of Civil War Military Pensions," 43–44.

to be placed under the direction of the Commissioner of Pensions. Also a competent clerk was to be sent to each pension district, to act in conjunction with the surgeon. The duty of the clerk was to take testimony in each case, review the evidence, and cross-examine the witnesses [in public hearings]. These two officials were to constitute a Commission on the part of the Government, before whom all pension applicants were to appear and submit whatever proof they desired in support of their claim. After obtaining all information relating to each claim, the case and its testimony was to be forwarded to the Pension Office for final settlement.[76]

Commissioner Bentley's remarkable proposal was in effect an effort to build up a stronger civil service organization able to conduct judicial-type proceedings, in order to control costs and promote regular standards in the granting of Civil War pensions. The example of France in the nineteenth century suggests that such an organization might have restricted the expansion of pensions. But Congress simply ignored Commissioner Bentley's plan, preferring instead to institute minor modifications in the existing system. During 1881 and 1882, it was stipulated that special pension examiners should hold hearings for those applications dependent upon parole evidence alone; and local boards of examining surgeons were substituted for affidavits from family physicians.[77] During the 1880s, the Pension Bureau in Washington was rehoused in a magnificent new building as it grew into what Commissioner of Pensions Green B. Raum called in 1891 "the largest executive bureau in the world"—with an office force of 2,009 persons "besides eighteen pension agents, with a clerical force of 419, and 3,795 examining surgeons stationed in various parts of the country."[78] Yet the application process remained rooted in local communities and regions. Applicants for pensions could apply credibly for more benefits than they might strictly deserve or even for pensions they had not earned at all—as long as they could obtain the collusion of friends and neighbors, who might themselves have an interest in a successful application and as long as they could secure the help of local doctors and lawyers, whose "natural disposition would be to favor the applicant. . . . There is little reason why they should feel called upon to protect the Government treasury."[79] The pension application system remained a classic example of a recurrent

[76] Ibid., 44–45.

[77] Ibid., 83–86.

[78] Green B. Raum, "Pensions and Patriotism," *North American Review* 153 (1891): 211. Raum was engaged in a bit of rhetorical exaggeration. See the description of the New South Wales (Australian) Department of Public Works, 12,000–15,000 strong as of the 1880s, in Desley Deacon, *Managing Gender* (Melbourne: Oxford University Press, 1989), 104.

[79] Smalley, "United States Pension Office," 430.

pattern in U.S. politics: a central agency linked with constituents and voluntary groups in thousands of local communities across America.

PENSIONS BECOME FUEL FOR CONGRESSIONAL AND PARTY PATRONAGE

The passage of the Arrears Act in 1879, accompanied by the failure in early 1881 of Bentley's Sixty Surgeon Pension Bill, transformed Civil War pensions from relatively straightforward compensation for wartime disabilities into fuel for patronage politics. Pension patronage flourished both through Congress and through party controls over the leadership and nonroutine practices of the Pension Bureau. An ideal distributive policy is one in which benefits are given to many particular recipients, and politicians have some discretionary control over the timing and targeting of those benefits. Civil War pensions may not seem to fit this profile very well, if one assumes that conditions of eligibility were set by statutory law and potential recipients exercised all the discretion: once they applied, they would automatically get the benefits if their qualifications fell within the statute. In fact, the statutes quickly became so bewilderingly complex that there was much room for interpretation of cases. Interior Department officials and commissioners of pensions might apply more or less stringent interpretations of existing statutes; they might even invite whole classes of old cases to be reopened to allow more generous pension awards.[80] In addition, individual cases (or groups of cases) might be speeded up or slowed down in their passage through the Bureau of Pensions. As a result of the many reapplications and new applications stimulated by the Arrears Acts, a backlog of several hundred thousand claims piled up for processing, and such massive backlogs continued to hang over over the system into the 1890s. This situation allowed considerable space for the manipulation of the timing of case processing.[81]

If a given applicant did not feel that his or her case had been correctly processed by the Pension Bureau, or if he or she thought that things were moving too slowly or that existing statutes did not quite cover the

[80] On reinterpretations across administrations, see *Decisions of the Department of the Interior in Cases Relating to Pension Claims and to the Laws of the United States Granting and Governing Pensions*, vol. 4, edited by George Baber of the Board of Pension Appeals (Washington, DC: Government Printing Office, 1891), iii. The editorial preface to this volume states that it is intended to highlight disagreements about legal interpretations with the previous administration of Democratic President Grover Cleveland, differences flowing "from a spirit of larger liberality exercised by the present administration [of Republican President Benjamin Harrison] in applying the pension system to those entitled to its benefits."

[81] Heywood T. Sanders, "Paying for the 'Bloody Shirt': The Politics of Civil War Pensions" in Barry S. Rundquist, ed., *Political Benefits* (Lexington, MA: Lexington Books, D.C. Heath, 1980), 146.

special merits of the case, a petition to a congressional representative might result. In 1882, Representative Roswell G. Horr of Michigan observed: "I think it is safe to say that each member of this House receives fifty letters each week; many receive more. . . . One-quarter of them, perhaps, will be from soldiers asking aid in their pension cases, and each soldier is clear in his own mind that the member can help his case out if he will only make it a special case and give it special attention."[82]

Robert M. La Follette estimated in his autobiography that he spent from a quarter to a third of his time in Congress from 1885 to 1891 "examining testimony and untangling . . . records" for the "many old soldiers" in his district. Such help to a veteran from a congressman could be just as important to the recipient's welfare as help to an unemployed worker from an urban political boss. As La Follette explained: "I recall one interesting case. An old man, by the name of Joseph Wood, living in Madison [WI], very poor, had a claim pending for an injury received at Pittsburg Landing. His case had been repeatedly rejected because the records of the War Department showed that his regiment had not arrived at Pittsburg Landing until forty-eight hours after the claimant swore he had been injured." La Follette found that his captain and twenty-five other soldiers agreed with the claimant, and so did the memoirs of General Sherman. But the War Department would not question its records.

> I seemed up against it, when it flashed across my mind that the [War Department] document looked too new to be the original record. Upon inquiry, I found this was true. The old worn records had been stored away some years before. Some one was detailed to examine them, and sure enough, there had been a mistake in copying. General Sherman and my old soldier friend were right. Thirty-six hundred dollars back pension brought comfort to that old man and his wife.[83]

With a proliferation of cases such as these, the "volume of correspondence between the Pension Bureau and members of Congress was immense. In 1880 it was reported as amounting to nearly 40,000 written and personal inquiries; in 1888 it had more than doubled (94,000 items); and in 1891 it reached a peak of 154,817 congressional calls for information on the condition of cases, an average of over 500 for each working day."[84]

[82] White, *Republican Era*, 72.
[83] Robert M. La Follette, *La Follette's Autobiography: A Personal Narrative of Political Experiences*, foreword by Allan Nevins (Madison: University of Wisconsin Press, 1968; orig. 1911), 37–38. For other instances of particular congressional representatives who took pride in helping pension applicants, see Heck, *Civil War Veteran in Minnesota*, 185–90.
[84] White, *Republican Era*, 75.

Usually the Pension Bureau was asked to reconsider or nudged to process cases more expeditiously. Yet when the bureau and the secretary of the interior ultimately ruled against applicants, Congressmen could sponsor "private pension bills" that added individuals to the pension rolls or—most often—increased benefits for existing pensioners. In the aggregate, private pension bills do not seem to have accounted in particular years for more than .5 percent to 2 percent of new pensioners or additional pension expenditures.[85] Nevertheless, Congress spent considerable time on them, and their numbers rose dramatically during the 1880s and again after 1900.[86] "In the 49th Congress [1885–1887], 40 percent of the legislation in the House and 55 percent in the Senate consisted of special pension acts. It was customary for Friday evening to be 'pension night' during congressional sessions."[87] "Passage of private pension bills was by general consent. Usually no quorum was present."[88] Eventually, congressional handling of private pension bills became fully routinized: pension committees in each house simply allocated members regular quotas of bills that they could put through without any real scrutiny.[89] When special pension bills were enacted at the highest rates in the early twentieth century, most raised the rates for individuals that congressional representatives found especially meritorious, even though these applicants' situations fell outside of existing statutes. Some special acts, however, actually changed the military records of former soldiers classified as deserters in order to make them eligible for pensions.

Pension patronage went beyond congressional interventions in individual cases. During the nineteenth century, when competitive patronage democracy was at its height, party-appointed leaders of the Pension Bureau exercised a certain amount of partisan discretion in the handling of categories of cases. In the words of the historian John Oliver,

there is evidence that as early as 1880 the influence of the pension system was felt in the political affairs of the nation. According to the testimony of one of the special agents of the Bureau, Mr. Thomas P. Kane, it was quite a common practice for the Pension Office to concentrate its forces on those claims coming from doubtful states, just before the general elections. . . . [And a] table submitted by the chief of the Records and Accounts Division shows that during the three months of July, August, and September, 1880, the average

[85] I base this conclusion on a memorandum prepared by Edwin Amenta, who used statistics available in the 1890, 1900, and 1910 Annual Reports of the Commissioners of Pensions.

[86] Glasson, *Federal Military Pensions*, 280.

[87] Morton Keller, *Affairs of State: Public Life in Late Nineteenth-Century America* (Cambridge, MA: Harvard University Press, 1977), 311.

[88] White, *Republican Era*, 76.

[89] Glasson, *Federal Military Pensions*, 275–76.

number of pensions issued was 1,661; but in October, the month preceding the national election, there were 4,423 original claims allowed.[90]

Appointed in 1881 by Republican President James A. Garfield, Commissioner of Pensions Colonel W. W. Dudley proved to be a key innovator in the political use of the Pension Bureau. Not only did Dudley champion the rapid expansion of the Pension Bureau to facilitate the processing of claims, he also worked with the Grand Army of the Republic to draw up lists of potentially eligible veterans in each state. He made lists of veterans' addresses available to new applicants so that they could locate witnesses. Commissioner Dudley determined that as of 1882 over a million living Union veterans and almost 87,000 pensionable relatives had not yet applied for benefits; and he realized that two-fifths of existing pensioners, along with over half of the 300,000 claims then pending at the bureau, came from the electorally crucial states of Illinois, Indiana, New York, Ohio, and Pennsylvania.[91] Moving from investigation of the political potential of the pension system to practical applications, Commissioner Dudley directed Pension Bureau officials not to refuse claims until after the 1884 presidential election and told them to speed up the processing of applications from Ohio and Indiana, where the election was sure to be very close. In September 1884, moreover, Dudley went on a paid "leave of absence" from Washington, taking large numbers of pension examiners first into Ohio and then into Indiana. Prospective pensioners were sought out, urged to apply, and told to vote for the Republican ticket to ensure the rapid processing of their claims. Several Democrats later told congressional investigators that they voted Republican in the election out of fear for their pension applications![92]

Commissioner Dudley's efforts may have helped the Republicans to carry Ohio by 15,000 votes, but they failed by about 6,500 votes in Indiana.[93] The Democratic presidential candidate, Grover Cleveland, was elected, and Dudley had to resign his post. Nevertheless, Colonel Dudley's "performance was not lost on the Republican Party. [Thereafter] the party used its incumbency of the White House as a vehicle for boosting the outputs and generosity of the Pension Bureau. . . . If the Republicans were able to create an enduring alliance with the ex-sol-

[90] Oliver, "History of Civil War Military Pensions," 77, discussing the testimony of Pension Bureau officials before Congress, published in *House Committee Reports*, 46th Congress, 3rd sess., no. 387, 389.

[91] Oliver, "History of Civil War Military Pensions," 107. My account of Dudley's activities draws on ibid., 105–117, and Sanders, "Politics of Pensions," 146–50.

[92] Oliver, "History of Civil War Military Pensions," 111–12, citing *House Report*, 48th Congress, 2nd sess., vol. 3, no. 2683, 6–9.

[93] Oliver, "History of Civil War Military Pensions." 112, 117.

diers and build a national political machine, it was largely because they were willing and able to employ the pension bureaucracy in a partisan fashion."[94] There were also reports of Democrats using the Pension Bureau to help old soldiers when they were in office and facing elections.[95] Nevertheless, Heywood Sanders presents rough evidence that the expansion of Pension Bureau budgets and personnel, and higher rates of approval for new pension claims, corresponded to years of Republican control of the executive branch between 1878 and 1899. "For the individual veteran," he concludes, "the choice was obvious. . . . Electoral support for Republican candidates promised a better pension, delivered more quickly."[96]

PARTY DIFFERENTIATION AND REPUBLICAN SPONSORSHIP OF THE DEPENDENT PENSION ACT

The Democrats and the Republicans increasingly parted company on the issue of pension generosity after the early 1880s. To be sure, many northern Democrats in Congress continued to vote in favor of private bills and general pension legislation. But from the time of Grover Cleveland's presidency onward, the national Democratic party and Democratic presidents stressed controls on pension expenditures, and the need to attack fraud in the system. Meanwhile, the Republicans waxed ever more eloquent in their advocacy of generosity to the Union veterans. As the 1888 Republican platform put it, "The legislation of Congress should conform to the pledges made by a loyal people and be so enlarged and extended as to provide against the possibility that any man who honorably wore the Federal uniform shall be the inmate of an almshouse, or dependent upon private charity. In the presence of an overflowing treasury, it would be a public scandal to do less for those whose valorous service preserved the government."[97]

"In the presence of an overflowing treasury. . . ." This phrase signals an important reason for major party differentiation on the question of further pension liberalization. After the 1870s, the rapid growth of the industrializing U.S. economy brought plentiful revenues into the federal treasury. As we saw in Figures 2 and 3, tariff revenues accounted for between 30 percent and 58 percent of all federal revenues between the

---

[94] Sanders, "Politics of Pensions," 150.

[95] According to Glasson, *Federal Military Pensions*, 224, President Cleveland's Commissioner of Pensions John C. Black attempted to use the bureau to aid the Democrats in 1888, especially in Indiana.

[96] Sanders, "Politics of Pensions," 147–50, quotation on 150.

[97] Donald Bruce Johnson, *National Party Platforms. Volume I: 1840–1956*, rev. ed. (Urbana: University of Illinois Press, 1978), 82.

Civil War and World War I, and the decade of the 1880s was a time of huge surpluses in the federal budget. Even with efforts made to "retire the outstanding national debt as quickly as possible," nevertheless, in the words of Morton Keller, "the most pressing fiscal problem of the 1880s was the large revenue surplus generated by rising tariff receipts."[98] This rising surplus easily covered the unanticipated costs of the Arrears Act and left high-tariff advocates, mostly Republicans, looking for new ways to spend money; advocates of lower taxes and tariffs could argue that the revenues were no longer needed.

The Democrats under the leadership of Grover Cleveland championed the cause of reducing excess taxation and backed off from competing with the Republicans on generous pensions in order to save money. Protective tariffs, the Democrats argued, constituted hidden taxes on consumers and on most southern and western producers. According to the Democrats, protection should be reduced, and in general only such moderate customs duties should be retained as might be necessary to raise revenue for a frugal federal government.[99] To the consternation of many Democratic regulars, President Cleveland also took up the cause of civil service reform as a way to reduce costly patronage corruption and make federal administration more efficient. For the Republicans of this era, the federal government functioned as a prime source of patronage resources. Of course, the Democrats also had patronage needs, but their most important party machines were centered in states and in major urban centers. In any event, Cleveland was a reformer by personal conviction, and he received support from many formerly Republican Mugwumps.[100]

Meanwhile, the Republicans understood themselves to be the party of those who had saved the nation and could best represent its postwar interest in a strong, growing economy.[101] The party benefited by the 1880s from an ideally complementary set of distributive policies, using some measures, such as protective tariffs and the expansion of federal services, to generate the money and jobs that could be distributed through other policies, including the pension system. By finding popular new uses for the surpluses piling up in the 1880s, the Republicans

[98] Keller, *Affairs of State*, 381.

[99] See R. Hall Williams, " 'Dry Bones and Dead Language': The Democratic Party" in H. Wayne Morgan, ed., *The Gilded Age*, rev. ed. (Syracuse, NY: Syracuse University Press, 1970). See also the Democratic party platforms of this period in Johnson, *National Party Platforms: Volume I*, 56–57 (1880), 65–68 (1884), and 76–78 (1888).

[100] See Allan Nevins, *Grover Cleveland: A Study in Courage* (New York: Dodd, Mead, 1944).

[101] See Lewis Gould, "The Republican Search for a National Majority" in Morgan, ed., *The Gilded Age*, 171–87; and (a contemporary party statement) *The Republican Party: Its History, Principles, and Policies*, John D. Long, ed. (n.p., 1888).

hoped to maintain the tariffs that helped them build coalitions across industries and localities. If a way could be found to spread Civil War pensions to still more people, that would be ideal. After the Arrears Act, many veterans and survivors had applied for pensions but could not prove that disabilities or deaths were directly connected to Civil War military service.[102] Additional pensions would flow overwhelmingly to the northeastern and midwestern states, where the Republicans were strong (and wanted to stay strong), including states where they found themselves in close competition with the Democrats.[103] Furthermore, pensions apparently would go disproportionately to townspeople and farmers, the sectors of the Republican coalition that did not benefit as directly from tariffs as many workers and businessmen did (or believed they did).[104]

Urged on by the Grand Army of the Republic and facing an electorate in which more than 10 percent of the potential voters were Union veterans, the Republicans moved toward reinforcing protective tariffs and fundamentally liberalizing the original Civil War pension law.[105] George Lemon's *National Tribune* and other Grand Army propagandists warned veterans across the North to beware of efforts at tariff reduction until all their needs were met. Initially, elements within the Grand Army and then in 1888 the national GAR itself endorsed calls for a new universal service pension that would simply make every Union veteran and all survivors eligible for monthly payments, regardless of disabilities or capacity for manual employment. Meanwhile, Democratic President Cleveland helped to galvanize the old soldier vote for the Republicans, because he became known as a determined enemy of pension liberality. Not only did Cleveland veto 228 bills (while allowing 1,871 to become law), he also rejected the Dependent Pension Bill of 1887, a forerunner of the measure that would pass in 1890.[106] Cleveland had earlier appeared to encourage such legislation, but he backed off when he saw what the costs might be and also because he claimed that the 1887 bill was vaguely worded.

For the 1888 election, the Republicans mobilized the Grand Army of

[102] Glasson, *Federal Military Pensions*, 204–205.

[103] See Bensel, *Sectionalism and American Political Development*, 68, map 3.1, and 62–73.

[104] We do not have good data on the precise social characteristics of pensioners, but suggestive findings along these lines appear in Sanders, "Politics," 151–52.

[105] My account of the events leading up to the election of Harrison in 1888 draws upon Dearing, *Veterans in Politics*, 364–89; Glasson, *Federal Military Pensions*, 204–225; and Donald McMurray, "The Political Significance of the Pension Question, 1885–1897," *Mississippi Valley Historical Review* 9 (June 1922): 19–36. The 10 percent figure comes from McConnell, "Social History of the Grand Army of the Republic," 15.

[106] Glasson, *Federal Military Pensions*, 278; and McMurray, "Political Significance," 28–29.

the Republic, whose membership stood at 372,960 in 1888.[107] They made strong promises about liberalized pensions and protective tariffs.[108] And they nominated a soldier president, General Benjamin Harrison, who ran a campaign that linked tariffs to appeals to the veterans, as illustrated by a political song of the day:[109]

> Let Grover talk against the tariff tariff tariff
> And pensions too
> We'll give the workingman his due
> And pension the boys who wore the blue.

This combination worked for the Republican party in 1888. In an across-the-board victory widely attributed to the old soldiers' vote, the Republicans took both houses of Congress; they won the presidency by detaching Indiana and New York from the states that had gone for Cleveland in 1884. In Indiana, the Republican victory was by the extremely narrow margin of 2,300 votes, and Harrison was surely helped by the presence of many thousands of present and potential pensioners along with a successful Republican gubernatorial candidate who was the leader of a major pension lobbying group. In New York, the Republicans won by some 13,000 votes in a state where "there were 45,000 federal pensioners in 1888 and the movement of service-pensions for all the Civil War soldiers was particularly strong."[110] Without controlled statistical studies, we cannot really tell whether pension politics made the differences in these states in 1890, but we do have the necessary kind of evidence for Republican fortunes across eighty-eight Ohio counties in elections from 1892 to 1895. Heywood Sanders found that even when the veteran population was controlled for, the prior distribution of pensions up to 1890 significantly affected both turnouts and election results in favor of the Republicans.[111]

After the 1890 national election, Republican President Harrison put "Corporal" James Tanner, a legless Union veteran and a member of the GAR Pension Committee, in charge of the Pension Bureau, and he resubmitted liberalized pension legislation to the Congress. During the election, Tanner had by his own account "plastered Indiana with promises" of more generous pensions under the Republicans. "God help the surplus revenue!" the new commissioner declared, as he set about hand-

---

[107] The GAR membership figure comes from Heck, *Civil War Veteran in Minnesota*, app. A, 356.

[108] See the 1888 Republican platform in Johnson, *National Party Platforms: Volume I*, 79–83.

[109] Quoted from Dearing, *Veterans in Politics*, 382–83.

[110] Glasson, *Federal Military Pensions*, 225.

[111] Sanders, "Politics of Pensions," 150–54.

ing out new and readjusted pensions with gusto.[112] Indeed, Tanner was so heedless of regular procedures that he soon had to be replaced by a slightly more cautious close friend of the soldiers, Green B. Raum, himself a GAR official and Republican politician from Illinois.[113] Meanwhile, as the Pension Bureau forged ahead with granting pensions under loose interpretations of existing laws, the Republicans' Billion Dollar Congress enacted monetary reforms that helped knit together western and eastern Republicans, along with the Dependent Pension Act and the McKinley Tariff of 1890, which embodied the highest rates up to that point in U.S. history.

The Dependent Pension Act was a service-disability measure, which relaxed the previous requirement that veterans must show disabilities originating in injuries actually incurred during the Civil War. Henceforth, monthly pensions could, in the words of the act, be obtained by "all persons who served ninety days or more in the military or naval service of the United States during the late war of the Rebellion and who have been honorably discharged therefrom, and who are now or who may hereafter be suffering from a mental or physical disability of a permanent character, not the result of their own vicious habits, which incapacitates them from the performance of manual labor. . . ."[114] With this watershed legislation, the door was opened for many new successful applicants—exactly what the Republican party wanted. Even the Grand Army's Pension Committee was pleased, declaring: "While not just what we asked, [the Dependent Pension Act] . . . is the most liberal pension measure ever passed by any legislative body in the world, and will place upon the rolls all of the survivors of the war whose conditions of health are not practically perfect."[115] This was prophetic.

Both the numbers of pensioners and overall expenditures on Civil War pensions leapt upward again after 1890 (see Figure 1 above). By 1893, there were 966,012 pensioners and the federal government was spending an astounding 41.5 percent of its income on benefits for them. This was the peak of expenditures, and, of course, natural attrition was pruning the ranks of actual and potential beneficiaries. But new veteran pensioners also continued to apply throughout the 1890s. As Table 1 documents, the percentage of Civil War veterans receiving benefits grew from 39 percent in 1891 to 74 percent in 1900. By 1915, 93 percent of

[112] Donald L. McMurry, "The Bureau of Pensions during the Administration of President Harrison," *Mississippi Valley Historical Review* 13 (December 1926): 343–64.

[113] William Barlow, "U.S. Commissioner of Pensions Green B. Raum of Illinois," *Journal of the Illinois State Historical Society* 60 (Autumn 1967): 297–313. For Raum's own point of view, see his "Pensions and Patriotism," *North American Review* 153 (1891): 205–14.

[114] Bureau of Pensions, *Laws of the United States Governing Pensions*, 38.

[115] Quoted in Glasson, *Federal Military Pensions*, 233.

Civil War veterans who were still living were signed up for federal benefits.

From the 1890s into the 1910s, the old-line Republicans continued to reap political rewards from the complementary interlock of high tariffs and generous pension expenditures. Yet the sudden expansion of pensions right after 1890, accompanied by all-too-evident excesses and corruption, helped Grover Cleveland be reelected president in 1892. The revenue situation also became tighter in the 1890s. Thereafter, especially once the national Democratic party went into decline, pension issues became less salient in national party competition.[116]

Over time, Civil War pensions became more and more obviously old-age and survivors' benefits for the veterans. Administrative rulings making age alone a "disability for manual labor" commenced soon after the Dependent Pension Act, and were later confirmed by a 1906 law that declared simply "the age of sixty-two years and over shall be considered a permanent specific disability within the meaning of the pension laws."[117] Further innovations in general pension legislation—the most important of which occurred in 1907, 1908, and 1912—conferred general benefit increases on age and length-of-service categories of veteran pensioners and addressed the needs of widows and other dependent survivors. Even when the Republicans were completely in control, a degree of moderation prevailed; not every new idea for more generous pensions was put into effect. In a situation in which huge revenue surpluses were no longer present (see Figure 3), we may surmise that the Republicans felt the intense criticism directed against pension profligacy, not only by Democrats but also by Mugwumps and progressive reformers. Since pension eligiblity had already been extended to virtually all Union veterans, further legal changes could not reach out to new categories of voters.

CONCLUSION

Looking back over the entire expansion of the Civil War pension system, it seems apparent that the dynamics of party-run patronage democracy spurred that expansion. We saw that close competition between the Republicans and the Democrats in the late 1870s helped to bring about the passage of the Arrears Act, whose effects in turn fueled the emergence of the Republican old soldiers' machine. The major parties continued to be very closely competitive until the mid-1990s, and in this context it was especially advantageous for the Republicans to combine tariff protection with the increased distribution of pension benefits under the Dependent Pension Act.

[116] McMurry, "Pension Question," 35–36.
[117] Bureau of Pensions, *Laws of the United States Governing Pensions*, 43.

To be sure, in any polity—and certainly in any democracy—there would have been pressures to provide for elderly and impoverished veterans toward the end of their lives. Such pressures in the 1830s and 1840s, for example, had led to modest and very belated benefits (more than fifty years after the war) for non-officer Revolutionary War veterans and their survivors. For Civil War veterans, however, this expectable movement toward universal-service coverage was speeded up and made much more generous. A military-disability system originally tailored to mobilize unprecedented masses of soldiers eventually became enmeshed in the intense competition of the distributively inclined parties that dominated both legislation and administration in the United States from the mid-1870s to the mid-1890s. Thus Civil War pensions became one of a handful of major distributive policies that helped to fuel and sustain late nineteenth-century U.S. patronage democracy, especially to further Republican fortunes within it.

Histories of U.S. social provision have mostly failed to notice that the national government was a major welfare provider at the turn of the century—no doubt because the relevant expenditures were officially categorized as military costs. Yet as Isaac Max Rubinow declared in 1913, five years after the British launched national old-age pensions,

> when our [Amercan] pension roll numbers several thousand more names than that of Great Britain. . . . [and] when the cost of our pensions is . . . more than three times as great as that of the British pension system, . . . it is childish to consider the system of war pensions as a sentimental problem only, and to speak of the millions spent for war pensions as the cost of the "Civil War." We are clearly dealing here with an economic measure which aims to solve the problem of dependent old age and widowhood.[118]

Rubinow was right. Civil War pensions became one of the politically most successful social policies ever devised and sustained in the United States. Expanded very significantly right at the beginning of the country's modern national history—during an era that most historians claim was dominated by limited government and rugged individualism—these pensions signaled the potential for honorable, crossclass, and crossracial social provision to flourish in American democracy. Civil War pensions at their height were America's first system of federal social security for the disabled and the elderly. This pioneering effort was not to be sustained beyond the lifetimes of the generation that fought to save the Union. But, politically speaking, it was a harbinger of things to come in American democracy.

[118] I. M. Rubinow, *Social Insurance, with Special Reference to American Conditions* (New York: Arno Press, 1969; originally 1913), 404.

CHAPTER THREE

Gender and the Origins of Modern Social Policies in Britain and the United States

with Gretchen Ritter

COMPARATIVE RESEARCH on the origins of modern welfare states typically asks why certain European nations, including Great Britain, enacted pensions and social insurance between the 1880s and the 1920s, while the United States "lagged behind," that is did not establish such policies for the entire nation until the Social Security Act of 1935. To put the question this way overlooks the social policies that were distinctive to the early twentieth-century United States. During the period when major European nations including Britain, were launching paternalist versions of the modern welfare state, the United States was tentatively experimenting with what might be called a maternalist welfare state. In Britain, male bureaucrats and party leaders designed policies "for the good" of male wage-workers and their dependents. Meanwhile, in the United States, early social policies were championed by elite and middle-class women "for the good" of less privileged women. Adult American women were helped as mothers, or as working women who deserved special protection because they were potential mothers.

Both Britain and the United States had liberal, electorally competitive polities, whose publics engaged in similar debates about potential social policies around the turn of the century. Consequently, a comparison between paternalist social policy accomplishments in Britain and contemporary maternalist policy breakthroughs in the United States can be very enlightening. This comparison sharpens our sense of what was distinctive about American social politics prior to the New Deal, and it also allows us to explore various explanatory approaches that should be applicable to developments in the United States compared to other nations.

Studies in American Political Development 5 (Spring 1991). © 1991 Cambridge University Press.

An earlier version of this paper was presented at the session on "Finding the Origins of Welfare States" at the Annual Meeting of the American Political Science Association, Washington D.C., September 1, 1988 and at the Social Science History Association Meeting, Washington D.C., November 1989. For suggestions and criticisms that helped us make revisions for publication, we thank fellow members of that panel, as well as Christopher Howard, Susan Pederson, Sylvia Walby, Michele Naples, Linda Gordon, and an anonymous reviewer for *Studies in American Political Development*.

What Is to Be Explained?: Divergent Policy Profiles

Table 1 provides an overview of the major kinds of regulations and social spending measures enacted for adults in Britain and the United States between the 1890s and the 1920s. For the unitary British polity, we can focus on what the national government did. For the United States, however, it is necessary to consider measures that were enacted across most of the states, because most nation-wide social policies took that form prior to the 1930s.

As Table 1 indicates, both Britain and the United States enacted workmen's compensation during the early twentieth century, enabling workers injured at the workplace to collect benefits without proving their employers to be at fault under the common law. The British legislation came earlier, was fully national in scope, and was soon extended to include industrial diseases, while the American laws that passed after 1910 in most but not all of the U.S. states covered only damage to specified parts of the body.[1] By including coverage for industrial diseases, British workmen's compensation in effect served as a bridge toward fuller health-related coverage through national health insurance, because employers were encouraged to see health insurance as a way to shift costs from the compensation system toward the state and the workers (both of whom "contributed" to insurance but not to industrial compensation funds).[2] In any event, workmen's compensation is the only area of social legislation in which the two nations were at all similar in the early twentieth century. With respect to public monetary benefits and regulations dealing with contractual conditions for adult workers, Britain and the United States took quite divergent paths.

Even before the outbreak of World War I, Great Britain had enacted a full range of modern social spending programs targeted on lower-income elderly people and on certain groups of wage-workers.[3] In 1908, Britain instituted old-age pensions for all needy elderly persons of worthy character. Soon after, the 1911 National Insurance Act established health and unemployment insurance for certain groups of industrial workers; these programs were funded one-third from general taxation, one-third from employer contributions, and one-third from the contributions of workers in the covered occupations. From the start, contributory health insurance

[1] Edward Berkowitz and Kim McQuaid, *Creating the Welfare State: The Political Economy of Twentieth-Century Reform* (New York: Praeger, 1980), p. 36.

[2] Roy Hay, "Employers and Social Policy in Britain: The Evolution of Welfare Legislation, 1905–14," *Social History* 4 (1977), pp. 449–50.

[3] On British social policies, see: A.I. Ogus, "Great Britain," *The Evolution of Social Insurance, 1881–1981*, edited by Peter A. Kohler and Hans F. Zacher (New York: St. Martin's Press, 1982) pp. 150–264; Bentley B. Gilbert, *The Evolution of National Insurance in Great Britain: The Origins of the Welfare State* (London: Michael Joseph, 1966); and Pat Thane, *The Foundations of the Welfare State* (London and New York: Longman's, 1982).

TABLE 1

Nation-Wide Labor Regulations and Social Spending Legislation for Adults in Britain and the United States, 1890s–1920s

Britain		United States
	1890s	Women's hour laws passed in 8 states
1897	Workmen's Compensation Act	
	1900–09	New or improved women's hour laws passed in 13 states
1906	Workmen's Compensation Act extended to cover industrial diseases and more occupations	
1908	Old Age Pensions Act	
	1909–17	New or improved women's hour laws passed in 39 states
1909	Trade Boards Act (Public boards established to set minimum wages in selected industries)	
	1911–19	Workmen's compensation laws passed in 38 states
1911	National Insurance Act (contributory unemployment and health insurance, including maternity benefits for wives of covered workers)	1911–20 · Mothers' pension laws passed in 40 states
1912–21	Trade Boards extended to cover 63 occupations	1912–23 · Minimum-wage laws for women passed in 15 states
1920	Unemployment Insurance Act (extends coverage to all manual workers)	1918–32 · Women's hour laws in 2 more states; 12 states make improvements
	1920–32	Workmen's compensation in 2 more states
1921	Unemployed Workers' Dependents Act (added benefits for spouses and children)	1923–28 · Mothers' pensions in 4 more states
1925	Widows', Orphans, and Old Age Contributory Pensions Act	
1927	Unemployment Insurance Act (established rights to open-ended benefits)	

included maternity benefits for the wives of workers who were part of the program. as well as for the few women workers who belonged to the covered occupations.[4] By the early 1920s, moreover, Britain had extended unemployment benefits to all workers and their dependents, regardless of previous contributions, and further liberalizations of benefits followed throughout the 1920s, a period of high unemployment. During the early 1920s, there was a campaign for "family endowments" that might have given benefits directly to all British mothers, but this effort failed as the government and trade unions reaffirmed their preferences for policies targeted on male breadwinners.[5] In 1925, Britain created an additional, contributory system of old-age coverage that included dependent benefits for the widows and orphans of contributing workers. In sum, the British social spending policies of the first decades of the twentieth century afforded some protection against market failures and life hazards not only to the elderly, but also to children and working-age adults. Most working-age women, however, were understood as dependents and benefited from social policies through their ties to wage-earning males.

In the United States, meanwhile, there were unsuccessful efforts to enact old-age pensions and contributory social insurance along British lines. From 1909 onward, noncontributory pensions for the needy elderly were supported by the American Federation of Labor and by a few individual reformers (although many reformers shied away from such pensions).[6] Not until the 1920s was a full-scale campaign waged across many states by the Fraternal Order of Eagles along with some labor unions and associations of reformers.[7] Despite this effort, only six U.S. states adopted optional, locally funded old-age pensions prior to the onset of the Great Depression in 1929.

During the 1910s and 1920s, the chief American proponents of contributory social insurance were social scientists, labor-law administrators, and social-work leaders. Having been influenced by European ideas and policy precedents, a few hundred such people banded together in 1906 to found the American Association for Labor Legislation (AALL).[8] After participating in the successful U.S. campaigns for workmen's compensation laws, the AALL in 1914–15 drafted an unemployment insur-

[4] Thane, *Foundations*, p. 85.
[5] Susan Pedersen, "The Failure of Feminism in the Making of the British Welfare State," *Radical History Review* 43 (1989): 86–110.
[6] For discussion and references, see Ann Shola Orloff and Theda Skocpol, "Why Not Equal Protection? Explaining the Politics of Public Social Spending in Britain, 1900–1911, and the United States, 1880s–1920," *American Sociological Review* 49 (December 1984), pp. 737–38.
[7] Jill Quadagno, *The Transformation of Old Age Security: Class and Politics in the American Welfare State* (Chicago: University of Chicago Press, 1988), pp. 64–72.
[8] Lloyd F. Pierce, "The Activities of the American Association for Labor Legislation in Behalf of Social Security and Protective Labor Legislation" (Ph.D. diss., University of Wisconsin, Madison, 1953).

ance bill modelled on the 1911 British program, and this bill was actually introduced in Massachusetts in 1916.[9] Similarly, the AALL devised a European-style proposal for health insurance and, along with labor and other reform groups, conducted lobbying campaigns between 1916 and 1920 for its enactment in various states, including New York, California, and Illinois.[10] But all of these efforts by early U.S. proponents of paternalist social insurance came to naught. No state legislature passed health insurance; and the first U.S. unemployment compensation programs were not instituted until the 1930s, after the onset of the Great Depression.

The one public social spending measure that did appear across the United States prior to the 1930s was the "mothers' pension," a type of social policy found only in three other nations.[11] Mothers' pensions were locally administered public stipends meant to enable respectable impoverished widows—and in some cases other categories of mothers or parents—to care for children in their own homes, rather than surrendering the children to the custody of institutions or foster homes. Between 1911 and 1920, forty states of the United States enacted laws to enable counties to establish mothers' pensions; and eighteen of these state laws were passed in one burst during 1913.[12] Four more U.S. states enacted mothers' pensions during the 1920s. After these laws appeared, certain American mothers could collect publicly funded social benefits, while virtually no U.S. adult male workers could collect such benefits, either for themselves or for their dependents.

In the area of industrial regulation, Britain and the United States at first travelled along parallel paths but then diverged in the early twentieth century, the former moving to regulate conditions for unorganized low-income workers and the latter focusing protective laws on women workers alone.

During the nineteenth century, both Britain and the pioneering U.S. industrial state of Massachusetts enacted legal limits on hours of factory work for minors and women; because these laws principally affected the textile industry, they set de facto limits to the workday for many male factory operatives as well.[13] At the end of the nineteenth century, Britain

[9] Daniel Nelson, *Unemployment Insurance: The American Experience, 1915–1935* (Madison: University of Wisconsin Press, 1969), pp. 17–18.

[10] Ronald Numbers, *Almost Persuaded: American Physicians and Compulsory Health Insurance, 1912–1920* (Baltimore: Johns Hopkins University Press, 1978).

[11] Laura A. Thompson, *Laws Relating to 'Mothers' Pensions' in the United States, Canada, Denmark, and New Zealand*, Children's Bureau, U.S. Department of Labor, Legal Series No.4, Bureau Publication No.63 (Washington D.C.: U.S. Government Printing Office, 1919).

[12] Children's Bureau, United States Department of Labor, *Mother's Aid, 1921*, Bureau Publication no.220 (Washington D.C.: U.S. Government Printing Office, 1933).

[13] Kathryn Kish Sklar, "'The Greater Part of the Petitioners are Female': The Reduction of Women's Working Hours in the Paid Labor Force, 1840–1917," *Worktime and Industrial-*

came close to enacting a statutory eight-hour limit for all workers, but did not do so.[14] Later industrial regulations in Britain developed through administrative action. The Trade Boards Act of 1909 authorized the establishment of public boards to promulgate minimum wages for workers in a few "sweated industries." Most of the workers initially affected were women, yet the legislation was phrased to include men as well, and during World War I five other British statutes extended trade board regulations to additional occupations, including some that were male-dominated.[15] Right after the war, the Trade Boards Act of 1918 extended the principle of public regulatory boards to all occupations not organized by trade unions, and increased the authority of the boards and the Minister of Labor to set minimum wages and regulate working conditions, including hours. By 1922, some sixty-three boards in thirty-nine trades set minimum wages for approximately three million male and female British workers. The boards also required overtime pay for work beyond eight- or nine-hour days and a forty-eight hour week, thus allowing unorganized workers to attain the hours standards enjoyed contractually by most unionized British workers.[16]

In the United States, progressive reformers and some labor leaders hoped to imitate the British approach to industrial regulation, using public power to protect all vulnerable employees. But this was not what happened. Instead, during the early twentieth century many U.S. states passed laws to limit working hours and (less frequently) establish minimum wages—not for workers in general, but usually for women workers in particular. Regulations for women workers were justified as protection for those who were, or might become, mothers. By 1921, forty-one American states had laws restricting daily hours of labor for women; most of this legislation came between 1909 and 1917, when 39 states passed new or improved women's hour laws.[17] Meanwhile, hours laws for adult males were narrowly restricted to a few occupations such as mining, railroad work, and public service.[18] Similarly, American male workers were protected by minimum-wage laws only through "prevailing-wage" laws applicable to certain public jobs, while women workers were the special beneficiaries of all of the general minimum-wage laws that were enacted in the early twentieth-century United States.[19] Be-

ization: An International History, edited by Gary Cross (Philadelphia: Temple University Press, 1988), pp. 103–33

[14] José Harris, *Unemployment and Politics: A Study in British Social Policy, 1886–1914* (Oxford: Clarendon Press, 1972), pp. 64–73.

[15] See Dorothy Sells, "The Acts of 1909 and 1918," *The British Trade Boards System* (London: P.S. King and Son, Ltd., 1923), pp. 1–6.

[16] Ibid., pp. 178–83.

[17] Elizabeth Brandeis, *Labor Legislation*, edited by John R. Commons et al., *History of Labor in the United States, 1896–1932* (New York: Macmillan, 1935), volume 4, chapter 3.

[18] Ibid., chapter 5.

[19] Ibid., chapter 4.

tween 1912 and 1923, fifteen states plus the District of Columbia enacted minimum-wage laws, some setting limits by statutes but most establishing British-style administrative boards to devise regulations. All but one'of these American minimum-wage laws for women were passed between 1912 and 1919.

Despite some areas of similarity, the overall contrasts between British and American social policies of the early twentieth century are clear. The early British welfare state featured regulations and benefits for workers and low-income dependent people. Although Britain ended up offering considerable help to mothers and widows, this typically happened through the extension of pensions and social insurance from male workers to their dependents. In the United States, meanwhile, direct ties were established between public authorities and widowed mothers, and between public authorities and women workers understood as potential mothers. Protective labor regulations were initially devised for a vulnerable gender rather than for the working class or low-income workers in general. U.S. "welfare" early took on the connotation of public help for mothers raising children without support from fathers.

This article seeks to explain why Britain and the United States took such divergent routes in creating the beginnings of modern social policies in the early twentieth century. In the next section, we briefly review existing theoretical approaches, finding them insufficient to account for the patterns of policy we have just specified. Then we introduce our own explanatory approach, which focuses on structural relations among states, political parties, and major social groups. Our approach accounts for the strategies followed—with varying degrees of success—by the politically active groups that contended to shape social policies in turn-of-the-century Britain and the United States.

EXISTING EXPLANATORY APPROACHES—AND AN ALTERNATIVE

Previous comparative research on the origins of modern social policies has relied upon theoretical approaches stressing the effects of socioeconomic modernization, national values and ideologies, or demands by working-class organizations. Whether considered separately or together, however, these factors cannot adequately account for the divergent policy profiles that we have outlined for Britain and the United States.

Modernization and Social Policies

Many cross-national theories of the welfare state begin with the view that social policies, especially social insurance programs, appear in response to the "modernizing" tempos of industrialization and urbanization. Arguments in this school of thought vary, of course.[20] But all hold that modernizing socioeconomic transformations create new social needs to which governments must respond; at the same time modernization generates the economic resources to finance such protections against market exigencies as workers' compensation, old-age pensions, health and unemployment insurance, and family allowances. Social insurance policies are expected to appear as nations industrialize and urbanize, and to expand in terms of population coverage and benefits as those nations experience further economic growth.

In general, arguments that tie the timing of social insurance innovations to relative levels of industrialization and urbanization do not explain cross-national variations very well, especially not for the period between the 1880s and the 1920s.[21] Moreover, the United States in particular has always proved an awkward case for modernization theories of social policy development, because nationwide social insurance measures did not emerge until the New Deal of the 1930s, when the United States was already much more advanced industrially than other nations which had created social insurance policies earlier. To handle this anamoly, modernization theorists have usually supplemented their explanations with arguments borrowed from the national values school (to be reviewed below).

A comparison between Britain and the United States in the early twentieth century may seem to confirm modernization arguments, because Britain industrialized earlier than the United States and Britain also created a comprehensive array of social insurance programs sooner than the U.S. federal government did. Yet it is misleading to juxtapose the two national governments in this period. Up until the mid-1930s, the various U.S. states were the arenas where social legislation was enacted, and where debates over social insurance proposals occurred. Within the United States, the state of Massachusetts exactly resembled

[20] For examples, see: Phillips Cutright, "Political Structure, Economic Development and National Social Security Programs," *American Journal of Sociology* 70 (1965): 537–50; Robert Jackman, *Politics and Social Equality: Comparative Analysis* (New York: Wiley, 1975); Clark Kerr et al., *Industrialism and Industrial Man* (New York: Oxford University Press, 1964); Harold Wilensky and Charles Lebeaux, *Industrial Society and Social Welfare* (New York: Free Press, 1965); and Harold Wilensky, *The Welfare State and Equality: Structural and Ideological Roots of Public Expenditures* (Berkeley: University of California Press, 1975).

[21] See Peter Flora and Jens Alber, "Modernization, Democratization and the Development of Welfare States in Western Europe," in *The Development of Welfare States in Europe and America*, edited by Peter Flora and Arnold Heidenheimer (New Brunswick: Transaction Books, 1981), pp. 37–80; and David Collier and Richard Messick, "Prerequisites versus Diffusion: Testing Alternative Explanations of Social Security Adoption," *American Political Science Review* 69 (1975): 1299–1315.

Britain in tempos and levels of industrialization and urbanization up to the 1920s. Thus the failure of Massachusetts to enact proposals for British-style pensions and social insurance cannot be attributed to the variables that the modernization school prefers to invoke.[22] By bringing additional U.S. states into the comparative argument, one can raise even more questions about the modernization approach. For reasons that go far beyond the socioeconomic variables highlighted in this perspective, U.S. states other than those at the forefront of industrialization, such as Wisconsin, Minnesota, North Dakota, Oklahoma, and Washington, often pioneered in developing social policies during the early twentieth century.[23]

In the final analysis, not only is socioeconomic modernization a poor predictor of the timing of enactment of social policies across nations, and across states within the United States, it also says little about the content of different national, or state-level, policy profiles, ignoring the particularities of program constituencies and the public rhetoric used to legitimate them. We can hardly learn from this perspective why Britain launched a paternalist welfare state, while the United States created maternalist regulations and social benefits. What is needed instead of modernization theory is an approach more sensitive both to the political causes and the programmatic forms of social policies in these two nations. Of course it was important that industrialization and urbanization transformed Britain and the United States; these processes did throw up new issues and social groupings that entered into political conflicts. But transformations in state structures, electorates, and party systems also occurred and these transformations as well affected the issues and groups that figured in social policy-making.

The Effects of National Political Culture

Instead of assimilating the U.S. case to a worldwide logic of industrialism, there have always been those who would stress "American exceptionalism," tracing the latter to the country's uniquely strong liberal values. In a classic formulation of this thesis, Louis Hartz argued that

[22] This argument is further specified in Orloff and Skocpol, "Why Not Equal Protection?"

[23] See, for example, the discussions in: Edwin Amenta et al., "The Political Origins of Unemployment Insurance in Five American States," *Studies in American Political Development* 2 (1987): 137–82; Keith L. Bryant, Jr., "Kate Bernard, Organized Labor, and Social Justice in Oklahoma During the Progressive Era," *Journal of Southern History* 35 (1969): 145–64; Robert L. Morlan, *Political Prairie Fire: The Nonpartisan League, 1915–1922* (Minneapolis: University of Minnesota Press, 1955); Joseph Frederick Tripp, "Progressive Labor Laws in Washington State (1900–1925)" (Ph.D. diss., University of Washington, 1973); and Richard M. Vallely, *Radicalism in the States: The Minnesota Farmer-Labor Party and the American Political Economy* (Chicago: University of Chicago Press, 1989).

the United States, a nation born in rebellion against British rule and without class divisions or a feudal heritage, developed an all-encompassing liberal culture in which individual rights are sacred, private property is honored, and state authority is distrusted.[24] Since Hartz, others have used liberal values to account, more specifically, for American social politics in contrast to the development of European welfare states. Comparative historian Gaston Rimlinger contrasts the traditional patriarchal values that encouraged Germany to launch pioneering social insurance programs in the 1880s, to the extreme laissez-faire, individualist values that delayed similar policy breakthroughs in the United States until the overwhelming crisis of the Great Depression.[25] Similarly, historian Roy Lubove attributes the failure of most social insurance proposals in the Progressive Era to the strength of voluntarist values.[26]

Plausible as invocation of the American liberal tradition might seem, such an approach does not satisfy the task at hand—explaining why Britain launched a paternalist welfare state in the early twentieth century, while the United States rejected similar measures and enacted maternalist social policies instead. Nineteenth-century Britain also trumpeted classic laissez-faire. The policies that laid the foundations of Britain's welfare state prior to World War I were devised by Liberals and justified by "new liberal" reworkings of established individualist values.[27] Contemporary Progressive reformers in the United States used very similar arguments, and invoked the same fundamental values as the British "new liberals."[28] Moreover, during the New Deal of the 1930s, when the United States finally did enact old-age and unemployment policies, reformers used liberal-individualist arguments to justify the new measures of "social security," thus proving that the American liberal tradition could be adapted to justify the institution of social insurance.

In general, theories that attribute particular policy outcomes to over-

[24] Louis Hartz, *The Liberal Tradition in America* (New York: Harcourt Brace, 1955).

[25] Gaston Rimlinger, *Welfare Policy and Industrialization in Europe, America, and Russia* (New York: Wiley, 1971).

[26] Roy Lubove, *The Struggle for Social Security, 1900–1935* (Cambridge: Cambridge University Press, 1968).

[27] Michael Freeden, *The New Liberalism: An Ideology of Social Reform* (London: Macmillan, 1973).

[28] Kenneth O. Morgan, "The Future at Work: Anglo-American Progressivism, 1870–1917," *Contrast and Connection: Bicentennial Essays in Anglo-American History*, edited by H.C. Allen and Roger Thompson (Columbus: Ohio University Press, 1976), pp. 245–71; and Charles L. Mowat, "Social Legislation in Britain and the United States in the Early Twentieth Century: A Problem in the History of Ideas," *Historical Studies: Papers Read Before the Irish Conference of Historians*, Volume 7, edited by J.C. Beckett (New York: Barnes and Noble, 1969), pp. 81–96.

arching national values suffer from several shortcomings. Any national political culture has space for many alternative "readings" and reworkings of core values. Competing political forces exploit and develop these possibilities; and changes occur over time.[29] The success or failure of any particular political project cannot be attributed solely, or primarily, to the value-laden justifications deployed in the political rhetoric of its supporters—or opponents. Instead, one must identify the groups active in politics, analyze the resources that they bring to bear in allying or conflicting with one another. One must also investigate how the changing institutional configurations of the national polity advantage some strategies and ideological outlooks and hamper others.

Working-Class Politics and the Origins of Modern Social Policies

Among comparative social scientists who attribute social policy developments to political struggles, theories that focus on the strength of the industrial working class have recently gained predominance.[30] Working-class "strength" may be understood as the proportion of manufacturing workers in the national workforce, as the percentage of workers who are unionized (especially in industrial as opposed to craft unions), or as the percentage of votes or number in years in government of a political party ostensibly devoted to furthering working class interests in politics. Sophisticated theorists use combinations of these measures. Yet the bottom line is always clear: business everywhere is understood to be, at best, reluctant to accept new public regulations or tax-supported benefits. Social spending programs, and modern welfare states in general,

[29] For example, in the United States during the late nineteenth century, there were two competing visions of organized labor's relationship to the state, one of which, producerism, envisaged a larger scope for state action to help labor. That the other tradition, pure and simple trade unionism, predominated by the turn of the century was due in large measure to the obstacles American labor groups (and intellectuals who wanted to cooperate with them) faced in achieving stable redistributive or regulatory gains through the U.S. governmental system. "Liberal values" in the abstract did not determine the outcome. Rather, distributively oriented political parties discouraged programmatic political alliances, and the courts were prone to reverse statutes favorable to organized labor. See Martin Shefter, "Trade Unions and Political Machines: The Organization and Disorganization of the American Working Class in the Late Nineteenth Century," in *Working Class Formation: Nineteenth Century Patterns in Europe and the United States*, edited by Ira Katznelson and Aristide Zolberg (Princeton: Princeton University Press, 1986), pp. 197–276; and Victoria Hattam, "Economic Visions and Political Strategies: American Labor and the State, 1865–1896," *Studies in American Political Development* 4 (1990):82–129.

[30] For surveys of this extensive literature, see Michael Shalev, "The Social Democratic Model and Beyond: Two Generations of Comparative Research on the Welfare State," *Comparative Social Research* 6 (1983): 315–51; and Theda Skocpol and Edwin Amenta, "States and Social Policies," *Annual Review of Sociology* 12 (1986): 139–43.

are therefore supposed to appear earlier and grow bigger in those nations where working-class strength is greater.

Evidence reveals, however, that working-class strength theories work best for the 1930s through the 1970s.[31] Trade unions and other workers' organizations were initially not strong advocates of social insurance. In Germany, Britain, and other nations that launched pioneering paternalist welfare states between the 1880s and 1920s, social insurance programs were devised by politicians and bureaucrats. Workers' organizations had to be persuaded to accept them. At that time, trade unions were often more concerned with other public policies, such as the legal rules affecting union organization. Moreover, unions realistically worried that social insurance programs might undercut their autonomy and empower bureaucrats. Only after early social insurance programs were launched did trade unions and labor-oriented political parties become strong advocates of their expansion—especially if benefits could be expanded without commensurate "contributions" taken directly from the paychecks of workers.

As we shall document below, differential labor strength as a single, unmediated factor cannot account for the divergent policy patterns in Britain and the United States between the 1890s and the 1920s. The British and U.S. trade union movements started out with similar orientations toward social legislation, and then diverged because of their experiences in very different national polities. In general, it cannot be taken as given that working-class groups will always fight for social insurance or any other given type of social policy. The political preferences and strategies of industrial workers—as well as those of other social classes and groups—are themselves partially shaped by the state structures, electoral contexts, and political party systems within which workers and their organizations find themselves at particular times and places. Thus institutional variables designed to explain working-class political strategies, as well as variables referring to working-class strength (however defined), need to be brought into cross-national explanations of welfare state development.

Theories stressing labor strength are, moreover, insufficient to explain social policies that are not targeted principally on industrial workers and their dependents. We cannot learn from such theories why Civil War pensions burgeoned into de facto old-age benefits for about a third of elderly men in the North in the late nineteenth-century United States.[32] Nor can they fully explain why the United States during the Progressive

---

[31] See Skocpol and Amenta, "States and Social Policies."

[32] An analysis of Civil War benefits appears in chapter 2, Theda Skocpol, *Protecting Soldiers and Mothers: The Political Origins of Social Policy in the United States* (Cambridge, MA: Belknap, Harvard University Press, 1992).

Era enacted social policies aimed at mothers and at female workers understood as potential mothers. Gender identities and relationships are
simply not treated as analytically central in theories that derive political
conflicts and outcomes straightforwardly from balances of power between capitalists and organized industrial wage earners. Unless we can
bring the politics of gender as well as class into our comparative analysis of British and U.S. social politics, we will not be able to explain the
policy patterns of interest here.

Political Institutions, Social Groups, and Politics

This brings us to the approach we find most useful. We identify the
major actors involved in political struggles over possible social policies.
Then we analyze how their identities, strategies, and capacities were
affected by social and institutional circumstances. Socioeconomic and
political arrangements alike must enter into an adequate specification of
the institutional contexts within which groups were defined and within
which political conflicts about possible social policies proceeded. Actors
situated within political organizations, both governmental institutions
and political parties, must be analyzed along with social groups such as
organized labor and women. The result of this approach is a better
understanding than one can gain from alternative theories of how various acting groups defined their identities and interests. In addition, we
gain a much better understanding of the political alliances formed, and
not formed, by the various groups engaged in policy debates; and we
can explain the successes and, failures of groups and alliances in shaping actual policy outcomes.

The actors that contended over social policies in Britain and the
United States around the turn of the century included working-class and
business organizations, political party leaders, women's organizations,
certain public officials, and reformist professionals. The terrain on
which these groups operated included not only the economies and social
structures of Britain and the United States, but also these nations'
changing electoral and political party systems, their legislatures, executive bureaucracies, and courts. In the American case, relevant institutional configurations existed at state (and sometimes local) as well
as the national level. Indeed, the American political system as much
involved relationships between levels and branches of government
as it did processes within the particular parts of the overall state structure.

In the remainder of this essay, we develop cross-national comparisons
centered on comparable sets of actors—those who were centrally involved in the turn-of-the century political processes leading to the enact-

ment of paternalist benefits and regulations in Britain, and to the failure of paternalist policies and the enactment of maternalist benefits and regulations in the United States. We begin with the reformers and public administrators who first devised proposals for social insurance and labor regulations in both nations. Then we examine the strategies and role of trade unions. Finally, we analyze the political activities of women's groups, exploring the reasons for the special impact of certain women's associations and outlooks on early modern social legislation in the United States.

REFORMIST ELITES AND THE POLITICS OF SOCIAL POLICYMAKING

In both Britain and the United States from the late nineteenth well into the twentieth century, certain reformers, public officials, and political leaders participated in transnational discussions about "workingmen's social insurance"—that is, public benefits for workers and their families when their market incomes were interrupted by old age, ill health, or unemployment. Such people also debated possibilities for new or extended administrative regulations to limit hours of labor and shore up minimum wages for the most vulnerable and least unionized sectors of the working class. Trade unionists and other popular forces entered into these policy debates, but the initiative tended to rest with reform-minded upper- or middle-class professionals, public officials, and politicians. At this point in world history in many industrializing nations, such elites were often attracted to pensions, social insurance, and labor regulations as possible tools for ameliorating class conflict, promoting economic efficiency, and, in general, furthering "the national interest" as they understood it.

Yet Britons and Americans interested in workingmen's benefits and labor regulations at the turn of the century had to work for such measures in polities with very different constitutional structures and prior histories. Britain had a centralized state, with national sovereignty concentrated in Parliament, whereas the United States had a federal state, with authority dispersed among local, state, and federal governments. Authority in the United States was also divided among legislatures, executives, and—last but not least—extraordinarily interventionist courts. Historically, the suffrage was extended in different phases and social patterns in Britain and the United States, profoundly influencing the orientations of political parties and the mobilization of groups into politics through or outside of parties and elections. Males were admitted to the British electorate in protracted, socioeconomically defined stages, a process that encouraged working-class political consciousness and facilitated programmatic party competition. In the United States, by contrast, all free men regardless of class were admitted to the electorate in the early nineteenth century, in a development of cross-class male democracy that discouraged political class consciousness and facilitated the institutionalization of patronage-oriented political parties. It also prompted electorally excluded American women to become extraordinarily gender-conscious and to find extraelectoral styles of political engagement.

In addition to their constitutional and electoral differences, moreover, Britain and the United States moved away from patronage-dominated politics toward public bureaucratization at different phases of industrialization and democratization, so that they had contrasting civil administrative structures and political party systems by the early twentieth century. These two liberal polities also had different social policies already in place, which would serve as reference points for debates over future policy alternatives. By the early 1900s, Britain had a reformed civil service, competing political parties willing to make programmatic appeals to working-class organizations and voters, and policy legacies of centralized welfare coordination to react against and build upon. Especially from the point of view of new-liberal elites in Britain, social spending and regulatory policies directed to wage-workers or lower-income people complemented the organizational dynamics of civil administration and political parties at that historical conjuncture. Meanwhile, however, the United States lacked established civil bureaucracies and was deeply embroiled in the efforts of progressive reformers to create professional regulatory agencies that would be free from the control of "corrupt" party politicians. The new agencies would also be free from immediate supervision of courts committed to case-by-case decisions about economic and social issues. At this juncture in U.S. political history, modern social spending programs for the working class were neither administratively feasible nor politically acceptable to elites and the middle-class public. What is more, new regulatory policies could advance only as far as the state and federal courts, armed with powers of judicial review, would allow them to go. Thus U.S. reformers had to trim their preferences in this area, backing away from aspirations for wage and hour regulations designed to cover all workers.

"Workingmen's Insurance" from Above in Britain

Britain's polity in the nineteenth century started out as a liberal oligarchy, ruled by and for landlords and their commercial allies.[33] During the

---

[33] R.K. Webb, *Modern England: From the Eighteenth Century to the Present* (New York: Dodd, Mead, 1970), pp. 53–57.

course of the century, this polity underwent several intertwined transformations, which—institutionally speaking—lay the basis for the Liberal welfare breakthroughs of 1908–1911: the expansion of national
administrative activities, especially in the realm of social-welfare policy;
the reform of the civil service; the step-by-step partial democratization
of the male parliamentary electorate in the 1830s and 1860s; and transformations in the modes of organization and electoral operation of the
major political parties.

In British civil administration during the eighteenth and early nineteenth centuries, oligarchic patronage predominated and "the public
services were the outdoor relief department of the aristocracy."[34] Industrialization and urbanization, along with the geopolitical exigencies
of maintaining British imperial domains and coping with growing international economic competition, generated pressures for the British government to become more efficient and technically competent than
patronage would allow.[35] Governmental change did not come automatically, reform advocates were initially frustrated by those with a vested
interest in the existing system.[36] Yet, finally, proposals for civil service
reform succeeded politically in the 1870s. Prior changes in universities
made them plausible as agencies for training and certifying civil servants. Once it became clear that working-class political influence might
grow as the electorate expanded, the landed and business groups and
the existing governing elites of Britain came together in order to maintain the elite civil service on a new basis.[37]

Civil service reform in Britain did *not* ensure that bureaucrats would
subsequently become policy innovators, however. At both the Local
Government Board (L.G.B.) and the Home Office, two of the departments most concerned with questions of domestic social policy, there
developed after 1870 a "general inertia and disinvolvement from reform," accompanied a view of the civil service "as a source of income
and status."[38] But the British state structure was not administratively
monolithic in this period. The Board of Trade, a competing agency out-

[34] K.B. Smellie, *A Hundred Years of English Government* (London: Duckworth, 1950), p.
69.

[35] Ibid., pp. 69–70.

[36] Emmeline Cohen, *The Growth of the British Civil Service, 1790–1939* (London: Allen
and Unwin, 1941), chapter 7; and Herman Finer, *The British Civil Service* (London: Allen
and Unwin, 1937), pp. 45–49.

[37] Cohen, *Growth of Civil Service*, pp. 81–83; H.R. Greaves, *The Civil Service in the
Changing State* (London: George C. Harrap, 1947), pp. 21–32; and Martin Shefter, "Party
and Patronage: Germany, England and Italy," *Politics and Society* 7 (1977): 434–37.

[38] Roger Davidson and R. Lowe, "Bureaucracy and Innovation in British Welfare Policy,
1870–1945," *The Emergence of the Welfare State in Britain and Germany, 1850–1950*,
edited by W.J. Mommsen (London: Croom Helm, 1981), pp. 268–69.

side of the control of L.G.B. and the Home Office, was able during the 1880s and 1890s to develop independent capacities in the collection and use of labor statistics.[39] The Board's activities expanded rapidly and it recruited a remarkable core of young, progressive-minded officials, eventually including William Beveridge, an expert on labor markets and issues of unemployment, who had gone from Oxford into settlement house activities, journalism, and unemployment relief work, before coming into government service under the Liberals in 1908.

Finally, and perhaps most important, civil service reform along with step-by-step electoral democratization had important implications for the organization and operations of the political parties. With the credentialization of the civil service, the parties had to stop relying on elite patronage and develop new methods of raising funds and rewarding activists as well as new ways of winning votes in an expanding electorate. In the 1870s and 1880s, both the Liberal and Conservative parties created constituency organizations and at the same time began to formulate programs to appeal through activists to blocs of voters and financial subscribers.[40]

The administrative arrangements and party system in place in Britain by the early twentieth century facilitated the Liberal welfare breakthroughs of 1908 to 1911. From the 1890s onward, there was widespread elite and popular disgruntlement with the way members of the respectable working class who became impoverished due to old age, ill health, or unemployment were handled by the poor laws. National politicians, Conservative and Liberal alike, became interested in reforming or replacing the New Poor Law of 1834 to deal better with the problems of the "worthy poor."[41] Some of their concerns were generated from administrative dilemmas within established relief programs and also by the threat to the whole edifice of local government finance posed by the rising and uneven costs of the law. Other concerns arose from the political fact that the votes of working class people—and the support of their organizations, the unions and friendly societies—had to be contested by parties engaged in increasingly programmatic competition.

During the 1890s, the voluntarist resistance of the friendly societies

---

[39] Roger Davidson, "Llewellyn Smith and the Labour Department," in *Studies in the Growth of Nineteenth Century Government*, edited by Gillian Sutherland (London: Routledge and Kegan Paul, 1972), pp. 227–62.

[40] Roy Douglas, *The History of the Liberal Party, 1895–1970* (London: Sidgwick and Jackson, 1971), pp. 1–17; H.J. Hanham, *Elections and Party Management: Politics in the time of Disraeli and Gladstone* (London: Longmans Green, 1959); Barry McGill, "Francis Schnadhorst and the Liberal Party Organization," *Journal of Modern History* 34 (1962): 19–39; and Shefter, "Party and Patronage," pp. 438–41.

[41] D. Collins, "The Introduction of Old Age Pensions in Great Britain," *Historical Journal* 8 (1965): 246–49; and Harris, *Unemployment and Politics*.

to old age pensions helped to delay new welfare breakthroughs, and then the Boer War of 1899 to 1902 provided political diversion and financial excuses for avoiding new domestic expenditures.[42] But after the war, the Liberals' welfare reforms—which bypassed the New Poor Law without abolishing or fundamentally reforming it—crystallized by two routes in the context we have outlined. In the face of the cross-class campaign waged by the National Committee of Organized Labour on Old Age Pensions, the Liberals devised their noncontributory and need-based old age pensions as a tool of programmatic competition with the Conservatives. The Liberals hoped to retain the loyalty of working-class voters and reinforce their party's alliance with the Labour Representation Committee. After the passage of pension legislation, proposals for contributory unemployment and health insurance came through initiatives from Liberal Cabinet leaders allied with civil administrators at the Board of Trade and the Treasury. For unemployment and health insurance alike, intragovernmental elites took the initiative in persuading both working-class and business interests to go along. Once this persuading was done and the Cabinet was set on its course, the discipline of the Liberal Party in Parliament ensured passage of the National Insurance Act, and there were no independent courts to which disgruntled parties could appeal.

Stepping back, to put these policy departures in broader context, we must underline that the administration of social spending as such was not fundamentally problematic for British elites in this period. The "corruption" of patronage politics was behind them, and disputes were now focused on levels and forms of spending, and especially on direct versus indirect taxation.[43] The Labour Party was not yet a major actor in British politics, and both Liberal and Conservative leaders were concerned to attract or retain working-class electoral support in programmatic party competition. Parts of the British state bureaucracy had the capacities and the personnel to take the initiative in devising new social policies. In this context and conjuncture, pensions and social insurance looked like good ways to circumvent for the respectable working class the cruelties, inefficiencies, and costs of the New Poor Law of the nineteenth century. Such policies also looked like appropriate programs to appeal to—and, in the case of the social insurance measures, newly *tax*—the working class, involving them more fully in the life of a united nation, yet under the hegemony of enlightened professional middle-class leadership.

---

[42] Gilbert, *Evolution of National Insurance*, pp. 179–88, 196.

[43] H.V. Emy, "The Impact of Financial Policy on English Party Politics before 1914," *Historical Journal* 15 (1972): 103–31.

The Obstacles to Pensions and Social Insurance in the United States

America's polity in the nineteenth century has been aptly described as a polity of "courts and parties" operating in a multi-tiered federal framework.[44] The courts adjudicated rights of contract and private property, and highly competitive political parties provided a modicum of integration across the various levels and branches of government. Crucially, U.S. electoral politics was fully democratized for white males in the Jacksonian era. Thus, political parties were able to rotate the "spoils of office" to reward their cadres and followers as the parties swept into and out of office in the constant rounds of close-fought elections characteristic of nineteenth-century American democracy.[45] The system worked best at all levels when governmental outputs took the form, not of programs devised to appeal to functionally organized collectivities, but of politically discretionary *distributional* policies, such as financial subsidies or grants of land, tariff advantages, special regulations or regulatory exceptions, construction contracts and public works jobs.[46]

Ideal sets of distributional policies combined measures that raised revenues—or created jobs—with those that allocated them. Especially from the point of view of the Republicans, the post-Civil War pension system was an excellent example of a policy generated by the distributional proclivities of nineteenth-century patronage democracy. It allowed the Republicans to confer on individuals in many localities pensions financed out of the "surplus" revenues from the constantly readjusted tariffs sponsored to benefit various industries and sections of industries. Not surprisingly, Civil War pension laws and practices were broadly liberalized from the late 1870s to the 1890s, when electoral competition between the Republicans and the Democrats in the North was especially intense.[47] A few hundred votes could make the difference

[44] Stephen Skowronek, *Building a New American State: The Expansion of National Administrative Capacities, 1877–1920* (Cambridge and New York: Cambridge University Press, 1982), chapter 2.

[45] Morton Keller, *Affairs of State: Public Life in Nineteenth Century America* (Cambridge, Mass: Harvard University Press, 1977), chapters 7, 8, 14. See also the relevant chronological portions of Martin Shefter, "Party, Bureaucracy, and Political Change in the United States," *Political Parties: Development and Decay*, edited by Louis Maisel and Joseph Cooper (Beverly Hills, CA: Sage Publications, 1978), pp. 211–65, and Richard McCormick, "Political Parties in American History," *The Party Period and Public Policy* (New York: Oxford University Press, 1986), chapter 4.

[46] Richard McCormick, "The Party Period and Public Policy: An Exploratory Hypothesis," *Journal of American History* 66 (1979): 279–98.

[47] Keller, *Affairs of State*, pp. 311–12; Donald M. McMurry, "The Political Significance of the Pension Question, 1885–1897," *Mississippi Valley Historical Review* 9 (1922): 19–36; and Heywood Sanders, "'Paying for the Bloody Shirt': The Politics of Civil War Pensions," *Political Benefits*, edited by Barry Rundquist (Lexington: D.C. Heath, 1980), pp. 137–60.

in states like Ohio, Illinois, and New York, so in addition to supporting recurrent legal liberalizations of the terms of eligibility, Congressmen intervened with the Pension Bureau to help people prove their eligibility and sponsored thousands of special pension bills tailored for individual constituents. Moreover, the Republicans were known to dispatch pension commissioners into states and localities during crucial election battles.

In significant contrast to Britain, there was no national poor law in the nineteenth-century United States, either in theory or in administrative fact. Instead, mixtures of Elizabethan and New Poor Law practices were institutionalized in diverse forms in thousands of individual local communities, where the prime responsibility lay both financially (as in Britain) and legally.[48] Reactions against poor law practices would not so readily converge into a series of national debates as they did from the 1830s on in Britain—although the final decades of the nineteenth century did witness the emergence of state-level administrative supervision and policy debates in places such as Massachusetts.[49] At all levels of American government there were, however, growing reactions against the "inefficiency" and "corruption" of nineteenth-century patterns of patronage democracy. As the United States became a truly national economy and society in the decades after the Civil War, problems faced by public policymakers challenged the distributional style of patronage democracy, and vociferous demands emerged for civil service reform. The initial proponents were "Mugwumps," mostly upper and upper-middle class reformers located in the Northeast, especially Massachusetts, as well as in some parts of the Midwest. Like the successful British civil service reformers of the 1870s, the Mugwumps wanted public administration to be taken out of patronage politics, so that expertise and predictability could prevail.

At first, however, the Mugwumps' reform proposals made only limited headway, for the regular American party politicians could rely upon well-developed organizational machineries and deep-seated party loyalties to resist reforms they did not like, or to pervert the implementation of early civil service measures.[50] What is more, in contrast to the situation in Britain, there was no impending threat of further electoral democratization to prod political and social elites into civil service reform. Not until the Progressive Era of the early twentieth century did administrative reform really make significant headway in the United States, and then

[48] Josephine Brown, *Public Relief, 1929–1939* (New York: Henry Holt, 1940), chapter 1.
[49] Ibid., pp. 22–23.
[50] Skowronek, *Building a New American State*, part II.

more at municipal and state levels than at the national level.[51] Social demands for new kinds of collective policies "in the public interest" and for reforms in government to ensure their proper implementation broadened out from the very elite ranks of Mugwumpry to include the growing ranks of the educated, professionalizing middle class and (in many places) farmers, organized women, and organized workers as well.[52]

The legacies of nineteenth-century patronage democracy and the conjuncture of its crisis in the Progressive Era created a much less favorable context for advocates of old-age pensions and social insurance in the early twentieth-century United States than the one enjoyed by their counterparts in Britain. Most basically, there was the sheer weakness of public administration, due to the original absence of state bureaucracy in America, the limited achievements of civil service reform in the nineteenth century, and the dispersion of authority in U.S. federalism. In contrast to the situation in Britain, there were in the early twentieth-century United States no influential high-level public officials strategically positioned to formulate new social benefits policies with existing administrative resources, press them on political executives, and work out firm compromises with organized interest groups. Typically, reforms in the Progressive Era were not autonomous initiatives from either civil servants or politicians. They were usually urged upon state legislatures by broad coalitions of reform and interest groups.

This made sense, and not only because of the weakness of public administration. After the failure of the Populists and their allies to establish a national programmatic party system, party organizations as such were weakened, even as the Republicans and Democrats remained jointly dominant.[53] Moreover, the structure of the U.S. electoral arena at the turn of the century made the construction of party coalitions with programmatic reform outlooks very difficult. Three features of electoral competition during the Progressive Era stand out. First, after the election of 1896, the electoral system was demobilized and became much less competitive than in the nineteenth century, entrenching party oligarchies at local levels and establishing Republican hegemony at the national level. Thus party leaders in many places were not under competitive pressure to devise programs for less privileged constituents. Secondly, although recurrent third party efforts within the "system of

---

[51] Martin Schiesl, *The Politics of Efficiency: Municipal Administration and Reform in America, 1880–1920* (Berkeley: University of California Press, 1977).

[52] John D. Buenker, *Urban Liberalism and Progressive Reform* (New York: W.W. Norton, 1970); and Robert Wiebe, *The Search for Order, 1877–1920* (New York: Hill and Wang, 1967), chapter 6.

[53] Walter Dean Burnham, *Critical Elections and the Mainsprings of American Politics* (New York: W.W. Norton, 1970); and Shefter, "Party, Bureaucracy, and Political Change."

1896" demonstrated the urges toward reform stimulated by rapid industrialization, these efforts invariably fell short. Established electoral rules, along with the dominance of the existing major parties, placed overwhelming obstacles in the way of third-party efforts—including the effort to launch a nation-wide Progressive Party committed to certain social insurance programs for workingmen. Third party efforts succeeded only in particular states and localities.

The ability of the established parties to fend off challengers was partly due to a third factor that weighed against programmatic reform coalitions. Especially in large urban centers, working-class electoral politics in this period often remained under the control of party machines. The hold of patronage-oriented politicians over locally circumscribed and (often) ethnically defined blocs of working-class voters worked against the political pursuit of policies designed for workers in general. It also alienated middle class reformers, who might otherwise have been willing to ally with unions and work through political parties for social reforms. Instead, American reformers in this period sought to break party controls in many cities and states.[54] They sought to "avoid politics" rather than face the fact that the new governmental policies they hoped to see would depend upon the mobilization of cross-class political support, such as that which the British Liberals enjoyed.

During the Progressive Era, the challenge for elected U.S. legislators was to find ad hoc—and often nonpartisan—ways to propitiate reform-minded pressure groups, while still retaining the loyalty of working class supporters. New social spending measures usually did not fit this formula; American politicians would not have been able to get support for such programs from broad coalitions including middle- and upper-class groups. Contemplating the precedent of Civil War pensions, even reform-minded members of these groups feared that social spending programs would quickly expand and fuel the "corruption" of established party politicians. As John Graham Brooks explained:

> the condition of our politics is the first difficulty in the way of the working of a pension scheme. . . . We have no end of illustrations of the way that we pension off all sorts of persons in the army; while there are a large number of deserving, there are many thousands who are not,—and pensions are given on account of politics. I do not see how we can save any pension system in this country from running into politics.[55]

[54] Samuel P. Hays, "The Politics of Reform in Municipal Government in the Progressive Era," *Pacific Northwest Quarterly* 55 (October 1964): 157–69.

[55] Quoted in *Report of the Commission on Old Age Pensions, Annuities, and Insurance,* Massachussetts House Document Number 1400 (Boston, MA: Wright and Potter, State Printers, 1910), p. 238.

As this comment indicates, fears about new social spending legislation were most openly expressed about proposals for non-contributory old-age pensions, the very measures for which it was easiest to mobilize broad popular support, including support from the American Federation of Labor.

U.S. elites sometimes used public investigatory commissions to throw cold water on proposals for new social spending. This happened with the 1910 Massachusetts *Report of the Commission on Old Age Pensions, Annuities, and Insurance*, which, since Massachusetts was traditionally a trailblazing state in U.S. social legislation, effectively derailed a potential nation-wide movement for old-age pensions during the Progressive Era.[56] Even when social spending proposals made it to the legislative agenda, as happened with contributory social insurance bills in a number of states, the broad elite and middle-class public failed to put enough pressure on legislatures to overcome opposition from business groups (and, in the case of health insurance, opposition from doctors). At the height of the Progressive Era, *regulatory* reforms often did receive sufficiently widespread and intense public support to pass in the face of business opposition. But such was not the case with proposals for old-age pension or social insurance.

In contrast to what happened in early twentieth-century Britain then, the common denominator of reform in the United States remained the struggle against "political corruption." Most elites and middle-class people doubted that social spending measures could be implemented honestly, and feared that they might well reinforce the hold over the electorate of patronage politicians. This political opposition, along with the absence of strong civil bureaucracies, made it impossible for American reformers to imitate the British patterns of constructing a nascent paternalist welfare state from above. Unlike their British counterparts, American reformers who favored "workingmen's insurance" lacked the opportunity to work with programmatic political parties, broad cross-class coalitions, or enlightened civil servants.

The Contrasting Scope of British and U.S. Labor Regulations

According to the argument just developed, it is reasonable that Britain launched social spending measures for workers, while the United States witnessed only the enactment of workers' compensation.[57] These laws passed in America at the level of the states as regulatory measures re-

---

[56] Ibid; and Alton A. Linford, *Old Age Assistance in Massachusetts* (Chicago: University of Chicago Press, 1949).

[57] Brandeis, *Labor Legislation*, edited by John R. Commons et al., *History of Labor in the United States, 1896–1932*, chapters 6 and 8; Berkowitz and McQuaid, *Creating the Welfare*

quiring businesses to compensate injured employees, not as mandates for the collection of taxes or for governments to hand out recurrent monetary benefits to citizens. Workers' compensation laws dealt in new ways with issues already under court jurisdiction in the United States, and were, in due course, accepted by the courts because they were enacted in ways that did not coercively infringe on the rights of private enterprises. Fitting the Progressive Era's formula for legislative success, workers' compensation bills typically gained broad public support from coalitions that included business, reformers, labor unions, and women's groups. Finally, the new kinds of public intervention in the marketplace required to administer early U.S. workers' compensation did not go beyond what progressive reformers actually achieved in most places: the creation of tiny new "islands" of bureaucracy staffed by professional experts like themselves. These new "regulatory agencies" did not have to work closely with politicians or establish direct ties to individual citizens eligible to receive continuing benefits (such as old-age pensions). They merely had to supervise the granting of fixed compensatory payments by businesses.

According to the logic explaining the success of workers' compensation in the United States versus the failure of pensions and social insurance, we might also expect the American states to have enacted additional industrial regulations during the Progressive Era. Presumably, expert-led administrative agencies rather than public spending could have been used to protect wageworkers from the worst vagaries of market capitalism, going beyond merely accident compensation and safety rules to place limits on daily and weekly hours of work and legal floors under wages for the sake of workers' health and family life. Indeed, the leaders of the two most prominent American associations of labor-law reformers—the American Association for Labor Legislation (AALL), and the National Consumers' League (NCL)—were strong proponents of such hours laws and minimum-wage regulations.[58]

American labor-law reformers would have liked the United States to go at least as far in regulating conditions of industrial labor as Britain did through the Trade Boards Acts of 1909 and 1918.[59] The first of

State, pp. 37–40; and Lawrence M. Friedman and Jack Ladinsky, "Social Change and the Law of Industrial Accidents," *American Law and the Constitutional Order: Historical Perspectives*, edited by Lawrence M. Friedman and Harry N. Scheiber (Cambridge, Mass: Harvard University Press, 1978), pp. 269–82.

[58] Pierce, "Activities of the American Association for Labor Legislation," especially chapter 4; and Louis L. Athey, "The Consumers' Leagues and Social Reform, 1890–1923" (Ph.D. diss., University of Delaware, 1965), especially chapters 6–8.

[59] On the aspirations of American labor law reformers, see ibid., along with Florence Kelley, "Minimum-Wage Laws," *Journal of Political Economy* 20(10) (December 1912): 999–1010; Henry Rogers Seager, "Minimum Wage as Part of a Program for Social Reform,"

these British laws, which authorized tripartite commissions to arrive at minimum wages in "sweated" trades, was promoted by politically active reformers, Liberal Party ministers, and civil servants in the Labour Department Board of Trade—similar forces to those that brought about labor exchanges and unemployment insurance in Britain. Along with contemporary extensions of social benefits in Britain, the second Trade Boards Act was the culmination of a series of wartime extensions of industrial regulation and public social provision negotiated among the Liberals, the trade unions, and the growing Labour Party. This 1918 act authorized the regulation of minimum wages and other working conditions for workers in many nonunionized industries. The new Ministry of Labour pursued these possibilities actively for several years, until the Treasury hobbled it with cuts in resources.

In contrast to British-style labor regulations, however, what the United States got was a series of state-level minimum-wage and maximum-hour laws targeted almost exclusively on women workers. In many American states during the 1910s, regulatory agencies were created (or expanded) and charged with supervising the treatment that businesses afforded their employees. But when it came to matters of wages and hours, matters which involved the heart of the labor contract, these U.S. labor bureaus were restricted by statute to dealing with women (and child) laborers, rather than with all low-wage or unorganized workers, as the British Trade Boards could do.[60]

The causes of this outcome are complex, and include the politics of labor movements and women's organizations, matters to be dealt with in the next two sections of this article. Yet the primary reason why American reformers could not imitate the approach of the British Trade Boards system lay in the special role of the U.S. courts, especially state high courts and the U.S. Supreme Court.[61] Armed with powers of judicial review that were unavailable to British judges, and often adhering to doctrines of "due process" and "freedom of contract" for private property holders, American courts were able to strike down industrial regulations passed by the state legislatures when aggrieved private parties, especially businessmen, challenged those laws.

Annals of the American Academy 48 (July 1913): 3–12; and Seager, "Theory of the Minimum Wage," *American Labor Legislation Review* 3 (February 1913): 81–91. On the British Trade Boards laws, see Sells, *British Trade Boards Systems*, pp. 93–94 and Thane, *Foundations of the Welfare State*, pp. 148–50. On the fascination of American reformers with New Zealand's even more comprehensive regulatory system for working conditions and labor disputes arbitration, see Peter J. Coleman, *Progressivism and the World of Reform: New Zealand and the Origins of the American Welfare State* (Lawrence: University Press of Kansas, 1987).

[60] For an overview, see Brandeis, *Labor Legislation.*

[61] Ibid., chapter 9.

By the height of the Progressive Era, when new labor laws were likely to be passed by state legislatures, most U.S. state high courts, and certainly the U.S. Supreme Court, had made it clear that they would not let stand protective regulations covering adult male workers as a class. According to the majority of America's judges at this time, private contractual conditions for adult males could be modified by public regulations only for certain narrow occupational categories. These exceptions included public employments, where the state was deemed a direct party to the contractual agreements about wages and hours, along with a new private occupations—e.g., especially dangerous jobs, such as mining; and jobs touching public safety, such as transportation work— where the state's "police powers" were deemed to override private contractual rights.[62] Other than in these special cases, adult male workers were to be left "free" to bargain with employers about their own wages and hours. The U.S. Supreme Court put it as follows in a five to four 1905 decision in *Lochner v. New York*, striking down a New York state law limiting the work hours of bakers to ten per day and sixty per week:

> We think there can be no fair doubt that the trade of a baker, in and of itself, is not an unhealthy one to the degree which would authorize the legislature to interfere with the right to labor. . . . Statutes of the nature of that under review, limiting the hours in which grown and intelligent men may labor to earn their living, are mere meddlesome interferences with the rights of the individual.[63]

The "Lochner decision," explained labor historian Elizabeth Brandeis, "was of the greatest significance because it was the first in which the United States Supreme Court held a statute to protect labor unconstitutional. It demonstrated that the Court might outdo the state courts in construing the Fourteenth Amendment as forbidding such legislation. . . . The effect of the Lochner decision was to circumscribe rather narrowly the occupations in which hours might be limited."[64] Eventually, in its 1917 decision in *Bunting v. Oregon*, the Supreme Court unanimously upheld an Oregon ten-hour law covering male workers. *Lochner* was not explicitly overturned in this decision, however, and two further circumstances also rendered the 1917 ruling less significant than it might have been. In the first place, the standard set in the Oregon law—ten hours with permission for three hours overtime— was so loose as to render it without much practical impact.[65] In the

[62] Ibid., chapter 5.
[63] Quoted in ibid., pp. 670–71.
[64] Ibid., p. 671.
[65] Ibid., p. 681.

second place, this ruling came too late to affect political strategies and coalitions at the height of the Progressive Era. After 1905, reform groups had refocused their efforts away from class-wide hours laws, and in 1914 the American Federation of Labor had officially come out against legislative means for setting maximum hours (or minimum wages).[66] The national AFL's stance made it politically awkward for would-be middle-class allies of labor to mount nation-wide agitation for labor regulations covering unionized men; and the 1917 *Bunting* decision did not really change this situation, especially since the Supreme Court remained ambiguous about how far labor regulations for adult men could go.

Even as the U.S. Supreme Court ruled out class-wide labor regulations during most of the Progressive Era, it opened the door after 1908 to gender-specific protective laws for adult women workers, no matter how "grown and intelligent." At first, it seemed that U.S. courts would apply to females the free contract rights they attributed to workers in general, as the Illinois Supreme Court did in *Ritchie v. People*, 1895, which overturned an 1893 law mandating an eight-hour day for women in manufacturing. But quite a few other state high courts refused to follow the Illinois precedent and upheld hours limitations for women. As Judge Cray of the Pennsylvania Supreme Court reasoned in 1900: "Surely an act which prevents the mothers of our race from being tempted to endanger their life and health by exhaustive employment can be condemned by none save those who expect to profit by it. . . ."[67] Then, in 1908, the U.S. Supreme Court rendered a decisive ruling in *Muller v. Oregon*, upholding a previous ruling by the Oregon high court that found valid a ten-hour law for women workers. In this ruling, the Supreme Court unanimously decided not to apply the *Lochner* precedent to women. In the words of Mr. Justice Brewer's opinion for the Court:

> That woman's physical structure and the performance of maternal functions place her at a disadvantage in the struggle for subsistence is obvious. This is especially true when the burdens of motherhood are upon her. Even when they are not, by abundant testimony of the medical fraternity continuance for a long time on her feet at work, repeating this from day to day, tends to injurious effects on the body, and, as healthy mothers are essential to vigorous offspring, the physical well-being of women becomes an object of public interest and care in order to preserve the strength and vigor of the race. . . . Differentiated by these matters from the other sex, she is properly placed in a

[66] Ibid., pp. 556–57.

[67] Justice Gray's opinion in *Commonwealth* v. *Beatty* 15 Pa.Super.5, 8, 16(1900) is quoted in Melvin I. Urofsky, "State Courts and Protective Legislation during the Progressive Era: A Reevaluation," *Journal of American History* 72(1) (June 1985): 74.

class by herself, and legislation designed for her protection may be sustained, even when like legislation is not necessary for men, and could not be sustained.[68]

After 1908, the Supreme Court consistently upheld hours laws for women, including the California eight-hour statute of 1913; and state high courts, including the Illinois Supreme Court, also fell into line. Moreover, during the Progressive Era, American courts seemed to apply reasoning similar to that of *Muller* to uphold minimum-wage laws for women. Thus, in 1914, the Oregon Supreme Court ruled in favor of that state's 1913 minimum-wage statute, arguing that "[e]very argument put forth to sustain the maximum hours law or upon which it was established applies equally in favor of the constitutionality of the minimum wage law as also in the police power of the state, and as a regulation tending to guard the public morals and the public health."[69] In 1917, the U.S. Supreme Court technically upheld this Oregon judgment in an evenly divided decision (with Justice Brandeis not participating, because he had formerly argued such cases for the National Consumers' League). Despite uncertainties about the judicial acceptability of minimum-wage laws which certainly undercut their political momentum, many reformers continued for some years after 1917 to assume that minimum-wage laws for women were constitutional in the same terms as maximum-hour laws. Not until 1923, when it ruled a District of Columbia minimum-wage law unconstitutional on free-contract grounds, citing the 1905 decision in *Lochner v. New York* as precedent, did the Supreme Court rule out the possibility of public regulations to shore up wages for low-paid women workers.[70] And even then, the Court did not back off from its 1908 decision to allow legal limitations on women's working hours.

Court decisions had a major impact on the political strategies of American reformers who worked for protective labor regulations during the Progressive Era. After the U.S. Supreme Court upheld a Utah eight-hour law for miners in the 1898 decision in *Holden v. Hardy*, U.S. reformers were very hopeful that they would be able to pursue labor regulations applicable to all workers, male and female alike.[71] But these

[68] From the Supreme Court's opinion in *Muller* v. *Oregon*, 208 U.S. 412(1908), reprinted in Louis D. Brandeis and Josephine Goldmark, *Women in Industry*, introduced by Leon Stein and Philip Taft (New York: Arno Press and the New York Times, 1969), pp. 6–7.

[69] As quoted in Athey dissertation, "Consumers' Leagues and Social Reform," p. 226.

[70] *Adkins* v. *Children's Hospital*, 261 U.S. 525(1923).

[71] On the reformers' hopes between 1898 and 1905, see Josephine Goldmark, *Impatient Crusader: Florence Kelley's Life Story* (Urbana: University of Illinois Press, 1953), pp. 144–49; and Henry Rogers Seager, "The Attitude of American Courts Toward Restrictive Labor Laws," *Labor and Other Economic Essays*, edited by Charles A. Gulick, Jr. (New York: Harper and Brothers, 1931), pp. 52–78.

hopes were dashed a few years later by *Lochner v. New York*. In the wake of the *Lochner* decision in 1905, reformers searched for reasons to set subsets of workers apart as "special classes" particularly deserving of public protection. Soon it became obvious that the broadest protective regulations the courts would allow were for women workers in general. Thus American reformers, while continuing to admire the British Trade Boards system, turned their practical legislative lobbying, and their efforts to defend new laws before the courts, toward gender-specific rather than class-wide laws.[72]

Finally, too, as we shall see in the following sections, the American progressive reformers concentrated on the proposed labor regulations and other social policies for which there was the most consistent and nationwide political support. Across much of the early-twentieth-century United States, women's associations were more likely to provide such support than were workers' organizations—exactly the opposite situation from the one that prevailed in contemporary Britain.

THE POLITICS OF INDUSTRIAL LABOR

Nowhere were simple "demands" from industrial labor directly responsible for launching modern welfare states between the 1880s and the 1920s. All the same, organized labor did matter. Through political alliances, labor could help to enact, shape, and expand modern labor regulations or social expenditures. Alternatively, trade union opposition could hurt possibilities for proposed social policies.

Developments over the course of the first two decades of the twentieth century reveal sharp divergences in the strategies and impact of labor organizations on social policymaking in Britain and the United States. In Britain, trade unions and Labour representatives in Parliament proceeded from supporting workmen's compensation and old-age pensions and acquiescing in Liberal-initiated labor-market regulations and

---

[72] The National Consumers' League, especially, sponsored research on the special physical vulnerabilities of women workers and became the nationally visible champion of maximum-hour and minimum-wage hours particularly applicable to females. The League's leaders did not entirely give up broader hopes for protective laws for all workers; and they even acted on these aspirations when they could. But its eyes were riveted above all on what the state courts and the U.S. Supreme Court would support in review. Until the bitter comeuppance of the 1923 *Adkins* decision, the League's leaders along with other American reformers presumed that the U.S. courts definitely would accept ever-stronger state interventions on behalf of women workers, while they would not accept hours limits or minimum-wage regulations encompassing adult males. Even after the 1917 *Bunting* decision, it was not clear that the American courts would permit gender-neutral labor regulations with any teeth. Many reformers hoped that regulations for women would eventually prove to be an "entering wedge" for legal hours restrictions and minimum wages for all workers. On these matters, see the Athey dissertation, "Consumers' Leagues and Social Reform," especially chapter 8 on "Legal Defense of Labor Legislation."

social insurance between 1906 and 1914, to becoming the chief promoters of public social provision after World War I.[73] In the United States, state Federations of Labor often helped to achieve workers' compensation laws and women's hour limitations during the 1910s, but proved ineffective when they supported state-level proposals for old-age pensions or social insurance. Meanwhile, at the national level, the American Federation of Labor unsuccessfully backed old-age pensions and otherwise opposed outright new social legislation. The Federation took an official stand against hour and wage regulations in 1914; its leader, Samuel Gompers, testified before Congress in 1916 in emotional opposition to an investigation that might have promoted a national system of social insurance.[74]

Arguably, for social insurance and labor regulations to have had any real chance in the early twentieth-century United States, the national AFL and its state affiliates would had to have been *more* consistent, enthusiastic, and effective proponents than were labor forces in Britain. In U.S. politics of the Progressive Era, reformist laws could not be promoted from the top down by bureaucrats, ministers, and parliamentary leaders, rather, they had to be—and in certain instances were—enacted through widespread, moralistic public pressure on legislatures across many or all of the forty-eight states. Yet during the same years that the mainstream British labor federation, the Trades Union Congress (TUC), along with the emerging Labour Party became fully involved in expanding a paternalist welfare state for workers and their dependents, the national American Federation of Labor (AFL) was little engaged in this sort of venture, and labor organizations in the states were pushing in many different directions.

Why did the nationally federated trade unions in the United States refuse to support reformers' efforts to achieve public social insurance and general labor regulations? A comparison of the American Federation of Labor with the British Trade Unions Congress suggests that the reasons lay to some extent in the characteristics of American unions, but mostly in the experiences those unions had during that period within the U.S. polity.

Class Structures and Labor Movements

There were obvious differences between the age and composition of the British and American trade union federations. "Continuous trade

[73] Arthur Marwick, "The Labour Party and the Welfare State in Britain, 1900–1948," *American Historical Review* 73 (1967): 380–403.

[74] Gompers' remarks appear in *Commission to Study Social Insurance and Unemployment, Hearings Before the Committee on Labor on H.J. Res. 159, House of Representatives, Sixty-Fourth Congress, First Session, April 6 and 11, 1916* (Washington D.C.: Government Printing Office, 1916). On the AFL and hours legislation, see Brandeis, *Labor Legislation*, pp. 554–57.

unionism"—the formation of national unions that persisted—dated from the 1850s in Britain, and a conference called in 1867 became the precursor of the modern Trades Union Congress.[75] The American Federation of Labor was founded in 1886 through a revolt by craft unions against the Knights of Labor.[76] Although certain truly industrial unions, notably the Mine Workers and the Brewery Workers, came over to the AFL from the Knights, by 1910 only about 16 percent of AFL members were organized into industrial unions oriented toward expansion into the unskilled labor force.[77] In comparison, at this time over sixty percent of British workers organized under the Trades Union Congress were members of industrial unions. As labor historian Andrew Thomson explains:

> In Britain, . . . the main centers of unionism were in the staple industries of the Industrial Revolution, serving not only national but international markets. . . . In the United States, the reverse was true. There were important national product market industries, notably in coal, clothing, glass, and the foundry trades, where unionism was well represented, but for the most part unionism's greatest strength was in the local product market industries of building, newspaper printing, street railways, baking, and local haulage.[78]

Certain analysts of social policies have argued that craft unions found it easier to protect the interests of their skilled worker members through workplace and market actions; thus such unions would not see as much need as industrial unions to work for legislative solutions.[79] This argument does help to make sense of the greater propensity of the British TUC to support public social provision, and helps explain why the AFL's strongest industrial affiliate, the United Mine Workers (UMW), was the center within the American trade union movement of similar agitation. Mine Workers were among the pioneering advocates at AFL conventions of old-age pensions and, during the 1910s and 1920s, con-

---

[75] G.D.H. Cole, *A Short History of the British Working-Class Movement, 1789–1947*, revised edition (London: George Allen and Unwin, 1948), part II.

[76] Philip Taft, *The A.F. of L. in the Time of Gompers* (New York: Harper and Brothers, 1957), p. 23, and chapter 2 generally.

[77] Leo Wolman, "The Extent of Labor Organization in the United States in 1910," *Quarterly Journal of Economics* 30 (1916): 506.

[78] Andrew William John Thomsom, "The Reaction of the American Federation of Labor and the Trades Union Congress to Labor Law 1900–1935" (Ph.D. diss., Cornell University, 1968), p. 75.

[79] This argument is featured in Quadagno, *Transformation of Old Age Security*, pp. 10–12, and chapter 3. For a classic formulation, see Michael Rogin, "Voluntarism: The Political Functions of an Antipolitical Doctrine," *Industrial and Labor Relations Review* 15(4) (July 1962): 521–35.

ducted official pension campaigns in many states.[80] UMW Secretary-Treasurer, AFL Vice-President William Green, was a vocal advocate of contributory social insurance, breaking with President Gompers to offer support to the AALL's drive for public health benefits for workers.[81] Still, one cannot argue that only industrial unionists supported public social provision in the early twentieth-century United States, because delegates from craft unions, not just leaders of Mine Workers, were among those who supported old-age pension legislation within national AFL debates from 1902 onward.[82]

Was it, perhaps, also the case that British unionists were simply much stronger than U.S. trade unionists in this period, thus inclining the British unions to work more through politics? Overall "union density"— the proportion of the total labor force organized—was consistently lower in the United States, because fewer workers were available for organization in a country that still had a much higher proportion of its workforce in agriculture.[83] Nevertheless, during the respective period of greatest social policy innovation in the two nations—1906 to 1911 in Britain and 1910 to 1920 in the United States—union densities were reasonably similar, ranging from nine to sixteen percent in both countries. And union densities were very similar between Britain and such highly industrialized and urbanized U.S. states as Massachusetts.

As is often noted in analyses of the development of the American labor movement, ethnic and racial divisions constrained possibilities for classwide politics. In Britain there were divisions between English and Irish workers but otherwise the working class was relatively socially homogeneous. In the United States, however, the period of intensive industrialization coincided with the height of foreign immigration, so that by the turn of the century about forty percent of the residents of the nation's twelve largest cities had been born outside the country.[84] Sectional and racial divisions also prevailed among native-born American workers, and employers often used ethnic and racial divisions to undercut unionization. Unionists themselves often allied with nativist

[80] Quadagno, *Transformation of Old Age Security*, pp. 64–72.

[81] William Green, "Trade Union Sick Funds and Compulsory Heath Insurance," *American Labor Legislation Review* 7(1) (March 1917): 91–95; and Nelson, *Unemployment Insurance*, p. 71.

[82] See *Reports of Proceedings* for Annual Conventions of the American Federation of Labor.

[83] Between 1910 and 1919, 31 percent of the U.S. labor force and 12 percent of the British labor force was employed in agriculture. For a series of tables comparing the socioeconomic characteristics and union densities of Britain, the United States, and the state of Massachusetts, see Orloff and Skocpol, "Why Not Equal Protection?," pp. 733, 736.

[84] Samuel P. Hays, *The Response to Industrialism, 1884–1914* (Chicago: University of Chicago Press, 1957), p. 95.

groups calling for immigration restrictions, rather than pursuing more inclusive strategies for organizing unskilled laborers.[85]

As for the proportions of total national electorates the two union movements could potentially mobilize, we must of course consider that under the male householder franchise that prevailed until 1918 only about half of British union members could vote. In contrast, virtually all American male unionists were eligible voters. Taking this and other factors into account, one scholar has estimated that the TUC included about ten percent of the British electorate in 1906, while the AFL included about five percent of the total American electorate (voters plus others eligible to vote). U.S. trade unionists appear, moreover, to have accounted for about eight percent of those who actually voted in the 1908 election.[86] Although this was a period of electoral demobilization in the United States, organized workers, disproportionately skilled, still turned out for elections more often than the unorganized.[87] Further, union voters were much more weighty in the industrialized states and localities. Sheer numerical voter potential does not, then, seem to have put the U.S. trade union movement at much of a disadvantage compared to the British movement before World War I.

In the final analysis, we should beware of any simple social, economic, or ecological determinism in assessing American labor's political prospects. The early twentieth-century AFL unions certainly had less numerical strength, both relatively and absolutely, than the contemporary British unions of the TUC. But neither union movement had anything close to majority power at the time early modern social policies were debated in the British and U.S. polities, both having had to enter into alliances with nonworking-class forces to make headway in politics. Important questions thus remain to be answered. As minority forces, how much political clout could British and American labor muster—to contribute to the achievement of their own political objectives and to carry their weight in alliances? What were the objectives these labor movements pursued in politics, alone or through alliances? How did labor's political objectives evolve over time, and under what circumstances did they come to include various sorts of social policies? To answer these questions, we need to explore how the labor federations

[85] This point is developed in Gwendolyn Mink, *Old Labor and New Immigrants in American Political Development* (Ithaca: Cornell University Press, 1986). This book does not, however, accurately present the full range of things the AFL unions were doing in politics.

[86] Thomson dissertation, "Reaction to Labor Law," pp. 672–73.

[87] Mark Lawrence Kornbluh, "From Participatory to Administrative Politics: A Social History of American Political Behavior, 1880–1918" (Ph.D. diss., The Johns Hopkins University, 1987), pp. 254–57, and chapter 5 generally.

intersected with the contrasting political institutions of their respective nations.

Governmental Institutions and Political Possibilities for Labor Organizations

British and American trade unions got into politics first and foremost for defensive reasons—and only if, and when, their defensive objectives were realized were they likely to move on toward broader demands that state power be used positively for the welfare of organized and unorganized sectors of the working class. As they grew up over decades, both British and American unions faced recurrent legal threats, sometimes from hostile legislatures, but more often from judges who were interpreting and applying received doctrines in disputes brought before the courts by threatened employers. It would take us too long to detail the precise timing and arguments of all of these judicial challenges to organized labor in Britain and America.[88] Suffice to say that by the early twentieth century American unions were agitated by a broad range of adverse judicial rulings, but especially by federal court interpretations of the Sherman Act, allowing the use of injunctions to stop strikes. Meanwhile, having apparently overcome earlier legal threats, British unions were up in arms about the Law Lords' 1901 Taff Vale decision, which rendered union assets liable to seizure in damage suits filed by employers hurt economically by normal union tactics. Although British labor was not beseiged by as wide a range of adverse rulings as the American movement, the Taff Vale judgment alone had the potential to ruin the unions.[89]

Faced with these court decisions, British and American unions naturally searched for ways to get around or reverse them. The structure of British politics made it relatively straightforward for British labor to do this, and to reap rewards from ever deeper involvement in national politics. But the structure of U.S. politics had exactly the opposite effect. Two contrasts in national political arrangements were, together, especially significant—the relations of legislatures and courts; and the or-

[88] For excellent histories and analyses, see: Thomson dissertation, "Reaction to Labor Law," part 2; Victoria C. Hattam, "Producers Into Workers: Changing Conceptions of Class and American Political Development, 1806–1896" (Princeton: Princeton University Press, forthcoming); William E. Forbath, "The Shaping of the American Labor Movement," *Harvard Law Review* 102(6) (April 1989): 1111–1256; and William E. Forbath, "Law and the Shaping of Labor Politics in the United States and England" (Unpublished paper, UCLA Law School, 1990).

[89] Cole, *History of British Working Class*, pp. 291–96; and Thomson dissertation, "Reaction to Labor Law," pp. 209–13.

ganization and orientation of established political parties. Before tracing what happened when the British and American unions tried to use politics to counter adverse court rulings, let us first contrast these aspects of the institutional terrain on which the two movements had to operate.

Parliament was the sovereign center of British politics. This supreme legislature did not share law-making powers with subnational legislatures, and, as the nineteenth century progressed, was increasingly preeminent over local governments. Parliament (and eventually the House of Commons) was also constitutionally able to reverse by statute even the highest level of court rulings.[90] Given Parliament's preeminence, the British unions had little choice but to focus political efforts on influencing it. This was no easy task; yet once legislative victories were won, they were not limited by federalism or subject to judicial reversal. In the United States, on the other hand, the national Congress was far from politically preeminent, for it divided lawmaking powers with forty-eight state legislatures and could not directly intervene in local governments. Around the turn of the century, by custom and court rulings, many issues of social and labor policy were still considered solely in the domain of the states, while Congress dealt with foreign policy, with aspects of economic and labor policy that were clearly part of "inter-state commerce," and with labor regulations for federal employees. To the degree that American unions needed or wanted to influence legislation, therefore, they had to focus efforts not on one sovereign national center but on forty-nine separate legislative bodies, each with its own rules, political composition, and distinctive relations to lower levels of government (including towns or cities that sometimes had their own powers of home rule).

Even if U.S. labor—or any other politically active group—could successfully negotiate the federally divided legislative maze, it might not matter. Where labor and social policies were concerned, the late nineteenth- and early twentieth-century American polity has aptly been labelled "court dominated."[91] There were forty-nine jurisdictionally distinct but intellectually and procedurally intertwined state and federal systems of courts, and the highest court in each system had long since successfully claimed powers of review over the constitutionality of legislative enactments. Such judicial powers were exercised with special vigilance when disputed cases touched on government control of markets or business enterprises, or government regulation of labor contracts and disputes. Thus, even when unions and their political allies obtained laws on these subjects through legislatures—including laws expressly in-

---

[90] Thomson dissertation, "Reaction to Labor Law," pp. 43–56. The following several paragraphs also draw upon this comparative discussion of the structure and operations of the British and U.S. polities.

[91] This label is used by both Hattam and Forbath. See note 88.

tended to reverse the effect of earlier adverse court rulings—the judges often proceeded to have the last word. Although U.S. courts could be politically influenced—particularly where judges were elected, or when public opinion was overwhelmingly on one side of an issue—the Supreme Court and the highest state courts were the least subject to outside pressures. Even the narrowest majorities of judges in these courts could, in effect, legislate or relegislate major social policies for entire states or the entire nation.

Political parties also mattered in Britain and the United States. In the administratively reformed and partially democratized British polity, both conservative and liberal M.P.s from these increasingly programmatic parties were willing to offer votes on legislation of special interest to labor in return for union endorsements and working-class votes. After 1900, the Liberal Party was particularly ready to make such concessions, because "new liberals" who believed the state should ameliorate industrial excesses gained leadership positions and because the party was anxious to head off the growth of an independent Labour Party.[92]

Meanwhile in the United States, where the electoral system had long been fully democratized for white males, the period of politically viable, independent farmer or labor parties had ended in the late nineteenth century, and intense electoral competition between the dominant Republicans and Democrats had waned in most parts of the nation. By the 1910s large segments of the population were no longer voting.[93] In contrast to the situation in Britain, there were no programmatic parties to attract labor's allegiance. Democrats and Republicans in many areas were still rooted in local machines that dispensed patronage in return for across-the-board political loyalty, a situation especially prevalent in the more industrialized states and large cities where, numerically speaking, unions and their members had the most potential political clout.[94] Leaders of local craft unions—of the kind that predominated in the AFL—had every reason to make deals with local political machines who could offer them and their followers such particularistic benefits as public jobs and jobs in private enterprises that employed local workers; influence in cases before local or state judges; and regulatory favors that were crucial, for example, to the construction trades.

Let us now see how these contrasting structural situations in Britain

[92] Freeden, New Liberalism.

[93] See Walter Dean Burnham, "The Appearance and Disappearance of the American Voter," Current Crisis in American Politics, edited by Walter Dean Burnham (New York: Oxford University Press, 1982); and Burnham, Critical Elections and the Mainsprings of American Politics (New York: W.W. Norton, 1970), chapter 4.

[94] Thomson dissertation, "Reaction to Labor Law," pp. 689–708. See also the excellent discussion in Richard Oestreicher, "Urban Working-Class Political Behavior and Theories of American Electoral Politics, 1870–1940," Journal of American History 74(4) (March 1988): 1257–86.

and the United States were implicated in the evolution of organized labor's political strategies and capacities.

The Rewards of Parliamentary Politics in Britain

Mobilizing politically to win victories through Parliament was difficult for the British unions. Like the American AFL, the British TUC confederation was loose and decentralized; its leadership was originally cautious about potentially divisive political entanglements, and many British union members could not vote even after the 1867 enfranchisement of working-class male householders. Yet English workers traditionally had a certain political class consciousness because they were originally excluded from the franchise and had to fight for political rights as a class.[95] Furthermore, the British unions were spurred into politics by the threats they felt in common from laws and judicial rulings to which they were all simultaneously subject in the unitary, nonfederal polity. In response to the convening in 1867 of a government commission on union affairs, the British unions created the TUC, called upon the working classes to organize for political objectives, began systematically questioning parliamentary candidates, and set up a national committee to lobby and monitor Parliament. Soon after the broadening of the franchise in 1867, Parliament passed laws between 1871 and 1876 to reverse adverse judicial rulings and ensure the unions basic institutional security.[96]

Following the 1870s, the British unions for a time were content with their existing political involvements, and they gradually gained greater direct representation through working-class M.P.s and other sympathizers in the Liberal Party. However, the subsequent rise of "new unions" and moderate socialists, employer offensives against unions, and a worsening judicial climate, all helped bring about the establishment in 1899–1900 of the Labour Representation Committee (LRC), precursor to the Labour Party. It was still not clear that the British labor movement as a whole would go further into politics—until the Taff Vale decision of 1901 aroused the unions, all of whom were threatened by this nationally binding ruling that rendered their assets liable to seizure in damage suits filed by employers hurt economically

[95] Reinhard Bendix, *Nation Building and Citizenship* (New York: John Wiley and Sons, 1964); and Ira Katznelson, "Working-Class Formation and the State: Nineteenth–century England in American Perspective," *Bringing the State Back In*, edited by Peter B. Evans, Dietrich Rueschemeyer, and Theda Skocpol (Princeton, NJ: Princeton University Press, 1985), pp. 757–84.

[96] Cole, *Short History*, pp. 200–205; and Thomson dissertation, "Reaction to Labour Law," pp. 502–505.

by normal strike tactics.[97] After Taff Vale, individual unions and the LRC raised new levies for national political activities, and placed renewed emphasis on electing Labour or "Lib-Lab" M.P.s, as well as on "pledging" other M.P.s, especially Liberals, to support legislation overturning the Law Lords' decision. Prior to the 1906 and 1910 elections, both of which prominently featured programmatic issues of vital interest to labor, the unions and the LRC entered into explicit political alliances with the Liberal Party. The Liberals swept the 1906 election and won more narrowly in 1910; and in both elections Labour forces and Labour-supported Liberals did well. The Liberal-Labour alliances triumphed electorally across class lines especially in the British industrial centers, which were dispersed across many parliamentary districts and not as concentrated in large cities as in the United States.[98]

British labor's fuller entry into national parliamentary politics after 1900 thus proved rewarding. The unions were able to work together in ways that led to quick electoral payoffs. The political alliance with the Liberals led at once to the reversal of Taff Vale's consequences in the 1906 Trade Disputes Act, and to the enactment of certain pieces of social legislation the unions had previously sought, including old-age pensions. All of this reconfirmed British labor's historically rooted belief that good things could be done through parliamentary action and state politics. This belief, along with short-term needs to continue working with the Liberals, allowed most of the unions and most of the Labour M.P.s to go along with the enactment of welfare-state measures about which they were not so enthusiastic—especially contributory social insurance—and to participate in implementing these measures once enacted. The British unions could cooperate with a strong administrative elite committed to "rationalizing" labor markets and overcoming the worst exploitative excesses of capitalism. The upshot of the policy orientations mutually worked out during the Liberal-Labour alliance of 1906–1914 was that later after World War I switched the balance between Liberals and Labour, making the latter dominant—British labor would become the chief proponent of comprehensive welfare-state expansion, especially in ways that would protect the autonomy of unions and insure the flow of benefits through the male breadwinners, who were the unions' and the Labour Party's most powerful constituents.[99] None of this would necessarily have happened—and certainly the many innovative British social policies of 1906–1911 would not have passed

[97] The following account is based upon ibid., pp. 505–33; and Cole, Short History, pp. 286–316.

[98] Thomson dissertation, "Reaction to Labor Law," pp. 675–77.

[99] Susan Pedersen, "The Failure of Feminism in the Making of the British Welfare State," Radical History Review 43 (1989): 86–110.

in the first place—had not the TUC, from the 1870s through the 1910s, found it both internally feasible and externally rewarding to use parliamentary politics to attain its most immediate political objective, the defense against threats to union existence coming from the courts.

U.S. Trade Unions in a Court-Dominated, Federal State

In the United States, meanwhile, things did not work as well for the AFL when it tried to work through national politics, for reasons arising both from the federation's internal operations and from the institutional and party dynamics of U.S. politics. In 1906, spurred by an Illinois court's use of an injunction against the Typographers' Union, and inspired by British labor's electoral gains, AFL President Gompers called a conference to draw up a list of legislative demands which included relief from the Sherman Act, an anti-injunction law, an eight-hour day for government workers, and anti-immigration measures.[100] The list reflected the AFL's defensive priorities as well as the constitutional limits of what Congress might do for labor. In the 1906 and 1908 elections, Gompers tried to mobilize AFL voters to elect representatives willing to support labor's priorities and defeat selected Congressmen holding key committee seats who had previously obstructed legislation on the injunction issue. Yet he could not get unanimous support from other national union leaders in the AFL; his appeals for union contributions to a central fund for electoral and lobbying activities netted less than $10,000 in each election; and local unions were reluctant to break their ties to local machines in order to further national AFL political objectives.[101]

Although some friends of labor did well in 1906, the Congressional "enemies" targetted by the AFL were re-elected, and no favorable legislation ensued, even as adverse judicial decisions continued. Moreover, the 1908 presidential election brought a whopping victory for anti-labor Republican William Howard Taft—a victory fuelled in part by strong, locally brokered labor votes for the Republicans across the industrial states.[102] After 1908, Gompers and the national AFL retreated from national politics, only to reenter sporadically in some later elections, such as the 1916 reelection campaign of Woodrow Wilson, who had proved friendly to the AFL's agenda in his first term. But in this and later elections, the AFL could never reliably deliver the vote to its friends (or withold it from its enemies) in Congress and the Presidency. Not until the 1920s, after the progressive tide had passed, did the AFL

---

[100] Thomson dissertation, "Reaction to Labor Law," pp. 262–63.
[101] Ibid., pp. 266–67.
[102] Ibid., p. 276.

even develop continuous organizational mechanisms for participating in elections.[103] Thus, the AFL could not keep in office even halfhearted friends, like the Democrats, with their predominant base in the South and West. It could not prevent the Republicans from acquiescing to the hostility of employers and judges to organized labor. Even purported legislative victories—like the 1914 Clayton Act, passed by a Democratic Congress and signed by Wilson, and designed to nullify the use of the injunctions under the Sherman Act—were soon reinterpreted by the federal courts to harm organized labor.[104] Anti-labor offensives intensified after World War I, a response to labor and radical gains during and right after that conflict, and a shrunken AFL survived mainly by focusing its efforts more than ever on the narrow labor-market interests of the craft unions of skilled workers.[105]

Through all of the vagaries of the AFL's frustrating ventures into national politics during the first decades of the century, Gompers and many other national AFL leaders remained distrustful of potential state controls over unions and preoccupied by the need for improved defenses against the judiciary. This is understandable. If the national AFL could not even win legislative protections for unions, or be sure that legislative victories would survive scrutiny by the courts, why risk giving further powers to government—such as regulatory powers to set hours and wages, or taxes for social insurance benefits and administrative control over their implementation? Only old-age pensions were not objectionable, because they would reach only retired workers and would not involve the collection of tax contributions from those covered. Thus between 1909 and 1914 the AFL endorsed federal noncontributory old-age pensions, dropping the issue only when they got nowhere with proposals in Congress.[106]

During the Progressive Era, such official support as organized labor gave to general hours regulations and social insurance came in individual states, for several reasons.[107] The states were the level of American government where social policy initiatives could be most readily under-

[103] Ibid., p. 296.

[104] Ibid., p. 287; and Taft, *AFL in Time of Gompers*, pp. 403–11.

[105] David Montgomery, *The Fall of the House of Labor* (Cambridge and New York: Cambridge University Press, 1987), pp. 452–54.

[106] See *Reports of Proceedings* for Annual Conventions of the American Federation of Labor from 1908 through 1914. The story of the national AFL's support for noncontributory old-age pensions is analyzed in Theda Skocpol, "Trade Unions and Social Legislation," chapter 4, *Protecting Soldiers and Mothers*.

[107] On the state federations and social legislation, see Christopher Anglim and Brian Gratton, "Organized Labor and Old Age Pensions," *International Journal of Aging and Human Development* 25(2) (1987): 91–107; Gary M. Fink, "Toward a New View of Labor and Politics," *Labor Search for Political Order: The Political Behavior of the Missouri Labor*

taken with some hope of surviving judicial review. One labor historian has argued, in fact, that because they could hope for more at this level, state Federations' legislative agendas tended to resemble those of the early British TUC much more closely than the national AFL agenda ever did.[108] The AFL's decentralization made this possible, and state Federation leaders often had different concerns than the national leaders.[109] Industrial unions were influential in some state leaderships, and state leaders were more likely than national AFL leaders to be concerned with nascent unions and not-yet-organized workers. Both of these factors might make state Federations more open to endorsing labor regulations or new social benefits for workers. Above all, state federations worked quite consistently for eight-hour limits and, as they took up the issue in the teens and twenties, for noncontributory old-age pensions.

Perhaps most important, state AFL leaders were normally part of political coalitions (albeit in most states constantly shifting ones) that sought to influence the state legislatures. Available allies—such as farmers' groups, women's associations, middle-class reform groups, party factions, or reformist professionals and civil administrators— could pull state Federations toward endorsements of social policy proposals that unions influential in given Federations did not find threatening. In many states women's groups encouraged AFL leaders to work with them for women's hour laws and sometimes even persuaded state Federations to support women's minimum-wage regulations over strong national AFL opposition.[110] In Massachusetts, New York, and elsewhere, reformist professional experts persuaded the respective Federations to ignore Gompers' opposition and endorse proposals for health or unemployment insurance.[111] In Wisconsin, the expert-led state industrial commission, along with Progressive Republicans and moderate Socialists based in Milwaukee, ensured that that state's unions would favor labor regulations and social insurance.[112] Agrarian movements in

---

Movement, 1890–1940 (Columbia: University of Missouri Press, 1973); and Philip Taft, *Labor Politics American Style: The California State Federation of Labor* (Cambridge: Harvard University Press, 1968), Introduction.

[108] Thomson dissertation, "Reaction to Labor Law," pp. 678–79.

[109] Brandeis, *Labor Legislation*, p. 557.

[110] Ibid., chapters 3 and 4; and Theda Skocpol, "Safeguarding the 'Mothers of the Race': Protective Legislation for Women Workers," chapter 7 of *Protecting Soldiers and Mothers*.

[111] Nelson, *Unemployment Insurance*, pp. 18, 70–71; Numbers, *Almost Persuaded*, p. 79; Paul Starr, *The Social Transformation of American Medicine* (New York: Basic Books, 1982), p. 250; Horace C. Tishler, *Self-Reliance and Social Security, 1870–1917* (Port Washington, NY: Kennikat Press, 1971); and "Labor Getting Behind Health Insurance," *The Survey* 39 (1918): 708–709.

[112] Nelson, *Unemployment Insurance*, chapter 6.

peripheral states sometimes drew tiny local Federations into alliances on behalf of a wide array of strong governmental measures, including labor regulations; this happened for example during the ascendancy of the Nonpartisan League in North Dakota.[113] In about a dozen states during the 1920s, labor groups joined hands with the cross-class Fraternal Order of Eagles in campaigns on behalf of old-age pensions for the most needy.[114]

Even at the level of the states, however, U.S. trade unions did not provide any strong push toward a British-style paternalist welfare state, centered in labor regulations and with social spending measures targeted on adult male workers and their dependents. Arguably, the U.S. labor movement voiced earlier and more consistent support than any other social force for noncontributory old-age pensions. But it did not spearhead movements across the states in favor of gender-neutral wage and hour laws, or unemployment and health insurance. Usually, non-labor political allies influenced organized labor's social policy agenda more readily than labor influenced the agendas of its helpers in state-level legislative lobbying, which led to great diversity across America's decentralized polity. What is more, no matter how their policy goals came to be defined, state labor Federations were never strong enough to mobilize all or even most of organized labor's potential resources on behalf of any legislative objective. State Federations had to rely on voluntary support from local unions and their members; and in many states individual unions tended to ignore the Federations and approach legislators directly on behalf of their own narrow craft interests.[115] At either the national or the state level U.S. organized labor could be at best a junior partner in a multifaceted legislative coalition.

In the context of the U.S. political system of the early twentieth century, organized labor had neither the capacity nor the incentive to pursue a national political program that included social legislation, and a pro-welfare-state alliance of reformers and unionists failed to come together as it did in Britain. Until the Great Depression unleashed changes from below within the labor movement, and until the New Deal's administrative state building and party realignment reworked the ties be-

---

[113] Elizabeth Sanders, "Farmers and the State in the Progressive Era" (Department of Political Science, New School for Social Research, Spring 1989); and Morlan, *Political Prairie Fire*, pp. 65–66.

[114] Quadagno, *Transformation of Old Age Security*, chapter 3.

[115] For some examples, see: Thomas Ray Pegram, "Progressivism and Partisanship: Reformers, Politicians, and Public Policy in Illinois, 1870–1922" (Ph.D. diss., Brandeis University, 1988), p. 123; Lorin Stuckey, *The Iowa State Federation of Labor*, Bulletin of the State University of Iowa, Studies in the Social Sciences, Volume 4(3) (August 1916), p. 17; and Irwin Yellowitz, *Labor and the Progressive Movement in New York State, 1897–1916* (Ithaca: Cornell University Press, 1965), p. 24, and chapter 2 generally.

tween the unions and the Democratic Party, organized labor in America would not become a significant force for constructing a paternalist welfare state for male workers and their dependents.

THE POLITICS OF MATERNALIST SOCIAL POLICIES

Most comparative studies of the origins of modern social policies have ignored gendered dimensions of politics as well as the roles that women's organizations may have played in bringing about particular sorts of measures. "Public" life is typically presumed to have been an exclusively male sphere, with women regarded as "private" actors confined to homes and charitable associations. Debates have centered on the relative contributions of male-dominated unions, political parties, and bureaucracies to the shaping of labor regulations and of social spending laws targetted on male breadwinners. Established approaches often overlook maternalist social policies directed at mothers and potential mothers (as well as children); and they fail to notice the contributions of female-dominated modes of politics, some of which were not dependent on action by parties, trade unions, or official bureaucracies.

Unfortunately, the unconsciously gendered premises of cross-national research on welfare state origins have blinded scholars to patterns of politics and policy that were especially important in the United States. If bureaucratic initiatives and class-conscious politics were largely absent from the Progressive Era, certain styles of women's politics were central to the period's reform agendas and actual legislative accomplishments, especially across the states. Meanwhile, during the construction of the British paternalist welfare state, there were socialists and women's groups who advocated even more far-reaching maternalist policies than those enacted in America. But British advocates of a universal "endowment of motherhood" were defeated by civil servants and the Labour movement; and benefits to women increasingly flowed to "dependents" on account of male breadwinners' "contributions" through waged labor.

The historically evolved positions of American and British women in relation to political institutions, higher education, and turn-of-the-century possibilities for different styles of politics can help us to understand the early triumph of a range of maternalist social policies in the United States in contrast to the failure of the campaign for the "endowment of motherhood" in Britain.

Conditions for Women's Politics: The United States in Contrast to Britain

In nineteenth-century America, women—above all, middle-class married women—were relegated to a "separate sphere" of domesticity and morality, charged with protecting the sanctity of home life and raising their children to be Godfearing, solid citizens.[116] Meanwhile, after the suffrage was extended to all white males, and once mass-based parties were organized in the Jackson era, formal politics became as strictly a male sphere as home life was a female sphere. This was true not only because women were excluded from voting, but more importantly, because rituals of male fraternalism were central during "the party period" of U.S. governance.[117] At the grass roots, partisan supporters associated in Democratic, Whig, or Republican clubs. The party faithful staged marches and parades replete with military trappings as "officers" mobilized the "rank and file" for electoral "battles." Campaigns "culminated in elections held in saloons, barber shops, and other places largely associated with men."[118] Voting rights and party loyalties tied men together across class lines in nineteenth-century America—so much so that partisan political participation was part of the very definition of American manhood.

Despite their exclusion from electoral and party politics—or perhaps we should say, in part because of such exclusion—American women became deeply involved in civic affairs. For "separate spheres," as ideology and practice simultaneously encouraged nineteenth-century American women to further domesticity and morality not only by staying at home—but by participating in community matters that had to do with religion, morals, and (as we would say today) social welfare. Throughout the nineteenth century elite and middle-class women, sometimes joined by working-class women, built organizations to promote virtues assigned as ideally feminine. Prior to the Civil War, such women's organizations became involved in church and charitable work, evangelical movements, moral crusades against prostitution, and the struggle to abolish slavery.[119] During the Civil War many women contributed

[116] Barbara Welter, "The Cult of True Womanhood: 1820–1860," *The American Family in Social-Historical Perspective*, edited by Michael Gordon (New York: St. Martin's Press, 1973), p. 225; Barbara Leslie Epstein, *The Politics of Domesticity* (Middletown, CT: Wesleyan University Press, 1981), p. 81; and Nancy F. Cott, *The Bonds of Womanhood: 'Woman's Sphere' in New England, 1780–1835* (New Haven: Yale University Press, 1977), especially chapter 2 on "Domesticity."

[117] Michael E. McGerr, *The Decline of Popular Politics* (New York: Oxford University Press, 1986), chapters 1 and 2; and Paula Baker, "The Domestication of Politics: Women and American Political Society, 1780–1920," *American Historical Review* 85(3) (June 1984): 627–29. The label "party period," referring to roughly 1830–1900, comes from Richard L. McCormick, "The Party Period and Public Policy: An Exploratory Hypothesis." *Journal of American History* 66 (September 1979): 279–98.

[118] Baker, "Domestication of Politics," p. 629.

[119] Carroll Smith-Rosenberg, *Disorderly Conduct: Visions of Gender in Victorian America* (New York: Alfred A. Knopf, 1985), part 2; William O'Neill, *The Woman Movement: Feminism in the United States and England* (London: Allen and Unwin, 1969), p. 20; and Ruth M. Alexander, "'We Are Engaged as a Band of Sisters': Class and Domesticity in the Washingtonian Temperance Movement, 1840–1850," *Journal of American History* 75(3)

in service efforts, and afterwards continued their activities in new ways.[120]

From the late nineteenth century, the transdenominational Women's Christian Temperance Union (WCTU) again expressed the will of many American Protestant women to reform society on feminine moral terms. Launched during 1873–74, the WCTU expanded to 27,000 members in over a thousand locals in twenty-four states by 1879, to reach over 168,000 dues-paying members in some 7,000 locals in every state of the union around the turn of the century.[121] With a motto declaring that "Woman will bless and brighten every place she enters, and will enter every place," the WCTU adopted a "do-everything policy."[122] The organization's various departments fought against prostitution, campaigned for female wardens and police matrons, worked for temperance propaganda in the schools, ran kindergartens for working mothers, and even supported labor reforms that might sustain respectable working-class homes.[123] The WCTU, writes historian Barbara Epstein, "pushed the women's culture of its time to its limits," turning women's subordination in a separate sphere into a resource for seeking political reforms of the nation as a whole.[124] Significantly, organized temperance activities in the United States were much more female dominated than contemporary temperance activities in England.[125]

Probably the largest proportion of married American women between the 1870s and the early 1900s confined their community participation, beyond church attendance, to literary clubs promoting what was known as "self culture."[126] Before long, however, these originally locally based

---

(December 1988): 763–85. See also Mary P. Ryan, *Cradle of the Middle Class: The Family in Oneida County, New York, 1790–1865* (Cambridge and New York: Cambridge University Press, 1981), chapters 2 and 3; and Nancy A. Hewitt, *Women's Activism and Social Change: Rochester, New York, 1822–1872* (Ithaca: Cornell University Press, 1984). Ryan's and Hewett's analyses differ from Smith-Rosenberg's, but they too emphasize women's activism in a variety of reform associations. Hewett offers intriguing insights into the possibly different class bases of different types of female-based associations.

[120] Lori D. Ginsberg, "Women and the Work of Benevolence: Morality and the Work of Politics in the Northeastern United States, 1820–1885" (Ph.D. diss., Yale University, 1985), chapters 5 and 6.

[121] Epstein, *Politics of Domesticity*, pp. 119–20.

[122] Quotations from Sheila Rothman, *Women's Proper Place* (New York: Basic Books, 1978), p. 67; and Ruth Borodin, "'A Baptism of Power and Liberty': The Women's Crusade of 1873–1874," in *Woman's Being, Woman's Place: Female Identity and Vocation in American History* (Boston: G.K. Hall, 1979), p. 121.

[123] Epstein, *Politics of Domesticity*, pp. 120–25; and Rothman, *Woman's Proper Place*, pp. 67–68.

[124] Epstein, *Politics of Domesticity*, p. 146.

[125] Borodin, "'A Baptism of Power and Liberty,'" p. 283.

[126] Karen J. Blair, *The Clubwoman as Feminist: True Womanhood Redefined, 1868–1914* (New York: Holmes and Meier, 1980).

and inwardly-oriented literary clubs became nationally organized and civicly assertive, following the route of earlier groups in parlaying women's separate sphere into political power. After 1890, these clubs coalesced into a national network, the General Federation of Women's Clubs (GFWC), which by 1911 claimed over one million members in locals spread across all 48 states, each of which also had its own state federation.[127] Clubwomen made the transition from cultural to reform activities not by abandoning the Victorian conception of women's special domestic sphere but by extending it into what came to be called "municipal housekeeping."[128] In the words of Rheta Childe Dorr, author of a 1910 book about clubwomen in politics entitled *What Eight Million Women Want:* "Woman's place is in the home. This is a platitude which no woman will ever dissent from. . . . But Home is not contained within the four walls of an individual home. Home is the community. The city full of people is the Family. The public school is the real Nursery. And badly do the Home and the Family and the Nursery need their mother."[129] Having decided that "all clubs, as bodies of trained housekeepers, should consider themselves guardians of the civic housekeeping of their respective communities,"[130] turn-of-the-century women's clubs worked for better libraries and schools, for measures to promote public health and consumer safety, and for new laws to ensure social welfare—above all, for mothers and children.

In this new set of endeavors, the GFWC often worked in tandem with the National Congress of Mothers, which was founded in 1897 to "carry the mother-love and mother-thought into all that concerns or touches childhood in Home, School, Church, State or Legislation."[131] By 1910 the Congress had 50,000 dues-paying members in twenty-one state branches; and by 1920, the Congress was organized in thirty-seven

[127] Margaret Gibbons Wilson, *The American Woman in Transition: The Urban Influence, 1870–1920* (Westport, CN: Greenwood Press, 1979), p. 100; and Mary I. Wood, *The History of the General Federation of Women's Clubs for the First Twenty-Two Years of Its Organization* (New York: History Department, General Federation of Women's Clubs), p. 353.

[128] See Mrs. T.J. Bowlker, "Woman's Home-Making Function Applied to the Municipality," *The American City* 6(6) (June 1912): 863. The entire issue of the journal contains valuable information on the civic activities of various women's clubs, as does Mary Ritter Beard's *Woman's Work in Municipalities* (New York: D. Appleton and Company, 1915).

[129] Rheta Childe Dorr, *What Eight Million Women Want* (New York: Kraus Reprint, 1971; originally 1910), p. 327. See also Marlene Stein Wortman, "Domesticating the Nineteenth-Century American City," *Prospects: An Annual of American Cultural Studies* 3 (1977).

[130] Attributed to the GFWC Civic Section in Wood, *History of the General Federation of Women's Clubs*, p. 116. This statement was part of a proposal made by the Section at the Fourth Biennial Convention of the GFWC in Denver, Colorado, June 21–27, 1908.

[131] This statement was for some years part of the "Aims and Purposes of the National Congress of Mothers," as listed in a box in each issue of the organization's official journal. See, for example, the October 1912 issue of *Child-Welfare Magazine*, p. 61.

states and had 190,000 members.[132] Obviously, this was a much smaller and somewhat less widespread association than the General Federation. Yet the National Congress could be extremely influential on matters of social legislation, because it had excellent relations with the newspapers and certain women's magazines, and because its leaders in the early years—like the leaders of the GFWC—tended to be social elites well connected in their communities and regions.

Not only were large numbers of married, domestically based American women well organized and civically active in the late-nineteenth and early-twentieth centuries, a hefty minority of American women also achieved higher education and college degrees. And a fraction of these went on—especially via the social settlement movement—to become leaders of reform efforts during the Progressive Era.

Despite the ideology of domesticity, the United States led the world in offering higher education to women through its decentralized and fast-growing system of colleges and universities. By 1870, some 11,000 women constituted over one-fifth of all American students in institutions of higher learning; and by 1880, some 40,000 women constituted a third of enrollees. Women's share increased to about 37 percent in 1900, with 85,000 enrolled, and rose to nearly half of all enrollees at the early twentieth-century peak in 1920, when some 283,000 women were in institutions of higher learning.[133] Some perspective can be gained on American women's considerable educational achievements, when we note that contemporary British women lagged far behind. In 1880, "only London University granted degrees to women scholars. The handful of the students in the women's colleges of Cambridge and Oxford (less than 200 in 1882) took the same examinations given to men, but were not allowed to receive degrees until after World War I."[134] Around 1890, there were more women students at Smith College alone than at all Oxford and Cambridge.[135] According to a list compiled by the Women's Institute, the total number of British women enrolled in women's colleges in 1897 was only 784—a miniscule number compared to the tens of thousands of American women.[136]

Those higher-educated American women who took jobs went over-

[132] These statistics come from *Golden Jubilee History, 1897–1947* (Chicago: National Congress of Parents and Teachers, 1947), p. 199; Harry and Bonaro Overstreet, *Where Children Come First: A Study of the P.T.A. Idea* (Chicago: National Congress of Parents and Teachers, 1949), p. 196; and Rothman, *Woman's Proper Place*, p. 104.

[133] Mabel Newcomer, *A Century of Higher Education for American Women* (New York: Harper, 1959), p. 46, Table 2.

[134] O'Neill, *The Woman Movement*, p. 44.

[135] Ibid., p. 57.

[136] Martha Vicinus, *Independent Women: Work and Community for Single Women, 1850–1920* (Chicago: University of Chicago Press, 1985), p. 127.

whelmingly into school teaching; and many worked only for a few years prior to marriage.[137] Nevertheless, the sheer extent of female higher education in America did produce large numbers, spread throughout the country, who could appreciate Progressive reform efforts justified in terms of both feminine values and the need for greater "professional expertise" in politics. This was important, even if most educated women simply served as rank-and-file supporters through such bodies as the American Association of University Women, professional associations, and the General Federation of Women's Clubs.

Higher education for American women also led a critical minority to become active reformers by way of the settlement movement. Significantly, from the 1870s through the 1920s, when only 10 percent of all American women did not marry, between 40 and 60 percent of women college graduates remained single.[138] Among those who obtained Ph.D.s between 1877 and 1924, fully 75 percent in this group remained single.[139] From the ranks of these mostly unmarried, educated women, including the elite few with graduate degrees, came the founders of many "social settlements" in American cities.[140]

Settlement houses were a British innovation. The first one, Toynbee Hall in the East End of London, was founded by Canon Samuel Barnett and Henrietta Barnett in 1884, and by 1911 there were 46 such houses in British cities.[141] Some British settlements were staffed by college women, but none of these became a leading center of reform; women were attracted to them as routes toward specialized types of charity work and, in due course, social work.[142] The more prominent British settlements, and especially Toynbee Hall, were mostly staffed by male graduates of Oxford and Cambridge who spent a few years engaged in social investigation and urban reform en route to careers in journalism, the universities, and the civil service. Nearly a quarter of the men who resided at Toynbee Hall between 1884 and 1914 went on to become

[137] Joyce Antler, "The Educated Woman and Professionalization: The Struggle for a New Feminine Identity, 1890–1920" (Ph.D. diss., State University of New York at Stony Brook, 1977), pp. 27, 380–82.

[138] Smith-Rosenberg, *Disorderly Conduct*, p. 253.

[139] Antler, "Educated Woman," p. 419.

[140] See John P. Rousmaniere, "Cultural Hybrid in the Slums: The College Woman and the Settlement House, 1889–1894," *American Quarterly* 22 (1970): 45–66.

[141] Allen F. Davis, *Spearheads for Reform: The Social Settlements and the Progressive Movement, 1890–1914* (New York: Oxford University Press, 1967), p. 8. See also Emily K. Abel, "Toynbee Hall, 1884–1914," *Social Service Review* 53(4) (December 1979): 606–32; and Werner Picht, *Toynbee Hall and the English Settlement Movement*, revised edition translated from the German by Lillian A. Cowell (London: G. Bells and Sons, 1914).

[142] Vicinus, *Independent Women*, p. 215. We do not mean to argue that British women settlers never became prominent reformers. Some did; for example, Eleanor Rathbone, who started out at the Liverpool Women's Settlement.

civil servants, and the proportion taking this career path increased with time.[143] In due course, four men who became prime ministers had close connections to Toynbee Hall.[144] As one observer commented sarcastically, "men who went in training under the Barnetts . . . could always be sure of government and municipal appointments . . . [They] discovered the advancement of their own interests and the interests of the poor were best served by leaving East London to stew in its own juice while they became members of parliament, cabinet ministers, civil servants."[145]

A telling instance was William Beveridge. After graduating from Oxford, Beveridge became subwarden of Toynbee Hall in 1903, writing to reassure his parents that "Toynbee Hall is not a cul de sac. It is known among men of position."[146] While at the settlement, Beveridge did economic research, served on private and public bodies dealing with unemployment in London, and became a regular writer on social issues for the *Morning Post* prior to joining the newspaper's regular staff.[147] All of this, of course, was prelude to Beveridge's achievement of many important national governmental assignments during a lifetime of shaping the British welfare state, including as the Board of Trade official behind the Liberal Party's plans for social insurance in 1911.[148]

Although early social settlements in the United States were directly modelled on Toynbee Hall, the American movement departed from the British settlement movement in a number of ways.[149] The American movement became much larger, encompassing over 400 houses by 1910.[150] Continuing to expand even as the British movement levelled off with the emergence of the official welfare state, the U.S. social settlement movement also developed a more democratic philosophy.[151] And if Canon Barnett and William Beveridge, leaders of Toynbee Hall in the British capitol of London, were the exemplary leaders of the British settlement movement, it is not accidental that Jane Addams, founder

[143] Abel, "Toynbee Hall," pp. 614–15.

[144] Robert C. Reinders, "Toynbee Hall and the American Settlement Movement," *Social Service Review* 56(1) (March 1982): 48.

[145] George Lansbury, as quoted in Vicinus, *Independent Women*, p. 215.

[146] As quoted in Abel, "Toynbee Hall," p. 623.

[147] Ibid., pp. 622–25.

[148] See Standish Meacham, *Toynbee Hall and Social Reform, 1880–1914* (New Haven: Yale University Press, 1987), especially chapter 6 on "William Beveridge: 'Benevolent, Bourgeois Bureaucrat'"; and Jose Harris, *William Beveridge: A Biography* (Oxford and New York: Oxford University Press, 1977).

[149] Davis, *Spearheads for Reform*, chapters 1 and 2; and Reinders, "Toynbee Hall and American Movement."

[150] Davis, *Spearheads for Reform*, p. 12.

[151] Reinders, "Toynbee Hall and American Movement," p. 45–50.

and long-term resident of Hull House in the midwestern U.S. city of Chicago, is the best known American settlement leader.[152] Women settlers predominated numerically in the U.S. movement; higher-educated, unmarried women like Addams were the most persistent American settlers, the ones who gave the houses and the movement staying power over time. While the median number of years spent by all residents of U.S. social settlements was three, unmarried women spent a median of ten years there, and many remained for their entire adult lifetimes.[153] The United States had numerous successful mixed-gender settlements in which women were leaders, while Britain had only six such in 1913 and these were not considered to work well.[154]

Perhaps most important, in contrast to the situation in Britain, many American women settlers were highly influential reformers and public figures—that is, leaders outside as well as within the settlement movement. The balance of opportunities offered to male and female reformers in the British versus the U.S. polity can help us to understand why these American women became prominent. Whereas British male graduates of Oxford and Cambridge could use settlement work as a predictable and quite direct route to elite careers in the political parties and the civil service, given the nature of parallel American institutions these opportunities were not regularly available to American male college graduates who went into settlement work. In the British settlements, women either operated in sex-segregated environments or else were treated as "helpers," without the establishment futures of their male counterparts, sporting Oxford and Cambridge degrees. In contrast, American settlement houses—such as Hull House in Chicago and Henry Street in New York—became settings from which talented women could create and pursue careers combining social research, public education, and civic activism. American men were not in a position to preempt all of the possibilities along this line, because, again, the kinds of institutions that in Britain increasingly took up the relevant "civic space," as we might label it—institutions such as expert bureaucracies, programmatic political parties, and in due course the "welfare state" itself—simply weren't there to the same extent in the United States. Through the settlements, intellectual American women at the

---

[152] See Daniel Levine, *Jane Addams and the Liberal Tradition* (Madison: State Historical Society of Wisconsin, 1971).

[153] Allen Freeman Davis, "Spearheads for Reform—The Social Settlements and the Progressive Movement, 1890–1914" (Ph.D. diss., University of Wisconsin, 1959), p. 5, including note 17; and Smith-Rosenberg, *Disorderly Conduct*, p. 254, note 20, citing a conversation with Allen Davis. The Davis dissertation contains material not subsequently included in Davis's book.

[154] Picht, *English Settlement Movement*, p. 102.

turn of the twentieth century could pursue long-term careers as professional reformers, supporting one another and cooperating with some male coworkers, without being crowded out by an official, male-dominated social policy establishment.[155]

Because American reformers, including the social settlement people, could not pursue reforms through programmatic parties and national bureaucracies as the British social policy establishment did, they built eclectic political coalitions capable of civic education and legislative lobbying. Settlement leaders were especially adept at knitting together coalitions—on the one hand among women from different classes, and on the other hand among women in the middle and upper classes.

Founded in 1903 by an alliance of women's trade union organizers, settlement house leaders, and some upper class matrons active in charity work, the U.S. Women's Trade Union League (WTUL) provided critical resources, including money and strike support, for women workers attempting to unionize.[156] In addition, to help make up for the weakness of women workers in labor markets and trade unions, the WTUL agitated for new laws to limit their hours of work, improve their wages, and regulate working conditions that might threaten women's health.[157] It also brought working women into alliances on behalf of female suffrage.[158] Significantly, the American WTUL was more devoted to legislative causes than was its British counterpart.[159] Operating in a national setting where unions were steadily gaining organizational and political strength, the British WTUL actively guided female unions into the national labor confederation. Indeed, in 1921 the British WTUL dissolved and became instead the women's section of the Trades Union Congress. Meanwhile, the American WTUL persisted as a basically gender-based

[155] This argument is developed in Kathryn Kish Sklar, "Hull House in the 1890s: A Community of Women Reformers" *Signs* 10(4) (Summer 1985): 658–77.

[156] Allen F. Davis, "The Women's Trade Union League: Origins and Organization," *Labor History* 5 (1964): 3–17.

[157] Diane Kirkby, "'The Wage Earning Woman and the State': The National Women's Trade Union League and Protective Labor Legislation, 1903–1923," *Labor History* 28(1) (1987): 54–74; and Nancy Schrom Dye, *As Equals and As Sisters: Feminism, the Labor Movement, and the Women's Trade Union League of New York* (Columbia: University of Missouri Press, 1980). These two scholars disagree about when and exactly why the WTUL became committed to campaigns for protective legislation; but they agree that it was a major emphasis for the organization.

[158] Robin Miller Jacoby, "The Women's Trade Union League and American Feminism," *Feminist Studies* 3 (1975): 126–40.

[159] Robin Miller Jacoby, "Feminism and Class Consciousness in the British and American Women's Trade Union Leagues, 1890–1925," *Liberating Women's History: Theoretical and Critical Essays*, edited by Berenice A. Carroll (Urbana, IL: University of Illinois Press, 1976) pp. 137–60. See also Gladys Boone, *The Women's Trade Union Leagues in Great Britain and the United States of America* (New York: Columbia University Press, 1942).

and fully cross-class organization devoted to legislation and the cause of women's suffrage, as well as to unionization. For American WTUL members, the rhetoric of "sisterhood" was more meaningful than the language of class.

Another small gender-based policy organization was the National Consumers' League (NCL), which involved many upper-class as well as middle-class women in economic boycotts and legislative struggles on behalf of working women. Some prominent male academics and reformers were titular officers of the NCL, but they often failed to show up for meetings, and the organization was clearly both run and energized by women.[160] The NCL—which had no British counterpart—was founded during the 1890s by Mrs. Josephine Shaw Lowell, Mrs. Maud Nathan, and other elite women who came together to agitate for better working conditions for shop girls.[161] Although the Consumers' League's membership never grew beyond a few thousand nationwide, the organization did claim 64 local leagues in 20 states in 1905. After that, the number of states organized dropped, with 15 states still claiming one or more local leagues by 1917.[162] Members of the Consumers' League were well connected socially in their states and communities and thus often strategically placed to press for legislative reforms. Moreover, the NCL took the bold step of hiring the remarkable socialist reformer and settlement resident Florence Kelley as its Executive Secretary.[163] Under her politically principled and technically expert leadership, the National League became an effective advocate of child labor legislation as well as protectionist legislation for women wage-workers.[164] Thus, even more than the WTUL, the National Consumers' League was a pure embodiment of gender politics, with a maternalist agenda, engaging women career reformers from the settlements and upper- and middle-class ma-

[160] According to William L. O'Neill, *Everyone Was Brave* (Chicago: Quadrangle Books, 1971), p. 95: "Except for the vastly larger NAWSA [National American Women's Suffrage Association], no other feminist group seems to have attracted upper-class women in such numbers." The NCL's Annual Reports show that President John Graham Brooks was often absent from Annual Meetings.

[161] Louis Lee Athey, "The Consumers' Leagues and Social Reform, 1890–1923" (Ph.D. diss., University of Delaware, 1965), chapter 2; and Maud Nathan, *The Story of An Epoch-Making Movement* (Garden City, NY: Doubleday, Page and Company, 1926).

[162] Information on numbers of state and local Consumers' Leagues appears in the NCL's Annual Reports.

[163] A comprehensive biography of Florence Kelley, placing her in the context of the gender politics of turn-of-the-century America, is being prepared by Kathryn Kish Sklar. Meanwhile, see Josephine Goldmark, *Impatient Crusader* (Urbana: University Press of Illinois, 1953), chapter 5.

[164] Allis Rosenberg Wolfe, "Women, Consumerism, and the National Consumers' League in the Progressive Era, 1900–1923," *Labor History* 16 (1975): 378–92; and Athey, "Consumers' Leagues and Social Reform."

trons on behalf of reforms deemed beneficial to working-class women and their children.

Settlement leaders also cooperated on many political issues with the larger and more widespread associations of elite and middle-class married women, especially the General Federation of Women's Clubs. Partnership between social settlement leaders and organized married ladies was possible during the Progressive Era in large part because both sides shared beliefs about women's roles in society and about the morally justifiable reforms needed in industrializing America. Ironically, although women leaders from the social settlement movement were often unmarried and childless, they thought of themselves as "public mothers."[165] Seeing mothers and children especially worthy of public help, they also believed that women had special proclivities for moral decision making and civic activity; thus women were the logical ones to lead the nation toward new social policies.[166] In sum, intellectual women from the American settlement movement ended up functioning as a kind of political vanguard of organized womanhood on reform issues understood to be part of women's special sphere of concern.

Victories for Maternalist Policies in the United States

Because American women did not have the vote in a polity where white men of all classes did, they viewed themselves as separate from the "corrupt" male realm of partisan politics. In contrast to contemporary British women, American women were not tempted to operate as auxiliaries of a strong working-class movement. Instead, reacting against a cross-class patronage democracy, American women developed an alternative style of politics emphasizing public education and moralistic lobbying for allegedly disinterested and nonpartisan legislative goals. During the Progressive Era, alliances that included women's groups and reformers from the social settlement movement used this political style to advocate social benefits for mothers and children. Many women's groups also promoted protective regulations for women workers, on the grounds that being positioned in the labor market they needed special help as potential mothers.

[165] The term "public mothers" comes from Smith-Rosenberg, who develops this argument in *Disorderly Conduct*, pp. 263–64.

[166] Not all of the women reform leaders of the Progressive Era believed that women thought differently from men. See the discussion of the views of Julia Lathrop in Lela B. Costin, *Two Sisters for Social Justice: A Biography of Grace and Edith Abbott* (Urbana and Chicago, IL: University of Illinois Press, 1983), p. viii. The fact remains, however, that even Lathrop was willing to speak to the General Federation of Women's Clubs as if she did believe that women had unique qualities.

Viewing matters from an equal-rights, feminist perspective that became prominent from the 1920s on, some scholars have argued that protective labor laws were detrimental to women workers. Scholars argue that such measures were often promoted by trade unions trying to exclude women from competition with male breadwinners.[167] Certain kinds of protective labor laws do fit this profile, particularly those intended to exclude women altogether from narrowly defined craft occupations.[168] But it should be remembered that, during the 1910s, groups such as the Women's Trade Union League advocated both limited hours and minimum wages for women workers, viewing such joint legal protections as ways to help vulnerable, nonunionized wage earners.[169] Not until the 1920s did it become clear that hours laws without minimum wages would have the effect of hurting many women by reducing their paychecks and shutting them out of some jobs. Moreover, as we discussed above, many reformers who supported protective labor laws for women during the Progressive Era saw them as an "entering wedge" for more general laws to protect all workers from low wages and too many hours of daily work.

Whether in the end they were really good for women or not, protective labor laws were enthusiastically supported by middle- and working-class womens' groups. Enacted in virtually all states during the 1910s, new or improved women's hour laws were often supported by state Federations of Labor, yet they were also advocated nationally and in the states and localities by the National Consumers' League, the Women's Trade Union League, the General Federation of Women's Clubs, and various other women's groups.[170] Minimum-wage laws for women were usually opposed by both organized labor and organized business, which helps to explain why they did not pass nearly as often

[167] Arguments along these lines appear in Susan Lehrer, *Origins of Protective Labor Legislation for Women, 1905–1925* (Albany: State University of New York Press, 1987); and Alice Kessler-Harris, *Out to Work* (Oxford: Oxford University Press, 1982).

[168] See the examples of the New York metal polishers and the New York and Massachusetts molders discussed in Clara M. Beyer, *History of Labor Legislation for Women in Three States*, Bulletin No.66-Part I, Women's Bureau, U.S. Department of Labor (Washington D.C.: United States Government Printing Office, 1929): 169–73.

[169] See Diane Kirkby, " 'The Wage-Earning Woman and the State': The National Women's Trade Union League and Protective Labor Legislation, 1903–1923," *Labor History* 28(1) (1987): 54–74.

[170] Supporting evidence is detailed in Theda Skocpol, "Safeguarding the 'Mothers of the Race': Protective Legislation for Women Workers," chapter 7 in *Protecting Soldiers and Mothers*. See also: Athey dissertation, "Consumers' Leagues and Social Reform"; Clara M. Beyer, *Labor Legislation for Women in Three States*; Bulletin No.66-Part I, Women's Bureau, U.S. Department of Labor (Washington, D.C.: U.S. Government Printing Office, 1929); and James T. Patterson, "Mary Dewson and the American Minimum Wage Movement," *Labor History* 5(2) (Spring 1964): 134–52.

as hours laws. Still, cross-class alliances of women's groups did manage to get such proposals on the agenda in most states, and fifteen legislatures actually enacted minimum-wage laws.[171] In the state of California, a broad alliance of women's groups in 1913 persuaded the legislature to enact a minimum-wage law, and they successfully defended it the next year in a state-wide referendum against concerted opposition from both business organizations and the California State Federation of Labor. The women's organizations used the slogans, "Let us be our sisters' keepers" and "Employed womanhood must be protected in order to foster the motherhood of the race."[172]

Women's politics during the Progressive Era achieved new public social spending for mothers, as well as protective legislation applying to women workers. Although in practice they were woefully underfunded, mothers' pensions would never have become the one kind of social spending measure to squeak through the Progressive Era's general bias against such policies had it not been for the early and persistent advocacy of women's voluntary associations. The National Congress of Mothers took up the cause in 1911.[173] At its 1912 Biennial Convention, the General Federation of Women's Clubs also endorsed the idea of mothers' pensions; and at least twenty state Federations of Women's Clubs lobbied state legislatures for the enactment of these measures between 1913 and 1919.[174] Despite opposition or lack of enthusiasm from other progressive reformers, the cause of mothers' pensions was also supported by leading women social settlement figures and aided by a series of vivid muckraking articles written for a women's magazine, *The Delineator*, by William Hard, a former social settlement worker and close friend of Jane Addams and Julia Lathrop.[175]

[171] Brandeis, *Labor Legislation*, chapter 4.

[172] Beyer, *Labor Legislation for Women in Three States*, pp. 129–31; and Norris C. Hundley, Jr., "Katherine Philips Edson and the Fight for the California Minimum Wage, 1912–1923," *Pacific Historical Review* 29 (1960): 271–85.

[173] The involvement of the National Congress with this issue can be traced in their official publication, *Child-Welfare Magazine*. See especially Mrs. G.H. Robertson, "The State's Duty to Fatherless Children," *Child-Welfare Magazine* 6(5) (January 1912): 156–60; and Mrs. Frederick Schoff, "The Evolution of the Mother's Pension," *Child-Welfare Magazine* 8(4) (December 1914).

[174] *Official Report of the Eleventh Biennial Convention, General Federation of Women's Clubs, June 25–July 5, 1912, San Francisco, California*, compiled and edited by Mrs. George O. Welch (General Federation of Women's Clubs, 1912), p. 600. See also the discussion on p. 185. Documentation about the activities of State Federations appears in chapter 8 of Theda Skocpol's *Protecting Soldiers and Mothers*, which offers a full analysis of the role of women's groups in campaigns for mothers' pension legislation. Preliminary results of a quantitative study now under way indicate that State Federations of Women's Clubs had a significant effect on the priority of state enactments.

[175] See Mark Leff, "Consensus for Reform: The Mothers' Pension Movement in the

Even though women were not able to vote in most states during the 1910s, feminine advocates of maternalist social policies were surprisingly effective at getting bills through state legislatures.[176] The widespread federated associations such as the General Federation and the National Congress of Mothers were skillful at highlighting a policy issue simultaneously across much of the nation. They mobilized local opinion makers to put pressure on legislators—not just in state capitols, or in Washington, D.C., but in their own home districts. The women's organizations could link local efforts to programs shaped nationally by their own leaders in conjunction with the social settlement reformers. Organized U.S. women were much better at using such tactics to shape public opinion and set legislative agendas than were the unionized workers of the AFL and the various state Federations of Labor. Women's politics in the early twentieth-century United States crossed class lines, linked local to supralocal efforts, and tied intellectuals to ordinary people much more effectively than contemporary U.S. labor politics did any of these things.

Whatever their party affiliations, members of state legislatures found women's moral rhetoric hard to publicly deny. Thus, when educational tactics and lobbying succeeded in getting proposals onto the legislative agenda, bills often passed by huge, lopsided majorities.[177] Of course, given the way U.S. politics operates, this might not have been enough to ensure victories for maternalist protective labor regulations—had not gender-based rhetoric also held sway in the American courts during the Progressive Era. As they revealed in their landmark 1908 ruling in *Muller v. Oregon*, the Justices of the Supreme Court were likewise persuaded that women as potential mothers were worthy of special public protection.

This 1908 decision, so crucial to the progress of women's protective legislation at a time when similar laws could not be passed for male workers, was partially shaped by the efforts of American women's organizations. At one level this is the case because the brief presented by Louis Brandeis on behalf of the Oregon hours statute at issue was initiated by the National Consumers' League and researched by its staff member, Josephine Goldmark.[178] Yet turn-of-the-century U.S. women's

---

Progressive Era," *Social Service Review* 47 (1973): 397–417. *The Delineator's* articles on mothers' pensions appeared from August 1912 through April 1913. On Hard's biography and connections to the settlement women, see Janet Marie Wedel, "The Origins of State Patriarchy During the Progressive Era: A Sociological Study of the Mothers' Aid Movement" (Ph.D. diss., Washington University, 1975), pp. 311–312.

[176] For a vivid example of the tactics used, see Elizabeth Hayhurst, "How Pensions for Widows Were Won in Oregon," *Child-Welfare Magazine* 7(7) (March 1913): 248–49.

[177] Leff, "Consensus for Reform," pp. 400–401, makes this point for mothers' pension legislation.

[178] Clement E. Vose, "The National Consumers' League and the Brandeis Brief," *Midwest*

politics also figured more tacitly in *Muller*'s ideological background. Judges did not simply accede to expert opinions from doctors and social scientists; in other cases they demonstrated the ability to ignore or legally controvert such "evidence."[179] Rather, as profoundly rhetorical institutions, courts were bound to be affected by moral understandings deeply embedded in political discourse. Thus, as Mr. Justice Brewer saw it, the expert opinions presented to the Supreme Court in *Muller v. Oregon* were

> significant of a widespread belief that woman's physical structure, and the function she performs in consequence thereof, justify special legislation restricting or qualifying the conditions under which she should be permitted to toil. Constitutional questions, it is true, are not settled by even a consensus of present public opinion. . . . At the same time, when a question of fact is debated and debatable, and the extent to which a special constitutional limitation goes is affected by the truth in respect to that fact, a widespread and long continued belief concerning it is worthy of consideration. We take judicial cognizance of all matters of general knowledge.[180]

In short, the justices of the Supreme Court, who unanimously decided in 1908 to treat women workers as a special class deserving public protection, were strongly affected by contemporary public understandings of gender differences. We can hypothesize that the justices saw women as mothers especially worthy of help from innovative public policies, because organized American women had taught civic leaders—and the educated public in general—to think in this way. If governmental paternalism was still suspect, maternalism had become much more acceptable by the Progressive Era, even to crusty judges still largely wedded to individualistic doctrines of free contract.

In both the legislative and the judicial realms, therefore, turn-of-the-century American women's politics—a politics based on extending rather than contravening ideals of separate spheres for the genders—was well suited to overcoming the obstacles that the U.S. polity placed in the way of advocates of new social policies. There was, for a time, an especially good fit between what politically active American women wanted and could do, and what the changing American state structure could accommodate. Thus, women's hour and minimum-wage laws

---

Journal of Political Science 1 (November 1957): 267–90; Athey dissertation, "Consumers' Leagues and Social Reform," pp. 205–13; and Goldmark, *Impatient Crusader*, chapter 13.

[179] See the discussion in Brandeis, *Labor Legislation*, p. 689 of the Supreme Court's dismissal of expert evidence in the 1923 decision it rendered in *Adkins v. Children's Hospital*.

[180] From the Supreme Court's opinion in *Muller v. Oregon*, 208 U.S. 412 (1908), reprinted in Louis D. Brandeis and Josephine Goldmark, *Women in Industry*, introduced by Leon Stein and Philip Taft (New York: Arno Press and the New York Times, 1969), p. 5.

were widely enacted, along with mothers' pensions, in a polity otherwise inimical to labor regulations and social spending measures.

British Counterpoint: The Failure of an Endowment for Mothers

Like their American sisters during the nineteenth century, British women also organized for civic action, inspired in many cases by similar Protestant values and by an analogous desire to extend ideals of Victorian domesticity into community service. But turn-of-the-century British women holding ideas about the moral superiority of their gender did not initially claim, or ever achieve, the same degree of influence in shaping social policies that such American women did.

Doctrines of women's moral superiority were initially weaker among British women, while Enlightenment-bred ideals of equal rights and ideologies combining working-class and women's concerns were stronger.[181] More consequential over time, there were differences in social movements as well. British temperance activities as a whole were not female dominated as were American temperance activities; nor did the female British temperance association endorse women's suffrage or promote such a wide range of social reforms as did the U.S. Women's Christian Temperance Union.[182] Before World War I, there were no true British counterparts to those nation-spanning U.S. associations, the General Federation of Women's Clubs and the National Congress of Mothers. Nor was there any British version of the National Consumers' League. Finally, even though there certainly was a British Women's Trade Union League, its reform agenda converged with that of the trade unions, and the British WTUL eventually dissolved as a separate organization, transforming itself into the women's arm of the Trades Union Congress.[183] Indeed, those British women who became politically active on behalf of political changes favoring women tended to do so either as equal-rights feminists or as socialists active in the labor movement.[184]

The social and political context in which civicly engaged British women and women's organizations operated was very different from the U.S. As we have seen, very few British women received higher education, so they could rarely follow the established path from Oxford and Cambridge into the British social and political establishment. Nor

---

[181] This is a major theme of the comparisons made between Britain and the United States in Olive Banks, *Faces of Feminism: A Study of Feminism as a Social Movement* (Oxford and New York: Basil Blackwell, 1986).

[182] Ibid., pp. 79–80; and Borodin, "Women's Crusade," p. 283.

[183] Jacoby, "British and American Women's Trade Union Leagues"; and Boone, *Women's Trade Union Leagues in Great Britain and the United States.*

[184] Banks, *Faces of Feminism*, parts II and III.

did British women become national leaders in or through the social settlements. Instead, British women active in charitable or political affairs typically gained prominence through individual ties of marriage or friendship to men, even moderate socialists, who were part of the British establishment. Beatrice Webb is the most celebrated example of a woman who gained access this way—and made the most of it, yet normally in ways that meshed with the viewpoints of labor leftists and administrative reformers.

Seen more broadly, the major obstacles facing British women in any quest to translate separate gender concerns into political issues were the prominence of paternalist competitors who took up most of the the "space" for reform efforts. American women were excluded from a cross-class male democracy, in which bureaucratic agencies were weak and unions and politicians remained entangled in patronage politics, but such a setting was ideal for mobilizing middle-class women representing the distinctive morality of their gender through nonpartisan styles of locally rooted politics—exactly the styles that paid off well during the Progressive Era. In contrast, British women's organizations had to operate in a polity where, from the 1850s through the 1920s, working class men (as well as all women) were collectively seeking initial political access through the vote, thus polarizing British politics along class lines. British women also had to relate to a strong and growing trade union movement. And they faced a political structure in which, especially after the 1870s, programmatic party politicians and civil administrators increasingly claimed to speak "in the public interest" about social welfare issues. As individuals and as local organizations, British women may often have spoken the same "maternalist" messages as their American sisters, but their voices tended to be absorbed into other choruses or simply drowned out in a national polity where male working-class leaders, politicians, and administrators were calling the tunes.

Developments from the nineteenth century onward were thus not propitious for any hegemonic British women's politics based on ideals of the separate, domestic sphere, even though particular movements and local women's groups often effectively used maternalistic ideas. What is more, social policies targetted on mothers and—especially—children were pushed forward by women working with and through other politically active forces. After the Boer War raised concerns about the physical fitness of the population, the Conservatives implemented some measures for children in the name of "national efficiency."[185] The "new" Liberals supported the cause of female suffrage and also initiated many

---

[185] Gilbert, *Evolution of National Insurance*, chapter 2.

welfare measures, including the 1911 National Insurance Act which provided some maternity benefits for wives of covered male workers.[186] Yet the Labour movement was most important for British women. As Olive Banks explains:

[W]hether because of its sympathy for feminist ambitions [including the suffrage] or its democratic basis, there is little doubt that women's groups and auxiliaries had much more influence on the policy of the Labour Party than similar groups within the other two main parties. . . .

The most strongly feminist of the women's auxiliaries, at least in the early years of the Labour movement, was the Women's Cooperative Guild. Ardent suffragists, they were also active campaigners for a number of other issues concerned specifically with women and children. In the years immediately before the first world war they ran influential campaigns for equal divorce laws for men and women, for better maternity and infant welfare and for maternity benefits to be paid to mothers. . . . The Women's Labour League founded in 1906 with the object of persuading women to take an active interest in political affairs, also concerned itself with issues affecting women and children. There were lengthy campaigns on school meals, medical inspections in schools, the provision of nursery schools, and pit-head baths. The League also played a major role in the passing of the Maternity and Child Welfare Act of 1918. . . .

The consequence of this pressure from within their own ranks was to make the Labour Party receptive to many policies that were also of importance to the feminists. Maternity and infant welfare, for example, which in the United States was almost entirely a feminist issue, was a significant aspect of Labour Party policy. . . . This alliance between feminism and the Labour Party was not paralleled in the United States until Roosevelt's New Deal, which ended the isolation of feminist reformers and social workers.[187]

Matters might have rested in the early British welfare state with piecemeal measures for mothers and babies had it not been for the impact of World War I on gender relations, particularly within the working class, and on organized women's politics, especially among middle-class feminists. During the War and the 1920s, calls for the "endowment for motherhood" reached the center of official welfare policy debates in Britain. At stake was a truly maternalist policy proposal much more sweeping than anything American women achieved—or even widely debated—during the Progressive Era. It is interesting to see how and why the possibility of this radically maternalist policy came up

[186] Thane, *Foundations of the Welfare State*, p. 85.
[187] Banks, *Faces of Feminism*, pp. 165–66.

in Britain, even after the foundation stones on the paternalist welfare state had been laid in 1906–11. Yet the "endowment for motherhood" idea failed to become law, and actually paved the way for the extension and consolidation of the paternalist welfare state. So this telling failure reveals, once again, the power of the bureaucratic and working-class political forces that successfully shaped British social policies through the 1920s, and afterwards.

In 1917, Eleanor Rathbone and other British feminists organized a "Family Endowment Committee," which a year later proposed to give regular allowances to all British women with young children.[188] This measure sought to make universal and permanent the "separation allowances" that had been paid to the wives and children of British soldiers and sailors during World War I. These wartime allowances had given working-class wives new economic independence, and the wartime experience had also helped to move British feminist thinking in the direction of advocating direct economic support for motherhood rather than just the equal wages or legally guaranteed share of male wages that had been feminist demands before the war.[189] Such "new feminism," based on separate spheres ideals gained ground in organized British women's politics during the 1920s after Eleanor Rathbone became President of "the most powerful feminist organization, the National Union for Societies of Equal Citizenship" in 1919.[190] Significantly, separate spheres ideals came to the fore in British women's politics just after all British males were finally enfranchised in 1918, while many women remained without the vote until 1928.

Despite widespread feminist support, however, a universal endowment for motherhood was not enacted in Britain, because the Labour Party and British civil servants, working from somewhat different paternalist premises, transmuted this demand into the contributory social insurance benefits for widows that were enacted in the Widows', Orphans', and Old Age Pensions Act of 1925. Advocates of the universal endowment could not get full support from the Labour Party. Even though Labour women's organizations were very interested in the endowment possibility, "[t]hrough the mediation of the women labor leaders themselves, the demands of the Labour women's organizations were scaled down to mesh with the traditional family policy of the Trades Union Congress," which called for protecting the male "family

[188] Susan Pedersen, "The Failure of Feminism," p. 90.

[189] See the discussion in Susan Gay Pedersen, "Social Policy and the Reconstruction of the Family in Britain and France, 1900–1945" (Ph.D. diss., Harvard University, 1989), chapter 2; and Susan Pedersen, "Gender, Welfare and Citizenship in Britain during the Great War" (Unpublished paper, Department of History, Harvard University, May 1989).

[190] Pedersen, "Failure of Feminism," p. 91.

wage" and channeling all benefits to married women through that wage.[191] Labour was prepared to support direct public payments to women only when the male breadwinner was absent. Conservatives and civil servants, meanwhile, wanted to keep down the state's direct cost of social benefits, so they favored contributory pensions paid out of earlier collections from male wageworkers; they also believed that elderly widows without children should receive support.

When Widows' Pensions were enacted in 1925 by a Conservative government, civil service preferences completed "the metamorphosis of 'mothers' pensions' from a step toward payment for motherhood to a necessary component of a welfare system constructed around men's right to maintain [their wives] . . . [T]he decision to finance pensions through insurance linked them both administratively and ideologically to the working man. Since eligibility turned on the man's insurance status and not [on] the woman's need, the system would exclude those women whom men had been least willing or able to support—deserted and separated wives, wives of uninsured casual laborers, and unmarried mothers."[192] The original British feminist proposals for endowment of motherhood had explicitly intended to include all such women when they were caring for children. It is worth pointing out that many or all of these categories of women *could be covered* by contemporary U.S. mothers' pension laws, depending on the precise provisions of statutes in individual states.[193]

As historian Susan Pedersen sums up the British developments from 1917 to 1925, "in the end . . . maternalist, 'separate but equal' ideology was pressed into service in the creation of policies encoding dependence, not the value of difference." The unsuccessful British women's "cam-

---

[191] Ibid., p. 95.

[192] Ibid., p. 102.

[193] See Children's Bureau, U.S. Department of Labor, Chart No.3, *A Tabular Summary of State Laws Relation to Public Aid to Children in Their Own Homes in Effect January 1, 1929 and the Text of the Laws of Certain States*, Third Edition (Washington D.C.: U.S. Government Printing Office, 1929). For example, the very liberal Michigan law allowed aid to any needy mother who was widowed, deserted, divorced, or unmarried, or "whose husband is insane, feeble-minded, epileptic, paralytic, or blind and confined in State hospital or other state institution; incapable of work because of tuberculosis; or inmate of State penal institution." (p. 12) To be sure, lack of fathers' economic support for children was the bedrock criterion here, so the "male breadwinner" norm was upheld. But as policy developments unfolded in contemporary Britain, that norm was adhered to by tying benefits to the absence of, specifically, a former wage-earning husband. Analysts of social policies for women need to investigate not only whether particular measures emphasized male breadwinning versus women's labor-force participation. Analysis should also look for alternative ways that policies may embody male-breadwinner norms. In this instance, the Michigan statute placed the emphasis on mothers' needs due to the absence of fathers for various reasons (including unwed parenthood), not on the wage-earning status of husband-fathers.

paign for the endowment of motherhood exposed where the real poli-cymaking power and political influence lay: with the civil service and the trade union movement."[194]

CONCLUSION

Organized labor, reformist intellectuals and officials, and women's groups all worked to launch modern social policies in Britain and the United States between the 1880s and the 1920s. But in the two nations such groups devised policy ideals and political strategies and contended or allied with one another—in the context of very different governmental institutions and party systems. The result was that distinctive kinds of politics flourished, leading to the enactment of contrasting sorts of social policies in Britain and the United States.

In Britain, social spending and labor regulations were furthered by civil service bureaucracies and by programmatic political parties competing for organized trade union support. In a unitary polity with a sovereign parliament, such forces were able to enact and implement social policies covering workers in general, regardless of gender. Over time, as the initial foundations of the British welfare state were laid in the teens and twenties, bureaucratic and organized working-class forces converged on social policies that reinforced and depended upon the ideal of the male-breadwinner, family wage. Meanwhile, radical maternalist demands for a universal endowment of motherhood were shunted aside in Britain.

In the United States during this period, bureaucratic forces and electorally involved trade unionists were too weak to push forward old age pensions or social insurance benefits for all workers. This was especially the case, because of middle-class and elite hostility during the Progressive Era toward the precedent of public social spending created by the earlier expansion of Civil War pensions. Progressive public opinion favored regulations rather than public social spending. Even so, reformers and labor groups were unable to enact public regulations setting limited hours or decent wages for all U.S. workers, because of the unwillingness of the independent and powerful U.S. courts to accept such "interferences" in contractual freedom for adult males.

Even as America's federal state of weak bureaucracies, patronage parties, and strong courts obstructed possibilities for paternalist labor regulations and social spending for the working class in general, it left space for forces advocating maternalist benefits and regulations targeted on women and children in particular. The courts were willing, for some

---

[194] Pederson, "Failure of Feminism," p. 105.

time, to accept legal hours limits and minimum-wage regulations for adult female workers as the potential "mothers of the race." And at the turn of the century, higher-educated women reformers and widespread associations of married ladies, both inspired by normative ideals of women's separate sphere of domesticity and motherhood, were able to shape public discourse and put effective simultaneous pressure on many state legislatures at once, encouraging bipartisan support for women's labor regulations and mothers' pensions. Some tentative beginnings toward a distinctively maternalist American welfare state were thus made at a time when the prospects were dim for an early paternalist welfare state along British or European lines.[195]

In ways that go beyond what we can describe and explain here, later policy developments in both Britain and the United States transformed as well as built upon the early paternalist, in contrast to maternalist, beginnings analyzed in this article. Our purpose here has not been to identify unchanging national essences. Rather, by contrasting these two liberal nations at a watershed period in their political histories, we have aimed to demonstrate the value of analyzing the politics of social policymaking from an historically grounded institutionalist perspective. Class and gender differences existed "in themselves" in both Britain and the United States. But class and gender identities and outlooks were expressed differently in British and U.S. social politics around the turn of the twentieth century. This happened in significant part because the British and U.S. polities selectively facilitated contrasting ideologies and political alliances. A paternalist social politics for and by the industrial working class was encouraged in the British polity. Meanwhile, the changing U.S. polity called forth and temporarily rewarded a nonelectoral style of social politics for and by women. These turn-of-the-century American maternalists were understood, by themselves and others, as members of a "separate sphere" charged with safeguarding family, morality, and community within U.S. capitalism and democracy. In the name of such values, American women sparked most of the social policy innovations that occurred at all during a time when the United States was refusing to follow Britain on the road toward a paternalist welfare state.

---

[195] In the end, a maternalist welfare state did not fully crystallize in the United States. See chapters 9 and 10 in Theda Skocpol's *Protecting Soldiers and Mothers* (Cambridge, Mass.: Belknap, Harvard University Press, 1992).

CHAPTER FOUR

The Road to Social Security

with G. John Ikenberry

ON 14 August 1935, President Franklin Roosevelt signed the Social Security Act, the charter law for the closest approximation the United States would achieve to a modern "welfare state," or system of public protections for citizens against the hazards of old-age, unemployment, ill health, disability, and poverty. The programs included in the "big bang" of reforms signed into law on this one watershed day had some very distinctive patterns that have largely survived and shaped the provision of public benefits in the United States to the 1980s.[1] Health insurance was omitted altogether from the Social Security Act, but there were three other major parts to the legislation as proposed and passed: unemployment insurance; public assistance; and old-age insurance.

Despite proposals for a more nationally uniform approach, unemployment insurance was instituted as a federal-state system, with authority left to the states to collect contributions from employers and employed workers and to provide benefits to eligible workers who later became unemployed. Over subsequent decades, taxation and benefits would become quite uneven across the states. It would also prove impossible to reform this system to pool risks of economic downturns on a national basis and to mesh the operations of unemployment insurance with Keynesian principles of national economic management.[2]

Public assistance was a set of programs already existing in certain states by the early 1930s, for which the federal government would henceforth share costs. Assistance for the elderly poor and for depen-

Political Science Quarterly 102(3) (Fall 1987) (Title changed).

[1] The conception of the Social Security Act as a "big bang" of policy innovations, thereafter enduring relatively unchanged, comes from Christopher Leman. "Patterns of Policy Development: Social Security in the United States and Canada," *Public Policy* 25 (Spring 1977): 261–91.

[2] See Joseph M. Becker, "Twenty-Five Years of Unemployment Insurance," *Political Science Quarterly* 75 (1960): 481–99; and Edward J. Harpham, "Federalism, Keynesianism, and the Transformation of Unemployment Insurance in the United States" in Douglas Ashford and E.W. Kelley, eds., *Nationalizing Social Security in Europe and America* (Greenwich, Conn.: JAI Press, 1986).

dent children were the most important programs. The states were accorded great discretion to decide benefit levels and, in practice, methods of administration. Over time, as old-age insurance expanded to cover virtually all retired employees in the United States, federal old-age assistance became proportionately less important than it was in the 1930s and 1940s. Meanwhile, by the 1960s the Aid to Dependent Children program (slightly retargeted to become Aid to Families with Dependent Children (AFDC), which provides benefits to caretakers as well as the children themselves), expanded enormously.[3] AFDC, often disparagingly labelled "welfare," has very uneven standards of eligibility, coverage, and benefits across the states, generally providing the least to the poorest and weakest people in the poorest states and leaving many impoverished men and husband-wife families without any coverage at all.[4]

The respectable part of American public social provision has now appropriated the term "social security," which originally encompassed the whole. The centerpiece of social security is the one program originally established on an entirely national basis in 1935: old-age insurance. Payroll taxes are collected from workers and their employers across the country and held in a special federal fund; ultimately, retired workers collect benefits roughly gauged to their employment incomes. After 1935, additional programs were added under this contributory insurance rubric: for survivors (1939); for disabled workers (1956); and for retirees in need of medical care (1965). What is more, old-age insurance expanded enormously in the United States, as more and more workers were incorporated by the 1950s, and then benefit levels were repeatedly raised by Congress.[5]

In sum, the American system of public social provision fashioned under the aegis of the Social Security Act of 1935 has never become comprehensive or truly national, and it has remained a system that only partially offsets the distributional profile of incomes and benefits generated by the private market.[6] In contrast to the situation in Britain since the Beveridge reforms instituted after World War II, national standards have not been established in the United States for all public benefits;

---

[3] See Winifred Bell, *Aid to Dependent Children* (New York: Columbia University Press, 1965).

[4] Norman Furniss and Timothy Tilton, *The Case for the Welfare State: From Social Security to Social Equality* (Bloomington: University of Indiana Press, 1977), 170; and Harrell R. Rodgers, Jr., *The Cost of Human Neglect: America's Welfare Failure* (Armonk, N.Y.: M.E. Sharpe), 56–62.

[5] Martha Derthick, *Policymaking for Social Security* (Washington, D.C.: The Brookings Institution, 1979).

[6] Furniss and Tilton, *Case for the Welfare State*, 179–83. This book develops overall contrasts among the British, Swedish, and U.S. systems for public social provision.

social security for deserving people has been firmly bifurcated, both institutionally and symbolically, from "welfare" for dubiously deserving ones. Equally in contrast to developments under Social Democracy in Sweden, there have been no possibilities in the federally uneven and fiscally insulated U.S. social benefits system for coordinating welfare provision with nationally rationalized public interventions in the macroeconomy and in labor markets. In the United States, various social benefits programs are operationally, fiscally, and symbolically separated from one another, and they are all kept quite apart from the other things the national government may be doing in the economy and society.

EXPLAINING PUBLIC SOCIAL PROVISION IN THE UNITED STATES

We will sketch an explanation for why public social benefits in the United States took the shape they did in the Social Security Act and its aftermath. Our primary contribution will be to trace the political and institutional underpinnings of the "political learning"—the "collective puzzlement on society's behalf" by reformers and policy-relevant experts[7]—from which the Social Security Act and its administration took their inspiration. Like Hugh Heclo, we take policy ideas and their carriers very seriously. But more than Heclo does, we stress how policy ideas about social insurance and other forms of public social benefits have been reworked over time as the carriers of these ideas dealt with the basic organizational features of the U.S. state structure and democratic polity. Decentralized federalism, the legacies of the patronage-oriented forms of democratic politics that prevailed in the nineteenth-century United States, the weakness and fragmentation of the new realms of public administration built from the late nineteenth century onward, and public policy-making processes centered in legislative log-rolling rather than in programmatic political parties or executive planning agencies—all of these features of the distinctive American state structure have affected the ideas and modus operandi of U.S. advocates of modern social benefits programs. They can, therefore, help us to account for the distinctive shape taken by social insurance and public assistance in the United States. Our analysis will begin in the Progressive Era, move through crucial state-level developments in the 1920s, and culminate in a discussion of the New Deal's Social Security Act and its subsequent administration.

It makes sense to highlight briefly how and why our explanatory ap-

---

[7] Hugh Heclo, *Modern Social Politics in Britain and Sweden* (New Haven, Conn.: Yale University Press, 1974), 305, and chap. 6 in general.

proach differs from another interesting line of argument about the formation of America's programs of public social provision. The United States has typically been interpreted as "exceptional" in international terms, because of the extreme strength of liberal values (or market-capitalist ideologies) and the "weakness" of organized labor as a distinctive political force.[8] At the same time—as the positive accompaniment to such explanations for why the United States did not experience public welfare developments paralleling those in major European nations—historians of U.S. social politics have often depicted corporate-capitalist business leaders as the arbiters of programmatic developments in the public sector. The most sophisticated version of this view to be published to date is Edward Berkowitz's and Kim McQuaid's 1980 book, *Creating the Welfare State*.[9]

Berkowitz and McQuaid creatively synthesize ideas from neo-Marxist arguments about the hegemonic role of liberal corporate-capitalists in modern American politics with the basic framework of the "organizational synthesis" school of historiography founded by business historian Alfred Chandler.[10] For this school, the master developmental trend of twentieth-century American history is the growth of functionally specialized bureaucratic organizations in the private economy and public spheres alike. According to Berkowitz and McQuaid, the key to understanding U.S. social welfare provision lies in the fact that large capitalist

[8] For a review and critique of explanations of American exceptionalism with respect to the development of the modern welfare state, see Ann Shola Orloff and Theda Skocpol, "Why Not Equal Protection?: Explaining the Politics of Public Social Spending in Britain, 1900–1911 and the United States, 1880s–1920," *American Sociological Review* 49 (December 1984): 726–750. For some characteristic treatments of the U.S. case, see Gaston V. Rimlinger, *Welfare Policy and Industrialization in Europe, America, and Russia* (New York: Wiley, 1971), 62–86, and chap. 6; Kirsten A. Gronbjerg, David Street, and Gerald D. Suttles, *Poverty and Social Change* (Chicago: University of Chicago Press, 1978); and John D. Stephens, *The Transition from Capitalism to Socialism* (London: Macmillan, 1979), 149–56.

[9] Edward Berkowitz and Kim McQuaid, *Creating the Welfare State: The Political Economy of Twentieth-Century Reform* (New York: Praeger, 1980). Classic statements of the corporate-liberalism thesis appear in Barton J. Bernstein, "The New Deal: The Conservative Achievements of Liberal Reform" in Barton Bernstein, ed., *Towards a New Past* (New York: Random House, 1968), 263–89; William Domhoff, *The Higher Circles* (New York: Vintage Books, 1970); Ronald Radosh, "The Myth of the New Deal" in R. Radosh and N. Rothbard, eds., *A History of Leviathan* (New York: Dutton, 1972), 146–87; and James Weinstein, *The Corporate Ideal in the Liberal State* (Boston: Beacon Press, 1968). A recent analysis of the origins of the Social Security Act that stresses the role of corporate leaders is Jill S. Quadagno, "Welfare Capitalism and the Social Security Act of 1935," *American Sociological Review* 45 (October 1984): 632–647.

[10] Louis Galambos, "The Emerging Organizational Synthesis in American History," *Business History Review* 44 (Autumn 1970): 279–90. Alfred Chandler's own most important work is *The Visible Hand: The Managerial Revolution in American Business* (Cambridge, Mass.: Harvard University Press, 1977).

corporations originally had an "organizational comparative advantage" over the federal government, and therefore took the lead in creating social benefits and other employee welfare programs and in fashioning the appropriate structures to administer them. Then, during the massive crisis of the Great Depression, corporate welfare capitalism faltered and the federal government, which had previously lagged in programmatic and bureaucratic development, was politically compelled to step into the breach. But liberal welfare capitalists were able to help shape the emerging Social Security system and, at least initially, the new public managers of old-age insurance had to borrow organizational techniques from private industrial corporations and insurance companies.[11]

Provocative and sophisticated though it is, Berkowitz's and Mc-Quaid's argument grounds the essential dynamics of U.S. social politics in the corporate-capitalist sphere, and ends up presenting an oddly nonpolitical explanation of both the agents and the structures that shaped the federal Social Security system. Contrary to the picture they present, the lineage of progressive capitalist experiments with intracorporate employee welfare programs was not the primary stream of policy intelligence and programmatic experimentation that fed into the formation of the Social Security Act. From the Progressive Era onward, professional experts and politically active reformers looking for policies to embody "the public interest" participated in transnational debates about social insurance and public welfare. These policy innovators were oriented not simply to business and its needs for profits and economic efficiency, but primarily to existing or potential structures of public administration and political decision making at federal and state levels.

Indeed, Berkowitz and McQuaid are remarkably vague and brief in discussing the structural and intellectual bases on which federal policy innovators in 1934–1935 actually built the new federal social insurance and public assistance programs. Nor do they highlight the central paradox of the Social Security Act from the point of view of welfare capitalists: the handful of liberal-capitalist leaders of large private corporations who participated in the drafting of the Social Security Act wanted a more *nationally uniform* system of unemployment insurance than the one adopted in the New Deal. If the federal government was going to displace the private efforts of corporations—something which ideally the liberal capitalists would have preferred to avert—then at least they wanted uniform taxes and benefits for employers and employees, putting all enterprises on the same competitive basis. However, the system of unemployment insurance actually proposed by the Roosevelt administration and legislated by Congress was a much more balkanized fed-

[11] Berkowitz and McQuaid, *Creating the Welfare State*, chap. 5.

eral-state system that frustrated such hopes for national economic rationalization. An approach that traces the distinctively *political* roots of U.S. social benefits can better explain their programmatic features.

THE FAILURE OF PROGRESSIVE SOCIAL INSURANCE REFORM

In the two decades preceding World War I, many social insurance ideas appropriated from abroad were studied and debated in the United States within a small but growing network of social reformers. Social insurance advocates self-consciously engaged in a form of public education and envisaged an American transformation of the sort occurring in Europe, with the national government—or many state governments[12]—sponsoring and underwriting social insurance programs. However, most proposals for social insurance reforms in the Progressive Era failed to take hold; only state-level laws requiring workers' compensation were successful. While social insurance ideas came to America and were given wide exposure during this period, fundamental political constraints restricted their practical political expression to state-level regulatory commissions.

The early students of social insurance were highly educated, most were social scientists or labor analysts, and they occupied a variety of university, government, and corporate positions.[13] Initial efforts by these individuals involved the detailed examination of European ideas and programs and the analysis of their relevance for the United States. An early American book on social insurance was published in 1898 by an economist working for the United States Department of Labor; it developed the theme that unemployment is beyond the control of individual workers and that various combinations of employers, employees, and government should provide protection.[14] Later, two of the most influential statements of social insurance ideas originated as a lecture series sponsored by the New York School of Philanthropy: one in 1910 by Columbia Professor Henry Rogers Seager, and the other in 1912 by Isaac Max Rubinow, chief statistician of the Ocean Accident and Guarantee Corporation and a former statistical expert at the U.S. Bureau of Labor.[15]

[12] On the Progressive reform strategy of seeking parallel laws across (especially adjacent) states, see William Graebner, "Federalism in the Progressive Era: A Structural Interpretation of Reform," *Journal of American History* 64 (September 1977): 331–57.

[13] Roy Lubove, "Economic Security and Social Conflict in America: The Early Twentieth Century," part II, *Journal of Social History* 1 (Summer 1968): 325–337.

[14] William Franklin Willoughby, *Workingmen's Insurance* (New York: Thomas Y. Crowell, 1898).

[15] Henry Rogers Seager, *Social Insurance: A Program of Social Reform* (New York: Macmillan, 1910); and Isaac Max Rubinow, *Social Insurance, With Special Reference to American Conditions* (New York: Henry Holt, 1913).

What is striking in these early indictments of private, voluntary, and individualistic schemes of worker protection was the major new role envisaged for the state. "The characteristic common to most of the policies I have advocated is that they call for vigorous governmental action . . ." Seager argued. "By cooperative action, impelled when necessary by the compulsory authority of the state, we can give stability to the incomes of wage earners and oppose that downward pressure which now so constantly recruits the army of standardless, casual labor."[16] This positive attitude toward the state—conceived as disinterested public authority capable of regulating capitalism and ameliorating its unnecessary inefficiencies and injustices—was especially prominent in Rubinow's remarks contrasting public with private insurance. Compulsory and state-subsidized insurance would necessarily depart from "the true scientific principles of business insurance," wrote Rubinow; such insurance ". . . may be and has been decried as rank paternalism, and this indictment must be readily admitted. For social insurance, when properly developed, is nothing if not a well-defined effort of the organized state to come to the assistance of the wage-earner and furnish him something he individually is quite unable to obtain for himself."[17]

Proposals and debates about social insurance found organizational expression in the American Association for Labor Legislation (AALL), established in 1906. The AALL's membership, primarily academic and nonacademic social scientists, understood the purpose of the association to be the introduction of objective expertise into industrial legislation. AALL members considered themselves uniquely able to define "the public interest" in industrial and social reform—better able than capitalist employers, trade unionists, socialists, or others. Thus, in addition to interpreting and advancing notions of social insurance, these reformers became actively involved in drafting "model" legislative bills to be pressed upon elected politicians.

But the crucial determinants of legislative success and failure for social insurance ideas in this period were set by the prevailing structures of government and the overall ideological atmosphere of Progressive reform, not by the cogency of ideas or "model" legislation. Reform struggles over social policy during the Progressive Era must be understood in the context of the broad Progressive reaction against nineteenth-century U.S. patronage democracy. Within a loosely integrated federal system of "courts and parties,"[18] disparate local systems of de

---

[16] Seager, *Social Insurance*, 150–51.

[17] Rubinow, *Social Insurance*, 11.

[18] Stephen Skowronek, *Building a New American State: The Expansion of National Administrative Capacities, 1877–1920* (New York: Cambridge University Press, 1982), chap. 2.

facto social provision flourished in post-Civil War America. Patronage-oriented political parties, seeking to incorporate and maintain constituencies and coalitions, drew upon public funds to disburse social benefits.[19]

Although the activities of these parties were grounded in local politics, nevertheless an extraordinary example of this sort of welfare provision depended upon federal social spending. This was the post-Civil War pension system which, through a series of extensions and revisions from the late 1870s onward, became a means through which politicians channeled benefits to crucial segments of the electorate. By the turn of the century about one out of every three native-born men in the North was receiving a de facto old-age pension under the guise of federal aid to Civil War veterans, and over a quarter of the federal government's budget was devoted to this purpose.[20] Congressmen, along with other party politicians, especially Republicans, vied to provide aid to "old soldiers" and their dependents.[21]

Contrary, then, to the image often held of nineteenth-century America as a total laissez-faire polity in which government left individuals on their own in the free market, the United States had a precocious system of extensive public social benefits that was already in place as the "modern welfare state" was born in Europe.[22] As late as 1913, five years after Britain established its national old-age pension system, the United States through "Civil War" pensions was covering "several hundred thousand" more people at over three times the cost to the national treasury.[23] Some social insurance advocates and labor leaders thought the post-Civil War pension system should simply be reworked into a more universalistic set of programs for old-age and disability coverage.[24]

[19] See Morton Keller, *Affairs of State: Public Life in Late Nineteenth Century America* (Cambridge, Mass.: Harvard University Press, 1977), chaps. 7, 8, and 14; Richard McCormick, "The Party Period and Public Policy: An Exploratory Hypothesis," *Journal of American History* 66 (September 1979): 279–98; and John W. Pratt, "Boss Tweed's Public Welfare Program," *New York Historical Society Quarterly* 45 (October 1961): 396–411.

[20] Keller, *Affairs of State*, 311. On the estimate of the proportion of men receiving pensions, see Orloff and Skocpol, "Why Not Equal Protection?," note 8. [Subsequent note: Better estimates appear in Skocpol, *Protecting Soldiers and Mothers* (Cambridge, MA: Belknap, Harvard University Press, 1992), chap. 2.]

[21] On the role of politicans in expanding Civil War pensions see Donald M. McMurry, "The Political Significance of the Pension Question, 1885–1897," *Mississippi Valley Historical Review* 9 (June 1922): 19–36; and Heywood T. Sanders, "Paying for the 'Bloody Shirt:' The Politics of Civil War Pensions" in Barry S. Rundquist, ed., *Political Benefits: Empirical Studies of American Public Programs* (Lexington, Mass.: Lexington Books, 1980), 137–59.

[22] On European developments see Peter Flora and Jens Alber, "Modernization, Democratization, and the Development of Welfare States in Western Europe" in Peter Flora and Arnold J. Heidenheimer, eds., *The Development of Welfare States in Europe and America* (New Brunswick, N.J.: Transaction Books, 1981), 37–80.

[23] Rubinow, *Social Insurance*, 404.

[24] For details see Orloff and Skocpol, "Why Not Equal Protection?"

Ironically, however, the opposition of Progressive Era reform opinion to the patterns of political corruption seen as associated with nineteenth-century patronage democracy severely limited the possibilities for modern social insurance innovations. Reform-minded upper- and middle-class people feared that new forms of public spending would get out of control and reinforce the corruption of political party bosses; this widespread fear hurt proposals for modern social spending. The fears of reformers and conservatives alike about the possible political abuse of government social expenditures were especially strong with regard to non-contributory old-age pensions, even though this was a modern welfare measure supported by organized labor and the general electorate.[25]

Progressive social insurance reformers shied away from non-contributory old-age pensions and were much more active in pushing for contributory insurance programs, especially for health and unemployment.[26] In Britain and continental Europe, executives and administrative bureaucracies were devising such programs of taxation and social expenditure and pressing them upon wary businessmen, labor leaders, and parliaments.[27] Yet because nineteenth-century American government had been dominated at all levels by patronage-oriented political parties, administrative apparatuses were weak and not closely tied to political executives.

During the Progressive Era, while campaigns for health and unemployment insurance failed, AALL-led campaigns for workers' compensation laws were successful. Between 1911 and 1920, forty-five states and territories passed workers' compensation laws that survived constitutional tests. Compensation disputes, previously resolved within the courts in unpredictable ways unsatisfactory to both employers and employees, were brought under the control of state legislation and in many states were administered by expert-dominated industrial commissions.[28] The industrial commission could be justified to all parties by its purported expert-based "rationality" and "efficiency."[29] The commission

[25] Ibid., 43–45.

[26] Ibid., 45–46; "Social Insurance," *American Labor Legislation Review* 4 (December 1914): 573–80; and "Unemployment Survey, 1914–1915," *American Labor Legislation Review* 5 (November 1915): 473–595.

[27] See Heclo, *Modern Social Politics*; Bentley Gilbert, *The Evolution of National Insurance in Great Britain: The Origins of the Welfare State* (London: Michael Joseph, 1966); and Deltev Zollner, "Germany" in Peter A. Kohler and Hans F. Zacher, eds., *The Evolution of Social Insurance, 1881–1981* (New York: St. Martin's, 1982), 1–92.

[28] Berkowitz and McQuaid, *Creating the Welfare State*, 33–36; and Lawrence M. Friedman and Jack Ladinsky, "Social Change and the Law of Industrial Accidents," *Columbia Law Review* 67 (January 1967): 50–82.

[29] Elizabeth Brandeis, "Labor Legislation" in Don D. Lescohier and Elizabeth Brandeis, eds., *History of Labor Legislation in the United States, 1896–1932*, vol. 3 (New York: Macmillan, 1935), 650–53.

mechanism worked around the edges of the prevailing market system, insinuating modest levels of public arbitration and standards into social and economic life.

Thus, while there were important state-level innovations in the area of industrial regulation, the efforts of Progressive Era social insurance reformers fell short of instituting actual public spending to help citizens deal with the vagaries of ill-health, unemployment, or old age. The failure of the one Progressive campaign for social insurance that was most intense and came closest to success in key states, the campaign for health insurance, turned out to be decisive for the long run.[30] The modern medical profession in the United States consolidated its economic power and cultural hegemony in a context free of public health insurance and the kinds of public administrative leverage over health-care delivery that might have accompanied it. By the 1930s, doctors, the American Medical Association, and private insurance companies had the political clout, even in the midst of the Great Depression, to frighten New Deal reformers away from including public health insurance in the Social Security Act, for fear that opposition to it might jeopardize the entire legislative package.

In contrast, proposals for old-age benefits and unemployment insurance were to be successfully revived again after the Progressive Era. But to understand exactly how and in what distinctive forms, we must now analyze the conditions that led during the 1920s and 1930s to the triumph of one particular lineage of policy intelligence, that associated with the political and academic reformers of the state of Wisconsin.

"WELFARE CAPITALISM" AND THE DEVELOPMENT OF THE WISCONSIN SCHOOL

In the United States, the aftermath of World War I brought to an abrupt end the period of reform ferment known as the Progressive Era. During the war itself, many reform intellectuals found themselves working in or with new national administrative agencies set up to mobilize economic and human resources for the duration of the national military effort. As the example of the United States Employment Service demonstrated, reformers associated with such wartime administrative efforts could briefly hope that they were laying the basis for permanent extensions of the federal government's social and economic role after the

---

[30] See Ronald Numbers, *Almost Persuaded: American Physicians and Compulsory Health Insurance, 1912–1920* (Baltimore, Md.: Johns Hopkins University Press, 1978); and Paul Starr, *The Social Transformation of American Medicine* (New York: Basic Books, 1982).

war.[31] Such hopes were soon dashed when the end of the war brought sharp reactions against federal programs and agencies from Congress, local governments, and many economic interests. The U.S. Employment Service—which, following the British pattern, might have created the administrative facilities for a national system of unemployment insurance—suffered draconian funding cuts by Congress right after the war and had to give up its state and local offices.[32] Most other wartime federal agencies were similarly curtailed.

Insofar as the United States would respond at all to the socioeconomic insecurities of industrialism, it would do so through "welfare capitalism" and a federal government functioning as an "associative state." Welfare capitalism refers to the entire complex of innovative labor-management practices adopted by certain highly visible U.S. companies during the 1920s—companies such as Proctor and Gamble, Eastman Kodak, and General Electric.[33] Provisions for stock ownership by workers, for employee representation plans, and for "human relations" techniques of worker supervision were typical welfare-capitalist efforts, which were, of course, often intended to preclude or supersede trade unions. In the social welfare area, moreover, many progressive managers believed that enlightened corporate action could forestall any need for public social insurance: company pension plans for loyal workers would provide for needs in old age; company safety and health-insurance benefits would prevent or compensate for injuries or sickness; and company guarantees of stable employment for workers, perhaps backed by promises to pay benefits to employees temporarily laid off, would cope with the evils of industrial unemployment.

[31] I.W. Litchfield, "United States Employment Service and Demobilization," *Annals of the American Academy of Political and Social Science* 81 (January 1919): 19–27. A fuller discussion of the rise and fall of the U.S. Employment Service during World War I appears in Theda Skocpol and John Ikenberry, "The Political Formation of the American Welfare State in Historical and Comparative Perspective," *Comparative Social Research* 6 (1983): 87–148. For a fascinating pre-war proposal to establish a federal system of public employment offices, see William M. Leiserson, "A Federal Reserve Board for the Unemployed," *Annals of the American Academy of Political and Social Science* 69 (January 1917): 103–17.

[32] Carroll H. Woody, *The Growth of the Federal Government, 1915–1932* (New York: McGraw-Hill, 1934), 371–73. Throughout the 1920s, Congress continued to block efforts to establish a national system of public employment offices, and when the coming of the Depression finally spurred Congress to pass a bill in 1931, President Hoover vetoed it. By 1929, all major industrialized nations except the United States had adopted national agencies of this sort. See Paul H. Douglas and Aaron Director, *The Problem of Unemployment* (New York: Macmillan, 1931), 289–91.

[33] On "welfare capitalism" (or the "New Emphasis") see Nelson, *Unemployment Insurance*, chaps. 2, 3, and pp. 73–78; Berkowitz and McQuaid, *Creating the Welfare State*, chap. 3; Stuart D. Brandes, *American Welfare Capitalism, 1880–1940* (Chicago: University of Chicago Press, 1976); and especially David Brody, "The Rise and Decline of Welfare Capitalism," in his *Workers in Industrial America: Essays on the 20th Century Struggle* (New York: Oxford University Press, 1980), 48–81.

The federal executive did its part during the decade of the 1920s to meld a continuation of the Progressive spirit of civic betterment into government-sponsored activities strictly in tune with the ideals—and limits—of welfare capitalism. Convening a national Conference on Unemployment during the severe recession of 1921, President Warren Harding made it clear that he would "have little enthusiasm for any proposed relief which seeks either palliation or tonic from the federal treasury."[34] Instead, Herbert Hoover (initially as secretary of commerce and then as president) conducted the federal government as an anti-bureaucratic "associative state."[35] Professional experts, businessmen, and leaders of industrial associations and responsible trade unions were urged by Hoover to cooperate with one another in a search for non-statist solutions to the nation's economic and welfare problems.

Within the ideological and practical limits set by welfare capitalism and the associative state in the 1920s, a few expert reformers gained influence and experience that would give them a central role when nationwide conditions for welfare reforms again became propitious in the 1930s. The balance of ideas and influence within the U.S. social insurance movement was profoundly affected by the fact that during the 1920s further legislative innovations occurred only in a few states. In this situation, "capitalist regulation," defined and administered by state-level industrial commissions and led by the Wisconsin school of reform, emerged to dominate debates on social policy during the years leading into the Great Depression. An alternative "Ohio plan," envisaging a much stronger public role in social insurance, finally developed, but only as a minor counterpoint to the greater influence of Wisconsin reform ideas.

The centrality of Wisconsin experts and politicians to American social insurance debates after the Progressive Era is not comprehensible in terms of prevalent theories of welfare-state development.[36] Wisconsin was never the leading industrial state in the United States. It was not the headquarters of prominent welfare-capitalist corporations. Nor was it the leading center of trade unionism or labor radicalism. The state of Wisconsin was, however, the earliest center of successful state-level

[34] Quoted in William L. Chenery, "Unemployment at Washington," *The Survey* (8 October 1921), 42.

[35] See Ellis W. Hawley, "Herbert Hoover, the Commerce Secretariat, and the Vision of an 'Associative State,' 1921–1928," *Journal of American History* 61 (June1974): 116–40; and Joan Hoff Wilson, *Herbert Hoover: Forgotten Progressive* (Boston: Little, Brown, 1975), chap. 4.

[36] Available theories primarily emphasize socioeconomic determinants, viewing the development of public welfare policies either as a by-product of industrialization and urbanization, or as the political achievement of strong unions and working class-based parties. See the discussion in Orloff and Skocpol, "Why Not Equal Protection?" 4–14. See also Edwin Amenta, Elisabeth Clemens, Jefren Olsen, Sunita Parikh, and Theda Skocpol, "The Political Origins of Unemployment Insurance in Five American States," forthcoming in *Studies in American Political Development* 2 (1987) (New Haven: Yale University Press).

Progressive reform, dating from the 1890s and the election of Robert La Follette as governor in 1901.[37] Wisconsin Progressivism was not purely an urban phenomenon either, for farmers, especially those of Scandinavian ethnic stock, were important supporters of La Follette and other Wisconsin reform politicians.[38]

Even more important, Wisconsin was the state where reform-oriented professional experts and academic intellectuals worked out the earliest, most sustained, and practically most effective relationships with state-level politicians, including the members of successive state legislatures as well as both progressive and conservative governors.[39] Before the 1920s, these relationships were well institutionalized in the ties among the state legislature and executive branch; the University of Wisconsin, a nationally prestigious research university that was simultaneously devoted to public extension work, popular education, and public service in its home state;[40] the Wisconsin Industrial Commission established in 1911 to administer workers' compensation and all other labor regulations in the state; and the Wisconsin Legislative Reference Library, established to allow qualified experts to help Wisconsin legislators draft laws and research their policy ideas.[41] The ideas and the students of University of Wisconsin labor economist John R. Commons were at work throughout this remarkable nexus of policy expertise and political and administrative practice.[42]

[37] See David P. Thelen, *The New Citizenship: The Origins of Progressivism in Wisconsin, 1885–1900* (Columbia: University of Missouri Press, 1972); Robert S. Maxwell, *La Follette and the Rise of the Progressives in Wisconsin* (Madison: State Historical Society of Wisconsin, 1956); and Herber F. Margulies, *The Decline of the Progressive Movement in Wisconsin, 1890–1920* (Madison: State Historical Society of Wisconsin, 1968).

[38] David L. Brye, "Wisconsin Scandinavians and Progressivism, 1900–1950," *Norwegian-American Studies* 27 (1977): 163–93.

[39] See Charles McCarthy, *The Wisconsin Idea* (New York: 1912); and Theron F. Schlabach, *Edwin Witte: Cautious Reformer* (Madison: State Historical Society of Wisconsin, 1969), chap. 3.

[40] See Laurence R. Vesey, *The Emergence of the American University* (Chicago: University of Chicago Press, 1970 paperback edition; first published 1965), 107–109; Henry F. May, *The End of American Innocence* (Chicago: Quadrangle Books, 1964; originally 1959), 99–101; Arthur J. Vidich and Stanford M. Lyman, "Secular Evangelism at the University of Wisconsin," *Social Research* 49 (1982); 1068–70; and (for general background) Merle Curti and Vernon Carstensen, *The University of Wisconsin: A History, 1848–1925*, 2 vols. (Madison: University of Wisconsin Press, 1949).

[41] See Schlabach, *Edwin Witte*, chap. 3; John R. Commons, "Constructive Investigation and the Industrial Commission of Wisconsin," *The Survey* 29 (4 January 1913): 440–48; A.J. Altmeyer, *The Industrial Commission of Wisconsin* (Madison: University of Wisconsin Studies in the Social Sciences and History, no. 17, 1932); and J.H. Leek, *Legislative Reference Work: A Comparative Study* (Ph.D. dissertation, Department of Political Science, University of Pennsylvania, 1925). Leek shows that Wisconsin was a leader in legislative reference work and unusually combined both bill-drafting and research services in a single agency.

[42] Schlabach, *Edwin Witte*, chaps. 2 and 3.

The distinctive mode of social reform articulated by Commons and embodied in Wisconsin's social policy nexus came to be known as the "preventive approach."[43] Its essential premise was the notion that employment could be stabilized, industrial accidents reduced, and the general welfare of workers enhanced through the crafting of labor regulations that offered financial rewards to employers who behaved in efficient and humane ways. Commons called for regulatory laws offering rewards or punishments for individual firms according to their performance. He also emphasized the central role of state-level industrial commissions; staffed by experts, these would insure the continuous, coordinated enforcement of labor regulations through negotiation with responsible employers and unions. Commission researchers could also investigate labor conditions and recommend administrative and legal innovations.[44]

Above all, Commons's preventive approach sought to apply to problems of industrial unemployment governmental methods that the Wisconsin Industrial Commission had already applied in the area of workers' compensation for industrial accidents. "Professor Commons was struck by the pressure which workmen's compensation had placed upon employers to reduce accidents in order to reduce premium payments. He came to believe that if unemployment were made a burden upon the employers they would seek in a similar fashion to reduce it."[45] Consequently, proposals for unemployment insurance in Wisconsin— destined to lead to the nation's first unemployment insurance law in 1932—taxed employers *only* for the purpose of setting up "unemployment reserves" for individual industries or (ultimately) particular companies. Employers with stable employment would avoid further taxes. Those that laid off employees would have funds for temporary unemployment compensation. But there would be no industry-wide insurance pool, and the state itself would not insure workers with public funds. Laid-off workers not covered or those whose industrial or enterprise funds had exhausted their resources would have to seek other assistance.[46]

Throughout the 1920s, Wisconsin reform experts pushed for unemployment insurance proposals embodying Commons's preventive approach to industrial regulation.[47] Their vigorous and continuous legisla-

[43] Nelson, *Unemployment Insurance*, chap. 6; and Layfayette G. Harter, Jr., *John R. Commons: His Assault on Laissez-Faire* (Corvallis: University of Oregon Press, 1962).

[44] Commons, "Constructive Investigation."

[45] Douglas and Director, *Problem of Unemployment*, 488.

[46] John R. Commons, "Legislation as an Aid to Management in Stabilizing Employment," *American Labor Legislation Review* 11 (June 1921): 154.

[47] See Nelson, *Unemployment Insurance*, 107–28.

tive activity also shifted the center of gravity within the American Association for Labor Legislation itself toward the Wisconsin policy ideas. Before the 1920s, U.S. social insurance activists, no less than those in Europe, stressed the major role of the state in promoting societal welfare. In the original AALL model bills of the Progressive Era, government was called upon to tax both business and its employees and to add its own general revenues to insure the adequacy of benefits to sick or unemployed workers.[48] After World War I, however, AALL policy ideas increasingly deemphasized proposals for government-run and subsidized social insurance programs. By 1931, the AALL model unemployment insurance bill, the so-called American plan, had completely abandoned traditional social insurance ideas and adopted the Wisconsin preventive approach.[49] This break with orthodox social insurance principles had started back in 1921, when the first bill inspired by Commons's preventive approach was introduced in the Wisconsin legislature. Although not at first successful, revised versions of this bill were introduced during every Wisconsin legislative session until 1929. Finally, after the onset of the Depression and after difficult compromises were negotiated through the state legislature, a pioneering unemployment compensation system was finally passed and signed into law in January 1932 by Governor Philip LaFollette.

During the late 1920s and early 1930s, the Wisconsin model of unemployment reserves was taken up by reform groups in other states, including Massachusetts, New York, and Pennsylvania.[50] The Wisconsin model also became the vehicle for attempts at collaboration and consultation among states on unemployment insurance legislation. The governors of six large industrial states met in early 1932 to recommend the passage of legislation along the lines of the Wisconsin reserves plan.[51] But in other states, agreement on specific legislation was elusive in the early 1930s.

As the case of Ohio best dramatizes, not all social-insurance reformers acknowledged the practical merits of the Wisconsin approach.

---

[48] See American Association for Labor Legislation, "A Practical Program for the Prevention of Unemployment in America," *American Labor Legislation Review* 5 (June 1915): 189–91; Paul Starr, "Transformation in Defeat: The Changing Objectives of National Health Insurance, 1915–1980," *American Journal of Public Health* 72 (January 1982): 79; and Lubove, *Struggle for Social Security*, 168.

[49] American Association for Labor Legislation, "An American Plan for Unemployment Reserve Funds: Tentative Draft of an Act," *American Labor Legislation Review* 20 (December 1930): 349–56.

[50] Nelson, *Unemployment Insurance*, chap. 8.

[51] "Governor's Interstate Commission Urges Unemployment Reserves," *American Labor Legislation Review* 22 (March 1932): 19.

The emphasis on preventive taxing schemes had left the Wisconsin unemployment insurance plan unable to incorporate public financing or to offer uniform benefits for workers in all industries. Reformers unwilling to make these concessions, while no longer influential nationally inside the American Association for Labor Legislation, did find possibilities for developing their proposals in Ohio. With a vigorous tradition of urban progressivism and labor organizing, Ohio had been the site for the earliest network of employment bureaus. And by the end of World War I, Ohio had the most comprehensive system of public labor exchanges.[52] There was, however, nothing in Ohio comparable to the well-institutionalized policy-making nexus centered in Madison, Wisconsin, which tied the governor and the state legislature to an authoritative industrial commission and reformist, university-based social scientists.

Consequently, the foundations of unemployment reform in Ohio were laid much more in isolation from both the legislature and economic interest groups than in Wisconsin. Programmatic planning started only very late in the 1920s, when policy study and lobbying activities were organized by the Consumer League of Ohio, which brought together social workers and reformers interested in agitation and public education.[53] In 1930 the League organized a committee to study practical unemployment proposals. Although several businessmen were recruited in the initial period of deliberations, their relationship to the reformers was uneasy and they eventually resigned. Nonetheless, by January 1931, the Consumer League introduced a draft bill into the state legislature. This move toward legislative action prompted state politicians to seek yet more study and planning, and the governor responded by appointing the distinguished Ohio Commission on Unemployment Insurance.

This Ohio Commission was an ad hoc, special body of experts and reformers sympathetic to unemployment insurance. Many of the members were self-consciously seeking to provide an alternative to the Wisconsin plan. Isaac M. Rubinow, now estranged from the AALL, played a central role, and the eventual Ohio Commission report was written by economist William Leiserson. Although Leiserson was trained by Commons in Wisconsin, he was something of an apostate. Accepting the more traditional social insurance premises, he believed that unemployment was a naturally occurring phenomenon that must be "met by state

---

[52] Hoyt Landon Warner, *Progressivism in Ohio, 1897–1917* (Columbus: Ohio State University Press, 1964); and J. Michael Eisner, *William Morris Leiserson: A Biography* (Madison: University of Wisconsin Press, 1967), 30–31.

[53] This paragraph and the next draw upon Nelson, *Unemployment Insurance*, 180–82; and upon Ohio Commission on Unemployment Insurance, *Report of the Ohio Commission on Unemployment Insurance* (Columbus, Ohio: The State House, November 1932).

action."[54] The Ohio plan called for public revenues and a state-wide insurance pool sufficient to provide uniform benefits for all unemployed workers. Thus the Ohio approach to unemployment insurance acknowledged that unemployment could not be abated by firm-level incentives, but rather must be insured against by public sponsorship of pooled reserves.

As events turned out, however, the Ohio Commission's proposed legislation failed to pass in 1933. The Wisconsin version of unemployment insurance was more politically successful at the state level than the Ohio plan, even though the conditions of economic crisis at the depth of the Depression, when individual company funds could not cope with massive layoffs, pointed to the need for an approach to unemployment compensation much more along Ohio plan lines. Whatever its economic shortcomings, the Wisconsin program was the product of long-term interactions of reformers and experts with business and labor under the auspices of the Wisconsin Industrial Commission. By contrast, the ad hoc Ohio Commission could not draw on such well-established relationships. As a governor-appointed, investigatory body, it worked in isolation from established employer and union organizations, and it became involved with the state legislature only after its report was completed. In the end, although it passed the Ohio Assembly in June 1933, the commission bill was the subject of protracted delays and died in a Senate committee.

In sum, during the 1920s the possibilities for continuing intellectual and practical innovations in the American social insurance movement were centered in a few state capitals, where reformers along with labor and employer groups engaged in spirited debates over unemployment legislation. The Wisconsin reform group, inspired by John Commons, was the most successful of these state-level reform efforts, and by the early 1930s, Commons's preventive approach to unemployment was predominant within the American Association for Labor Legislation. The Wisconsin reserves plan was also the only form of unemployment insurance to achieve legislative embodiment at the state level before the election of Franklin Roosevelt to the presidency. The coming of the New Deal revived debates about social insurance and welfare at the national level.

New Deal Watershed: The Federal Government Promotes Public Social Benefits

The coming of the Great Depression suddenly expanded the political possibilities for social welfare reforms in the United States. Crisis condi-

[54] Eisner, *Leiserson*, 32.

tions stimulated a broad democratic upsurge and invigorated social movements, while at the same time the New Deal of 1932 to 1939 brought to power at the national level political leaders willing to deploy executive authority in new ways. In the midst of this critical juncture, Congress passed the Social Security Act of 1935, setting into place the institutions that have patterned U.S. public social provision for almost fifty years.

The Social Security Act was basically a substantive and organizational victory for the Wisconsin reformers and experts who had earlier consolidated and extended Progressive reforms at the state level. The Wisconsin group brought to Washington experience with legislative maneuvering and compromise. Willing to make concessions to Congress where necessary, the Wisconsin experts acknowledged the vested interests of state and local governments and settled for a state-centered unemployment insurance system. They also engaged in creative program building where they could, and after 1935 the Wisconsin experts presided over an enormous and disproportionate expansion of the old-age insurance program within the overall American system of public social benefits.

Radical proposals for unemployment insurance and old-age pensions advanced by social movements in the early 1930s reflected the new political space opened for public welfare innovations, once welfare capitalism and the minimalist role of the federal government of the 1920s were discredited by the Depression crisis. The Townsend movement organized a mass-based campaign for an "Old Age Revolving Pension Plan," which called for $200 to be paid monthly to every retired person over sixty, on the condition that the money be spent the same month.[55] The Lundeen Bill (or Workers' Bill for Unemployment and Social Insurance) called for universal, open-ended unemployment compensation, equivalent to wages lost, progressively financed by employers and the government, and locally administered by councils of workers and farmers. This bill gathered support from some local unions and several state labor federations, from reformist social workers, and from groups of unemployed workers organized under Communist auspices.[56]

Despite considerable popular support for these and other proposals, however, the policy process through which Social Security was planned and drafted in the mid-1930s was strikingly closed. The process did not involve the transmission into policy of programmatic preferences articulated by parties, unions, or voluntary groups. Rather, a small number of

[55] Abraham Holtzman, *The Townsend Movement: A Political Study* (New York: Bookman Associates, 1963), chap. 2.

[56] See "Social Insurance Spree: Lundeen Bill in Congress Attracts Left Wing Support," *American Labor Legislation Review* 24 (June 1934): 67–70; and Mary Van Kleeck, "Security for Americans, IV: The Workers' Bill for Unemployment and Social Insurance," *The New Republic*, 12 December 1934, 121–24.

experts and public figures were brought into national policy deliberations through a selective process of recruitment and consultation by executive branch leaders.[57]

Especially consequential for the eventual shape of the Social Security
proposals, therefore, were the orientations and backgrounds of key politicians and experts who were brought into the executive branch after
the 1932 Democratic victory. The Social Security Act was formulated in
1934 and guided to enactment in 1935 by Roosevelt himself and by
Labor Secretary Frances Perkins, who had been his industrial commissioner during his tenure as governor of New York. Turning to the state-
level social policy group that was most successful before 1933, Perkins
favored the Wisconsin versus the Ohio proponents of social insurance.
She gave the key post for policy planning and legislative drafting of the
Social Security Act to Edwin Witte, formerly the secretary of the Wisconsin Industrial Commission (1917–22) and chief of the Legislative
Reference Library for the state of Wisconsin (1922–33).[58] Witte, in
turn, recruited a staff of research, statistical, and actuarial experts num-
bering less than fifty. Together, Witte argued, these experts were "a
majority of all the people in the country who were considered to be
specialists on any aspect of social security."[59] However, many key personnel were from Wisconsin, or sympathetic to Wisconsin reform ideas,
and in any event the reins of policy control never slipped from the
hands of Edwin Witte and Frances Perkins. Despite their distinguished
intellectual and reform backgrounds, Ohio plan social insurance proponents such as I. M. Rubinow and Abraham Epstein were excluded from
serious planning for the Social Security Act. The Committee on Economic Security asked Rubinow to Washington only once, to lead a
round-table discussion on old-age security.[60]

The planning apparatus created for the preparation of the Social Security legislation consisted of several formally organized groups of par-

[57] On the co-optation of selected labor leaders into the processes leading to the Social
Security Act, and on labor's general lack of independent impact on Social Security, see Edwin
E. Witte, *The Development of the Social Security Act* (Madison: University of Wisconsin
Press, 1963), 49–51; Edwin E. Witte, "Organized Labor and Social Security" in Milton
Derber and Edwin Young, eds., *Labor and the New Deal* (New York: DeCapo Press, 1972),
241–74; and Derthick, *Policymaking for Social Security,* 111–13. Union leaders lacked access
to independent expertise on social policy in the 1930s, and in any event unions were
preoccupied with issues of organizing workers, gaining legal recognition, and ensuring
union-scale wage rates on federal relief projects. By the later 1930s, moreover, the split
between the American Federation of Labor and the Congress of Industrial Organizations
undercut organized labor's rising political effectiveness within the Democratic party.
[58] On Witte's Wisconsin background, see Schlabach, *Edwin Witte,* chaps. 1–3.
[59] Witte, "Organized Labor and Social Security," 251.
[60] J. Lee Kreader, "Isaac Max Rubinow: Pioneering Specialist in Social Insurance," *Social
Service Review* 50 (September 1976): 419.

ticipants.[61] The Committee on Economic Security (CES) was the formal decision-making body and was composed of key cabinet officials. An Advisory Council on Economic Security provided a forum for carefully selected business and labor leaders, along with professionals and representatives of other organized interests. In addition, there was a Technical Board on Economic Security, drawing on government statistical and actuarial expertise. Finally, Edwin Witte, as executive director of the committee, and his staff were charged with coordinating and drawing up the committee's report containing legislative proposals. It was within and among these organizational bodies that administration officials, professional experts, and public advisers debated issues of national standardization and national administrative control.

The key Roosevelt administration and staff participants in policy making for Social Security had prior backgrounds as progressive reformers in state governments, and so it is understandable that they shared a strict opposition to social programs that might entail politically uncontrollable and easily expanded public expenditures. Neoprogressive conviction in favor of "sound" financing was clearly reflected in strategic moves by Roosevelt to set the fiscal parameters for social security legislation. Roosevelt did not launch permanently institutionalized welfare programs at the moment when emergency relief expenditures were appropriated in the early New Deal. By waiting until the middle of 1934, Roosevelt made certain that old-age and unemployment insurance programs would be symbolically and institutionally separated from relief.[62]

Roosevelt's cautious views were shared by Edwin Witte as well. Indeed, Witte's contempt for the Townsend Movement and his fear that its ambitious agenda would threaten "sound legislation," led him to advocate cutting out the old-age insurance portion of the emerging Social Security legislation.[63] Popular outcry and pressures on Congress prevented this from happening. But the point remains that the key shapers of the new Social Security legislation saw themselves as bulwarks

[61] Witte, *Development of Social Security Act*, 8–9.

[62] Roosevelt was explicit about this crucial separation. Addressing the Advisory Council of business, labor, and "public" advisers to his Committee on Economic Security, the President outlined his cautious approach and reaffirmed the shibboleth of fiscal "soundness": "We must not allow this type of [unemployment] insurance to become a dole through the mingling of insurance and relief. It must be financed by contributions, not taxes . . . Let us profit by the mistakes of foreign countries and keep out of unemployment insurance every element which is actuarially unsound." Franklin D. Roosevelt, "Address to Advisory Council of the Committee on Economic Security," 14 November 1934, in Samuel I. Rosenman, *The Public Papers and Addresses of Franklin D. Roosevelt*, Vol. 3 (New York: Random House, 1938), 453–54.

[63] Schlabach, *Edwin Witte*, 110.

against social groups and political forces attempting to open up the federal treasury. Thus one distinctive imprint left by the Wisconsin reformers working with Franklin Roosevelt and Frances Perkins was an early and consistent insistence upon contributory and "sound" financing for unemployment and old-age insurance. Beyond this, the Wisconsin policy experts brought to the planning for Social Security their crucial prior experience in political maneuver and compromise. These skills were important, because during late 1934 and the first months of 1935 important provisions of the emerging Social Security system were still open to debate and negotiation.

THE DEFEAT OF NATIONALIZING HOPE FOR U.S. PUBLIC BENEFITS

Issues of national uniformity and degrees of administrative centralization and control dominated debates during the planning by the Committee on Economic Security and during Congress's deliberations on the proposed Social Security legislation. Such matters were even more important for the long term than the original patternings of taxes and benefits. As any welfare state develops over time, its forms of intervention are woven into the fabrics of economy and society and generate vested political interests in existing uniformities and differentials. Likewise, the placement of welfare administrators within an overall state structure is important, because it influences possibilities for future programmatic developments, as well as possibilities for coordinating public social benefits with other public policies.

The earliest of many defeats for would-be standardizers and nationalizers among those who launched the New Deal's Social Security Act came during the fall of 1934 in disputes about the kind of unemployment insurance program the Committee on Economic Security should recommend that Roosevelt propose to Congress.[64] Three alternatives were debated: a purely national system, in which the federal government would collect payroll taxes and provide uniform compensation to workers; a federal subsidy plan, in which the federal government would

---

[64] The following account of the formulation of the Social Security Act draws generally upon facts presented in ibid., 114–26; Witte, *Development of Social Security Act*, part I and III, 29; and J. Douglas Brown, "The Genesis of Social Security in America; an Intimate Account of a Critical Period, 1934–35," chap. 1 in his *An American Philosophy of Social Security* (Princeton, N.J.: Princeton University Press, 1972), 84. Perkins's views about what the Supreme Court would accept seem to have been based on a conversation "with Justice Stone at his wife's tea one afternoon." See Arthur J. Altmeyer, *The Formative Years of Social Security* (Madison: University of Wisconsin Press, 1968), 15. Moreover, the tax-offset method of federal "control" over the states had already been embodied in legislation found constitutional by the Supreme Court in *Florida v. Mellon*. The best discussion of the relevant history of the tax-offset approach appears in Lewis Meriam, *Relief and Social Security* (Washington, D.C.: The Brookings Institution, 1946), 185–88.

collect payroll taxes and distribute them to states operating unemployment compensation systems according to acceptable national minimum standards, perhaps also holding back some funds for a national pooling of risks to help regions especially hard hit by unemployment; and a federal tax-offset plan, in which the federal government would assess payroll taxes, but forgive 90 percent of them if employers paid required contributions to insurance systems set up according to states' individually-set standards for benefits, eligibility, and taxes.

In the debates of the fall of 1934, strong support for the more nationally uniform alternatives came from both the Technical Board and the outside Advisory Council of business, labor, and other public figures. Edwin Witte, however, personally preferred the tax-offset plan because it alone would respect variations in state measures and allow Wisconsin to preserve its distinctive system of individual employer reserves. In any event, Witte's job was to find a way to propose measures in accord with Roosevelt's and Perkins's convictions, and they firmly believed that only the most federal of the three plans for unemployment insurance could get through Congress and the Supreme Court.

The difficulties Witte faced in the disputes over the alternative unemployment insurance proposals indicate the strength of nationalizing hopes at the moment of creation of the New Deal's social-benefits programs. Most academic and social-work professionals of the early 1930s who had considered the arguments for adequate benefit levels and the pooling of risks in unemployment insurance were persuaded that a kind of Ohio plan at the national level would be best for workers and the country. Leaders of labor unions agreed, and, interestingly enough, so did the liberal welfare capitalists on the Advisory Committee for Social Security. Along with other businessmen in the Commerce Department's Business Advisory Council, these capitalists favored more, rather than less, national uniformity in the country's new unemployment insurance system.[65]

Welfare capitalists had always thought of government involvement in

[65] The liberal welfare-capitalists who served on the Advisory Council on Economic Security were Gerard Swope, president of the General Electric Company; Morris E. Leeds, president of Leeds and Northrup; Sam Lewisohn, vice president of the Miami Copper Company; Walter C. Teagle, president of the Standard Oil Company; and Marion B. Folsom, treasurer of the Eastman Kodak Company. These five businessmen all voted for the subsidy plan, because it would introduce more national uniformity than the tax-offset plan (see Witte, Development of the Social Security Act, 58). This happened in December 1934, well after Roosevelt had made his opposition to a purely national approach clear. For the position of the Business Advisory Council (BAC), see Altmeyer, Formative Years, 23. Of course, at this stage of the New Deal, most business leaders were feuding with the Roosevelt administration, and the BAC had only liberal welfare-capitalists left in its diminished ranks. But these are precisely the "far-sighted vanguard" capitalists cited by corporate-liberal theorists as the ones who were especially influential in shaping Social Security.

social insurance as primarily a way to keep "progressive" employers from being undercut by low-cost competitors. Wisconsin's labor regulations, too, had been designed to bring "less enlightened" employers up to the standards of the best. Yet once Wisconsin reformers moved from Madison to Washington, Edwin Witte's desire to protect the autonomy of the state of Wisconsin under the Social Security Act's unemployment insurance system ended up having very ironic consequences. For the federal tax-offset scheme—especially after Congress gave the states discretion to adjust unevenly effective business taxes through "merit rating" provisions—opened up possibilities for interstate balkanization, with employers in "less enlightened" states enjoying lower costs for unemployment insurance than employers in progressive states.[66] And this was exactly the kind of outcome feared by liberal welfare capitalists in 1934.

In the end, Witte and Perkins pushed the federal tax-offset scheme through the reluctant group of cabinet officers in the Committee on Economic Security by stressing congressional unwillingness to accept a more national program.[67] By the mid-1930s a number of states were enacting state-level unemployment insurance programs with varying provisions.[68] And in 1933 Congress had passed the Wagner-Peyser Act to provide federal inducements for the establishment of state-level public employment offices. As Paul Douglas pointed out, this prior legislation "helped to fix the mold into which the unemployment insurance system was to be cast."[69] Composed of representatives of the states and localities, Congress would indeed faithfully defend decentralizing administrative arrangements where related efforts already existed in the states. Southerners, who dominated key congressional committee chairmanships, were especially vigilant because of their desire to protect racist practices and low-cost patterns of labor control. But liberals in Congress also often shortsightedly supported federal rather than national arrangements in order to protect more progressive state-level practices. Thus, in the fashioning of America's unemployment insurance system, all of the nationalizing pressures inside and around the Roosevelt administration had to give way before the practical institutional obstacles

[66] See Becker, "Twenty-Five Years of Unemployment Insurance"; and Harpham, "Federalism, Keynesianism."

[67] See especially the account in Morton Grodzins, "American Political Parties and the American System," *Western Political Quarterly* 13 (December 1960): 978–80.

[68] See Theda Skocpol and Edwin Amenta, "Did Capitalists Shape Social Security?" *American Sociological Review* 50 (August 1985): 572–75.

[69] Paul Douglas, *Social Security in the United States* (New York: DaCapo Press, 1971; originally 1936), 32.

built into the federalism and congressional leverage characteristic of the overall U.S. state structure.

Historical accounts agree that the disputes over the administrative form of unemployment insurance were what preoccupied the formulators of the Social Security Act in the fall of 1934. The national or federal administrative shape of the other major elements of the Act—a national old-age insurance system, and federal grants-in-aid to help support state-level, need-based programs especially for the elderly poor and for dependent children—aroused less controversy. Various state-level programs offering help to poor children or old people were already in existence by the mid-1930s, so federal subsidization rather than direct administration by the national government was taken for granted, especially because Roosevelt was looking by 1935 for ways to push "relief" programs onto the states and localities to lighten the load on the federal budget.

As for the old-age insurance system, the experts who advised the CES argued that a federal-state system would be technically impossible.[70] Of course, similar arguments were made against the federal-state unemployment insurance system. But in the untrodden area of old-age insurance for regularly employed workers, there were no pre-existing state-level programs or administrative structures for Congress to protect. So the CES, despite certain constitutional trepidations, took the portentous step of recommending a purely national system.

For the federal parts of the proposed Social Security legislation, the CES attempted to include administrative provisions promoting standardization and nationalization. But these were undermined in Congress. The Senate relaxed the proposed requirement that unemployment compensation be paid only through unemployment offices, allowing states to propose alternative agencies, and it also loosened proposed restrictions on state decisions about employers' contributions to unemployment insurance funds.[71] Both of these moves worked against later development of a more nationally uniform unemployment compensation system.

Even more telling, to get the old-age assistance program through Congress, it was necessary, as Edwin Witte later put it, "to tone down all clauses relating to supervisory control by the federal government" because "some southern senators feared . . . [any] entering wedge for federal interference with the handling of the Negro question. . . . [and] did not want to give authority to anyone in Washington to deny aid to any state because it discriminated against Negroes. . . ."[72] Thus, federal

[70] Brown, "Genesis of Social Security" describes the ideas and activities of those who drafted the old-age insurance proposals.
[71] Witte, *Development of the Social Security Act*, 135–36, 141.
[72] Ibid., 143–44.

controls over states' methods of administration were loosened, and the all-important requirement that states "furnish assistance sufficient to provide, 'when added to the income of the aged recipient, a reasonable subsistence compatible with decency and health'" was simply eliminated from the Social Security Act.[73] Future possibilities for requiring national minimum standards in a major social welfare program were thereby severely curtailed, for the "elimination of this provision left the states free to pay pensions of any amount, however small, and yet recover 50 percent of their costs from the federal government."[74]

Finally, the original hopes of the CES to mesh Social Security with strong federal employment programs were also frustrated in Congress. For the many workers fortunate enough to be steadily employed until the 1970s, the system worked, and the New Deal public benefits served as an adequate back-up for temporary unemployment and promised basic income support for retirement. However, for the unlucky people who were willing to work, but unable to do so regularly or at adequate wage levels, the lack of a full governmental commitment to full employment was much more telling. For such people the social-insurance and public-assistance programs legislated at the height of the New Deal were left to bear much more weight alone than their formulators had ever intended.[75]

"SOCIAL SECURITY" AFTER 1935: BUILDING NATIONAL SOCIAL PROVISION THROUGH OLD-AGE INSURANCE

The only fully national program established by the Social Security Act of 1935 was contributory old-age insurance. Roosevelt originally insisted on this program because he hoped that its gradual expansion as a "sound" system based on payroll taxes would eventually result in much reduced costs for old-age assistance. Actually, because potential bene-

---

[73] Ibid., 144.

[74] Ibid., 144–45.

[75] On the triumph of "commercial Keynesianism" as the U.S. variant of public macroeconomic policy, see Margaret Weir and Theda Skocpol, "State Structures and the Possibilities for 'Keynesian' Responses to the Great Depression in Sweden, Britain, and the United States" in Peter B. Evans, Dietrich Rueschemeyer, and Theda Skocpol, eds., *Bringing the State Back In* (New York: Cambridge University Press, 1985); and Robert M. Collins, *The Business Response to Keynes, 1929–1964* (New York: Columbia University Press, 1981). See also Margaret Weir, Ann Shola Orloff, and Theda Skocpol, eds., *The Politics of Social Policy in the United States* (Princeton, N.J.: Princeton University Press, 1988). For an overview of the complex system of U.S. macroregulation put together out of New Deal legacies and private sector bargaining practices after World War II, see Michael J. Piore and Charles Sabel, *The Industrial Divide* (New York: Basic Books, 1984), chap. 4.

ficiaries had to pay taxes for some time before they could collect benefits, old-age insurance expanded so slowly that liberal or conservative proposals for doing away with it, or sharply modifying it in favor of a flat-rate, need-based pension, remained on the national political agenda until the mid-1950s. The old-age insurance program survived congressional revisions of the Social Security Act in 1939 only because its strictly contributory features, including the projected accumulation of a huge funding reserve, were somewhat modified, the payments of benefits speeded up, and coverage made slightly more generous.[76] Throughout the 1940s and into the early 1950s, old-age insurance had to be repeatedly defended against many critics; and not until the beneficiaries of old-age insurance had clearly outstripped those receiving old-age assistance was the system solidly entrenched.

Through all of the formative years of Social Security, the defense of the basic structure and the inexorable expansion of old-age insurance were masterfully managed by the leaders of what was originally the Social Security Board and became in 1946 the Social Security Administration. The key administrative leader from 1935 to 1954 was Arthur J. Altmeyer.[77] Educated at the University of Wisconsin, where he worked as John Commons's research assistant, Altmeyer served between 1920 and 1934 as chief statistician and then secretary of the Wisconsin Industrial Commission. In 1934, Frances Perkins brought him to Washington as her Assistant Secretary of Labor, and during the formulation of the Social Security Act, Altmeyer also headed the Technical Board under the CES. Then, once Congress passed the act and set up the autonomous Social Security Board, Altmeyer moved into what became in effect the strategic control center for the newly emerging American regime of public social provision.

[76] See Arthur J. Altmeyer, *The Formative Years of Social Security* (Madison: University of Wisconsin Press, 1968), chap. 4; Martha Derthick, *Policymaking for Social Security* (Washington, D.C.: The Brookings Institution, 1979), 214; and Edward D. Berkowitz, "The First Advisory Council and the 1939 Amendments" in Edward D. Berkowitz, ed., *Social Security After Fifty* (Westport, Conn.: Greenwood Press, 1987), 55–78.

[77] The preface to Altmeyer's *Formative Years* briefly recounts his life and career. Altmeyer's book is one of three complementary books that provide an excellent picture of Social Security's leadership and development after 1935. The second book is Derthick, *Policymaking*, which is especially good on the relationships of Social Security's administrators with Congress and organized interest groups. This book interprets events from a sophisticated neoliberal perspective. Finally, the third important work is Jerry R. Cates, *Insuring Inequality: Administrative Leadership in Social Security, 1935–54* (Ann Arbor: University of Michigan Press, 1983), which provides a very critical analysis from a left-liberal or social-democratic perspective. Cates highlights the biases of the Social Security administrators against public assistance programs. In the following discussion, we have drawn facts and insights (especially) from Derthick and Cates, whose strengths complement one another in our view.

From the start, old-age insurance was Altmeyer's favorite program—and, as the only national component of Social Security, it was the part most fully under the board's control. After a period of wariness until old-age insurance was found constitutional in 1937, Altmeyer spearheaded what surely deserves to be called a remarkable state-building drive to give the program a disciplined, efficient organization—for collecting payroll taxes, distributing benefits, and recording all such taxes and benefits on millions of individualized records—as well as an ideology that would help the program survive and grow politically.

The ideology that Altmeyer and other Social Security administrators fashioned for the old-age insurance system was individualistic and based on a (technically quite false) analogy to private savings or insurance.[78] In this ideology, old-age insurance was *not* portrayed as a program through which the government taxed workers and employers to pay benefits to retired people. It was portrayed instead as a huge set of public piggy banks into which individual prospective "beneficiaries" put away "contributions" for their own eventual retirements. Even though the national state legally required the payment of payroll taxes, invested them in public securities, and paid proportionately (modestly) higher pensions to poorer beneficiaries, none of this was openly discussed. Rather the old-age "social security" system was said to be based on its "fair return" to each individual according to his or her relative income standing during working years. The system supposedly established a kind of contractual bond or promise to repay with interest between the government and each individual contributor, thereby giving each person a sacred right eventually to collect the benefits he or she had earned.

Echoing the language used during the 1920s to talk about the Wisconsin version of unemployment insurance, Altmeyer and his Social Security propagandists called this sort of old-age provision a genuinely "American approach" to social insurance.[79] Indeed, it is easy to see in this ideology a transmutation into new programmatic circumstances of the Wisconsin approach to workers' compensation and unemployment insurance through capitalist regulation. Here government establishes its functional regulatory tie with individual contributors (as well as with the business enterprises that collect the payroll taxes), yet still tries to intrude minimally in the market economy.

[78] Derthick, *Policymaking*, 199, 204, 224–25; and Cates, *Insuring Inequality*, 13–17 and passim. For a nice statement of Social Security's ideology by a former commissioner of Social Security (1962–1973), see Robert M. Ball, "The American System of Social Security," *Journal of Commerce*, 15 June 1964.

[79] American Association for Labor Legislation, "An American Plan"; and also Nelson, *Unemployment Insurance*.

But it is important to understand that the Wisconsin contributions to state-building for Social Security consist of more than just ideological extensions and reworkings of preexisting ideas about social insurance. The really important qualities that Altmeyer, Witte, and other former Wisconsin reformers brought with them to Washington were not fixed ideas. Their crucial contributions were eagerness to carve out a viable political place for limited reforms and an experienced capacity to do this through the creative molding of public opinion and through the astute management of the flow of expert opinions and technical information to nominally superior political executives and to legislative decision makers. Such were the political practices encouraged by Wisconsin Progressivism and by such institutions as the Wisconsin Industrial Commission and the Legislative Reference Library.[80] Witte and Altmeyer simply brought the political skills they had honed in Wisconsin to Washington, where Witte used them to get the Social Security Act through Congress, and Altmeyer then used them to work out for Social Security a popular public image and a remarkable programmatic capacity to get presidents, cabinet officials, and congressional oversight committees to defend it and go along with the policy recommendations of its administrators.

Under Altmeyer's skilled guidance, the ideological myth of old-age insurance—as contributors saving through government to build up individually earned benefits—was deployed in many politically advantageous ways.[81] Payroll taxpayers did not have to be addressed as such; they could be individually told that they were building up rights to their own future benefits.[82] Resistance to old-age insurance taxes was thus lessened, and over time broad popular support was built up among voters for liberalized benefits. Social Security finances could be insulated from other government activities through the device of the supposedly sacrosanct trust fund. Again and again, funding for favored Social Security programs—benefit increases or extensions into new areas such as survivors' benefits and disability coverage—could be presented to politicians as "actuarially sound," because supposedly sufficient taxes were always being collected or sufficient tax increases proposed to cover future benefits.[83]

[80] Schlabach, *Edwin Witte*, chap. 3.

[81] Derthick, *Policymaking*, 170–82; Cates, *Insuring Inequality*, chap. 4.

[82] The early stages of this process are well described by Altmeyer, *Formative Years*, 53–55, 68–70. For example, in the initial assignment of Social Security numbers in 1937, Altmeyer writes that "every effort was made to use terminology that would inspire confidence rather than arouse suspicion. Thus the process was called 'assignment of social security account numbers' instead of 'registration,' The use of the word 'registration' was avoided because it might connote regimentation." See also Derthick, *Policymaking*, 198–99.

[83] Derthick, *Policymaking*, esp. chap. 2.

To preserve the rights and dignity of citizens and to safeguard the public purse, it was essential in the view of the Social Security administrators to make sure that programs resembling public assistance could not displace social insurance. So the Social Security administrators—who had federal oversight authority over old-age assistance, as well as control of contributory old-age insurance—used discretionary administrative decisions to prevent liberal states (like California) from making old-age pensions too automatic, too generous financially, or too dignified in their local implementation. In the process, Altmeyer and other Social Security administrators left many needy older Americans inadequately protected in order to sustain the idea of the indignities and inadequacies of "welfare" and leave political room for the continued gradual expansion of contributory old-age insurance, the true "social security."

From a broader historical perspective there have, of course, always been other forces at work to keep welfare forms of public assistance penurious and demeaning for needy Americans—and also to keep welfare identified with the fate of blacks in the United States. The great leeway left to the states in the legislation of the 1930s ensured that conservative or racist interests would be able to control welfare coverage, benefit levels, and methods of administration in large stretches of the nation, and especially in the South, where the vast majority of blacks lived at the time in poverty and political disenfranchisement. Much later, old-age public assistance was significantly nationalized through the 1974 Supplemental Security Income program.[84] But this was too late to alter the connotations or reality of "welfare," because by the 1970s the largest public assistance program was Aid to Families with Dependent Children. As U.S. blacks migrated in massive waves during the 1950s and 1960s out of the rural South and into northern and southern cities, many were unable to carve out secure economic niches in the mature industrial economy. As the major welfare program available to dependent people without adequate employment income, AFDC thus became strongly identified in the public mind with black urban poverty and with black welfare mothers, stereotyped as unwed and immoral.[85]

The brief outburst of Great Society efforts in the late 1960s to eradicate poverty in America did not succeed in overcoming the economic and social difficulties of either the white or black poor. Instead, one can

[84] See Jill Quadagno, "From Old Age Assistance to Supplemental Security Income: The Political Economy of Relief in the South, 1935–1972" in Weir, Orloff, and Skocpol, eds., *The Politics of Social Policy in the United States.*

[85] The historical and ideological processes involved here are discussed in Winifred Bell, *Aid to Dependent Children* (New York: Columbia University Press, 1965).

say that the entire belated process since the 1960s of incorporating blacks as full, voting citizens into the American polity has aroused bitter political controversies about special federal programs targeted for the poor or the black—and indeed about welfare in general, because of its symbolic identification with the fortunes of the black poor. Under the right-wing administration of President Ronald Reagan, both pro-black and public assistance programs have been targeted for disproportionate funding cuts, even though they constitute a much smaller part of federal social-benefits expenditures than the privileged programs associated with old-age insurance or Social Security.

CONCLUSION

Since the 1950s, the dynamic core of the U.S. system of public social benefits has been the administratively sovereign, politically privileged, and fiscally insulated Social Security program. This program certainly has proven durable and capable of expansion—both expansion of benefits and expansion into the vacuums of disability coverage and provision for elderly medical care left open by the absence of national health insurance in the United States. But the successes of Social Security have helped to leave other American public benefits programmatically underdeveloped, symbolically demeaned, and politically vulnerable. Furthermore, the fiscally privileged features of Social Security have stood—and may stand even more in the future—as obstacles to the development of government economic and social interventions that might promote the security of all Americans together.

Taking the long historical view, that the New Deal ended up channeling modern public social benefits disproportionately through the politically and fiscally privileged contributory old-age insurance program, is not so surprising. In Europe and elsewhere modern welfare states could be developed by reworking and extending preexisting administrative and political arrangements, with both state bureaucracies and labor-based political parties playing important roles. But in the United States the structure of the polity was always distinctive. Even though the patronage democracy of the nineteenth century elaborated the Civil War pension system into a de facto program of benefits to the many elderly and disabled Americans, a modern U.S. welfare state was not to be constructed on earlier foundations. Instead, America's nineteenth-century patterns of public social spending were attacked by movements for regulatory reforms in the "public interest" and the efforts of such Progressive movements to counter "corruption" helped to prevent the United States from adopting European-style public pensions and social insurance around the turn of the century.

Nevertheless, the way was not simply cleared for welfare capitalists to provide for social welfare through large corporations and through federal government efforts of their own choosing. Progressive reform victories in certain states made possible the distinctively American approach to capitalist regulation institutionalized most fully in the Wisconsin Industrial Commission and its surrounding political and academic appurtenances. Then, during the New Deal, Franklin Roosevelt and Frances Perkins, themselves progressive politicians from New York, called upon the well-established reformers of Wisconsin to help fashion viable new public benefits programs at the federal level. In the administration of the Social Security Act, moreover, the progressive form of the expert-run commission was adapted to the exigencies of running a national old-age insurance system and defending it against programmatic and political competitors. Using their Wisconsin-inherited skills in the politics of managing public opinion and technical advice, the Social Security administrators carved out an impregnable and expansionary niche for their preferred national social insurance program. Quite remarkably, such victories for Social Security in the United States were achieved inside a federal state structure and political party system otherwise uncongenial to generous and nationally uniform public welfare efforts.

CHAPTER FIVE

Redefining the New Deal: World War II and the Development of Social Provision in the United States

with Edwin Amenta

ACCOUNTS of the development of public social provision in the United States often focus on major periods of domestic reform, in particular the New Deal of the 1930s and the Great Society of the 1960s. By comparison, the period during and immediately after World War II seems inconsequential. When the wartime period is discussed, students of social policy frequently claim that it consolidated the changes wrought by the New Deal.[1] Yet this time brought some new departures and also saw the failure of bold plans to extend the social policies of the 1930s. The welfare aspirations of the New Deal were not realized as a result of the impact of war; they were redefined.

A comparison of the U.S. experience with that of Great Britain indicates that World War II could spur comprehensive innovations, for there the war catalyzed the reorganization and extension of social benefits and services. The British changes were largely mapped out in the Beveridge Report of December 1942 and put into effect between 1944

From *The Politics of Social Policy in the United States*, edited by Margaret Weir, Ann Shola Orloff, and Theda Skocpol (Princeton, NJ: Princeton University Press, 1988). © Princeton University Press.

For constructive criticism and comments, we thank James Cronin, Alfred Darnell, Jennifer Hochschild, Michael Katz, Barbara Laslett, Mark Leff, Sunita Parikh, Craig Reinarman, the members of the brown bag workshop at the Center for the Study of Industrial Societies at the University of Chicago, and the members of the 1986–87 Colloquium on American Society and Politics, held in Cambridge, Massachusetts.

[1] See, for instance, Richard E. Neustadt, "Congress and the Fair Deal: A Legislative Balance Sheet," in Carl Friedrich and John Kenneth Galbraith, eds., *Public Policy*, vol. 5, pp. 351–81; David Brody, "The New Deal and World War II," in John Braeman, Robert H. Bremner, and David Brody, eds., *The New Deal: The National Level* (Columbus, Ohio: Ohio State University Press, 1975), pp. 267–309; and Richard O. Davies, "Social Welfare Policies," in Richard S. Kirkendall, ed., *The Truman Period as a Research Field* (Columbia: University of Missouri Press, 1967), pp. 149–86. For different views, see Mary Hedge Hinchey, "The Frustration of the New Deal Revival, 1944–1946," (Ph.D. diss., University of Missouri, 1965), and Barton J. Bernstein, "America in War and Peace: The Test of Liberalism," in Barton J. Bernstein, ed., *Towards a New Past* (New York: Random House, 1967).

and 1949, as specified by White Papers sponsored by the wartime coalition government and a series of parliamentary acts passed by the post-war Labour government. The new and extended social policies were intended to protect all British citizens from want due to sickness, unemployment, disability, old age, family obligations, or lack of income. The sum of these innovations was called "the welfare state," a phrase coined to contrast the aspirations of Britain with the horrors of the Nazi "warfare state."[2]

Planning for a postwar American welfare state was detailed in various reports—most notably *Security, Work, and Relief Policies* (the "American Beveridge Plan"), released in March 1943. In it, the National Resources Planning Board (NRPB) proposed major reorganizations and extensions of U.S. social policies that would accompany measures to sustain a full-employment economy. With the Democrats in nominal control of Congress and President Roosevelt in office, reformers hoped to use the war to complete the New Deal. But their aims were not to be realized. New Deal public employment agencies were phased out, and the comprehensive plans of the National Resources Planning Board were thwarted.

Still, the World War II period in the United States was not entirely a missed opportunity, for some significant innovations were made. A new set of benefits for individuals was included in the 1944 GI bill, and other legislation for veterans followed. Like the reforms unsuccessfully advocated by the NRPB, the measures for veterans were comprehensive; they covered needs ranging from physical rehabilitation to employment assistance and health care, and offered grants or loans for education, for home ownership, and for starting a new business. This American welfare state for veterans and their families was administered primarily by the Veterans Administration. Although Congress dismissed comprehensive proposals for changes in employment policy and income transfers, the war brought a broadening of the base of the federal income tax and an increase in its progressiveness. The enhanced fiscal capacity of the national government enabled it to fund postwar veterans' benefits, as well as to spend higher sums for defense. Also funded were new domestic policies that indirectly met social welfare needs. Such measures as federal subsidies for housing and hospital construction signaled the beginning of a trend; until the 1960s U.S. social provision would rely heavily on federal funds channeled through states, localities, and businesses.

In short, a war that had brought comprehensive, nationalizing re-

[2] Peter Flora and Arnold J. Heidenheimer, "The Historical Core and Changing Boundaries of the Welfare State," in Peter Flora and Arnold J. Heidenheimer, eds., *The Development of the Welfare State in Europe and America* (New Brunswick, N.J.: Transaction Books, 1982), p. 19.

forms of social policy to Great Britain furthered the development of indirect and disjointed forms of public social provision in the United States. To understand why, we probe the gaps between the plans put forward in the United States during the war and the new legislation that survived the battles of wartime domestic politics. In the next two sections, we present an overview of American social policies as they stood in 1939 and a description of wartime plans and changes in social policies made during the 1940s. In an attempt to determine why events followed the course they did, we examine British policy changes and some theories about war and the welfare state that were inspired by the British example. Because we find these theories inadequate, we offer explanatory arguments of our own. By analyzing the impact of America's mode of mobilization on the evolving capacities of the national government, on the options available to business and industrial labor, and on the political alliances that vigorously debated the various social policy proposals, we attempt to explain why the United States did not fashion a comprehensive welfare state out of the crucible of war, as Britain did. Our analysis also reveals the ways in which the war and its immediate aftermath redirected the social policies of the New Deal.

U.S. SOCIAL POLICY AT THE END OF THE NEW DEAL

At the end of the 1930s, social policy in the United States consisted of a wide assortment of programs. In addition to veterans' benefits carried over from previous wars and state workers' compensation laws passed in the Progressive Era, there were job programs offering publicly funded employment, public works projects, a federal-state employment service, two newly established contributory social insurance programs, state-level public assistance programs (some of which were supplemented by federal funds), and housing programs, including subsidies for home building and a modest program for slum clearance and the erection of public housing. Most of these programs either had been created or were substantially altered during the first two administrations of President Franklin Delano Roosevelt.

By far the most important national welfare effort in 1939 was public employment, although it covered only approximately 3 million of the nearly 10 million out of work in that year. About 0.8 million young Americans were working for the National Youth Administration and the Civilian Conservation Corps (CCC); some 2.3 million workers were on the rolls of the Works Projects Administration (WPA), which was created in 1935 and made an independent agency in 1939. The WPA administered labor-intensive projects, such as the construction or rehabilitation of highways, streets, and public buildings. Congress provided financial resources and state and local governments sponsored the projects; the WPA decided which ones to fund and ran them. The cost of all these public employment programs was approximately $1.9 billion, which represented more than 20 percent of total federal expenditures and about 47 percent of federal social welfare expenditures in 1939.[3]

More people were receiving public assistance, but it was transmitted primarily through the states and localities. In 1933, the Federal Emergency Relief Administration (FERA) was established to provide financial relief to the unemployed. After the 1934 elections, the president decided to "quit this business of relief" and changed the focus to public employment. When FERA wound up its operations at the end of 1935, general assistance was back under the control of states and localities, with no federal controls or standards. To some extent, the 1935 Social Security Act brought the federal government back into the relief business. Washington would match state and local government expenditures up to specified maximums for means-tested old-age assistance and aid to the blind, and would provide one-third of payments for Aid to Dependent Children. The Social Security Act amendments of 1939 increased the federal share of ADC to one-half. In that year approximately 1.9 million were receiving Old Age Assistance, approximately 1 million were receiving ADC, and 1.7 million were still receiving general assistance.[4]

The Social Security Act also established old-age and unemployment insurance, with payments to begin in 1942. For unemployment insurance, a federal tax (that reached 3 percent in 1937) was levied on employers' payrolls. The law provided that this tax could be credited to the employer if the state in which the employer operated passed a suitable unemployment compensation law. By the middle of 1937, all states had passed such legislation; the result was a variety of benefit provisions, levels of taxation, and forms of administration. State unemployment insurance funds were intended to be sufficient without drawing on state revenues or federal general revenues.[5] For old-age insurance under the Social Security Act, a 1 percent payroll tax on a maximum wage base of $3,000 was levied on employers and employees. The tax was to begin in 1937 and was scheduled to increase in steps until 1949, when

[3] Committee on Long-Range Work and Relief Policies, *Security, Work, and Relief Policies* (Washington, D.C.: Government Printing Office, 1942), p. 604 (hereafter referred to as Committee, *Security*); Donald S. Howard, *The WPA and Relief Policy* (New York: Sage, 1943), chap. 4, pp. 854–57; *Historical Statistics of the United States from Colonial Times to 1976* (Washington, D.C.: Government Printing Office, 1976), p. 357.

[4] Searle F. Charles, *Minister of Relief: Harry Hopkins and the Depression* (Syracuse, N.Y.: Syracuse University Press, 1963), chap. 2; Howard, *The WPA and Relief Policy*, chap. 1; Josephine Brown, *Public Relief, 1929–1939* (New York: Henry Holt, 1940), chaps. 7, 13, 14; *Historical Statistics*, p. 356.

[5] Daniel Nelson, *Unemployment Insurance: The American Experience, 1915–1935* (Madison: University of Wisconsin Press, 1969), chap. 9.

both employers and employees were to be taxed at a rate of 3 percent. Old-age insurance was to be paid according to recipients' previous earnings and was to be financed solely with funds accruing from the payroll tax. The 1939 amendments added benefits for survivors and allowed payments to begin in 1940 rather than 1942. The amended legislation also postponed until 1943 a tax increase that was to have taken effect in 1940; according to 1939 projections, the tax postponement and the increased benefits would require the fund to be heavily supplemented by general revenues in later years.[6]

Reformers considered other New Deal social policy innovations as preliminary steps toward a comprehensive public policy. In the area of employment policy, an important new agency, the United States Employment Service, was established in 1933. The federal government provided grants-in-aid for states to set up employment offices, and the USES attempted to coordinate their efforts. In the area of housing policy, the first problem addressed by New Deal reformers was the foreclosure of mortgages; the National Housing Act of 1934 created the Federal Housing Administration, which insured individual home mortgages. By 1938, the emphasis had changed; legislation now provided modest funding for public housing and slum clearance. Also in that year, an administration-sponsored report called for, among other things, national hospitalization insurance. Roosevelt limited his health initiatives in 1939, however, to a bill for a WPA hospital construction project, which failed to pass Congress.[7]

The New Dealers attempted to cut back one category of social expenditures: benefits for military veterans. They believed that the needs of ex-soldiers should be met chiefly by programs directed at the entire population. In the 1920s, Congress had passed several laws to aid World War I veterans and made the Veterans' Bureau responsible for the administration of all such programs. The most expensive program was compensation to the disabled; in 1933 nearly 750,000 were receiving benefits for service- and nonservice-connected disabilities. The National Economy Act of 1933 gave Roosevelt the power (for two years) to issue executive orders to regulate veterans' benefits. Under this economy regime, the primary savings came from a reduction in compensation for veterans with service-connected disabilities, and the removal

[6] On the payroll tax, see Mark H. Leff, *The Limits of Symbolic Reform: The New Deal and Taxation, 1933–1939* (New York: Cambridge University Press, 1984), chap. 1.

[7] Joseph Huthmacher, *Senator Robert F. Wagner and the Rise of Urban Liberalism* (New York: Atheneum, 1968); Monte M. Poen, *Harry S. Truman versus the Medical Lobby: The Genesis of Medicare* (Columbia: University of Missouri Press, 1979); Richard O. Davies, *Housing Reform during the Truman Administration* (Columbia: University of Missouri Press, 1966).

from pension rolls of the vast majority having nonservice-connected disabilities.[8] Moreover, like his predecessor (though FDR did not use the Army against protesting veterans as President Herbert Hoover had done in 1932), Roosevelt attempted to stop the movement to redeem adjusted compensation certificates. These so-called bonuses, granted by Congress in 1924, were not to mature until 1945. But in 1935 Congress passed a measure allowing immediate redemption of the certificates and, in 1936, overrode Roosevelt's veto and disbursed or credited $3.2 billion to veterans. Nevertheless, by 1939 New Deal reformers had managed to slow special benefits to military veterans; the federal government was spending $606 million, mainly for disability pensions, compared with $825 million in 1932.[9]

Following its failure in 1938 to get comprehensive executive reorganization measures through Congress, the Roosevelt administration made a more modest and ultimately successful effort to coordinate social policies—specifically, to improve coordination of social-spending programs with employment programs and enhance the executive's ability to plan and reform social policies. The 1939 executive reorganization legislation incorporated the Works Projects Administration and the Public Works Administration (PWA) into a newly created Federal Works Agency, underscoring the administration's commitment to employment. The USES was placed under the Social Security Board (SSB), which controlled old-age insurance, unemployment insurance, and special assistance programs. The board itself was placed under the new Federal Security Administration. The Veterans Administration remained in control of veterans' programs, including hospitals. Although the administration hoped that spending for veterans would decrease and eventually end as World War I veterans died, there was no merger of programs for veterans with the nationwide programs for all citizens before the outbreak of World War II.[10]

[8] William P. Dillingham, *Federal Aid to Veterans, 1917–1941* (Gainesville: University of Florida Press, 1952); Daivs R. B. Ross, *Preparing for Ulysses: Politics and Veterans during World War II* (New York: Columbia University Press, 1969), chap. 1; *Historical Statistics*, pp. 1147–50.

[9] Irving Bernstein, *The Lean Years: A History of the Americna Worker, 1920–1933* (Boston: Houghton Mifflin, 1960), chap. 13; Dillingham, *Federal Aid to Veterans*; Ross, *Preparing for Ulysses*, chap. 1.

[10] Richard Polenberg, *Reorganizing Roosevelt's Government, 1936–1939: The Controversy over Executive Reorganization* (Cambridge: Harvard University Press, 1966); William E. Pemberton, *Bureaucratic Politics: Executive Reorganization during the Truman Administration* (Columbia: University of Missouri Press, 1979), pp. 11–14; Committee, *Security*, p. 33.

U.S. Social Policy in the 1940s: Plans and Accomplishments

When Franklin Roosevelt was reelected for a third presidential term in 1940, the United States was already informally involved in World War II as a result of its ties with Great Britain. Plans and partial measures for wartime mobilization of the economy had been discussed for many months before the Japanese attack on Pearl Harbor on December 7, 1941.[11] Early on, Roosevelt's New Deal reforms also set the stage for postwar developments. In November 1940, he instructed the National Resources Planning Board (NRPB), a nonadministrative agency located in the Executive Office of the President, to refrain from direct involvement in war mobilization and to concentrate on formulating national social and economic policies for the postwar period. In response, the NRPB sponsored a series of investigations concerning employment, relief, social insurance, housing and urban development, and benefits for World War II veterans. The resulting reports reveal the outlines of an American full-employment welfare state that might have emerged after World War II, had the New Deal planners achieved their aims. Before considering why they failed, let us examine the recommendations developed by the groups sponsored or otherwise supported by the NRPB.

The most important of these reports on social policy was *Security, Work, and Relief Policies*, submitted by the Committee on Long-Range Work and Relief Policies. Appointed by the NRPB at the end of 1939, this committee was chaired by William Haber, professor of economics at the University of Michigan; the director of research was Eveline Burns of the Economics Department of Columbia University. The committee included representatives from the Works Projects Administration, the Federal Security Administration, the Children's Bureau, and the Farm Security Administration, as well as leaders of private social work associations. It was charged with surveying all existing work and income-maintenance programs and designing ways to restructure them, and it proceeded without interference from the president or Cabinet members.[12] *Security, Work, and Relief Policies* was submitted three days before the attack on Pearl Harbor. The report was intended to be a

---

[11] Harold G. Vatter, *The U.S. Economy in World War II* (New York: Columbia University Press, 1985), chap. 1.

[12] Marion Clawson, *New Deal Planning: The National Resources Planning Board* (Baltimore: Johns Hopkins University Press, 1981), pp. 136–40; Philip W. Warken, *A History of the National Resources Planning Board* (New York: Garland, 1979), pp. 224–26. The NRPB added a 4-page introduction to the 640 oversized pages of the committee's report in which it endorsed the group's work and recommendations but made a stronger pitch for a national guarantee of work and emphasized the need for immediate action. The board also referred to matters not mentioned in the report, such as international trade, labor relations, and antitrust policies. See Committee, *Security*, pp. 1–4.

comprehensive study of U.S. social policy, and 50 of its 640 pages were devoted to recommendations for policy innovations.

In the report, relief, social insurance, and public employment programs were discussed together under the rubric of "public aid."[13] Echoing the sentiments of the Committee on Economic Security, the NRPB committee called for the assurance of an "American standard" of economic security as a *right* of every citizen. Through one or another of the programs of public aid a citizen should, the NRPB committee felt, receive at least the minimum wage as specified by the 1938 Fair Labor Standards Act.[14] Although it retained the distinction between "social insurance" and "public assistance" programs, the committee did not want insurance to gain at the expense of assistance; thus it proposed nationalization of public assistance as well as new social insurance policies to fill gaps in the Social Security Act. Measures to ensure full employment were a primary concern of the committee. Like most other observers of the American economy at that time, committee members expected high postwar unemployment. Like many other products of NRPB research, both the NRPB's introduction to the report and the committee's recommendations were couched in the rhetoric of Alvin Hansen's "stagnationist" version of Keynesianism, which presumed that private business activities alone would be insufficient to maintain full employment in the postwar era.[15]

The NRPB, like previous New Dealers, regarded public works and public employment as the solutions to the unemployment problem. For those in need of steady work that the private economy could not provide, the federal government should provide a job. The NRPB committee sought something as flexible as, yet more powerful than, the WPA, which at its peak of operations employed less than 40 percent of the unemployed. The committee proposed the permanent planning of projects, both the labor-intensive WPA kind of project and the capital-intensive PWA kind. Project work would be provided without a means test and would be similar to private employment in hours, wages, and conditions of employment; the prevailing wage would be paid where wages were high, and the security or minimum wage would be paid elsewhere.[16] The committee emphasized the value of the nation's youth.

---

[13] Committee, *Security*, p. 9.

[14] Ibid., pp. 514–15.

[15] Ibid., pp. 1–4, 502–3.

[16] The WPA at first compromised between the two and paid an hourly "prevailing" wage until a monthly "security" level of payments had been reached. The skilled worker did not have to work as many hours as the unskilled worker to get the full benefit. In 1939 Congress forced all WPA workers to work a certain number of hours per month, in effect legislating the security wage. See Charles, *Harry Hopkins*, pp. 150–52.

It proposed to keep those between sixteen and twenty-one years of age out of the labor force and in school; job programs for youths would supplement educational aid.[17] To guarantee employment would require organizational change. Because of the need to gather detailed information about employment and employment trends, a national employment service was deemed essential.[18] The committee wanted such a service to administer all work and training programs, as well as unemployment compensation.[19]

Because of the strong emphasis placed by the NRPB committee on public programs to combat unemployment, the failure of all such efforts during the 1940s represents the widest gap between social policy plans and accomplishments. The termination of public employment programs began in 1942 when Congress ended the Civilian Conservation Corps. Shortly after the 1942 elections, Roosevelt called for the end of the WPA; Congress abolished the National Youth Administration the following summer. In June 1943 Congress appropriated only enough funds for the NRPB to allow it to phase itself out of existence. This left the Bureau of the Budget as the only nonemergency department in the Executive Office of the President. Thereafter, no public employment or planning agencies were reestablished; federally financed projects were considered on their own political merits and were not incorporated into any national employment program.[20]

The Full Employment bill of 1945 would not have brought back public employment; at best the bill might have revived some of the NRPB's functions through the creation of certain executive budgeting procedures. But even this bill was watered down to specify that economists, who were not required to adhere to Keynesian principles, were to serve in a purely advisory capacity.[21] Perhaps more important, plans to permanently strengthen the United States Employment Service failed. Although the service was nationalized soon after Pearl Harbor, Congress

[17] Committee, *Security*, pp. 504–11.

[18] The employment offices would be expected to construct detailed work histories to classify applicants. Ibid., pp. 507, 513–14, 536.

[19] Ibid., pp. 523–24.

[20] Barry D. Karl, *Charles E. Merriam and the Study of Politics* (Chicago: University of Chicago Press, 1974), chap. 12; Clawson, *New Deal Planning*, chaps. 15–19; Warken, *National Resources Planning Board*, pp. 237–45; Richard Polenberg, *War and Society: The United States, 1941–1945* (Philadelphia: J. B. Lippincott, 1972), pp. 80–82.

[21] Stephen Kemp Bailey, *Congress Makes a Law: The Story behind the Employment Act of 1946* (New York: Columbia University Press, 1950). For the view that the full employment bill did not require the government to spend, see "What the Bill Proposes," in *The Road to Freedom: Full Employment*, special section of *The New Republic* (September 24, 1945): 396–97. The articles in this special section were written by Heinz Eulau, Alvin H. Hansen, Mordecai Ezekiel, James Loeb, Jr., and George Soule. No byline preceded any article, yet the various authors were not collectively responsible for the articles. This article clearly could not have been written by Hansen.

gave responsibility for public employment offices back to the states at the end of the war.[22]

In the area of public assistance, or "relief" for the poor, the NRPB committee was strongly committed to general assistance and the setting of national standards, rather than continued reliance on special-category programs such as Aid to Dependent Children and old-age assistance. Some things should remain as they were, in the committee's view: states would continue to contribute fiscally and to administer programs along with local authorities; means tests would continue to be used. But the committee wanted general public assistance to be a top priority and called for increased federal funding and strict controls.[23] Specifically, it proposed that all public assistance programs be administered by one agency in each state and that the federal government administer general public assistance according to national standards until every state had demonstrated the ability to do so independently.[24]

In its report, the NRPB Committee on Long-Range Work and Relief Policies adopted the term "social insurance," yet refused to embrace an analogy to private insurance. The committee did not want *only* unemployment and old-age benefits to be provided as a right. What is more, it opposed the way such programs were being funded: it considered the trust fund a drag on aggregate consumption (according to Keynesian theory), and it considered the payroll tax regressive. Although it preferred to see the tax eclipsed by general revenues, it suggested the continuation of the payroll tax, in a reduced form, chiefly for the sake of appearances.[25] The uncoupling of accrued taxes and payments would result in more generous benefits financed mainly through general revenues. The NRPB committee sought to improve unemployment insurance by nationalizing the program and extending benefits to twenty-six weeks. In addition, domestic, agricultural, and other formerly excluded workers were to be covered by contributory insurance programs, and social insurance was to cover both temporary and permanent disability.[26]

[22] Leonard P. Adams, *The Public Employment Service in Transition, 1933–1968: Evolution of a Placement Service into a Manpower Agency* (Ithaca, N.Y.: New York State School of Industrial and Labor Relations, 1969), chap. 3; Hinchey, "New Deal Revival," chap. 6

[23] The committee rejected the 1935 recommendations of the CES regarding relief and sided with the CES Advisory Committee on Public Employment and Relief, which was dominated by social workers and others concerned with public welfare. The NRPB committee proposed that all relief programs adhere to national standards of adequacy. Specifically, aid to dependent children should go to mothers and should be as adequate as aid to the aged and the blind. The report indicated that ADC benefit levels were significantly lower than those of other aid programs. For the views of the advisory committee, see J. Brown, *Public Relief*, pp. 306–6, and Committee, *Security*, pp. 518–20.

[24] In 1939, only a few states had control over general assistance.

[25] Committee, *Security*, pp. 522–28.

[26] Ibid., pp. 515–17.

National health insurance had been omitted from the Social Security Act of 1935, and the NRPB committee spent little time on health issues.[27] The NRPB endorsed health insurance, however, and undoubtedly supported many of the recommendations of the Roosevelt administration's Interdepartmental Committee to Coordinate Health and Welfare Activities, which in the late 1930s had called for increases in federal public health expenditures; expansion of maternal and child health services; federal grants to expand hospital facilities; federal aid to state programs for the medically needy; grants-in-aid to establish state-level temporary disability insurance; and a general program of publicly supported medical care.[28]

Wide-ranging as the NRPB committee's proposals were, few changes were made in U.S. public assistance and social insurance during and immediately after the war. The proposed reforms of public assistance had little impact on wartime political debates. The Wagner-Murray-Dingell bills of 1943 and 1945 did not provide for the federal reorganization of state assistance systems, but called for grants-in-aid for all the needy without respect to special assistance categories, eliminated the maximums on matching payments, and changed the matching formula to increase aid to poorer states. Such provisions might have increased the benefits provided under the public assistance system in some states to a level approximating those provided by national social insurance for the elderly, and preempted the expansion of other social insurance programs. But the Wagner-Murray-Dingell bills failed to pass, and Congress also refused to expand federal grants-in-aid to include another form of special assistance for unemployable adults. The main achievement was the creation of a new special assistance program for permanent disability, a risk that the NRPB committee had thought should be covered by social insurance.[29]

[27] Unlike employment and income maintenance programs, health services were given little attention. The committee nodded toward national health insurance but said little about it (about one-half page). It was more specific about two other services: school lunches (it called for free lunches for all) and surplus commodity distribution (it recommended replacement by the food stamp plan and elimination of the means test for it). Ibid., pp. 520–22, 528–39.

[28] Soon after the interdepartmental committee met, Senator Robert Wagner of New York introduced what would be an ill-fated bill that was consistent with its report. The bill's medical care provision included a *grant-in-aid* to states for health insurance and for expansion of medical services to the poor and public health programs. See Huthmacher, *Senator Robert F. Wagner*, pp. 263–67; Poen, *Truman versus the Medical Lobby*, pp. 19–24.

[29] Wilbur J. Cohen and Robert J. Myers, "Social Security Act Amendments of 1950: A Summary and Legislative History," *Social Security Bulletin* 13 (October 1950): 3–14. Jerry Cates argues that generous state-administered old-age assistance would have constituted a threat to old-age insurance; see *Insuring Inequality: Administrative Leadership in Social Security, 1935–54* (Ann Arbor: University of Michigan Press, 1983), chap. 5.

The social insurance reforms fared better in the bills brought before Congress, but the legislative gains were minimal. Proposals to make social insurance more comprehensive were the key provisions of the unsuccessful Wagner-Murray-Dingell bills, which emphasized the creation of health insurance and the nationalization of unemployment insurance. But rather than increasing social insurance without reliance on payroll taxes, which was the hope of the NRPB committee, the proposed bills called for stiff increases in payroll taxes. Later attempts to pass legislation establishing national health insurance also failed. Hard as the Truman administration pushed for such a program in 1946 and 1949, all it had to show for the effort were grants-in-aid for the building of hospitals, expansion of state public health systems, and medical research.[30] In the end, the only successful social insurance reform was that of Old Age and Survivors' Insurance (OASI), whose eligibility, coverage, and benefits were expanded in 1950.[31]

In the area of urban reform, the NRPB had a radical viewpoint. The "right to shelter" was included in its 1942 New Bill of Rights, which President Roosevelt cited in his 1944 reelection campaign. The NRPB was more concerned with comprehensive urban planning than with public housing and slum clearance.[32] It called for the coordination of national and local planning for slum clearance and public housing, but saw no organic connection between the two. Instead, the board wanted both kinds of projects incorporated in a comprehensive urban redevelopment program. The NRPB was concerned with the timing of public housing projects, for they were to be included in the approved public works for which it would be responsible.[33]

[30] Authorship of the 1943 Wagner-Murray-Dingell bill has been variously attributed. Wagner's biographer, J. Joseph Huthmacher, sees the bill as mainly the work of Wagner, who was influenced by many, including the NRPB. See *Senator Robert F. Wagner*, pp. 292–93. Martha Derthick claims that it was written entirely by Wilbur Cohen and I. S. Falk of the Social Security Board. See Derthick, *Policymaking for Social Security* (Washington, D.C.: The Brookings Institution, 1979), pp. 111, 114. For the bill, see *Congressional Record*, 78th Cong., 1st sess., June 3, 1943, pp. 5260–62. On Truman's battles over national health insurance, see Poen, *Truman versus the Medical Lobby*, chap. 6, and Donald E. Spritzer, *Senator James E. Murray and the Limits of Post-War Liberalism* (New York: Garland, 1985), pp. 133–35.

[31] On the 1950 amendments, see Arthur Altmeyer, *The Formative Years of Social Security* (Madison: University of Wisconsin Press, 1966), pp. 182–86. See also Cohen and Myers, "Social Security Act Amendments of 1950."

[32] In 1940, the NRPB contracted for and published a report entitled *Housing: The Continuing Problem*, but it did not endorse any of its conclusions.

[33] Phillip J. Funigiello, *The Challenge to Urban Liberalism: Federal-City Relations during World War II* (Knoxville: University of Tennessee Press, 1978), chap. 5; Clawson, *New Deal Planning*, p. 132. The most important report on urban planning sponsored by the NRPB was Charles S. Ascher, *Better Cities* (Washington, D.C.: Government Printing Office, 1942). See also NRPB, *National Resources Development, Report for 1943* (Washington, D.C.: Government Printing Office, 1943), pp. 14–16.

In different ways, both urban planning and public housing failed in the United States, however. The urban planners lost their bid to gain influence over reform efforts in 1943, with the abolition of the NRPB and the defeat of bills providing federal aid for state and local planning and redevelopment. Public housing proponents, who cared little about urban planning, eventually won their battle, but without a comprehensive program. Truman's public housing legislation did not pass until 1949, and by the end of his term only 60,000 dwelling units of public housing had been built. Moreover, Truman's policy to encourage home construction owed its limited success to subsidies for private builders and homeowners. In the absence of public planning, FHA insurance and "yield insurance" for builders of middle-class homes and apartment buildings facilitated a private construction boom; five million such housing units were built between 1946 and 1950.[34]

Not until late in the game did the National Resources Planning Board become concerned specifically with the problems of veterans. The NRPB committee did not include veterans' programs in its definition of "public aid," for instance. To coordinate planning aimed at meeting the readjustment needs of soldiers and war workers with long-range social planning, the NRPB organized the Postwar Manpower Conference, which met for the first time in July 1942 and included representatives from the NRPB; the Departments of Agriculture, Labor, Navy, and War; the Federal Security Agency; the War Manpower Commission; the Selective Service System; and the Veterans Administration. The NRPB representatives wanted to ensure that the emergency postwar provision for veterans would mesh with comprehensive plans to achieve full employment and to revamp the social security system. If possible, soldiers and war workers should be included in the same legislation; if not, special legislation for veterans was acceptable so long as it did not establish an administratively separate scheme of superior benefits and employment arrangements, thus undermining proposals for more comprehensive measures.

The recommendations of the conference's report of June 1943 were consistent with NRPB preferences, although most of its proposals pertained to short-term issues concerning munitions workers and the demobilization of veterans. The main proposals with regard to soldiers included three months' furlough pay at a maximum of $100 per month; provision of unemployment insurance administered by the USES for up to twenty-six more weeks; aid for education; and credit toward old-age and survivors' insurance for time spent in the armed services. These proposals underlined the concern of conference members and the NRPB

[34] See Davies, *Housing Reform*; Funigiello, *The Challenge to Urban Liberalism*, chap. 7.

with mitigating the high postwar unemployment that everyone expected. Providing educational opportunities for veterans was also consistent with the NRPB committee's proposal to use educational opportunities to keep young people out of the labor market.[35]

To some extent, the new wartime laws providing veterans' benefits corresponded with the ideas of the NRPB. The GI bill of 1944 did not include large bonuses for able-bodied veterans but instead offered "readjustment allowances," a type of unemployment compensation. The benefits offered for vocational or college study were considerably more generous than those the conference members had originally proposed.[36] These programs were supplemented by veterans' benefits that undercut demands for more comprehensive social programs for all citizens, however, especially in the areas of health and housing. The GIs could not be denied the benefits of World War I veterans; therefore, in the absence of national health and disability insurance, veterans with war-related injuries were granted free medical care and generous disability pensions. The GI bill also included incentives for able-bodied veterans to purchase homes, and, during the Truman administration, veterans were provided mortgage subsidies and insurance for the construction of cooperative housing.[37]

In sum, although the NRPB and like-minded planners pointed the way toward a national and comprehensive full-employment welfare state for the United States, and even though congressional liberals and the Truman administration were able to translate some of the plans into legislation, the social policy changes achieved during and after World War II were minor, except where veterans were concerned. They and their families now enjoyed a comprehensive set of benefits and services. Americans in general benefited primarily from extensions of OASI and from modest federal subsidies for home and hospital construction; but the unemployed could no longer depend on public jobs programs. Hence the war brought what the New Deal reformers had hoped to avoid: a special welfare state for a substantial sector of the population deemed especially deserving. The social reformism of the New Deal had been channeled into expanded public provision for veterans, making it henceforth less likely that establishment of a national welfare state

[35] National Resources Planning Board, *Demobilization and Readjustment: Report of the Conference on Postwar Readjustment of Civilian and Military Personnel* (Washington, D.C.: Government Printing Office, 1943).

[36] Ross, *Preparing for Ulysses*, chap. 4; Keith W. Olson, *The G.I. Bill, the Veterans, and the Colleges* (Lexington: University Press of Kentucky, 1974), pp. 10–15.

[37] President's Commission on Veterans' Pensions, *The Historical Development of Veterans' Benefits in the United States* (Washington, D.C.: Government Printing Office, 1956); Ross, *Preparing for Ulysses*, chap. 8; Davies, *Housing Reform*, pp. 41–47, 50–57.

could be completed along the lines envisaged by the Committee on Economic Security or by the NRPB committee.

COUNTERPOINT: WAR AND THE WELFARE STATE IN GREAT BRITAIN

In Britain, wartime planners had much greater success. The NRPB Committee on Long-Range Work and Relief Policies had its British counterpart in William Beveridge. A student of policy and former civil servant who had been involved with British social insurance since its inception, Beveridge was commissioned in June 1941 to study and make recommendations with regard to British social policy. His mandate came from Arthur Greenwood, the minister without portfolio in charge of reconstruction and a member of the coalition government's wartime Cabinet. Beveridge was to work with a committee of civil servants from the ministries involved in social policy. The Beveridge Report, *Social Insurance and Allied Services*, was released in December 1942 to widespread public acclaim. In sharp contrast to the influence of the NRPB's plans in the United States, the Beveridge Report, although it was not immediately adopted by the government, set the tone of comprehensive social policy changes in Britain.

Aside from the Beveridge Report, responsibility for reconstruction planning was at first scattered among the ministries of the wartime coalition government. Notably, the president of the Board of Trade, Hugh Dalton of the Labour party, formed his own reconstruction team. The government as a whole concerned itself with reconstruction in November 1943 when Prime Minister Winston Churchill appointed a minister of reconstruction. The Reconstruction Committee became the key standing committee; its ten members were divided equally among Conservative and Labour ministers. Churchill paid little attention and established the principle that no measures requiring Treasury funds would be passed until after a postwar general election. The compromises of this committee and its many subcommittees were embodied in a series of White Papers, issued in 1944, dealing with social insurance, health, and employment policy.[38] The first of these, *Social Insurance*, was largely consistent with the Beveridge Report.

Like *Security, Work, and Relief Policies*, the Beveridge Report ranged across many realms of social policy. Although the report was couched in visionary rhetoric, Beveridge's main recommendation was merely to

[38] J. M. Lee, *The Churchill Coalition, 1940–1945* (Hamden, Conn.: Archon Books, 1980), pp. 127–38; Ben Pimlott, *Hugh Dalton* (London: Jonathan Cape, 1985), chap. 13. For the view that postwar social policy developments were mainly due to the policies and actions of the coalition government, see Paul Addison, *The Road to 1945* (London: Jonathan Cape, 1975).

reorganize and revamp social insurance, including workmen's compensation. All programs would provide similar flat subsistence benefits and would be financed by equal, flat contributions from employer and employee, with the final third provided by the state, as in the original 1911 social insurance programs. Unlike the NRPB committee, Beveridge did not call for a high level of benefits and was not concerned about the incidence of taxation. He called for the end of the Assistance Board (which administered public assistance) as a separate entity, and expected that the scope of public assistance would be substantially reduced. He wanted all programs to be combined under one social insurance ministry. Finally, the nuts-and-bolts treatment of social insurance was annexed to three sweeping assumptions about postwar social policy: that it would include the introduction of family allowances, the creation of a national health service, and a commitment to maintain full employment.[39]

Beveridge's assumption regarding the creation of a national health service had been foreshadowed by wartime developments. In 1939 the Emergency Medical Service was organized, partly because of fears that bombings would leave large numbers of citizens in need of medical care. Under the emergency program, voluntary and local hospitals provided free treatment for an increasing number of patients, including servicemen, war workers, and those injured in bombing raids. In 1944, the coalition government's White Paper, written under the direction of the Conservative Henry Willink, the minister of health, called for a free national health system financed mainly by the Treasury, but also with a small payroll tax. The system would be administered by the national government and by local authorities, who would retain considerable authority. Voluntary hospitals would be coordinated with the system, but would remain private. Doctors connected to health centers would derive their income from salaries and capitation fees.[40]

After completing his report on social insurance, Beveridge turned to the study of employment policy, but this time the government beat him to the presses. His *Full Employment in a Free Society* was preceded by

---

[39] William Beveridge, *Social Insurance and Allied Services* (New York: Macmillan, 1942). Beveridge did not care that the flat rates of contributions for workers would take a larger proportion of the incomes of poor workers—even without consideration of employer contributions. See José Harris, *William Beveridge: A Biography* (Oxford: Clarendon Press, 1977), chap. 16.

[40] Almont Lindsey, *Socialized Medicine in England and Wales: The National Health Service, 1948–1961* (Chapel Hill: University of North Carolina Press, 1962), pp. 32–39; Roger Eatwell, *The 1945–1951 Labour Governments* (London: Batsford Academic, 1979), pp. 62–63; Henry Pelling, *The Labour Governments, 1945–51* (New York: St. Martin's Press, 1984), pp. 151–64; Derek Fraser, *The Evolution of the British Welfare State* (London: Macmillan, 1973), p. 214.

the 1944 White Paper, entitled *Employment Policy*, which called for the government to accept responsibility for ensuring high and stable employment. For short-run aims, the White Paper drew upon the 1940 Barlow Report, issued before formation of the coalition government. To move new industries to declining areas, the paper proposed to maintain munitions factories in depressed areas. It suggested that licenses, government contracts, and financial assistance be used to achieve this result, and that this industrial policy be coordinated by the Board of Trade.[41] With regard to long-run aims, *Employment Policy* called for the use of Keynesian spending categories to analyze economic trends and the use of public works projects to offset declines in private capital expenditure. The paper also included Keynesian proposals for the use of varying tax rates to regulate contributions for social insurance. In the matter of public works, local authorities were expected to submit five-year plans for public improvements and the national government was to use loans to speed or slow such projects.[42] The White Paper did not propose that the government fund the projects or development of the five-year plans, however. Nor were public employment programs suggested for postwar Britain.

Both American and British planners of social policy in the postwar period devised comprehensive sets of reforms, aiming to fill programmatic gaps, to merge social insurance and relief programs, and to further national economic growth—specifically, to achieve full employment. Yet the emphases of postwar planning efforts in the two nations differed considerably. The American plans dealt mainly with work and relief, and called for the creation of brand new social insurance programs along with the centralized administration of federal unemployment insurance. The British plans concentrated on the rationalization and extension of existing social insurance. The new British proposals for family allowances and for creation of a national health service had nothing to do with unemployment and economic depression, and relief reform seems to have been an afterthought. Moreover, the British plans for preventing postwar unemployment were conspicuously undeveloped compared with the elaborate American proposals for public works and public employment.

The achievements of American and British planners also differed sharply. In the area of social insurance, the Labour government adopted the Beveridge reforms in 1946, revamping old-age insurance, unemployment insurance, disability insurance, and workers' compensation. As to

[41] Ministry of Reconstruction, *Employment Policy* (New York: Macmillan, 1945), pp. 10–15; Kenneth O. Morgan, *Labour in Power, 1945–51* (Oxford: Clarendon Press, 1984), pp. 182–83.

[42] *Employment Policy*, pp. 20–24.

the related area of relief, Beveridge had called for the end of the locally rooted poor law, and in 1948 the Labour government nationalized public assistance. In establishing the new British National Health Service, the government followed the controversial recommendations for universal and free medical care specified in the coalition government's 1944 White Paper—and went beyond them. In 1946, the Labour government passed legislation nationalizing the hospitals, and induced the reluctant medical profession to join the system when the law took effect in 1948.[43]

Unambitious as they were, Britain's wartime plans for a postwar employment policy were also largely carried out. For the short run, the British planned to manipulate industrial policy to direct development to depressed areas. Under the Labour government, however, the use of Keynesian demand management was limited, partly because of Labour's preference for direct industrial controls and partly because of postwar inflation and high employment.[44]

British urban and housing planners achieved what their U.S. counterparts could only dream about. Although the coalition government could not agree on the compulsory purchase of land, the Town and Country Act of 1947 empowered planners to purchase sites for renewal and other projects. There was little coalition government planning with regard to public housing.[45] Yet postwar British housing policy provided for the construction of locally controlled and planned public housing. About 80 percent of the one million permanent housing units built from 1945 to 1951 were publicly owned.[46]

[43] On social insurance, see Pelling, *The Labour Governments*, p. 98; Morgan, *Labour in Power*, p. 143; and Fraser, *British Welfare State*, p. 220. On public assistance legislation, see Pelling, *The Labour Governments*, p. 101; Morgan, *Labour in Power*, p. 173; and Fraser, *British Welfare State*, pp. 212–13. On family allowances, see John Macnicol, *The Movement for Family Allowances, 1918–1945: A Study in Social Policy Development* (London: Heinemann, 1980), chap. 7. On the national health service, see Lindsey, *Socialized Medicine in England and Wales*, pp. 43–46; Pelling, *The Labour Governments*, pp. 102–8; and Morgan, *Labour in Power*, pp. 151–64.

[44] Alan Booth, "The 'Keynesian Revolution' in Economic Policymaking," *Economic History Review* 36 (1983): 103–23; Margaret Gowing, "The Organization of Manpower in Britain during the Second World War," *Journal of Contemporary History* 7 (1972): 147–67; Pimlott, *Hugh Dalton*, chap. 16.

[45] During the war, British urban planners urged that national legislation create sanctions whose effect would be to encourage comprehensive local land-use planning and redevelopment. The Uthwatt Report, which was commissioned by the Minister of Works and Buildings, called for government planning authorities to purchase land for redevelopment sites. The coalition government split over the issue of compulsory purchase of land, however, and did not issue a White Paper on postwar planning. Nor was the question of public housing covered in any White Paper. See J. M. Lee, *The Churchill Coalition*, p. 137, and Funigiello, *The Challenge to Urban Liberalism*, pp. 189–95.

[46] J. B. Cullingworth, *Town and Country Planning in Britain* (London: George Allen and Unwin), pp. 15–23; Pelling, *The Labour Governments*, pp. 110–13; Morgan, *Labour in Power*, pp. 163–70.

BRITISH THEORIES ABOUT WAR AND SOCIAL POLICY

Major reforms of British social policy were planned during World War II and were quickly put into effect after the war; social theory lagged only slightly behind. In 1955 at King's College in London, Richard Titmuss delivered a lecture on "War and Social Policy" in which he outlined a thesis about the positive relationship between modern "total" warfare and the development of the welfare state. Echoing Max Weber's dictum that "the discipline of the army gives birth to all discipline," and pointing out that modern wars rely on conscripts and civilians as well as specialized military castes, Titmuss concluded that "the waging of modern war presupposes and imposes a great increase in social discipline . . . [and] this discipline is tolerable if—and only if—social inequalities are not intolerable."[47] Titmuss also agreed with Arthur Marwick that the impact of modern wars on civilians must be taken into account.[48] The more civilians who are involved in wartime efforts, Titmuss concluded, the greater the equalizing effects achieved by new social policies and reforms of existing ones; the reforms should be universal, benefiting civilians as well as soldiers.

Provocative as Titmuss's arguments are, they constitute only a starting point for analysis, for comparative evidence indicates that the causal links are not as simple as Titmuss suggests. In neither Great Britain nor the United States did the first modern pension and social insurance policies *originate* during or right after the world wars. The Liberal party launched the major British social policies from 1906 to 1911. American progressives failed to gain passage of social insurance legislation before World War I; congressional Democrats gained passage of the Social

[47] Richard M. Titmuss, "War and Social Policy," in *Essays on the "Welfare State"* (Boston: Beacon Press, 1969), p. 85. Titmuss acknowledged that his formulation was similar to Stanislav Andreski's military participation ratio. See Andreski, *Military Organization and Society* (London: Routledge and Kegan Paul, 1954).

[48] Arthur Marwick, *War and Social Change in the Twentieth Century: A Comparative Study of Britain, France, Germany, Russia, and the United States* (New York: Macmillan, 1974). With the emergence of the small war in the second half of the twentieth century, scholars began to perceive a negative relationship between war and social policy. The result was a sort of academic consensus that large or total wars such as World War I and World War II help to strengthen and universalize social policy, whereas small wars and large standing forces tend to fragment social policy and drain resources away from it. For the most explicit statement of this view, see Harold L. Wilensky, *The Welfare State and Equality: Structural and Ideological Roots of Public Expenditures* (Berkeley: University of California Press, 1975), chap. 4. The evidence is sketchy, however. Wilensky's analysis of twenty-two industrialized nations shows that military spending between 1950 and 1952 is negatively correlated with social spending as a percentage of the GNP in 1966. Arthur Stein examines the four wars of the twentieth century in which the United States has participated and finds no evidence to support his hypothesis that mobilization leads to equality by way of social spending. See Stein, *The Nation at War* (Baltimore: Johns Hopkins University Press, 1978), chaps. 3, 7.

Security bill in 1935. An analysis of the *expansion* of social programs and expenditures reveals that in the United States, both world wars culminated in periods of conservative retrenchment and the frustration of virtually all wartime reform hopes for expanded federal social interventions, except those aimed at veterans. In Britain, by contrast, social insurance expanded rapidly right after World War I, to encompass veterans and civilian workers alike,[49] and all social policies were reorganized and extended soon after World War II. Even so, the British experience in that war does not bear out the Titmuss conclusion as to the influence of war on equality. The World War II effort put a premium on the participation and morale of British civilians as well as soldiers and, according to Titmuss's reasoning, should have led to policies funded by a more progressive income tax structure. Instead, the Beveridge reforms relied heavily on a regressive, flat payroll tax to finance the extension of flat benefits.

To give Titmuss his due, the destruction of World War II did affect British *civilians* more than their U.S. counterparts. In the United States there were only brief and false scares about Japanese attacks on the West Coast following Pearl Harbor. But British civilians were bombed by the Nazis; civilian deaths numbered 60,000.[50] This may help to explain the establishment of war-related health programs for British civilians. The Emergency Medical Service covered many civilians along with servicemen, and its formation was the basis of Beveridge's assumption that a national health service would be created.[51] In other policy areas, however, the differential impact of the war on the two civilian populations had little effect on public policy. For instance, the wartime boom in the U.S. domestic economy brought a mass migration of American workers from rural to urban areas and across regions. Had social policies been changed to reflect this situation, they would have included more generous and nationally uniform disability insurance, unemploy-

[49] See Bentley B. Gilbert, *British Social Policy, 1914–1939* (Ithaca, N.Y.: Cornell University Press, 1970), pp. 54–61.

[50] Marwick, *War and Social Change*, p. 155. In other ways, the U.S. and British experiences in World War II were similar. Both nations were winners, and both escaped occupation. In terms of casualties, the two countries did not differ much. The percentage of the British population killed during the war was 0.97; the percentage of Americans was 0.23. The British figure is larger, but much closer to the U.S. percentage than the percentages for Germany (6.42), Poland (9.66), or Yugoslavia (11.14). The British figure is also smaller than those for some other Western European countries, such as the Netherlands (2.44) and Finland (2.34). These data are from John Dryzek and Robert E. Goodin, "Risk-Sharing and Social Justice: The Motivational Foundations of the Post-War Welfare State," *British Journal of Political Science* 16:1–34.

[51] Richard Titmuss, *Problems of Social Policy* (London: His Majesty's Stationery Office, 1950), chaps. 11, 22–24.

ment insurance, and family support measures. But U.S. proposals for such policy changes failed, whereas similar British proposals were more successful, even though the uprooting of British workers was less dramatic.

Another British theory of war and the welfare state is the fiscal argument developed by Alan Peacock and Jack Wiseman.[52] Like Titmuss, these authors posit that wars lead to advances in social policy, but they emphasize a different causal mechanism: increases in the state's fiscal capacities through the "displacement effect." To prosecute a war, their argument goes, the state must raise taxes, and this is easier to do during national emergencies. When the crisis ends, the level of taxation remains higher than before, because the populace has grown accustomed to higher taxes. This situation facilitates new social policy initiatives or expansion of existing programs, for people always want higher public expenditures than they are willing to cover with increased taxes. In short, any crisis that loosens fiscal constraints will quickly lead to increased social expenditures.

Peacock and Wiseman's argument does not explain the differences in the two nations' social policy development. If this fiscal perspective were valid, the United States would have been able to achieve greater advances in social policy more rapidly than did Britain, for the United States benefited economically from the war whereas Britain was decimated. Indeed, Britain was forced to turn to the United States for loans immediately after the war. The United States ended the generous Lend-Lease Program in 1945 but in 1947 began to provide grants to Britain under the Marshall Plan. In effect, the United States helped to finance a series of nationalizing reforms of British social policy, while comparable reforms were rejected at home.[53]

Why did a more dramatic "displacement effect" not occur in the United States? A close look at tax politics and its relation to changes in social policy casts doubt on the applicability of Peacock and Wiseman's reasoning to the U.S. case. Their theory predicts tax increases throughout the war and no large tax cuts after the war. At first, the war did lead to tax increases. To pay for the war, Congress passed the U.S. Revenue Acts of 1941 and 1942, which broadened the base of the personal income tax and thus added 20 million people to the rolls, mainly

[52] Alan T. Peacock and Jack Wiseman, *The Growth of Public Expenditure in the United Kingdom* (Princeton, N.J.: Princeton University Press, 1961).

[53] Morgan, *Labour in Power*, pp. 143–51. On the British tax system during the war, see B.E.V. Sabine, *A History of Income Tax* (London: George Allen and Unwin, 1966), chaps. 12, 13. For a comparison of changes in U.S. and British income taxes during World War II, see Carolyn Webber and Aaron Wildavsky, *A History of Taxation and Expenditure in the Western World* (New York: Simon and Schuster, 1986), pp. 472–76.

by lowering exemptions. The income tax structure was also made more progressive.[54] In addition, these early tax acts established a "victory tax" surcharge and increased the corporate income tax and the excess profits taxes; altogether these revenues met about 45 percent of the costs of the war. All U.S. taxes did not increase throughout the war, however. Notably, previously scheduled increases in the payroll tax for old-age and survivors' insurance were consistently delayed.

The Roosevelt administration failed to gain much support for its tax proposals after 1942. Overriding Roosevelt's veto, Congress passed the Revenue Act of 1944, which yielded much less revenue than Roosevelt had demanded. Soon after the war, Congress passed a $5 billion tax cut that mainly affected the victory and excess profits taxes. In 1948, Congress passed, over Truman's veto, another $5 billion tax cut, this time affecting the personal income tax. It nearly erased an $8.8 billion surplus in fiscal 1948, although the 1941 and 1942 changes in the structure of the personal income tax largely remained on the books.[55] In sum, Peacock and Wiseman's theory is borne out in that the income tax system was strengthened during the war and was not severely weakened afterward, but the increased revenues were not automatically channeled into social spending, and previously scheduled increases in the OASI payroll tax were not made during the war.

Peacock and Wiseman also expect war to promote the permanent centralization of government functions.[56] The postwar fiscal predominance of the U.S. federal government would appear to be consistent with their thesis. In 1939, federal revenues were 7.4 percent of GNP, and state and local revenues were 10.6 percent. In 1946, the tables were turned: federal revenues amounted to 18.7 percent of GNP, and state and local revenues constituted 6.2 percent.[57] But in terms of social policy, centralizing reforms failed; states and localities gained greater control over existing social programs. Moreover, the additional federal revenues brought by wartime tax increases (and not rolled back by postwar tax cuts) were used to fund veterans' benefits and grants-in-aid to states and localities, rather than national social programs covering all citizens. Why are Peacock and Wiseman's expectations incorrect?

[54] The income tax structure was not made as progressive as the Roosevelt administration would have liked, however. See John F. Witte, *The Politics and Development of the Federal Income Tax* (Madison: University of Wisconsin Press, 1985), pp. 114–19.

[55] Ibid., pp. 132–37. See also Roland Young, *Congressional Politics in the Second World War* (New York: Da Capo Press, 1972), pp. 128–30, and Herbert Stein, *The Fiscal Revolution in America* (Chicago: University of Chicago Press, 1969), pp. 206–10.

[56] Peacock and Wiseman, *Public Expenditure in the United Kingdom*, chap. 6. On the centralization of American government in wartime, see A. Stein, *The Nation at War*, pp. 55–63.

[57] *Economic Report of the President, 1980* (Washington, D.C.: U.S. Government Printing Office, 1980), pp. 203, 288.

The war had an ironic effect on the relative fiscal capacities of the various levels of government. In the early New Deal period, the initial impetus toward federal control over relief policy had been the fiscal crisis of the states and localities, both of which had relied heavily on property taxes. When all levels of government were fiscally hurt by the Depression, the federal government gained a relative advantage because of its greater ability to tolerate deficits.[58] During the war, although the absolute and relative size of federal revenues greatly increased, the high employment rate ended the fiscal crises of the states and localities.

In ways not revealed by the highly aggregate approach of Peacock and Wiseman, preexisting U.S. social policies and their associated fiscal instruments discouraged the channeling of wartime federal revenues toward more generous citizen benefits. Overall, because national social programs relying on payroll taxes were not fully developed before the war, it was difficult to expand them through fiscal sleights of hand during and right after the war. An almost politically costless way to extend social insurance programs is to spend the unexpected surpluses in earmarked trust funds. In Britain the prior, long-term existence of payroll taxes that funded a number of national social insurance programs doubtless made it easier for the wartime coalition government to agree on their expansion and rationalization, and to put into effect the concrete proposals of the Beveridge Report beginning in 1944. In the United States, however, unemployment insurance was not nationalized, and there were no national programs for health and disability insurance. Only old-age and survivors' insurance benefited from the fiscal dividends of the increased employment and higher wages brought about by the war. Although Congress rejected scheduled OASI tax increases during the war, by 1949 the program's financial prospects were so favorable that Congress could increase benefits and extend coverage with only a slight increase in the payroll tax (and without projecting any use of general revenues).[59]

In sum, neither the ideas of Titmuss about the impact of war on a population, nor the argument of Peacock and Wiseman about the effects of war mobilization on the state's aggregate fiscal capacities, can explain the differences between American and British development of so-

[58] States now rely primarily on sales and income taxes, not property taxes, which are still the main source of revenue for local governments. See James A. Maxwell and J. Richard Aronson, *Financing State and Local Governments*, 3d ed. (Washington, D.C.: The Brookings Institution, 1977), pp. 18–21; Joseph A. Pechman, *Federal Tax Policy*, 3d ed. (Washington, D.C.: The Brookings Institution, 1977), chap. 9; Henry J. Bitterman, *State and Federal Grants-in-Aid* (New York: Mentzer, Bush, 1938), chap. 1; and I. Bernstein, *The Lean Years*, chap. 7.

[59] Derthick claims that conservative actuarial estimates regarding the OASI program facilitated its expansion throughout the postwar period. See *Policymaking for Social Security*, chap. 17.

cial policy during and after World War II. Such theories, based on what apparently happened in Britain, do not explain why the United States failed to forge a national welfare state despite the renewed solidarities and increases in federal fiscal capacity brought about by the war. In the following section, we explore the impact of specifically political processes on social policy outcomes in the two countries.

EXPLAINING THE IMPACT OF WORLD WAR II ON SOCIAL POLICY IN THE UNITED STATES AND GREAT BRITAIN

Wars are not fought by "the state" in the abstract, but by particular states with different institutional structures, prior policies, and contending political coalitions. Preexisting institutional structures and political coalitions influence the choices national leaders make about how to plan for the postwar period and how to mobilize the nation for war. The exigencies of war and the mode of mobilization reinforce some political forces and undermine others, in part by changing the agenda of problems discussed by the nation's politicians and in part by changing the goals and capacities of politically active groups.

Taking this approach, we compare the impact of World War II on social policy plans and outcomes in the United States and in Great Britain. First, we examine the effects of prior social policies on the content of new policy proposals and on the ability of planners to translate them into proposed legislation during the war. Next, we analyze the different strategies used to mobilize the people and the economies for war. The modes of mobilization in Britain and the United States influenced social policy agendas, support for political parties, and possibilities for extending wartime controls into postwar reforms. Finally, we discuss political coalitions and the role of industrial labor in them during and right after the war, examining how mobilization strengthened the position of those advocating certain policy alternatives and weakened the position of others at critical moments.

The comparisons in this section clarify why World War II affected social policy outcomes differently in the United States and in Britain. In brief, the administrative and political forces strengthened by America's participation in World War II worked against the extension and nationalization of many social policies and their coordination with planning to achieve full employment. The national role in the formulation and administration of social policy began to expand during the New Deal but was redefined during the 1940s. Thereafter the trend was away from public assistance and employment programs, and toward national social provision primarily for veterans and the elderly.

PRIOR SOCIAL POLICIES AND WARTIME PLANNING

As has been noted, sweeping social policy reforms were proposed in both Britain and the United States. The heightened sense of public purpose in wartime encouraged national planning, and the projections of Beveridge and the NRPB were released within a few months of one another, in December 1942 and March 1943. Yet the central emphases of the Beveridge Report and the NRPB's *Security, Work, and Relief Policies* differed considerably. The latter called for the use of progressive general revenues to improve public employment, public assistance, and public works, as well as for nationalized and more generous unemployment insurance; the former recommended rationalizing social insurance and establishing family allowances and a national health service. The plans fared differently in the two countries. The characteristics of the British reform plan helped it to gain a favorable public and administrative reception. By contrast, the NRPB proposals seemed irrelevant to American problems after 1942, and fell prey to bureaucratic rivalries within the executive branch.

American planners relied more heavily than the British on Depression era tools to fight unemployment and this difference of approach reflected overall differences in the prior social policies of the two countries. The U.S. policies were of more recent origin; most nationwide social policies had been created in the 1930s. British social policies had been in existence since the 1910s and 1920s. Moreover, the two nations had previously coped in contrasting ways with economic crisis, including mass unemployment. During the 1920s and 1930s, the British government had avoided public works and jobs programs and had provided relief to the unemployed through extensions of social insurance programs that had always been financed by contributions from general public revenues as well as payroll taxes. The United States government, however, stressed emergency public relief and employment programs to help the unemployed during the Depression, and kept its new contributory social insurance programs separately based on payroll taxes without immediate contributions from general revenues.

When they turned to postwar planning, British and American reformers built on what they considered the best of their respective systems. The Beveridge Report did not include public works or employment programs, leaving for later consideration what appeared to be less pressing questions about full employment. Because the British had long experience with nationally organized social insurance, Beveridge could assess the previous performance of various programs and suggest what appeared to be adjustments, extensions, and rationalizations of existing social insurance policies, accomplished by tripartite financing.[60] The Committee on Long-Range Work and Relief Policies, however, considered all New Deal programs experimental and held no financing technique sacred. It saw no major distinction between supposedly emergency programs such as the WPA and the supposedly permanent programs of the Social Security Act.[61] Moreover, in the late 1930s and early 1940s, providing adequate benefits to the needy and work for the unemployed seemed more important than preserving and extending strict contributory financing by imposing taxes on employers and employees. Unlike British reformers, who had experienced the 1930s as a period of conservative muddling through, New Deal planners hoped to use the wartime period to realize their aims by adding new programs and nationalizing old ones, mainly along the lines projected by the 1934–35 Committee on Economic Security.

But the impact of wartime realities on the projections of the planners shattered the hopes only of the Americans. Although the unemployment crisis of the Depression came to an end in both countries, the wartime surge of full employment had different effects on their plans for postwar social policies. In Britain, social insurance, the central concern of the Beveridge Report, remained important throughout the war, and this helped to overcome the initial reluctance of the coalition government to enact its provisions.[62] Because the American plans for social policy reform were grounded in late-1930s thinking, they were soon undercut by the skyrocketing wartime employment rates, which minimized the importance of the employment and relief programs stressed by the NRPB committee. Probably for these reasons, a lack of enthusiasm for *Security, Work, and Relief Policies* was registered in public opinion polls taken soon after its release in early 1943. Surveys found that 76 percent of the public approved of the principles in the report, but 58 percent thought its proposals would not affect them personally.[63]

---

[60] Fraser, *British Welfare State*, pp. 185–97; B. Gilbert, *British Social Policy*, pp. 180–92.

[61] Warken, *National Resources Planning Board*, p. 229.

[62] The coalition government supported the Beveridge reforms only in principle. In February 1943, when the House of Commons began to consider the report, 121 Labour backbenchers supported an amendment calling for immediate implementation of the plan, the first time since formation of the coalition that Labour had taken issue with the coalition government. See Henry Pelling, *Britain and the Second World War* (Glasgow: Collins, 1970), pp. 168–73.

[63] A week after *Security* was transmitted to Congress, 58 percent of a random sample of the public had heard of the plan. Only 34 percent felt that it would help them personally. See Jerome Bruner, *Mandate from the People* (New York: Duell, Sloan and Pierce, 1944), chap. 8. The lack of enthusiasm was not due to the committee's rejection of conventional social insurance. According to survey data compiled by Michael E. Schiltz, public approval ratings of old-age insurance and old-age pensions in the middle 1930s were similar; ratings for old-

In other ways, British and American experiences with preexisting social policies helped Beveridge's proposals and hurt the NRPB's plans. The British plan employed visionary rhetoric, yet what was envisioned did not differ significantly from existing administrative and fiscal arrangements. The American plans were comprehensive and visionary only because they did not build upon and elaborate the undeveloped fiscal and administrative arrangements specified by existing U.S. social policies, with the exception of those pertaining to employment. Although ultimately answerable to himself, Beveridge met with an interdepartmental committee of administrators familiar with the details of each area of social policy, and his report coincided sufficiently with their views to make its proposals seem practicable to the British government.[64] In contrast, the NRPB committee was heavily weighted with academicians and leaders in the field of social work. Because there was less long-term administrative experience to draw upon in formulating social policy, U.S. planners had no solid base within the executive branch, and their proposals were vulnerable to bureaucratic rivalries.

One rivalry was with the newly established Social Security Board (SSB). The thinking of the NRPB Committee on Long-Range Work and Relief Policies partially clashed with the postwar plans of the SSB, the agency established in 1935 to administer the Social Security Act's provisions. This disagreement led to a battle over proposed legislation. Although the SSB and the NRPB committee shared many goals, including permanent nationalization of the United States Employment Service and unemployment insurance and the creation of disability and health insurance, the SSB's reception of *Security, Work, and Relief Policies* was lukewarm. A firm supporter of contributory insurance based on payroll taxes, the SSB objected to the NRPB committee's criticism of payroll taxes and its attempts to uncouple benefits from contributions. The SSB was not opposed to some contribution to social insurance from general revenues, but it wanted payroll taxes to provide most of the funding, and considered the adequacy of benefits strictly a secondary goal. Although the SSB was in favor of a new federal grant-in-aid as a form of general assistance to the states, it could not agree to the extension and

---

age pensions were perhaps higher. For instance, 89 percent of respondents approved pensions for the needy (December 1935), whereas polls of different samples revealed that 68 percent (September and November 1936) and 77 percent (January 1937) approved of old-age insurance. In 1941, 93 percent approved of old-age pensions; in 1943, 97 percent approved of old-age insurance. See Schiltz, *Public Attitudes toward Social Security, 1933–1965* (Washington, D.C.: Government Printing Office, 1970), p. 36.

[64] José Harris, "Some Aspects of Social Policy in Britain during the Second World War," in W. J. Mommsen, ed., *The Emergence of the Welfare State in Great Britain and Germany* (London: Croom Helm, 1981), pp. 247–62.

partial nationalization of general assistance, for this might transform
the aid into a sort of guaranteed income, displacing contributory social
insurance.[65] If results are judged in terms of legislation passed in the
mid-1940s, neither the SSB nor the NRPB committee realized anything
close to their policy goals. But in terms of proposed legislation the SSB
outmaneuvered the committee; the Wagner-Murray-Dingell bills called
for large payroll tax increases, to be channeled into a single trust fund.

The National Resources Planning Board also had to contend with the
Veterans Administration, another autonomous organization in the federal bureaucracy with authority over matters central to postwar social
policy. The NRPB got what it wanted only insofar as its ideas did not
conflict with VA-supported programs for veterans. After the NRPB organized the Postwar Manpower Conference, it achieved some of its
goals through the GI bill: veterans received readjustment allowances,
improved unemployment benefits, and educational subsidies, rather
than bonuses. But in matters such as health insurance and disability
programs, the jealous control maintained by the VA over national programs for veterans prevented the NRPB from realizing its vision of national programs for all citizens, even in areas where the SSB favored the
NRPB's ideas.[66] In Britain, the increase in the number of World War II
veterans who were covered by existing national health programs increased the possibility that a comprehensive national health service
would be established.

To summarize, in wartime Britain, Beveridge presented a vision of
welfare state reforms grounded in previously well developed social insurance measures. In the United States, NRPB planners did not have
well-developed social policies upon which to build, and, in the spirit of
1930s reformism, they tried to expand the New Deal employment and

[65] The debate between Eveline M. Burns and Edwin E. Witte over the future of social
security reflects the debate between the NRPB and the SSB. See Burns, "Social Insurance in
Evolution," *American Economic Review* 34, no. 1 (supplement): 199–211; Witte, "What to
Expect of Social Security," *American Economic Review* 34, no. 1 (supplement): 212–21. See
also Edwin E. Witte, "American Post-War Social Security Proposals," *American Economic
Review* 33 (December 1943): 825–38. For the views of the SSB and of people associated
with it, see Arthur Altmeyer, "War and Post-War Problems," in Wilbert Cohen, ed., *War
and Post-War Social Security: The Outlines of an Expanded Program* (Washington,
D.C.: American Council on Public Affairs, 1942), pp. 20–30; Arthur Altmeyer, "Desirability of Expanding the Social Insurance Program Now," *Social Security
Bulletin* 5, no. 11 (November, 1942): 5–9; and George E. Bigge, "Social Security and Post-
War Planning," *Social Security Bulletin* 5, no. 12 (December 1942):4–10. For the SSB's view
of Committee, *Security*, see "Social Security in Review," *Social Security Bulletin* 6, no. 3
(March 1943):1–2.

[66] On the operation of the separate veterans' social policy system, see Sar A. Levitan and
Karen A. Cleary, *Old Wars Remain Unfinished: The Veteran Benefits System* (Baltimore:
Johns Hopkins University Press, 1973).

public assistance programs during the wartime employment boom. Inside the executive branch, the Social Security Board and the Veterans Administration promoted their visions of social policy at the expense of key NRPB plans. In contrast to the Beveridge Report, the NRPB's *Security, Work, and Relief Policies* had neither public enthusiasm nor bureaucratic backing.

STATE CAPACITIES, POLITICAL SYSTEMS, AND NATIONAL MOBILIZATION FOR WAR

During World War II, the United States and British governments had to mobilize people and economies. Yet the mobilization effort was managed quite differently in the two nations, in part because of their different political systems and state structures. The British government was run politically by a formal coalition, and the imposition of strong controls over the wartime economy was facilitated by the greater capacities of the British state. In the United States, the wartime political coalition was informal, and federal control over the economy was weak. As we show in this section, these differences in mobilization help to explain why the postwar expansion of social policies was accomplished more easily in Britain than in the United States.

The British parliamentary system of government allows the creation of formal governing coalitions, and a Conservative-dominated bipartisan directed British participation in the war. The formalization of a bipartisan coalition opened the Conservatives to reforming influences. Labour party leaders were brought into the wartime Cabinet and, more important, were placed in key ministerial positions. Arthur Greenwood commissioned the Beveridge Report in his capacity as minister without portfolio; trade union leader Ernest Bevin was given responsibility for the Ministry of Labour and Hugh Dalton was put in charge of the Board of Trade. Throughout the war, these ministers were able to use their positions to advance reform. Equally important, formalization of the coalition promoted the explicit agreement concerning postwar health and social insurance reforms embodied in the White Papers of 1944.[67]

The British coalition government imposed comprehensive public controls that were administered by the permanent ministries of the long established national civil service. Soon after its inauguration in May 1940, the British coalition government obtained passage of the Emergency Powers Act, which required conscription of property, control of labor, and rationing of food. Every year the controls were extended,

[67] J. M. Lee, *The Churchill Coalition*, chap. 5.

and in 1944 the Conservative and Labour parties agreed to continue them for two years after the war. Moreover, the relative importance of British ministries changed during the war. The Ministry of Labour, which was historically identified with social policy improvements, played an important role in British war mobilization.[68] The use of manpower budgeting had come into its own by 1943, allowing the role of the Ministry of Labour to eclipse that of the Treasury, with its long history of thwarting social reforms.[69] For British social policy making, there were direct advantages to be gained from the strong role the government played in war mobilization. The wartime controls were crucial to the establishment of planning for industrial location and housing, and the continuation of controls into the postwar period allowed the Labour party to follow the wartime reforms in planning and employment with vigorous new programs for public housing and industrial location.[70]

In contrast to the British parliamentary system, the U.S. governmental system ensured that wartime cooperation between the Republicans and Democrats would be merely informal. President Roosevelt named Henry Stimson secretary of war and appointed many Republican-leaning businessmen, or at least businessmen acceptable to Republicans, to the planning bureaus in charge of wartime production. But Roosevelt received no explicit promise of support in return; Republicans remained free to attack the administration whenever there was an opportunity. The same was true of Southern Democrats, who generally supported the president on war matters, but not on the continuation of New Deal programs or social initiatives.[71]

The fact that U.S. wartime bipartisanship was tacit and limited to immediate war issues helped, in the course of the war, to undermine Roosevelt's base of power in Congress. Partisan electoral politics could not and did not cease in the United States, whereas British elections were suspended. In both countries, the unpopularity of various aspects of the war reflected on the party in power. Thus public support for the British Conservatives was low at the time of the 1942 U.S. elections,

---

[68] W. K. Hancock and M. M. Gowing, *British War Economy* (London: His Majesty's Stationery Office, 1949). On the role of the Treasury, see Henry Roseveare, *The Treasury: The Evolution of a British Institution* (New York: Columbia University Press, 1969); Robert Skidelsky, "Keynes and the Treasury View: The Case For and Against an Active Employment Policy," in Mommsen, ed., *Emergence of the Welfare State*, pp. 167–87, and James E. Cronin, "The Resistance to State Expansion in Twentieth Century Britain," Center for the Study of Industrial Societies Occasional Paper no. 24 (Chicago: University of Chicago, 1986).

[69] Gowing, "Organization of Manpower in Britain," p. 155.

[70] On British housing and planning policies, see note 46 to this paper.

[71] V. O. Key, *Southern Politics in State and Nation* (New York: Knopf, 1949), chaps. 16, 17.

and the Conservatives lost a few by-elections in the first half of 1942. In June 1943, about one-half year *after* the war had started to go in the Allies' favor, a Gallup poll found that if British elections were held, 38 percent would vote for the Labour party as opposed to 31 percent for the Conservatives.[72] But the British did not hold midwar elections. In the United States the electorate had a chance to act on its grievances. Congressional elections came as usual in November 1942—soon after Allied armed forces had suffered loss after loss in the Pacific theater, and after Americans at home had been covered by a crazy quilt of controls. The U.S. electoral result was about twice as bad for the presidential party as that of the typical off-year election; the Democrats lost 50 seats in the House. Because almost all of the losses were non-Southern Democrats, the midwar election weakened the reform element of the Democratic party, and at a crucial point.[73]

In the United States, the existence of a nonparliamentary system and the division of sovereignty within the federal government also hurt the prospects for enacting social policy reforms. Policy struggles between Democrats and Republicans took place both outside and inside Congress. When Roosevelt put the New Deal on the back burner so that he would have a freer hand to run the war, struggles over social policy did not end. Instead, liberals in Congress, not in the administration, took the initiative and constructed their own postwar reform plans, with the help of appropriate administrative agencies. For instance, the Wagner-Murray-Dingell bills were influenced by the Social Security Board, and Senator James Murray relied on the Bureau of the Budget in formulating the 1945 Full Employment bill. Congressmen working with the Veterans Administration and military agencies were key proponents of veterans' legislation. Despite such liberal initiatives, however, U.S. social policy initiatives could progress no further than Congress would move them.

This situation resulted in the removal of many administration proposals from the postwar social policy agenda. After the 1942 elections, the conservatives in Congress were strong enough to roll back the New Deal, first by eliminating public employment agencies. By 1943, moreover, Congress had claimed the initiative in questions of reconstruction;

[72] Paul Addison, "By-Elections of the Second World War," in Chris Cook and John Ramsden, eds., *By-Elections in British Politics* (London: Macmillan, 1973), pp. 165–90; *The Gallup Poll in Britain, 1935–1951*, p. 73.

[73] Hadley Cantril and John Harding, "The 1942 Elections: A Case Study in Political Psychology." The authors argue that the Democratic loss can be explained by a low Democratic voter turnout. They suggest that the reason for their political indifference is that these voters had grown more comfortable as a result of high war employment, but they were also apathetic because of the lackluster running of the war.

it made postwar planning the province of congressional committees and abolished executive planning agencies, including the NRPB. Congressional planning committees were so weighted by conservatives that a Republican, Robert Taft, was named to head one key Senate subcommittee.[74] Accordingly, by the time Harry Truman became president in April 1945, Congress had already reached unfavorable decisions on several questions important to the liberal social policy planners of the late New Deal and early war periods.

In the United States, the weakness of most federal controls over the wartime economy made it likely that controls would not be converted into postwar reforms. As in Britain, economic mobilization for war meant centralization, but in the United States centralization was accomplished mainly by temporary bureaucratic agencies intended to coordinate the activities of industries and government, or to coordinate federal activities with those of the state and local governments. Roosevelt relied heavily on businessmen to staff these emergency agencies, partly because the U.S. state lacked sufficient administrative capacities and partly because he wished to avoid re-creating the political divisions of the late 1930s. Military agencies retained control over much of the weapons procurement process and over the flow of some key materials.

At the apex of the U.S. war-time government, several oversight agencies were created within the Office of Emergency Management, a temporary division of the Executive Office of the President. Notably, however, the National Resources Planning Board was kept out of the war mobilization effort, as was the Bureau of the Budget. Had the NRPB been involved it would have at least outlived the war and might have been in a better position to gain support for some postwar social policy reforms.[75] In short, the Roosevelt administration never achieved the degree of control over the wartime economy that the British coalition government did. In the United States, direct controls were imposed on profits, prices, and raw materials; secondary controls were placed on wages; but there was almost no control over costs.[76] And the administration had no instrumentalities such as a national service or manpower controls by which to manage industrial labor.

Because, politically and administratively, Britain and the United

[74] Young, *Congressional Politics in the Second World War*, chap. 8.

[75] On the reform potential of U.S. wartime controls, see Brody, "The New Deal and the Second World War"; Herman Miles Somers, *Presidential Agency: OWMR, the Office of War Mobilization and Reconversion* (New York: Greenwood Press, 1950), pp. 76–80; and Edward Berkowitz and Kim McQuaid, *Creating the Welfare State: The Political Economy of Twentieth-Century Reform* (New York: Praeger, 1980), chap. 7.

[76] See John Morton Blum, *V Was for Victory* (San Diego: Harcourt Brace Jovanovich, 1976), chap. 4; Vatter, *The U.S. Economy in World War II*, chap. 4.

States managed their mobilization effort in different ways, plans for postwar social policy improvements were formulated throughout the war in Britain and protected from backlashes, whereas in America they were not. Although the British Conservatives did not agree to many left-wing positions on postwar social policies, the makeup of the coalition and the British approach to economic mobilization ensured that some agreements would be reached and that some plans could be put "on hold" for possible postwar enactment. Furthermore, the continuation of strong governmental controls into the postwar period facilitated a number of British reforms.

In the United States, however, there were few such controls to continue, and the informality of the wartime coalition hurt liberal Democrats. War spurred visionary social planning in America, but the political system allowed no bureaucratic continuity for, or moratorium on, the social policy plans that had been devised early in the war. After the effective authority in postwar planning was appropriated by Congress, congressional liberals incorporated only a few aspects of the plans, in watered-down forms, in their legislative proposals. This ensured that many ideas of the NRPB would not survive the war in their original form, if they survived at all.

But even the ability of plans to survive the war and the existence of strong wartime controls would not have been enough to bring about post-war reforms. After all, the federal government had managed to nationalize the employment service during the war, yet was forced to return control to the states afterward. In addition to the conditions discussed in this section, social policy changes in the United States depended on the congressional coalitions that could be constructed to pass or obstruct bills. By influencing such coalitions, as some theories of the welfare state suggest, industrial labor and its champions could significantly affect social policy innovations. What, specifically, was the role of the American labor movement in the wartime and postwar struggles over social policies?

LABOR, POLITICAL COALITIONS, AND SOCIAL POLICIES

In the social science literature on modern welfare states, theories about how industrial labor can influence social policy are of two general types.[77] According to arguments in the first category, if labor has a strong or increasingly strong societal presence in relation to capital—as

[77] For a discussion of these two approaches, see Francis G. Castles, *The Working Class and Welfare: Reflections on the Political Development of the Welfare State in Australia and New Zealand, 1890–1980* (Wellington: Allen and Unwin, 1985).

evidenced by the growth of unions or the launching of strikes, for instance—whatever party happens to be in power must take this strength into account and respond with prolabor social policies. According to the second type of argument, social policy innovations are likely only when a political party that represents or is allied with the labor movement is in a position to rule. We find that the relevant experiences of the United States and Britain during World War II do not entirely support either argument. Rather, the different modes of wartime mobilization determined the influence of social groups and political coalitions on social policy.

To some extent, what happened in America compared with what happened in Britain was inconsistent with the first argument, which stresses labor organization and strikes. The organized labor movements in Britain and the United States were growing at similar paces, but labor's organizational power was increasing more rapidly in the United States. Union density, or the percentage of the labor force belonging to unions, increased by 49.4 percent between 1939 and 1946 in the United States, while in Britain the growth was 36.1 percent.[78] As far as strikes are concerned, from 1939 to 1945 American labor was on the offensive much more than British labor. The volume of strikes—the average number of man-days lost (times 1,000) as a percentage of the labor force—was almost three times as large in the United States as in Britain.[79]

More important than organizational gains or collective action was how American and British labor were incorporated into wartime mobilization effort and the politically structured compromises between capital and labor. American labor was not as influential in the mobilization effort as British labor, and the way American labor was incorporated into the wartime administrative machinery worked against attempts at social reform. Strikes in the United States were provoked by weak wartime controls, and U.S. strike activity worked against the possibility of

[78] In the United States, union density increased from 15.8 percent in 1939 to 21.9 percent in 1945 to 23.6 percent in 1946. In Great Britain, union density increased from 31.6 percent in 1939 to 38.6 percent in 1945 to 43.0 percent in 1946. The data for the United States are from *Historical Statistics*, p. 178. The data for Britain are from James E. Cronin, *Labour and Society in Britain, 1918–1979* (New York: Schocken Books, 1984), pp. 241–42.

[79] In the years 1939 to 1945, the strike volume in the United States was 261.5. In Great Britain the strike volume in the same period was 93.7. In 1946, the strike volume in the United States was 1901.8, compared with 105.4 in Britain. Calculated from data in *Historical Statistics*, pp. 178–79, and Cronin, *Labour and Society in Britain*, pp. 241–42. On the influence of the postwar strike wave in the United States on antilabor legislation, see R. Alton Lee, *Truman and Taft-Hartley: A Question of Mandate* (Lexington: University of Kentucky Press, 1966), and Arthur F. McClure, *The Truman Administration and the Problems of Post-War Labor, 1945–1948* (Cranbury, N.J.: Associated University Press, 1969).

passing social policy legislation. Democratic administrations were forced to turn their attention to the management of labor unrest. Wartime strikes tended to decrease public support for labor and to harm chances for the passage of social policy legislation.

Government controls over labor were strong in Britain, but they were administered by a friendly leadership. Ernest Bevin, the leader of Britain's major trade union and an official of the Labour party, was made minister of labour in 1940 and added the national service to his portfolio. He strove to treat servicemen and war workers equally and had the power to direct labor. In 1941, Bevin froze the number of workers in war-related jobs (but only if he found their wages and working conditions to be satisfactory) and established worker and management production boards. He allowed collective bargaining to continue and relied on the moderation of demands for increases in wages rather than an incomes policy.[80]

In contrast, American organized labor had little say as to the administration of war production. Although labor was well represented on the Office of Production Management (OPM), which was established in January 1941 and was the first of many such coordinating bodies, the OPM did not create the sort of management-labor production committees prevalent in Britain. Moreover, labor was not well represented on the OPM's successor, the War Production Board (established in January 1942), which was dominated by businessmen. To some extent, organized labor was consulted on manpower questions. The War Manpower Commission was in charge of manpower mobilization, and representatives of organized labor and business and farm associations formed the Management-Labor Policy Committee to advise it. The management and labor representatives joined forces to help defeat the selective service legislation supported by the president, however.[81]

In the United States, the compromise between capital and labor on unionization and wages was less favorable to labor than that reached in Britain. After Pearl Harbor, organized labor gave Roosevelt a no-strike pledge. The National War Labor Board (NWLB) was established in January 1942 to aid in the settling of industrial disputes. It included four labor representatives, four industry representatives and four persons presumed to represent the public. The key compromise called for organized labor to receive "maintenance of membership" guarantees (unionized workers had to remain in unions or forfeit their jobs) in return for

[80] Alan Bullock, *The Life and Times of Ernest Bevin*, vol. 2, *Minister of Labour, 1940–1945* (London: Heinemann, 1967); Gowing, "Organization of Manpower in Britain," pp. 160–66.

[81] Mathew Josephson, *Sidney Hillman: Statesman of American Labor* (Garden City, N.Y.: Doubleday, 1952); Brody, "New Deal and the Second World War."

wage restraint. According to the so-called Little Steel formula, workers were allowed 15 percent cost-of-living raises. Roosevelt's hold-the-line order, issued in April 1943, prevented wage increases beyond this level. On wages and unionization, capital and labor did not agree; these decisions were made by the public members, who sided with capital on wages and with labor on maintenance of membership. This quasi-corporatism did not extend to other realms, such as social policy, because the NWLB had little authority beyond the mediation of industrial disputes. To the extent that the wage freeze had an effect on social policy issues, it encouraged agreements on private fringe benefits for workers in a favorable bargaining position.[82]

Federal labor policies also encouraged disputes—and the strikes helped to undermine the chances that Congress would accept social policy proposals. For instance, organized labor sponsored the Wagner-Murray-Dingell bills of 1943 and 1945, but, as mentioned, wartime strikes turned the attention of Congress away from social policy to anti-labor legislation. Large-scale strike activity took place after the 1943 hold-the-line order; and again after the war when the no-strike pledge was no longer in effect.[83] Congress passed, over Roosevelt's veto, the antistrike Smith-Connally bill in June 1943, after strikes had begun in the coal mining industry. The strike wave that began at the end of 1945 provoked Truman to propose antistrike legislation and led Congress to pass, over Truman's veto, the 1947 Taft-Hartley bill limiting the power of the 1935 National Labor Relations Act.

With respect to the second theoretical argument, about how labor can influence social policy, which focuses on the importance of the rule of parties allied to labor, we find that war and the mobilization for war mediated the effect on social policy of dominant political parties supported by labor. According to this view, the political makeup of the U.S. wartime government should have led to greater gains in social policy than were achieved in Britain. In America, a reformist Democrat occupied the presidency and enjoyed a Democratic majority in Congress. The British wartime coalition government was voluntary on the part of the dominant Conservatives; when Britain entered the war, the Conservatives had a more than 200-vote margin in the House of Commons. The British partnership furthered the possibility of successful social policy reform during the war, however.

[82] Joel Seidman, *American Labor from Defense to Reconversion* (Chicago: University of Chicago Press, 1953), chaps. 6–7.

[83] For a summary of arguments concerning the positive effect of strikes and civil unrest on social policy and cross-national evidence that opposes these arguments with respect to the quality of old-age pensions, see John Myles, *Old Age in the Welfare State: The Political Economy of Public Pensions* (Boston: Little, Brown, 1984), pp. 89–91, 96.

The prospects of the British Labour party were not adversely affected by the wartime predominance of the Conservatives and the agreement to postpone elections, because of the influence over social policy that wartime coalitions tend to give to the minority partner. The preoccupation of the dominant party with war and world issues means that its leaders pay less attention to domestic concerns. In the United States, "Dr. New Deal" became "Dr. Win the War," as Roosevelt's post-1939 administrations put social policy aside. Similarly, Churchill, who was minister of defense as well as prime minister, was chiefly concerned with the war and left reconstruction questions to others. The British Standing Committee on Reconstruction and its subcommittees were much more heavily weighted toward Labour than either the party's parliamentary delegation or its ministerial representation.[84] They could make and officially protect plans for the postwar period.

During the immediate postwar period in Britain, the direct rule of a party directly allied with organized labor proved important. The Labour party's 1945 victory (a majority of 146) ensured that legislation resembling all of the coalition government's White Papers on social policy would pass. Yet, to some extent this was also constraining, for the Labour government was forced to accept the fairly conservative Beveridge plan. If it had considered social policies on its own, the postwar Labour government might have opted for a progressive tax system, such as the one it chose for the creation of the National Health Service. The Labour victory ensured continuation of the National Health Service, and it also won the day for advocates of local planning. The 1945 election may have doomed Keynesian full employment planning, however, for Labour had a wholehearted commitment to the direct controls used during the war and an indifferent commitment to Keynesianism. These controls could influence the location of new industry, but they were no basis for achieving full employment in the long run.

In the United States, throughout the war and into the postwar period, Democrats, including reformist presidents, were reelected. But even though the Democratic party was heavily subsidized by organized labor in the electoral campaigns of 1940, 1944, and 1948, the Democrats were not a functional equivalent of the Labour party. To achieve a balance that would be even close to the Labour majority of 1945, Americans would have had to elect a left-wing Democratic president and a majority of *urban* Democrats to Congress.[85] In the 1940s, there was a

[84] A.J.P. Taylor, "1932–1945," in David Butler, ed., *Coalitions in British Politics* (New York: St. Martin's Press, 1978), pp. 74–94; J. M. Lee, *The Churchill Coalition, chap. 5.*

[85] For an analysis of organized labor's influence on U.S. farm policy in which urban Democrats are seen as the allies of labor, see Karen Orren, "Union Politics and Postwar Liberalism in the United States, 1946–1979," in Karen Orren and Stephen Skowronek, eds.,

split between urban and rural constituencies and between Republicans and Democrats over prolabor social policies. Congressional Republicans and rural Democrats were especially opposed to policies advocating centralized controls, such as presented in the NRPB proposals and the liberal bills based partly on them. Democrats won the 1944 election and won again in 1948, but in neither case was there sufficient liberal strength in Congress to legislate general social reform.

The main problem was that the House, which was weighted in favor of rural areas, killed almost all of the reform bills that survived consideration by the Senate. Although Roosevelt's reelection in 1944 brought with it a 52-seat Democratic majority in the House, it was not close to the 106-seat majority he had brought with him after his reelection in 1940, or even to the 97-seat majority returned in the 1938 congressional elections, which were considered a disaster for the Democrats.[86] Truman picked up 74 seats in the House when he was elected in 1948. This victory gave him a 91-vote majority overall, a margin comparable to Roosevelt's in 1938. Moreover, in every House throughout the 1940s, 105 Democrats came from the former states of the Confederacy, whose representatives had always tended to oppose national standards and centralized social policies. To achieve the kind of majority that the Labour party received in 1945, the Democrats needed to win almost all of the House districts dominated by urbanites or labor, for, in the 1940s, there were fewer than 240 of these. The Democrats did not even come close to succeeding.[87]

Even had the House had a majority of urban Democrats in 1944, not all the proposals of the New Deal planners would have been enacted, because many of their recommendations had been removed from the political agenda by then. Had there been such a majority, the second Wagner-Murray-Dingell bill would have passed, giving America a comprehensive system of social insurance financed by payroll taxes. All of the improvements in public assistance and the financing changes for social insurance envisaged by the Committee on Long-Range Work and Relief Policies still would not have been achieved, however. Although the Full Employment bill of 1945 would also have been passed, it seems

---

Studies in American Political Development, vol. 1 (New Haven, Conn.: Yale University Press, 1986), pp. 215–52.

[86] On the decline of congressional support for the New Deal reforms, see David L. Porter, *Congress and the Waning of the New Deal* (Port Washington, N.Y.: Kennikat Press, 1980), and James T. Patterson, *Congressional Conservatism and the New Deal: The Growth of the Conservative Coalition in Congress, 1933–1939* (Lexington: University Press of Kentucky, 1967).

[87] David R. Mayhew, *Party Loyalty among Congressmen: The Difference between Democrats and Republicans, 1947–1962* (Cambridge: Harvard University Press), chap. 1; Key, *Southern Politics.*

unlikely that Congress would have reestablished the NRPB or the WPA, both necessary to the committee's plans, unless there were double-digit unemployment. Moreover, after 1944 no one could have demanded the return of benefits already voted for veterans.

The American system of political representation and the composition of political coalitions after the end of the New Deal thus made it difficult for post-1942 Democratic victories to be translated into majorities that would demand new social benefits, except those aimed at veterans. Conservative coalitions that opposed other strong federal measures collapsed on the issue of generosity toward veterans. Conservatives were mollified by the fact that the Veterans Administration would administer the programs, and they could not resist veterans' lobbying groups, especially the American Legion, which was locally organized throughout the nation and actively appealed to wartime sentiments favoring soldiers.[88]

The narrow margin of the Democratic victory in 1948 meant that President Truman could obtain passage of only part of what was left of the wartime social policy agenda. By then, many issues had receded from prominence. Truman could have gained passage of the new health and disability insurance measures only if there had been a larger urban-liberal majority in Congress. In the end he could get only small funding for public housing, without national controls, and accompanied by measures that appealed to private home builders. The period did bring one successful nationalizing reform of social insurance: the revamping of OASI to include more contributors and beneficiaries. This change, however, was an improvement of an already existing program championed by the Social Security Board. To these reforms, Congress attached a new grant-in-aid for public assistance to the permanently disabled; this legislation contradicted wartime proposals to include benefits for the disabled in social insurance.[89]

In sum, the different positions of labor in Britain and the United States during and right after the war resulted in different governmental approaches to social policy making. In most cases, however, the results were not those predicted by the two most prevalent theories about the influence of labor on social policy. American labor was organizing at a more rapid pace and was more militant during the war than was British labor. Nevertheless, the way labor was incorporated into wartime mobilization was more important. The U.S. government's weak controls provoked labor militancy, and this militancy undercut the support of labor in American public opinion and made more likely the defeat of social policy legislation supported by labor.

[88] Ross, *Preparing for Ulysses*, pp. 283–86.
[89] Cohen and Myers, "Social Security Act Amendments of 1950."

The American wartime political coalition was dominated by a reform Democrat and the British coalition was dominated by Conservatives. Yet the war ensured that these partisan configurations would have an effect on social policy different from that predicted by existing theories. In Britain, the minority coalition partner had a stronger influence on social policy, for questions of postwar reconstruction were decided in executive committees weighted to the advantage of the Labour party. In 1945, a strong Labour government inherited these plans and put them into effect, creating the British welfare state. Postwar American elections returned reformist presidents, but the political system ensured that no majority urban-liberal coalition would be formed in Congress. Except for policies benefiting veterans, Congress would not channel income tax revenues into establishment of a more national and comprehensive welfare state for all Americans. Instead, it preferred to preserve or initiate domestic policies that were under the control of states, localities, and private enterprises. In addition, it pledged much of the nation's postwar public wealth to American military power and global economic influence.

CONCLUSION: REDEFINING THE NEW DEAL

In the United States, World War II and its aftermath did not bring consolidation of the New Deal, but rather its failure and redefinition. Various liberal plans for completing New Deal socioeconomic reforms were thwarted; health insurance failed; and public assistance was not nationalized. The federal government quit the business of administering public employment programs; even the less ambitious Keynesian public works projects of the NRPB failed to become institutionalized.

At the same time, American social policy developed different emphases. Although the original aim of New Deal social policy was to provide employment and relief, old-age insurance became the centerpiece of U.S. social policy. And although the New Dealers had attempted to downplay separate veterans' programs, after the war the Americans benefiting most from public social provision were veterans and their families. They were eligible for housing, health, and educational benefits that made the civilian welfare state conspicuous by its absence. The principle of treating veterans much better than other citizens, which originated immediately after the Civil War, was reestablished.

If the politics of the New Deal did not resemble the politics of the wartime period, it is partly because there were profound differences between the Depression and World War II as national crises. During the Depression, nationalizing social reforms were promoted by the fiscal crises of the states and localities. But during and after the war, even though the national government put itself on a relatively stronger fiscal footing with the expanded income tax, the states and localities were no longer financially insecure; moreover, local interests could work through Congress in an attempt to ensure that new domestic policies would have decentralized controls. The Depression forced the Roosevelt administration to give social policy its undivided attention, whereas during the war the same president focused on foreign policy. The Allied victory ensured that foreign policy would remain a central concern of all postwar U.S. presidents.

The decline of presidential interest in social policy was accompanied by the resurgence of congressional strength and the lack of coordination of the agencies in charge of social policies. The reassertion by Congress had begun before the war, with Roosevelt's post-1936 battle to reorganize the executive branch and the increasing restrictions placed on the WPA; thereafter, the administration's concern with the war reinforced the process. The assumption of control by congressional committees and individual senators over the planning of postwar social legislation led to scrambling among agencies and bureaus of the executive branch. No longer under the close control of the administration, these agencies found that they could increase their influence over delimited realms of policy—*if* they could make themselves useful to congressmen.

The only national civilian program strengthened during the immediate postwar period, Old Age and Survivors' Insurance, predicted the future of American social policy. In a number of ways, the war aided the bureaucratic fortunes of the Social Security Board and set the stage for OASI to become the keystone of postwar U.S. public social provision. The reluctance of the executive branch to introduce new social policy legislation during the war gave the SSB room to maneuver in Congress. Through its Bureau of Research and Statistics, the SSB supplied "technical help" to those formulating the Wagner-Murray-Dingell bills, in the process influencing their provisions to protect the payroll tax. The demise of the National Resources Planning Board also contributed to the program's strength, for it was the only governmental body to sponsor expert criticisms of the SSB's priorities.[90] Finally, the high employment rates of the war and its aftermath aided the OASI program. According to the 1939 Social Security Act amendments, the tax should have reached 6 percent in 1949, but instead remained at 2 percent. Yet the many delays in the increase of the payroll tax became less

---

[90] Derthick notes that one reason for the success of the SSB was that it was rarely confronted by the criticism of experts, which the NRPB undoubtedly would have continued to provide. See *Policymaking for Social Security*, chap. 7.

significant when employment and wage rates turned out to be much higher than had been projected in 1939.

After the war, the Social Security Board formed ties to the congressional taxing committees; it provided technical assistance to a Senate Advisory Council on Social Security and was able to influence the direction of its recommendations. The Democratic majority swept in with Truman in 1948 provided just enough strength to gain passage of some extensions of the OASI program. The 1950 legislation extended coverage to domestic workers and some categories of agricultural workers and increased benefits to keep up with inflation. Although nationalized unemployment insurance and temporary disability insurance were lost for good, OASI survived despite the wartime delays of its tax increases and gained new life in 1950. Afterward, the (now renamed) Social Security Administration found it easiest to pursue the goal of comprehensive social insurance by making improvements in the OASI program. Its sights were set on permanent disability insurance and health insurance for the retired.

At the end of a decade of war and reconversion, a comprehensive national welfare state had been created in Great Britain; meanwhile, the United States had settled into other patterns. Despite the dreams of New Deal and early wartime planners for a distinctively American full-employment welfare state, nearly all possibilities for nationalized social policy had been eliminated from the agenda of mainstream politics by the beginning of the 1950s. Thereafter, for civilians, national public social provision would be restricted to those contributory social insurance programs that the Social Security Administration already managed, or would devise, primarily for elderly retired workers. A postwar American welfare state of sorts would be established for the elderly veterans of industry, comparable to the one already established for the veterans of war. But the New Deal dream of national social and economic policies to meet the many needs of all Americans had been dissolved by the domestic politics of the war years. The dream would not soon reappear, and never again in the same way.

CHAPTER SIX

The Limits of the New Deal System and the Roots of Contemporary Welfare Dilemmas

DURING the past two decades, the social policies of the U.S. national government have been the focus of heated political controversies that have gone well beyond mere tinkering with the terms of the 1935 Social Security Act, the charter legislation for America's social insurance and public assistance programs. These controversies are far from over. Debates about the rising costs of old-age insurance and medical coverage, about the adequacy or efficacy of welfare, and about the basic legitimacy of national public efforts to cope with social dependency promise to be with us for some time to come. The United States is unmistakably in the midst of a watershed in its public social policies.

From the 1960s through the early 1970s, the United States looked to many observers as if it might soon complete—in its own peculiar way—a belated progress toward a European-style welfare state.[1] The "War on Poverty" of Lyndon Johnson's Great Society promised to address the special needs of groups left beyond the reach of the New Deal's social legislation.[2] An array of special programs was launched to address the difficulties faced by inner-city blacks and inhabitants of non-urban "de-

From *The Politics of Social Policy in the United States*, edited by Margaret Weir, Ann Shola Orloff, and Theda Skocpol (Princeton, NJ: Princeton University Press, 1988). © Princeton University Press.

Final revisions of this paper benefited from astute comments and criticisms by Christopher Jencks, Jennifer Hochschild, Robert Kuttner, and Craig Reinarman.

[1] Until recently, the comparative social science literature on welfare states has been remarkably evolutionist, assuming that sooner or later all welfare states would establish a full array of five types of programs—accident, old-age, sickness, unemployment, and family allowance—and expand benefits and population coverage for each type of hazard. In addition, welfare states were expected to integrate such programs with universally available public assistance for low-income people, overcoming the lingering stigma attached to public assistance from the era of pre-industrial poor laws. Sweden, Great Britain, and other Western European nations were implicitly the models for "full welfare state development," and the United States and other industrial or industrializing nations were expected, perhaps with delays due to peculiar national values or class relations, to follow in their footsteps.

[2] For overviews of Great Society efforts, see Sar A. Levitan and Robert Taggart, *The Promise of Greatness* (Cambridge, Mass.: Harvard University Press, 1976), pts. 1 and 2, and James T. Patterson, *America's Struggle Against Poverty, 1900–1980* (Cambridge, Mass.: Harvard University Press, 1981), pt. 3.

pressed" areas, and efforts were made to nationalize income supports for the poor. Manpower and public employment programs were fashioned to cope with "structural unemployment." Reformers inside and outside of government hoped that national health insurance would soon follow the enactment of Medicare for the elderly and Medicaid for the poor.

But the liberal-reformist controversies of the 1960s soon gave way to the conflicts over social policy retrenchment that dominated the national political agenda after the 1980 presidential election. During the 1970s, formerly liberal academics led the way in attacking Great Society programs as overambitious and costly failures, and Keynesian tenets of macroeconomic management came under increasing criticism from economists and publicists who argued that excessive government spending and regulation hurt economic growth.[3] An effort at national welfare reform petered out during Jimmy Carter's presidency.[4] Thereafter, the main preoccupation of social policy advocates became the shoring up of existing programs, especially retirement insurance and Medicare for the elderly, in the face of rapidly rising costs.

Political forces gathered to reverse the trends of thirty years of social policymaking. In 1975, David Stockman, the man who became President Reagan's budget director in 1981, attacked what he called the "great social pork barrel" and called for major cuts in federal social spending on the grounds of equity and economic efficiency.[5] Once in power, the Reagan administration found that it was not politically feasible to cut major middle-class entitlement programs such as Social Security. But the first Reagan administration did manage to achieve other domestic spending cuts, primarily by shrinking programs that were started or expanded during the Great Society period.[6] During its second term, moreover, the Reagan administration conducted an in-house re-

[3] For representative critiques of the Great Society efforts, see Henry Aaron, *Politics and the Professors* (Washington, D.C.: The Brookings Institution, 1977), and Daniel Patrick Moynihan, *Maximum Feasible Misunderstanding* (New York: The Free Press, 1970). The retreat from Keynesianism is discussed in Ira Katznelson, "A Radical Departure: Social Welfare and the Election," in Thomas Ferguson and Joel Rogers, eds., *The Hidden Election: Politics and Economics in the 1980 Presidential Campaign* (New York: Pantheon Books, 1981), pp. 313–40.

[4] Laurence E. Lynn, Jr., and David deF Whitman, *The President as Policymaker: Jimmy Carter and Welfare Reform* (Philadelphia, Pa.: Temple University Press, 1981).

[5] David A. Stockman, "The Social Pork Barrel," *The Public Interest* no. 39 (Spring 1975): 3–30.

[6] See David A. Stockman, *The Triumph of Politics: The Inside Story of the Reagan Revolution* (New York: Avon Books, 1987); Jack Meyer, "Budget Cuts in the Reagan Administration: A Question of Fairness," in D. Lee Bawden, ed., *The Social Contract Revisited* (Washington, D.C.: The Urban Institute, 1984), pp. 33–64, and Edward J. Harpham, "Fiscal Crisis and the Politics of Social Security Reform," in Anthony Champagne and Edward J. Harpham, eds., *The Attack on the Welfare State* (Prospect Heights, Ill.: Waveland Press, 1984), esp. pp. 26–32.

view of all public assistance programs for the poor, with the rhetorical emphasis upon finding ways to "reduce welfare dependency" while de-emphasizing the role of the national government.[7]

The unsettledness of American social politics from the 1960s to the present must be understood in relation to what the Social Security Act did, and did not, achieve—and, indeed, in relation to the whole array of social and economic reforms that the New Deal did, and did not, accomplish. The New Deal's accomplishments and shortcomings created the matrix for subsequent political struggles over public social policies in America. Only against this historical background—with history understood not just as past events but as processes over time leading into the present—can we properly understand the nature of the contemporary political debates about U.S. social provision.

In the following sections, I analyze social and political patterns that can help us to understand the present controversies over public social provision. Rather than attempt a single chronological narration, I move back and forth between the New Deal era and the period since the 1960s, suggesting under a number of thematic headings how earlier institutional and policy patterns have fed into the ongoing dilemmas of contemporary U.S. social politics.

"SOCIAL SECURITY" VERSUS "WELFARE": A LEGACY OF THE NEW DEAL

Social scientists may use the term *welfare state* to refer to the entire set of social insurance and public assistance programs operating in virtually every industrial nation, the United States included. Obviously, though, the term has an inappropriate ring about it in the case of the United States. For in practical political rhetoric, Americans make a sharp conceptual and evaluative distinction between "social security" and "welfare." *Social security* refers to old-age insurance and the associated programs of survivors', disability, and medical coverage for the elderly; and these programs are seen as sacred governmental obligations to deserving workers who have paid for them through "contributions" over their working lifetimes. *Welfare*, by contrast, is often discussed as a set of governmental "handouts" to barely deserving poor people who may be trying to avoid honest employment—trying to get something for nothing.

[7] *Up From Dependency: A New National Public Assistance Strategy*, Report to the President by the Domestic Policy Council Low Income Opportunity Working Group (Review Draft, December 1986). During the mid-1980s, in fact, state governments became the chief loci of debates over such social policy initiatives as reforming welfare by adding work requirements. See the discussion of several states' programs in Michael Wiseman, "Workfare and Welfare Policy," *Focus* (Newsletter of the University of Wisconsin's Institute for Research on Poverty) 9, no. 3 (Fall and Winter 1986): 1–8.

"Welfare state" as a political slogan originated in Britain during World War II.[8] It indicated an aspiration to integrate all forms of income assistance, social services, and social insurance into a complete system of social protection for all British citizens, and it was held up as an ideal worth fighting for in the conflict with Nazi Germany. Tellingly, no such ideal has ever gained currency in American social politics. Americans do not think of the federal government's public benefits as adding up to an integrated system, applicable to *all* citizens. Instead, they sharply distinguish welfare programs from Social Security. And only Social Security has positive legitimacy as a state activity and comes close to being identified with full citizenship rights for Americans.

The exact programs connoted by Social Security versus those connoted by welfare have shifted over time since the 1930s, but the bifurcation itself was implicit in the original Social Security Act and was deliberately emphasized by the administrators of the act after 1935.[9] The framers of the Social Security Act made sure that unemployment insurance and old-age insurance would start to pay out benefits only after workers or employers had paid in taxes for some years. And they tried to minimize the federal government's outlays for public assistance to the poor by putting one-half to two-thirds of the fiscal obligation onto the hard-pressed states and leaving the states responsible for setting benefit levels and eligibility rules. Those who formulated the Social Security Act hoped that, over time, most Americans would earn protections from contributory social insurance programs and cease to need public assistance at all.

After the Social Security Act was passed, its administrators worked hard from 1936 through the 1950s to build up contributory old-age insurance, the only fully national program they controlled, and simultaneously to reduce the popular appeal of federally subsidized old-age public assistance.[10] This was not easy. Until the 1950s, more older Americans received old-age assistance (one-half funded by their states, one-half by the federal government) than were covered by contributory old-age insurance. Moreover, there were recurrent political efforts by Townsend Movement advocates of flat-rate pensions, by Keynesians, and by conservatives to substitute need-based old-age pensions for con-

---

[8] Peter Flora and Arnold J. Heidenheimer, "The Historical Core and Changing Boundaries of the Welfare State," in Flora and Heidenheimer, eds., *The Development of the Welfare State in Europe and America* (New Brunswick, N.J.: Transaction Books, 1981), p. 19.

[9] This draws upon Theda Skocpol and John Ikenberry, "The Political Formation of the American Welfare State in Historical and Comparative Perspective," *Comparative Social Research* 6 (1983): 92–119.

[10] Jerry R. Cates, *Insuring Inequality: Administrative Leadership in Social Security, 1935–54* (Ann Arbor: University of Michigan Press, 1983).

tributory insurance. But in their dealings both with the public and with Congress, the Social Security administrators presented old-age insurance as an "earned right," an honorable "contract" between each working citizen and the government. What is more, they used administrative discretion to make sure that public assistance remained niggardly, as well as difficult and demeaning to obtain. Many states, especially in the South, treated welfare in this way without federal encouragement; but the Social Security administrators also reined in would-be liberal states like California to make sure that public assistance did not become too easily available or too appealing.

During the 1950s, beneficiaries of Social Security old-age insurance finally overtook those receiving welfare assistance for the elderly, as more and more retiring workers became eligible for social security payments. Social Security was becoming politically popular and sacrosanct. Under Republican and Democratic administrations alike, working alliances between the Social Security Administration and key congressional committees led to the expansion of coverage, higher benefits, and the addition to Social Security of new disability and medical-insurance programs.[11] By the early 1970s, social security was sufficiently extended and liberalized to function as a true retirement wage for regularly employed workers, including many middle-class Americans.[12]

Meanwhile, a public assistance program that had been quite minor at the time it was brought into the Social Security Act of 1935 expanded greatly in response to unanticipated social and economic changes. This program—Aid to Families with Dependent Children (AFDC), whose rolls grew steadily in the 1950s and early 1960s and exploded after that[13]—primarily dispenses grants to mothers without husbands to support them and their children. Since the 1950s, AFDC clients have been marginal participants in labor markets and thus not able to build up social insurance rights of various kinds.

By the 1960s, AFDC became the visible embodiment of welfare understood in contrast to social security, and Great Society programs targeting the poor tended to be incorporated into the welfare rubric. Iron-

---

[11] Martha Derthick, *Policymaking for Social Security* (Washington, D.C.: The Brookings Institution, 1979).

[12] On Social Security as a retirement wage, see John Myles, "Postwar Capitalism and the Extension of Social Security into a Retirement Wage," pp. 265–84 in *The Politics of Social Policy in the United States*, edited by Margaret Weir, Ann Shola Orloff, and Theda Skocpol (Princeton, NJ: Princeton University Press, 1988).

[13] Winifred Bell, *Aid to Dependent Children* (New York: Columbia University Press, 1965); Patterson, *America's Struggle Against Poverty*, chap. 11. As Patterson points out (p. 171), the "number of Americans on public assistance grew from 7.1 million in 1960 . . . to 14.4 million in 1974," and "all of this growth came in the numbers on AFDC, which increased from 3.1 million in 1960 . . . to 10.8 million by 1974."

ically, the efforts the Social Security Administration had made over the years to differentiate two kinds of old-age coverage were in effect transferred into the bifurcations of the current period—between public benefits for the elderly, on the one hand, and public benefits for the unemployed and underemployed poor, on the other. As the first years of the Reagan administration clearly demonstrated, this symbolic and programmatic bifurcation built into the American scheme of public benefits really matters. Even though low-income public assistance programs accounted for less than 18 percent of federal social spending, far less than the proportions for Social Security and Medicare, these welfare programs took the brunt of the Reagan efforts to trim the "social pork barrel."[14] The expanding ranks of the poor, primarily mothers and children, have suffered while the elderly clients of Social Security have continued to improve their economic standing.[15]

THE FAILURE OF SOCIAL KEYNESIANISM AND FULL EMPLOYMENT

The Social Security Act of 1935 was originally planned in 1934–35 by a body of Roosevelt administration officials and selected expert advisors called, not incidentally, "the Committee on Economic Security." Although the committee's report to the president was careful to maintain throughout a firm distinction between "social insurance" for nondependent, employable people and "relief" or "public assistance" for dependent unemployables, it was also eloquent in insisting that this approach would work only if the federal government permanently committed itself to providing guarantees of suitable public employment for willing workers who exhausted unemployment benefits, or were not covered, or could not find private employment.[16] Patterns of social-welfare provision, in short, were seen as inextricably tied to complementary public policies to ensure full employment. Such plans and hopes of the Committee on Economic Security were not realized, however.

At the time the Social Security Act was proposed, its formulators thought that the appropriate larger economic framework could be insti-

[14] John Palmer and Isabel Sawhill, *The Reagan Experiment* (Washington, D.C.: The Urban Institute, 1982), p. 373.

[15] See Samuel H. Preston, "Children and the Elderly: Divergent Paths for America's Dependents," *Demography* 21, no. 4 (November 1984): 437–57, and the overview of current findings on "The Relative Well-Being of the Elderly and Children: Domestic and International Comparisons," *Focus* (Newsletter of the University of Wisconsin's Institute for Research on Poverty) 9, no. 3 (Fall and Winter 1986): 10–14. See also Irwin Garfinkel and Sara McLanahan, *Single Mothers and Their Children: A New American Dilemma* (Washington, D.C.: The Urban Institute, 1986).

[16] *Report to the President of the Committee on Economic Security* (Washington, D.C.: U.S. Government Printing Office, 1935), p. 1 and passim.

tutionalized simply through extensions of New Deal public works and public employment programs, and through the establishment of the National Resources Board as a permanent executive agency for social and economic planning by the federal government. Later, beginning in the late 1930s, many liberal New Dealers also became "social Keynesians," adopting the view that permanently high levels of federal social spending should be coordinated with macroeconomic stimulation to ensure steady growth with full employment.[17] During World War II, social Keynesians drew up the Full Employment bill of 1945.[18] This measure would have reorganized federal budgeting and economic planning capacities and unequivocally committed the national government to using public spending and other appropriate governmental means to ensure jobs for all Americans willing to work.

But the New Deal did not culminate in social Keynesianism or in government guarantees to pursue full employment through public action. Instead, from the late 1940s to the 1970s, mainstream American Keynesians with the greatest academic prestige and most access to national policy planning through the Council of Economic Advisors stressed the fine-tuning of fiscal and monetary adjustments within relatively limited parameters of government action and domestic social spending.[19] Such "commercial Keynesians" understood their finest moment to be the decision by President John Kennedy in 1962 to cut taxes in order to stimulate economic growth.[20]

The New Dealers who originally planned and proposed the Social Security Act believed that unemployment was the most basic hazard that would be addressed by the nascent American welfare state they were launching; yet the timid commercial Keynesianism with which the federal government addressed this problem after the defeat of the Full Employment bill of 1945 fell far short of the guaranteed "employment assurance" originally envisaged by the Committee on Economic Security. Nevertheless, following World War II the U.S. national economy was reasonably healthy. Its steady growth with but moderate inflation and unemployment was propelled by limited federal efforts at macroeconomic management, by wage and benefit bargains in the private cor-

---

[17] See Dean L. May, *From New Deal to New Economics: The American Liberal Response to the Recession of 1937* (New York: Garland, 1981); Richard V. Gilbert et al., *An Economic Program for American Democracy* (New York: Vanguard Press, 1938); and Robert M. Collins, *The Business Response to Keynes* (New York: Columbia University Press, 1981), chaps. 1 and 2, esp. pp. 10–12 and 51, on "stagnationist Keynesianism."

[18] On the Full Employment Bill, its background, and its fundamental modification before passage, see Stephen Kemp Bailey, *Congress Makes a Law: The Story Behind the Employment Act of 1946* (New York: Columbia University Press, 1946).

[19] Collins, *Business Response to Keynes*, pt. 3.

[20] Robert Lekachman, *The Age of Keynes* (New York: Vintage Books, 1966), chap. 11.

porate sector that kept consumer purchasing power high, and of course by the temporarily privileged position of the U.S. economy within the postwar international economy.[21]

The postwar U.S. political economy, including the New Deal's Social Security system, worked well enough to meet the expectations of the majority of American workers who were steadily employed. As more and more employees became covered by contributory old-age insurance, they could look forward to basic public support in retirement, perhaps supplemented by private-sector benefits gained through union bargaining. Federal unemployment insurance was markedly uneven across the states and not easily coordinated with Keynesian macroeconomic management; nevertheless, it served the steadily employed as a back-up for temporary periods of unemployment.[22]

Even during the 1950s and 1960s, however, the lack of a U.S. national commitment to ensure full employment was telling for those unlucky people who were willing to work but unable to do so regularly or at adequate wage levels. For such Americans, including residents of depressed regions and blacks migrating out of the rural South, the New Deal's social programs were left to bear much more weight than their formulators had ever intended. The persistent ranks of black males marginal to the labor market and the growing ranks of dependents on AFDC were indications, even in the prosperous parts of the postwar era, of the prescience of those New Deal reformers who had doubted that social security's social insurance programs could be adequate without what they called federal "employment assurance."

Briefly during the 1960s, federal labor market and job training programs emerged as part of the Great Society's War on Poverty, yet these programs remained adjuncts of the predominant "anti-poverty" and "welfare reform" themes of the period.[23] Equally damaging, these policies were never accepted as part of overall federal strategies for managing the economy as such. Commercial Keynesian macroeconomists re-

---

[21] See Michael J. Piore and Charles Sabel, *The Industrial Divide* (New York: Basic Books, 1984), chap. 4, and Charles S. Maier, "The Politics of Productivity: Foundations of American International Economic Policy after World War II," in Peter Katzenstein, ed., *Between Power and Plenty* (Madison: University of Wisconsin Press, 1978), pp. 3–49.

[22] On the unevenness of unemployment coverage, see Joseph M. Becker, "Twenty-five Years of Unemployment Insurance," *Political Science Quarterly 75* (1960): 481–99; on the difficulties of meshing unemployment insurance with Keynesian macroeconomic management, see Edward J. Harpham, "Federalism, Keynesianism, and the Transformation of Unemployment Insurance in the United States," in Douglas Ashford and E. W. Kelley, eds., *Nationalizing Social Security in Europe and America* (Greenwich, Conn.: JAI Press, 1986), pp. 155–79.

[23] See Margaret Weir, "The Federal Government and Unemployment: The Frustration of Policy Innovation from the New Deal to the Great Society," pp. 149–90 in *The Politics of Social Policy in the United States*, edited by Weir, Orloff, and Skocpol.

mained in charge—until the puzzlingly persistent "stagflation" of the 1970s raised questions about their ability to predict and manage the national economy.

The discrediting of Keynesian certainties in the 1970s was accompanied by the rising political credibility of "monetarist" and "supply-side" arguments that too much—not too little—"government spending" and "interference with the free market" lie at the root of any U.S. economic difficulties.[24] By the 1980s, it became apparent that even periods of economic recovery and growth were unlikely to bring the United States as close to full employment as it was in the 1950s and 1960s. For the foreseeable future, unemployment rates—which do not even include the large numbers of "discouraged workers" who have dropped out of the labor market altogether—seem unlikely to drop below 5 or 6 percent at best. And structural declines in heavy industries are displacing many formerly privileged industrial workers. Yet even in the face of these developments, calls for the federal government to devise bold, new full employment strategies have been but faintly heard in academic and political discourse.

In historical perspective, this is not surprising. Back during the founding period of its modern interventionist state, from 1930 through 1946, the United States originally opted not to closely coordinate "social" and "economic" interventions. Throughout the postwar period, U.S. macroeconomic managers de-emphasized public spending and did not work to coordinate manpower and labor market interventions (or any other sectorally specific interventions) with the fiscal and monetary adjustments used to encourage economic growth. The technical and intellectual capacities of the federal government to devise and implement targeted industrial or labor market interventions were not improved during the era of commercial Keynesian dominance. Little intellectual or political legitimacy was built up for the notion that the federal government could—or should—pursue economic, employment, and social-welfare objectives through the same public policies or through deliberately coordinated public policies.

Thus, when economic growth faltered and stagflation persisted in the 1970s, moderate Democrats and conservative Republicans understandably perceived trade-offs between economic growth and social protection (including protection against unemployment). Predictably, too, they responded—starting during the Democratic presidency of Jimmy Carter—by advocating at least the appearance of a reduced role for government in relation to the economy. Under President Reagan, many de facto Keynesian measures certainly were used to stimulate economic

[24] See Katznelson, "A Radical Departure."

demand, but they were not labeled as such. And the labeling was significant, for it was part of an overall effort by conservatives in the 1980s to
de-legitimate public spending and governmental interventions as "economically inefficient."

In one sense, of course, such Reagan administration tactics reacted
against the logic of American public policies in the commercial Keynesian era of the 1940s to the 1970s. But, in another sense, they were an
understandable culmination of the original failure of the New Deal to
institutionalize social Keynesian policies and full employment guarantees as complements to social policies premised on the notion that all
able-bodied Americans would be able to work at well-paid jobs in a
growing national economy. The commercial Keynesianism with which
the postwar United States muddled through was, it is now clear, only a
fair-weather support for the social needs of American workers. By
downplaying the role of the state in coping with economic problems,
the policies and rhetoric of the commercial Keynesian era paved the
way for further retreats from public solutions once their own efficacy
became questionable.

The Unstable Place of Blacks in the New Deal System

If the framers and—especially—the administrators of the Social Security Act established a bifurcation between "social security" and "welfare," the New Deal as a whole laid the basis for the eventual politicization of this division along racially charged lines. This politicization
would become especially bitter in a political economy without the will
or the means to ensure full employment, since blacks are disproportionately the victims of insufficient employment opportunities for the
least skilled and poorest Americans.

In effect, blacks were only marginally included in the Social Security
programs launched by the New Deal, for in the 1930s they were still
mostly at the bottom of a racist caste system and a backward economy
in the South. Yet New Deal economic interventions ended up facilitat-
ing structural transformations in the southern economy that would urbanize black poverty. What is more, the Democratic party that sponsored and benefited from the New Deal began to mobilize urban blacks
into electoral coalitions. By the 1960s, the Democratic party would
have to cope with political contradictions engendered by the shifting
socioeconomic status and rising political demands of blacks. From the
Great Society to the recent efforts to revitalize Democratic coalitions to
do battle with Reagan Republicans, the Democratic party has grappled
with these racially charged political contradictions.

The core social insurance programs established by the New Deal—
old-age insurance and unemployment insurance—did not reach most

American blacks. The agricultural and service occupations open to most blacks at that time were simply excluded from social insurance taxes and coverage. Had this not been done to propitiate politically powerful southern Democrats and representatives of commercial farmers, it is doubtful that the Social Security Act could have gotten through Congress.[25] Likewise, the Social Security Act's institutionalization of federally subsidized public assistance programs gave free rein to state-level variations in benefits and eligibility, and allowed state and local officials to exercise administrative discretion. This meant that blacks in the South could be deprived of adequate welfare assistance. Southern economic interests were left free to enforce labor discipline on their own terms and retain competitive advantages in relation to higher-wage industries in the North.

Although Franklin Roosevelt and the New Deal facilitated and benefited from the expansion of urban liberalism in the Democratic party during the 1930s, they never could escape dependence on the southern party oligarchs whose local sway partially rested on the exclusion of blacks from electoral politics. When it came to appealing to black voters, the New Deal Democrats confined their efforts to the northern cities, where they were building multi-ethnic coalitions in tandem with the growing trade unions. Northern blacks were the last and the most marginal group to join the New Deal electoral coalition.[26] Fatefully for the future of the Democratic party, they had gained a toehold through which black demands could be pressed more aggressively in the future, after black urban populations grew.

Ironically, New Deal agricultural programs facilitated major transformation of southern agriculture that ultimately helped to undermine segregation and swell the ranks of urban blacks, leading to new demands on the national Democratic party for civil rights and economic assistance. Among New Deal liberals were radical reformers who wanted to aid tenant farmers and agricultural laborers, including southern blacks; but these reformers were defeated by the American Farm Bureau Federation and by allied officials in Congress and the Agriculture Department.[27] From the mid-1930s onward, federal farm subsidies and other

[25] See Edwin E. Witte, *The Development of the Social Security Act* (Madison: University of Wisconsin Press, 1963).

[26] Kristi Andersen, *The Creation of a Democratic Majority, 1928–1936* (Chicago, Ill.: University of Chicago Press, 1979), chap. 6; Harvard Sitkoff, *A New Deal for Blacks* (New York: Oxford University Press, 1978), esp. chap. 4.

[27] See Richard S. Kirkendall, "The New Deal and Agriculture," in John Braeman, Robert H. Bremner, and David Brody, eds., *The New Deal: The National Level* (Columbus: Ohio State University Press, 1975), pp. 83–109; Raymond Wolters, "The New Deal and the Negro," in Braeman, Bremner, and Brody, eds., *The New Deal: The National Level*, pp. 170–78; Paul E. Mertz, *New Deal Policy and Southern Rural Poverty* (Baton Rouge: Louisiana State University Press, 1978); and Christiana McFadyen Campbell, *The Farm Bureau and the New Deal* (Urbana: University of Illinois Press, 1962).

interventions in the agricultural sector aided richer commercial farmers and spurred the mechanization of southern farming. During World War II, moreover, military spending promoted urbanization and industrialization in the South.

From the 1940s through the 1960s, blacks migrated in huge waves into southern and northern cities.[28] The shift of blacks from a predominately rural South to heavily populated urban areas located in the South and the North created the preconditions for the civil rights struggles of the 1950s and 1960s.[29] At last, American blacks had won the right to vote in all areas of the nation, and from the 1960s to the Jesse Jackson movement of the current period they have been mobilizing for fuller participation in local and national politics.

Yet the migration of blacks from the rural South transformed their electoral status more thoroughly and quickly than it changed their economic status. For blacks arrived in America's central cities and heavy industries at a point when opportunities for upward mobility after starting in unskilled industrial jobs were much less available than they were for earlier ethnic immigrants into American cities.[30] Thus urban blacks experienced extraordinary rates of unemployment or marginal employment, and to survive economically they called in disproportionate numbers upon welfare programs, especially AFDC.

By the 1960s, blacks were pressing the federal government and the Democratic party for expansion of the few social programs within the New Deal system for which impoverished blacks were eligible—and for new programs to address their special needs. Reformers of the 1960s realized that the original New Deal framers of the Social Security Act had been wrong to suppose that contributory old-age insurance and contributory unemployment insurance would, over time, include virtually all Americans and leave only shrinking ranks of non-employable and truly destitute people dependent on public assistance. This comfortable illusion of the Social Security framers had been premised upon the exclusion of most blacks from America's nascent and partial welfare state—and the illusion crumbled as soon as blacks gained political rights and black poverty gained urban visibility. The Democratic party,

[28] See Doug McAdam, *Political Process and the Development of Black Insurgency, 1930–1970* (Chicago, Ill.: University of Chicago Press, 1982), Tables 5.2 through 5.4, pp. 78–80.

[29] Ibid. McAdam's overall argument connects the changing structural circumstances of blacks to the development of the civil rights protests.

[30] Stanley Lieberson, *A Piece of the Pie: Blacks and White Immigrants Since 1880* (Berkeley: University of California Press, 1980), esp. chap. 10 and 11; John D. Kasarda, "The Changing Occupational Structure of the American Metropolis: Apropos the Urban Problem," in B. Schwartz, ed., *The Changing Face of the Suburbs* (Chicago, Ill.: University of Chicago Press, 1976); John D. Kasarda, "Caught in the Web of Change," *Society* 21 (November-December 1983): 41–47.

above all, had to do something to cope with the contradictory socio-economic and political tendencies that the New Deal had fostered.

The Great Society programs of Lyndon Johnson's War on Poverty can be understood as an effort by the national Democratic party to address the political demands and economic needs of blacks—especially urban blacks—by tacking onto the Social Security system a whole new layer of programs especially targeted for the poor, both whites and blacks.[31] The idea was that healthy growth in the U.S. economy would allow the continued expansion of Social Security protections for the elderly and increased funding for social programs appealing to the predominately white middle classes, at the same time that new, ostensibly nonracial programs to overcome poverty were launched. Although AFDC rolls continued to expand, reformers during the Great Society period and for some years afterward hoped to do better than just expand the demeaning welfare programs originally established by the New Deal. Rather, they hoped to use programs such as Food Stamps, Medicaid, federally subsidized housing, and job training to overcome racial divisions by eliminating poverty once and for all.[32] Many reformers also intended to nationalize and reform public assistance into permanent, universal income subsidies for the working and non-working poor.

In *America's Hidden Success*, John Schwarz argues that Great Society anti-poverty efforts did achieve remarkable successes, reducing poverty by about half compared with what it would have been in the absence of such federal interventions in the private economy.[33] Newly upwardly mobile black politicians and middle-class professionals also gained employment opportunities through these efforts.[34] With some justice, Schwarz argues that the failure of the Great Society to eradicate poverty was due as much to the under-funding and early abandonment of many of its programs as it was to fundamental flaws in their conception.

Nevertheless, political time-bombs were built into these special anti-poverty efforts from the start. Federal interventions further provoked

[31] Carl M. Brauer, "Kennedy, Johnson, and the War on Poverty," *Journal of American History* 69 (1982): 98–119; Frances Fox Piven and Richard Cloward, *Poor People's Movements* (New York: Pantheon Books, 1977), chap. 5; Guida West, *The National Welfare Rights Movement: The Social Protest of Poor Women* (New York: Praeger, 1981).

[32] See note 2. Along with Medicare, Medicaid was considered by its proponents to be a "second best" alternative to national health insurance, and many reformers hoped that national health insurance would then soon follow.

[33] John Schwarz, *America's Hidden Success: A Reassessment of Twenty Years of Public Policy* (New York: Norton, 1983), pp. 32–35.

[34] Michael K. Brown and Steven P. Erie, "Blacks and the Legacy of the Great Society: The Economic and Political Impact of Federal Social Policy," *Public Policy* 29 (Summer 1981): 299–330.

rather than propitiated black demands—demands both for "affirmative action" to benefit the employed and for more generous assistance to those on welfare. In turn, black demands continually aroused fearful reactions among established white groups, especially the working-class ethnics who are socially closest to blacks in urban residential and employment settings.[35] In addition, Great Society reformers did not foresee that the Vietnam War and America's shifting international economic position in the 1970s would undermine their original supposition that ever-increasing federal funding could be made simultaneously available for middle-class programs and antipoverty efforts. As soon as fiscal constraints did become an issue, politicians responding to white working- and middle-class fears could easily castigate the Great Society's anti-poverty programs for being costly and unnecessary welfare handouts (this criticism was usually accompanied by the unstated presumption that these programs benefited only overly demanding and often undeserving blacks). Such programs were all the more vulnerable because they clearly had not achieved the apocalyptically declared objective of "abolishing poverty" in America.

Originally an effort to correct for the New Deal's omissions and shortcomings in public social provision, the Great Society ended up reinforcing the programmatic bifurcation of Social Security and welfare and deepening American political divisions along racial lines. It is hard to avoid the conclusion that the Great Society's attempt to complete by rhetorically overblown patchwork the partial system of social protections inherited from the New Deal inadvertently opened the door to powerful critiques of the aims and practices of public social provision in the United States. It especially opened the door to attacks against those policies implicated in the troubled realm of welfare for the unemployed or marginally employed.[36]

THE VULNERABILITY OF SOCIAL POLICIES WITHOUT COLLECTIVE JUSTIFICATION

To the degree that any nationally organized political force is actively working in the 1980s to defend the lines of social provision launched in the New Deal, it is the Democratic party. Yet we have seen that the Democratic party of today is laboring to overcome the ulterior political effects of tensions built into the New Deal's original accomplishments

[35] On "white backlash," see Jonathan Rieder, *Canarsie: The Jews and Italians of Brooklyn Against Liberalism* (Cambridge, Mass.: Harvard University Press, 1985).

[36] A vivid example of the kind of sweeping attack against federal social programs that can be launched by those who stress the failures of the Great Society efforts is Charles Murray, *Losing Ground: American Social Policy, 1950–1980* (New York: Basic Books, 1984).

and shortcomings: the bifurcation of social insurance and public assistance, the holding out of political promises to blacks not originally included in New Deal social provision, and the failure to join full employment and social spending in a socioeconomically comprehensive welfare state. Finally, the party must cope with yet another problematic legacy of the New Deal: the absence of effective collective symbols to legitimate the social policies with which it is identified.[37]

In an excellent essay entitled "The New Deal and the American Anti-Statist Tradition," James Holt has analyzed the evolving symbols and arguments that were invoked by New Dealers during the 1930s to characterize and justify their new federal interventions. Holt explores "the difficulty of explaining and defending a complex and novel program of federal action in the face of deeply entrenched anti-statist traditions" in the United States.[38]

The New Deal was up against anti-statist traditions in the 1930s not just because Americans were ideologically prejudiced against strong public authority, but also because, historically, they had not experienced for good or ill the impact of a bureaucratic national state. There was no such thing in nineteenth-century America, and even though realms of public administration did expand markedly in the first decades of the twentieth century, Congress and the federal system always circumscribed direct, coordinated "national state" activities.[39] Americans thought of political sovereignty as divided and considered ultimate sovereignty to reside abstractly in "the law" and "the Constitution," because these ideas in fact made the most sense of the actual political organization within which they lived.[40]

The New Deal made direct federal governmental activities an immediate reality for all Americans, *and the justification and portrayal of the new economic and social programs in New Deal rhetoric was a portentous ideological development in U.S. history.* As Holt shows, in the early New Deal, Franklin Roosevelt and his political allies relied heavily on images of social cooperation combined with constant emphasis on the "experimental" activism of federal governmental efforts. Things had

[37] This section draws from my "Legacies of New Deal Liberalism," *Dissent* (Winter 1983): 33–44.

[38] James Holt, "The New Deal and the American Anti-Statist Tradition," in Braeman, Bremner, and Brody, eds., *The New Deal: The National Level*, pp. 27–49.

[39] See Stephen Skowronek, *Building a New American State* (Cambridge, England, and New York: Cambridge University Press, 1982).

[40] See the discussions of American political culture in J. P. Nettl, "The State as a Conceptual Variable," *World Politics* 20 (1968): 559–92, and in Ira Katznelson and Kenneth Prewitt, "Constitutionalism, Class, and the Limits of Choice in U.S. Foreign Policy," in Richard Fagen, ed., *Capitalism and the State in U.S.-Latin American Relations* (Stanford, Calif.: Stanford University Press, 1979), pp. 27–33.

to be done to promote economic recovery and relieve distress; only a distant, heartless federal government would fail to act boldly. Roosevelt's government would "roll up its sleeves" and "keep them rolled up," acting not out of ideological or intellectual certainties, but out of value of neighborliness that would bring the whole nation together in response to the emergency. As Holt astutely points out, this early New Deal rhetoric, although rather thin and expedient in many ways, did have a component of moral regeneration. For early New Dealers called upon Americans to put aside selfish, competitive individualism in the name of solidarity across regional and class lines.

Yet as the early New Deal—launched around the ultimately unsuccessful National Recovery Administration—gave way to the second, reformist New Deal of 1935 and after, the official rhetoric changed. It became more focused on *political conflict*—the people against the "economic royalists"—and on *social security* for "the one-third of a Nation ill-fed, ill-housed, ill-clothed." In these ways, the rhetoric of the later New Deal became undeniably more radical. But as Holt underlines, in another way it simultaneously became more conservative. For the New Deal after 1935 mostly gave up the rhetoric of collective solidarity as an antidote to excessive individualism and instead sought to justify New Deal reforms as better means for achieving or safeguarding traditional American individualistic values of liberty and "getting ahead." Their socioeconomically interventionist state, later New Dealers told Americans, was not the attack on basic American values that conservatives were saying it was. Rather, it was merely an excellent instrument for furthering those values because it struck down the excessive privileges and power of "economic autocrats" and relieved economic necessity so that Americans could really be free to exercise their individual rights to equality of opportunity.

This approach to legitimating the new state activities established by the New Deal was probably the surest way to stabilize and moderately extend such policies in U.S. domestic politics from the 1930s to the 1970s. Between 1937 and 1940, liberal New Dealers were not able to best conservatives in head-on collisions, so rhetorical retreat was prudent. After World War II, liberal Democratic gains usually depended upon taking advantage of the rosy climate of national economic expansion and international hegemony to push through social spending programs that would benefit not only blue-collar workers and the poor but also the more middle-class and suburban groups who might swing to the Republicans.[41] In these circumstances—even during the break-

---

[41] The political constraints on liberal Democrats and the policy patterns that resulted are cogently discussed in John Mollenkopf, *The Contested City* (Princeton, N.J.: Princeton University Press, 1983).

throughs of the War on Poverty—it was politically safest to avoid collectivist visions of a welfare state in favor of suggestions that social policies could help every individual and category of individual to get ahead in a non-zero-sum economy.

But when the political going gets rough for public social policies, as it has in the United States since the 1970s, policies that lack clear political and cultural legitimation as expressions of social compassion and collective solidarity are difficult to either defend or extend against individualist, market-oriented, and anti-statist attacks. Hard public choices are called for now that federal interventions are no longer automatically associated with a steadily growing economy. In this situation, the vulnerabilities of instrumentally justified social policies become apparent— especially to the political heirs of the New Deal in the Democratic party. Political coalitions become difficult to sustain across urban and rural populations, Northeast and Southwest, blacks and whites, and middle class and poor. For Americans are not habituated to the notion that, as Michael Walzer eloquently puts it, "the welfare state . . . expresses a certain civil spirit, a sense of mutuality, a commitment to justice."[42]

The rhetoric of the 1984 presidential campaign revealed that the Democrats are, indeed, seeking new moral imageries to overcome the vulnerabilities of instrumentally justified social policies. In his widely praised keynote address to the Democratic National Convention in July 1984, Governor Mario Cuomo invoked the notion of "the family of America" to "explain what a proper government should be."

> We believe we must be the family of America, recognizing that at the heart of the matter we are bound to one another, that the problems of a retired school teacher in Duluth are our problems. That the future of a child in Buffalo is our future. The struggle of a disabled man in Boston to survive, to live decently is our struggle. The hunger of a woman in Little Rock, our hunger. The failure anywhere to provide what reasonably we might, to avoid pain, is our failure.

Obviously, Cuomo was invoking a new political metaphor in order to justify a Democratic defense of activist government under attack: "We believe in only the government we need, but we insist on all the government we need."[43]

Yet the rhetoric of Cuomo and of the Democratic party's 1984 nominees also indicated how cautious they felt they had to be in defending America's threatened social policies in the current conjuncture. Presi-

---

[42] Michael Walzer, "The Community," *The New Republic* (March 31, 1982): 11.
[43] Governor Cuomo's address is reprinted in the *New York Times*, July 17, 1984, p. A16.

dential nominee Walter Mondale talked mostly about budget deficits and about the need not only to raise taxes but also to cut public spending for the sake of the economy. Vice-presidential nominee Geraldine Ferraro both discussed and symbolized the hope that the traditional American and Democratic theme of opening the doors for individual achievement might be realized one more time, for women. Even the family imagery invoked by Cuomo was, after all, minimally solidaristic—much less so than the rhetoric of neighborliness, national community, and mutual sacrifice invoked in the early New Deal.

Tellingly, Governor Cuomo tried to join in one ambiguous image the conservative, almost patriarchal notion of each individual family struggling to get ahead as a single unit with the more collectivist idea of a national family "feeling one another's pain. Sharing one another's blessings. Reasonably, honestly, fairly, without respect to race, or sex, or geography or political affiliation." But the analogy was severely strained, for families do not bridge races (except in very few cases); nor do families operate by public principles of fairness. It also remains to be seen whether many Americans can be persuaded to extend the protective feelings they have (or feel they should have) toward their own children, siblings, parents, and spouses to encompass the "other people's children," disproportionately Hispanic or black, who along with their mothers now crowd the ranks of the American poor.[44]

In sum, Governor Cuomo's imagery (which he continued to use well after 1984) revealed the problematic thinness of the collective vision invoked by mainstream Democrats as they currently try to revitalize broad support for a strong federal social role.[45] In the shifting political circumstance of the 1980s, advocates of a revitalized American system of social provision have yet to find political metaphors of collective compassion simultaneously appealing to blacks and whites, to traditional and newly structured families, and to the middle classes and the poor.

CONCLUSION

Ironically, especially for the Democratic party, many of the contradictions that now bedevil efforts to build strong social policy coalitions across races and social strata represent the playing out of the New Deal's partial accomplishments in shaping and justifying nationwide patterns of public social provision for the United States. As this discus-

---

[44] Preston, "Children and the Elderly" (see note 15).

[45] See the "Transcript of Cuomo's Inaugural Address for His Second Term," *New York Times*, January 2, 1987, p. B4.

sion has tried to show, only if we understand historically the limits and the internal contradictions of modern U.S. public purposes and social policies—with the New Deal as the pivot of our analysis—can we properly understand the roots of the critical juncture those purposes and policies face today.

The legacies of New Deal achievements and, even more, the problems left unresolved by its shortfalls, have interacted with postwar changes in American society and politics to produce passionate debates—from the 1960s through the present—about what government should do for poor women and children, for unemployed black youths, and for displaced industrial workers. Neither the Democratic party nor any other national political force—including the Republicans under Ronald Reagan—has as yet come up with politically self-sustaining solutions. Consequently, the unresolved dilemmas posed by the Great Society's efforts to transcend the limits of the New Deal system continue to arouse intellectual and political conflict. Alternative possible futures for social policy in the United States remain very much at issue.

CHAPTER SEVEN

"Brother, Can You Spare a Job?"
Work and Welfare in the United States

THE United States recently marked the fiftieth anniversary of the Social Security Act of 1935, the federal law that established the enduring framework for modern public social provision in America. This act established the major programs of public assistance, unemployment insurance, and old-age retirement insurance that add up to America's peculiar and incomplete version of a modern "welfare state." With the exception of Medicare, Medicaid, and Food Stamps, which were added in the Great Society period, the framework established by the Social Security Act has remained largely unmodified. Yet the legislation that Franklin Delano Roosevelt signed on August 14, 1935, was proposed by a Cabinet-level Committee on Economic Security (CES) that saw this measure as but one part of a set of commitments by the federal government that would be needed to address "the problem of economic security for the individual" in the United States.[1]

If the policy planners of the CES were to return to our midst to look back over the evolution of public social provision since the New Deal, they would be highly pleased that "social security's" program of old-age insurance has expanded and become politically entrenched—to the point that not even the ultraconservative president Ronald Reagan was able to cut it back. But at the same time, the members of the CES would surely be unhappy that what they considered the federal government's most basic role—providing "employment assurance" to the American people—has never been institutionalized.

To the CES policy planners the huge expansion of welfare payments to the poor since the 1950s would be little cause for celebration. They would see this expansion as an indication of the government's failure to assure jobs to all able-bodied American adults. For the CES members believed that if everyone who could work had a decent job, only a modest residuum of truly dependent people would need or want outright

From *The Nature of Work: Sociological Perspectives*, edited by Kai Erikson and Steven Vallas (New Haven, CT: Yale University Press, 1990). © Yale University Press.

[1] *The Report of the Committee on Economic Security of 1935, and Other Basic Documents Relating to the Development of the Social Security Act*, Fiftieth Anniversary Edition (Washington, D.C.: National Conference on Social Welfare, 1985), 23.

"No, keep the dime. But Brother,
could you spare a job?"

Source: Cartoon by Kevin Wachs (WOX.) From William A.
Gamson and Kathryn Lasch, "The Political Culture of Social Pol-
icy," in *Evaluating the Welfare State*, ed. Shimon E. Spiro and
Ephraim Yuchtman-Yaar (New York: Academic Press, 1983).

public assistance. Essentially, the CES members adhered to one of the
major perspectives that William Gamson has identified as constitutive
of the "political culture of welfare policy" in America.[2] According to
this perspective—which the CES members believed was widely held by
the American people—the poor person is thought to prefer a job to a
handout. The cartoon in Figure 1 (borrowed from Gamson) captures
the essence of this perspective.

Few people realize that the planners of Social Security placed such a
great emphasis on the federal government's role in assuring jobs for all
who needed them. Yet in their *Report of the Committee on Economic
Security* (January 1935), the very first policy recommendation, preceding even the recommendation for unemployment insurance, was about
"employment assurance." It read as follows:

Since most people must live by work, the first objective in a program of
economic security must be maximum employment. As the major contribution

[2] William A. Gamson and Kathryn Lasch, "The Political Culture of Social Welfare Policy,"
in *Evaluating the Welfare State*, ed. Shimon E. Spiro and Ephraim Yuchtman-Yaar (New
York: Academic Press, 1983), 397–415.

of the Federal Government in providing a safeguard against unemployment, we suggest employment assurance—the stimulation of private employment and the provision of public employment for those able-bodied workers whom industry cannot employ at a given time. Public-work programs are most necessary in periods of severe depression, but may be needed in normal times, as well, to help meet the problems of stranded communities and overmanned and declining industries. To avoid the evils of hastily planned emergency work, public employment should be planned in advance and coordinated with the construction and developmental policies of the Government and with the State and local public works projects.

We regard work as preferable to other forms of relief where possible. While we favor unemployment compensation in cash, we believe that it should be provided for limited periods . . . without governmental subsidies. Public funds should be devoted to providing work rather than . . . relief.[3]

How was the federal government to implement employment assurance? In the mid-1930s, reformers devoted to institutionalizing such a commitment by the federal government thought in terms of an updated, expanded, rationally planned system of public works projects on which the unemployed could, if necessary, do useful work at public expense.[4] This took an old idea in American politics and transferred it from the local to the national level.[5] By the late 1930s, another idea of what the federal government could do had emerged and coexisted with this earlier conception. So-called stagnationist Keynesians both within and without the executive branch argued that federal spending on socially useful projects should be expanded when necessary to maintain the economy at "full employment equilibrium."[6] In this way, private investment and job creation would be maximally stimulated by federal deficit spending, and some of that spending could simultaneously be used to provide public jobs to workers in industries or communities with especially severe and persistent unemployment.

[3] *Report of the Committee on Economic Security*, 23–24.

[4] See National Planning Board, *Final Report, 1933–1934* (Washington, D.C.: U.S. Government Printing Office, 1934), secs. I and II.

[5] Leah Hannah Feder, *Unemployment Relief in Periods of Depression: A Study of Measures Adopted in Certain American Cities, 1857 through 1922* (New York: Russell Sage Foundation, 1936).

[6] Robert M. Collins, *The Business Response to Keynes, 1929–1964* (New York: Columbia University Press, 1981), 10–11, 51; Dean L. May, *From New Deal to New Economics: The American Liberal Response to the Recession of 1937* (New York: Garland Press, 1981); Richard V. Gilbert et al., *An Economic Program for American Democracy* (New York: Vanguard Press, 1938); Alvin H. Hansen, *After the War—Full Employment*, a National Resources Planning Board publication (Washington, D.C.: U.S. Government Printing Office, 1942); and National Resources Planning Board, *Security, Work, and Relief Policies* (Washington, D.C.: U.S. Government Printing Office, 1942).

Still later, in the post-World War II period, some American "manpower economists" became attracted to ideas for "active labor market policies."[7] These would be policies tailored to particular industries or areas, policies used to train or retrain workers and to help them find jobs and if necessary relocate with public assistance so they could take those jobs. Ideally, such active labor market interventions could be closely coordinated with Keynesian macroeconomic stimulation and with projects offering temporary public employment. By the 1960s, therefore, at least three sets of recognized policy instruments—public employment, deficit social spending, and active labor market policies—were potentially applicable, singly or in combination, in the task of realizing a federal government commitment to employment assurance.

From the 1930s through the 1970s, repeated efforts were made to commit the U.S. national state to coordinating such policy instruments for employment assurance, yet every one of those efforts failed. The most notable efforts happened in 1945–46, 1967, and 1976–78:

- Around the end of World War II, the stagnationist Keynesian vision was embodied in the Full Employment bill of 1945. This called upon the federal government to guarantee jobs for all who were willing to work and to use public spending for stimulative purposes and, if necessary, to provide public employment. However, the bill was eviscerated in Congress and became merely the Employment Act of 1946. The 1946 law endorsed "high" rather than "full" employment; it no longer mandated public spending as a priority policy instrument; and it backed off from institutionalizing planning around an annual National Production and Employment Budget.[8]

- In what historian Bonnie Schwartz has called "the first major push for public employment since the Great Depression," Senators Joseph Clark and Robert Kennedy proposed in 1967 an Emergency Employment bill that would have given the secretary of labor $2.5 billion to assist public and private agencies to offer new work opportunities in health, education, and related fields.[9] But even though this proposal came along with the Great Society's antipoverty efforts, the Johnson administration was opposed, and the legislation failed to pass.

- In 1976, the Humphrey-Hawkins Full Employment and Balanced Growth bill was introduced into the Congress. Like the Full Employment bill of

[7] See the discussion in Margaret Weir, "The Federal Government and Unemployment: The Frustration of Policy Innovation from the New Deal to the Great Society," in *The Politics of Social Policy in the United States*, ed. Margaret Weir, Ann Shola Orloff, and Theda Skocpol (Princeton: Princeton University Press, 1988), 168–80.

[8] The evolution of the 1945 bill into the 1946 act is analyzed in Stephen Kemp Bailey, *Congress Makes a Law* (New York: Vintage Books, 1950).

[9] Bonnie Fox Schwartz, *The Civil Works Administration, 1933–1934: The Business of Emergency Employment in the New Deal* (Princeton: Princeton University Press, 1984), 268–69.

1945, this would have committed the federal government to guaranteeing jobs to everyone able and willing to work. Humphrey-Hawkins authorized $15 billion the first year for enhanced federal employment services and for temporary public-service jobs, and it required the president to submit every year a "full employment and national purpose" budget embodying plans to keep the unemployment rate below 3 percent. But two years later, in 1978, Humphrey-Hawkins passed as a mere resolution, with all the operative provisions excised with the unemployment goal raised to 4 percent and with the goal of reducing inflation also mandated in the purely symbolic resolution that was enacted.[10]

Across the western, advanced-industrial world in the post–World War II decades, the full employment welfare state came into its own, at least symbolically if not always actually. In this context, the United States stood out not only for its relatively high unemployment rates in the 1950s, 1960s, and 1970s, but even more for its passive governmental approach to managing the national economy. The variant of Keynesianism that held sway intellectually and in public policy practice after the defeat of the Full Employment bill in 1945 was "commercial Keynesianism."[11] This emphasizes the use of tax cuts and automatic stabilizers as tools of macroeconomic stimulation, rather than the use of increases in public social spending. U.S. policymakers officially aimed to fight inflation as much as to keep unemployment rates down, and social-welfare expenditures were not planned in coordination with macroeconomic management. Moreover, despite some minor efforts at manpower programs after World War II and again during the Great Society period, active labor market interventions have been much more extensively and effectively used in Sweden and several other West European nations than in the United States.[12]

In short, compared to most European welfare states in the postwar period, the United States has been profoundly reluctant both in political precept and in practice to use active governmental measures (spending, public employment, active labor market policies) to promote a full employment economy with decent jobs for all who want them. After the advent of Ronald Reagan's presidency, this reluctance became en-

[10] See the discussion in Margaret Weir, *Politics and Jobs: The Boundaries of Employment Policy in the United States* (Princeton: Princeton University Press, 1992), chap. 5.

[11] This term comes from Robert Lekachman, *The Age of Keynes* (New York: McGraw-Hill, 1966), 287.

[12] *European Labor Market Policies*, Special Report no. 27 of the National Commission for Manpower Policy (September 1978); Beatrice G. Reubens, *The Hard-to-Employ: European Programs* (New York: Columbia University Press, 1970); and Margaret S. Gordon, *Retraining and Labor Market Adjustment in Western Europe* (Washington, D.C.: Department of Labor, Office of Manpower, Automation, and Training, 1965).

shrined as official policy. From 1946 through 1979, lip service was paid to the goal of keeping unemployment rates down, and when they were rising or stubbornly high, pressures accumulated on the federal government to devise new measures to combat unemployment. Under Reagan, however, unemployment persisted for some years at 7 percent or above, yet the official goals of the administration were to reduce government's role in the economy and "unleash" private market forces through tax cuts and reductions in federal social programs. Nor was the Reagan administration isolated, for many members of the opposition Democratic party have endorsed these goals and the comprehensive anti–public sector rhetoric that accompanied them. The U.S. national government today is thus further than ever from pursuing the goal of employment assurance articulated by the planners of Social Security in 1935.

How can we explain the failure of the modern U.S. state to use public instrumentalities to pursue full employment assurance? I will eventually point out that the failure is not as complete as it might seem, because the U.S. federal government has always, in one way or another, functioned to distribute job opportunities to the local constituents of congressional representatives. But such "job creation politics" has not been explicitly debated that way at the national level, and it has never been possible to supplant congressional pork barrel with deliberate and selectively targeted national strategies. The peculiarities of administrative statebuilding in the United States since the nineteenth century have left national leaders without effective means to devise or implement explicit full-employment planning. And because of the nature of U.S. political parties, the great new waves of democratic electoral mobilization that came in the 1930s and 1960s ended up creating backlashes against potential commitments to a full-employment welfare state at the very moments when the balance of forces seemed to be swinging in that direction.

Before elaborating this argument centered on the U.S. state and political parties, let me briefly consider two alternative perspectives that might appear to account more straightforwardly for the absence of public employment assurance in America. Could we perhaps dismiss the entire issue on the ground that basic American values—and therefore public opinion in U.S. democracy—rule out the possibility of government taking responsibility for full employment? Or might we invoke the flip side of the variables that many political economists have used to explain Sweden's full employment welfare state, arguing that the American working class has been relatively weakly organized and thus business interests have held sway in the national political process, blocking possibilities for public employment assurance?

Do American Values Rule Out Employment Assurance?

Arguments that basic American values rule out social-welfare activities have always flourished in periods of conservative reaction because it is easy enough for right-wing propagandists to invoke one possible reading—an antistatist reading—of values that surely are at the core of American culture. Americans believe in getting ahead through self-reliance and hard work—so we would all agree. Therefore, Americans do not want help from government, or so the right-wing propagandists attempt to conclude from the agreed-upon premise. But evidence from social history and modern opinion polling alike demonstrates that many Americans, including large majorities at times for which appropriate evidence exists, have held to a perspective more congruent with the core notion of the cartoon reproduced above. Americans have believed that simple "welfare" handouts, whether from private or public sources, were inappropriate (undeserved and demeaning) for those able to work. Yet they have also felt that public authorities had a special responsibility to help able-bodied people get jobs.

In short, many Americans believe that while people are helping themselves, government should also help the unemployed to acquire the jobs through which they can then get ahead through hard work. A complete review of the evidence on this point would take a lengthy paper of its own, but consider the following empirical findings, stretching from the nineteenth century to the late 1970s:

- In her research on the origins of urban political machines, Amy Bridges shows that nineteenth-century party politicians responded to demands for jobs from the unemployed. In New York City during the hard times of the 1850s, "mass meetings of the unemployed" discussed remedies; "private charity was declared both inadequate and degrading. Instead, unemployed workers demanded. . . [that] the city government. . . increase public works to provide employment, without partisan preference and with a guaranteed minimum wage."[13] By 1857, Mayor Fernando Wood responded positively to these demands, despite strong business opposition, and his organization gained electoral strength as a result. Similar developments occurred in Newark, Philadelphia, and Baltimore. In Bridges's words, "the depression of the 1850s brought demands for public works and public relief [through jobs] . . .; these demands won concessions from city governments and pressured politicians into a kind of pre-welfare-state-ism."[14]
- Social historian Alex Keyssar has studied unemployment and working-class

[13] Amy Bridges, *A City in the Republic: Antebellum New York and the Origins of Machine Politics* (Cambridge and New York: Cambridge University Press, 1984), 116.
[14] Ibid., 123.

responses to it in the state of Massachusetts. He documents that in every depression from the 1870s to the 1920s Massachusetts unionists "demanded that government offer direct aid to the unemployed by launching public works programs during depressions."[15] These demands spread upward from cities to state government to the federal government. In the depression of the 1890s, "the national executive council of the A.F. of L. sent a memorial to the President and to Congress asking for public works" and "similar demands were voiced in 1907–08, 1913–14, and most vociferously after World War I . . . [when, according to labor spokesmen,] a nation that sent men into battle had a moral and political obligation to make sure they had jobs when they returned home."[16] During this same period, the national A.F. of L. firmly opposed public unemployment insurance on the grounds that it would undermine workers' independence and subject them to the state. But the state's role in providing work for the unemployed was understood more positively, and the values invoked are revealing. According to Keyssar, "unionists stressed that public works programs were preferable to simple poor relief in three respects: they paid workers a living wage rather than a pittance; they permitted jobless men and women to avoid the demoralizing consequences of accepting charity; and they performed a useful public service."[17]

- According to a social historian who has looked at elite views toward unemployment during the same period covered by Keyssar's study of workers, by the time of the depression of 1913–15, "reformers were learning to recognize that the unemployed wanted jobs, not charity," and they were willing to support public works projects along with public labor exchanges and (as a last resort for those not given work) public unemployment insurance as a right, not a handout.[18]

- During the New Deal of the 1930s, of course, many governmental efforts to combat unemployment were launched—including the public employment programs of the Civil Works Administration, the Works Progress Administration, and the Public Works Administration—and many historians have documented the popularity of these efforts. Public opinion polling also started in this decade. A poll conducted by *Fortune* magazine in July 1935 reported that three-fourths of the public agreed that "the government should see to it that any man who wants to work has a job."[19] And a 1939

---

[15] Alexander Keyssar, *Out of Work: The First Century of Unemployment in Massachusetts* (Cambridge: Cambridge University Press, 1986), 211.

[16] Ibid., 212.

[17] Ibid.

[18] Paul T. Ringebach, *Tramps and Reformers, 1873–1916: The Discovery of Unemployment in New York* (Westport, Conn.: Greenwood Press, 1973), 178 and chaps. 5, 6.

[19] Cited in Lloyd A. Free and Hadley Cantril, *The Political Beliefs of Americans: A Study of Public Opinion* (New York: Simon and Schuster, 1968), 10.

Roper poll reported that 76 percent of the unemployed, 73 percent of blue-collar workers, 60 percent of lower white-collar workers, and 46 percent of upper white-collar workers agreed that the government should guarantee jobs to everyone.[20]

- In the 1960s, there was strong public support for the few targeted "active market" programs that were tried. In 1963–64, "a special survey done by . . . Gallup . . . demonstrated that three-fourths of the public favored Federal aid to 'depressed areas, that is, where unemployment has been high over a long period,' either at the present or an increased level."[21] And in 1967, even after a conservative electoral reaction had begun, 75 percent of Americans in a Gallup poll favored present or increased levels of federal funding for "retraining poorly educated people so they can get jobs."[22]

- In a mid-1970s survey of the U.S. urban workforce, including employed and unemployed respondents of all strata, Kay Schlozman and Sidney Verba found 77 percent agreeing that "the government should end unemployment."[23] Overall, only 30 percent agreed that the government should end unemployment if, in order to do so, it had to hire all of the jobless. Yet the proportions agreeing at each socioeconomic level were higher among the themselves, and about half of those unemployed at the lower would have the government hire all of the jobless.

- In a study (published in 1979) of public attitudes toward who should receive social services, Fay Lomax Cook found that, in general, respondents were loath to support public services for able-bodied poor adults, who were seen as responsible for themselves. But there was an exception if the services would help such people achieve independence. Thus, "when respondents feel they help poor adults under 65 to escape their plight by providing them with education services, support is very high."[24] Cook did not ask directly about public employment opportunities, but the logic of her findings certainly would apply to job training efforts.

- Finally, Robert Shapiro and his associates have explored American attitudes toward public social provision in some detail. They find that "there has always been overwhelming support for work in place of welfare," even though the U.S. public is ambivalent about public works jobs.[25] These au-

[20] Cited in Kay Lehman Schlozman and Sidney Verba, *Injury to Insult: Unemployment, Class, and Political Response* (Cambridge: Harvard University Press, 1979), 220.

[21] Cited in Free and Cantril, *Political Beliefs*, 11.

[22] Cited in ibid., 12.

[23] Schlozman and Verba, *Injury to Insult*, 202–5.

[24] Fay Lomax Cook, *Who Should Be Helped? Public Support for Social Services* (Beverly Hills, Cal.: Sage Publications, 1979), 170.

[25] Robert Y. Shapiro, Kelly D. Patterson, Judith Russell, and John T. Young, "The Polls—A Report: Employment and Social Welfare," *Public Opinion Quarterly* 51 (Summer 1987): 269. See also Robert Shapiro et al., "The Polls: Public Assistance," *Public Opinion Quarterly* 51 (1987): 120–30.

thors have compiled available findings from prior social surveys. In one telling question that has been posed since the 1950s, Americans have been asked whether they agree or disagree that "The government in Washington [or "the federal government"] ought to see to it that everybody who wants to work can find a job." Remarkably, during the 1970s agreement with this idea grew, reaching 74 percent in 1978.[26] Shapiro and associates also show that Americans are broadly supportive of job training programs for the unemployed, work requirements for people on welfare, and child care for working women—all measures that embody expectations that able-bodied adults should be helped to get ahead through work, rather than being left dependent on relief.

Although the evidence just sampled is only suggestive and does not represent all the evidence that could be marshaled, it seems sufficient to allow us to reject any notion that basic American values rule out government efforts at employment assurance. On the contrary, from the nineteenth century to the present, many Americans have called upon government to fight unemployment by using a variety of direct and indirect means to generate jobs for those who need work. Recurrently, moreover, the theme of government ensuring work or job training rather than providing relief has echoed through American politics. Thus the CES planners of 1934–35 *were* operating on value premises broadly shared by a substantial majority of their fellow citizens.

DOES POLITICAL CLASS STRUGGLE EXPLAIN THE FAILURE OF EMPLOYMENT ASSURANCE IN THE UNITED STATES?

If basic U.S. values have not ruled out a strong state role in employment assurance, perhaps the trouble has been in the balance of power between business and organized labor. Adherents of the most fruitful recent approach to the comparative study of Western welfare states—the working-class strength or social-democratic approach—would certainly direct our attention to the relative weakness of U.S. industrial unions and to the absence of a labor-based political party in U.S. democracy.[27] Given these weaknesses of working-class organization, the argument goes, U.S. capitalists have been able to use direct and indirect pressures to prevent governments at all levels from undertaking social-welfare efforts, and especially from undertaking labor market interventions or

[26] Shapiro et al., "Polls: Employment and Welfare," 274–75.

[27] For overviews of this literature, see Michael Shalev, "The Social Democratic Model and Beyond: Two Generations of Comparative Research on the Welfare State," Model *Comparative Social Research* 6 (1983): 315–51; and Theda Skocpol and Edwin Amenta, "States and Social Policies," *Annual Review of Sociology* 12 (1986): 131–57.

public works projects that would interfere with the prerogatives or profits of private businesses.

Unquestionably, political class struggle does partially help explain why the U.S. national state has not committed itself to full employment assurance. Swedish-style policies would probably have come about in the United States had American workers been as highly unionized as Swedish ones or had the modern Democratic party been a truly social-democratic party based in the organized working class. Moreover, American business groups have consistently pressured against the inception or extension of many welfare-state efforts. It would be pointless to deny that such business pressures—as well as the alternative public policy ideas championed by business-sponsored intellectuals—have had their effect on policy outcomes. For example, after the defeat of the essentially social-democratic stagnationist Keynesian ideas embodied in the Full Employment bill of 1945, commercial Keynesian prescriptions were instead put into effect. These policies had been partly developed and propagated under the auspices of two business organizations, the Committee on Economic Development and the U.S. Chamber of Commerce.[28]

Nevertheless, for several reasons it would be a mistake to attribute the failure of employment assurance entirely to the political class struggles of strong business versus weak labor. First, a focus exclusively on political conflicts of interest between capitalists and industrial workers deflects our attention from other partially socioeconomically grounded forces that have shaped and limited state activities in the United States. Agricultural interests in the South and West have always been very much a part of American politics, and regional and racial conflicts have been just as critical in shaping and limiting U.S. state activities in economic planning and labor market intervention as have conflicts between business and labor.[29] Moreover, business and labor groups have often united to work for or against governmental policies that would affect employment in particular areas. As I argue below, the structure of the U.S. federal state and the character of U.S. political parties have especially encouraged local solidarities and interregional and racial/ethnic conflicts over economic interventions by the national government.

Second, the political class struggle approach applied to the case of the United States proves insensitive to the peculiar evolution of American political history. Any approach that focuses our attention on the rise of industrial unions fails to explain why U.S. party patronage democracy

[28] Collins, *Business Response to Keynes.*

[29] This theme is developed in several of the essays in Margaret Weir, Ann Shola Orloff, and Theda Skocpol, eds., *The Politics of Social Policy in the United States* (Princeton: Princeton University Press, 1988).

in the nineteenth century actually functioned as a precocious (albeit uneven) welfare state, distributing social benefits that included permanent or emergency jobs for many middle- and working-class men.[30] Ironically, America in the twentieth century may in many ways have retreated from the employment assurance efforts that certain nineteenth-century urban party machines were prepared to make for their popular constituents.

Finally, an approach that stresses political class struggle fails to explain the politics of employment assurance at those critical conjunctures in twentieth-century American politics—especially the mid to late 1930s and the 1960s—when U.S. business interests were politically vulnerable, when working-class and more broadly democratic forces were on the rise, and when many social-welfare policies that business strongly opposed actually did pass and become a permanent part of the federal government's activities. Why didn't employment assurance efforts become institutionalized as goals and programs at these conjunctures—when policies were actually proposed and debated, and U.S. public opinion (as we have seen) favored work over relief for the unemployed and the impoverished? A political class struggle approach alone will not explain the missed possibilities for national commitments to employment assurance during the special conjunctures of the thirties and sixties.

Thus, by paying attention to conflicts between capitalists and labor we can explain some features of modern U.S. social-welfare policies—especially in contrast to the social democracies of post–World War II Western Europe. Yet analysis from another perspective is also required if we are to understand fully why American democracy has not institutionalized full employment assurance as a goal and activity of the national state.

The Politics of Job Creation versus Employment Assurance in America's Federal Democracy

Many of the answers to the questions and puzzles I have posed lie in the history of U.S. state building and in the peculiar structures of U.S. federal democracy and party politics. As I cannot fully elaborate or prove

[30] See Bridges, *City in the Republic*, passim; Martin Shefter, "Trade Unions and Political Machines: The Organization and Disorganization of American Working Class Life in the Late Nineteenth Century," in *Working-Class Formation: Nineteenth-Century Patterns in Western Europe and the United States*, ed. Ira Katznelson and Aristide R. Zolberg (Princeton: Princeton University Press, 1986), 267–72; and Steven P. Erie, *Rainbow's End: Irish-Americans and the Dilemmas of Urban Machine Politics, 1840–1985* (Berkeley: University of California Press, 1988), chap. 2.

my case in a short essay, let me make three bold propositions about how these matters relate to employment politics in major phases and key conjunctures of U.S. history. My propositions should be considered working hypotheses in need of further research and exploration. I lay them out here to provoke discussion and debate.

Proposition Number One: A "distributive" politics of job creation has always been an important part of public policymaking in the United States. But this kind of politics was explicit at all levels in the party-patronage democracy of the nineteenth-century and has become a nationally unacknowledged politics of local subsidies and regional competition in the U.S. state structure of the twentieth century.

Both social commentators and social scientists have often fundamentally mischaracterized American society and politics in the nineteenth century, suggesting that Americans back then were all hardy individualists and that governments did little to "interfere" in the economy or society. In truth, nineteenth-century America was the world's first mass democracy, and the polity was dominated at all levels by patronage-oriented political parties that were intensely competitive with one another and had elaborate organizations capable of getting out virtually all eligible white, male voters for incessant rounds of local, state, and national elections. These patronage-oriented parties specialized in distributive public policymaking—that is, they constantly looked for ways to generate divisible material benefits to pass out to their key cadres and supporters in as many states and local communities as possible.[31] Land grants, Civil War pensions, and tariff advantages were some of the distributive policies that characterized party-patronage democracy in the nineteenth century. But the most obvious distributions were of public jobs themselves. Thus national party managers distributed postmasterships and customs house jobs, and state and local party bosses distributed proliferating numbers of posts at those levels of government. Finally, as we have seen from Amy Bridges's work, urban political machines responded during crises to the demands of the unemployed for expanded public works projects to provide work for the jobless. All in all, it is fair to say that the central political organizations of nineteenth-century America, the parties, unabashedly worked at all levels to generate and distribute jobs in government or at public expense. Especially because it was dealing with such political parties, the emergent American working class learned to hope that government would provide work rather than charity.

In the twentieth century, however, patronage-oriented political par-

---

[31] Richard L. McCormick, "The Party Period and Public Policy: An Exploratory Hypothesis," in *The Party Period and Public Policy* (New York: Oxford University Press, 1986), chap. 5.

ties have been on the defensive, as wave after wave of elite reformers from the Progressives on have sought, with considerable success, to weaken their organizations and reorient electoral democracy toward the expectations of upper-middle-class ideals of good government. Yet the politics of creating and distributing jobs has not disappeared. Rather it has survived in the operations of Congress at the federal level, and in the way congressional politics links up to local politics and regional interests.

The U.S. national state structure of the twentieth century has remained remarkably decentralized because national administrative structures have only rarely supplanted the powers of state and local governments, and because Congress, with its state and local constituencies, has used its committee system to retain great influence over both legislation and actual policy implementation.[32] Politically speaking, shifting congressional coalitions, often brokered through committee negotiations, are much more important than political party divisions as such in modern American politics. For public policy outcomes, this means that the bread-and-butter interests of many localities typically have to be brokered into most laws that get through Congress. Once laws are passed, individual congressional representatives will work with the federal bureaucracy to make sure that benefits are channeled to their localities.

The upshot of all this is that many modern U.S. public policies that appear to be about national problems—such as defense or health care or urban renewal—are really mechanisms for spreading federal subsidies to as many congressional districts as possible. Back home, each congressperson presents these policies as ways to generate or protect jobs for local people. But in national policy debates, they are not explicitly treated as employment assurance policies. And that matters, because if full employment were the explicit goal, alternative kinds of policies, more carefully targeted on selected areas of the country or aimed at helping people to move around more freely, might be preferred. As it is, congressional brokering has repeatedly spent a lot of national resources on job creation for the middle classes and construction and defense workers across many, many localities. But people in especially depressed regions and localities (that is, inner cities) have been left in place, insufficiently helped to find employment. Yet those people do not

---

[32] Background for this and the following paragraph comes from Stephen Skowronek, *Building a New American State* (Cambridge and New York: Cambridge University Press, 1982); Samuel P. Huntington, "Congressional Responses to the Twentieth Century," in *The Congress and America's Future*, 2d ed. (Englewood Cliffs: Prentice-Hall, 1973), 6–38; Morris P. Fiorina, *Congress: Keystone of the Washington Establishment* (New Haven: Yale University Press, 1977); and R. Douglas Arnold, *Congress and the Bureaucracy: A Theory of Influence* (New Haven: Yale University Press, 1979).

feel even as entitled to ask for political help as the unemployed workers of the 1850s in New York City did—because U.S. politics in the twentieth century is not *openly* about job creation and distribution!

Proposition Number Two: Efforts at bureaucratic state building and administrative reform since the Progressive Era have not facilitated national economic planning for full employment. Actually, through their failures and halfway successes, such efforts have created obstacles to the implementation of nationally coordinated public works, to Keynesian macroeconomic management through social spending, and to active labor market policies.

The reformist American elites who have worked since the Progressive Era to displace patronage-oriented parties and politicians from their formerly dominant role in American democracy have also had positive state building goals. Middle-class professionals, including social scientists, have always been prominent among such good government reformers, from the Progressives through the New Dealers to the New Politics reformers of the 1960s. These reformers have sought to create professional-bureaucratic agencies of government through which rational policies in the public interest could be pursued free from the clutches of mere politicians, especially those in Congress and in political party organizations. For our purposes here, the point to be made about efforts at administrative reform is that they have never succeeded in creating state capacities for national full employment assurance.

During the Progressive Era, reformers were determined to undermine patronage-oriented party politicians. Thus they favored the establishment of regulatory commissions free from political control but opposed new state activities that would allow politicians to channel money or jobs to popular constituents.[33] Working-class demands for public works to employ people during depressions met with a cautious response from reformers. Until city and state governments or federal agencies were reorganized under expert control, most reformers did not want them to have enhanced spending powers.

The one relevant reform that the Progressives did strongly favor was the establishment of a strong national system of employment bureaus, and had this succeeded it would have facilitated the later implementation of both public works and active labor market policies. But despite the setting up of a temporary federal Employment Service during World War I, this Progressive state building effort failed.[34] Local business and

---

[33] Skowronek, *Building a New American State*, part 3; and Martin Shefter, "Party, Bureaucracy, and Political Change in the United States," in *Political Parties: Development and Decay*, ed. Louis Maisel and Joseph Cooper (Beverly Hills: Sage Publications, 1978), 211–65.

[34] I. W. Litchfield, "The United States Employment Service and Demobilization," *Annals of the American Academy of Political and Social Science* 81 (1919): 19–27.

labor groups working through Congress dismantled the national system right after World War I, and the nation was subsequently left until the 1930s with no effective means to monitor or intervene in labor markets.

During the 1930s, of course, New Dealers resumed efforts to build new governmental agencies to serve the public interest—and many of their efforts were directly oriented to dealing with massive unemployment in the Great Depression. Throughout the New Deal and into the 1940s, however, there was an ongoing political struggle between New Dealers in the executive branch and Congress, with its ties to state and local interests. The struggle was over who would control enhanced federal spending and new federal activities; basically Congress won in the end. Key New Deal programs and failed efforts at administrative reform ended up enhancing federal and congressional controls at the expense of centralized national planning and coordination. Thus:

- Public employment agencies were established as a state-controlled federal system, rather than as a national system; and right after World War II, Congress defeated an attempt to maintain the nationalization of these services that had been necessary to implement wartime manpower policies.[35]
- The various emergency public works and public employment programs of the New Deal were constantly wracked by local objections to Washington's initiatives and requirements. Consequently, some of the most efficient programs, like the Civil Works Administration and the Public Works Administration, aroused opposition from local and state politicians and from Congress and ended up being dismantled or hobbled in their ability to fight unemployment in a nationally coordinated way.[36]
- What perhaps did the most to undercut the possibility of the permanent institutionalization of either public works or Keynesian social spending was the failure of the sweeping budgetary and administrative reforms that Roosevelt attempted to put through in 1937–38. Southerners feared too much federal intervention in their agricultural labor relations and in race relations, and southern congressional committee chairmen thus opposed efforts to strengthen the New Deal executive. Further, congressional representatives generally, including liberals, were anxious to protect their branch's established ties to parts of the federal bureaucracy and their branch's controls over the federal budgeting process. Thus Congress eviscerated Roosevelt's proposed administrative reforms.[37]
- In related moves, Congress step by step undercut and then abolished the

[35] See the discussion and references in Weir, "Federal Government and Unemployment," in *Politics of Social Policy in the United States*, 166–67.

[36] Schwartz, *Civil Works Administration*.

[37] Richard Polenberg, *Reorganizing Roosevelt's Government, 1936–1939: The Controversy over Executive Reorganization* (Cambridge: Harvard University Press, 1966).

National Resources Planning Board that Roosevelt had hoped to make central to long-range national economic planning for full employment. This happened during World War II, and it was just a prelude to Congress's defeat of the Full Employment bill of 1945, which was a last attempt by New Dealers interested in institutionalizing a commitment to employment assurance to beef up the capacities of the president and executive branch to plan and coordinate social spending and public works for that purpose.[38]

In the aftermath of the struggles between the executive and the Congress during the New Deal and World War II, federal policies relevant to employment proceeded on two tracks, neither well coordinated with the other. One track was congressionally managed spending programs, which tended to be presented to local constituencies as ways to bring jobs into particular localities, but not as national strategies to combat unemployment as such. The other track involved presidentially sponsored initiatives to combat either unemployment or inflation. These overtly national, macroeconomic strategies were devised by the Office of the President and the Council of Economic Advisors, which were the purely advisory bodies established after the New Deal administrative reforms and the Full Employment bill had been emasculated. Yet, because these bodies had little administrative authority and no capacity to control Congress, they tended to gravitate toward passive, commercial Keynesian strategies that used tax cuts and automatic stabilizers, rather than toward social spending or active labor market interventions.[39]

As Margaret Weir shows in her important book about U.S. employment policies from the 1960s to the 1980s, the established bifurcation —built into the post–New Deal state structure—between congressionally controlled programs and executive commercial Keynesian macroeconomic management meant that it was hard during the War on Poverty of the 1960s for proponents of active labor market interventions to succeed.[40] During the sixties and early seventies, some manpower economists in the Labor Department wanted to devise new national approaches to unemployment, approaches that combined public employment with federally sponsored training programs and with the use of

[38] Marion Clawson, *New Deal Planning: The National Resources Planning Board* (Baltimore: Johns Hopkins University Press, 1981); and Philip W. Warken, *A History of the National Resources Planning Board* (New York: Garland Press, 1979).

[39] Further discussion appears in Edwin Amenta and Theda Skocpol, "Taking Exception: Explaining the Distinctiveness of American Public Policies in the Last Century," in *The Comparative History of Public Policy*, ed. Francis G. Castles (Oxford: Polity Press/Basil Blackwell, 1989), 305–9.

[40] Weir, *Politics and Jobs*.

enhanced spending for the redevelopment of depressed areas. Under President Kennedy, however, the Council of Economic Advisors chose to use tax cuts to stimulate overall growth in the national economy, assuming that this alone would address unemployment.

Within the executive branch, the Labor Department economists could not sell their approach to the economic advisers or to presidents. Within Congress, the only kinds of manpower and spending programs that could get through were *not* programs that enhanced Labor Department controls over efficiently targeted training efforts. They were, instead, programs that would channel funds for administration by many local governments and agencies. President Johnson, moreover, was a president who thought in congressional terms, and he believed that the War on Poverty could best be fought by channeling some funds to many established local authorities and others (for example, Community Action grants) to newly mobilized blacks in the cities. Johnson did not support Labor Department ideas for targeted, centrally managed employment policies. Like other presidents, he relied on the Council of Economic Advisors for strategies to further national economic growth without specifically addressing structural unemployment as a national economic problem.

Proposition Number Three: The peculiarities of American political parties, and the internal contradictions of the Democratic party in particular, have made it impossible to translate upsurges of popular political participation in the 1930s and the 1960s into broad political alliances that could provide support for full employment policies. Instead, conservative backlashes occurred in each time period.

Whatever the difficulties of building and reorganizing the American national state in the twentieth century so as to facilitate full employment policies, one might still suppose that—if Americans really do prefer work to welfare—popular preferences for such policies would have prevailed, especially in the New Deal or in the aftermath of the civil rights revolution of the 1960s. Indeed, one can point to *potential* broad popular coalitions favoring employment assurance in both the 1930s–40s and the 1960s–70s.

In the 1930s, industrial workers were newly organized into increasingly powerful unions allied with urban-liberal Democrats, and masses of new voters were joining the Democratic electoral base. Moreover, during the New Deal, at least initially, poor farmers in the South and Midwest were potential recruits to a Democratic–popular coalition that could have furthered a broad social program, including full employment planning and policies.

In the 1960s and early 1970s, American blacks were finally fully mobilized into the Democratic electoral coalition, and the potential was opened for an ascendant liberal coalition of workers, blacks, and some middle-class people as southern and farm-area conservative control of Congress was finally broken. However, in both these critical periods, the Democratic party was the key to any enduring pro-full-employment alliance. Yet the Democratic party's internal contradictions, as they played out within the U.S. federal state structure and electoral system, doomed possibilities for further reforms and triggered conservative reactions.

During the 1930s, the growth of urban-liberal forces within the Democratic party had to coexist with the entrenched conservative power of southern Democratic representatives of agricultural and racially segregationist areas.[41] For Roosevelt and the New Dealers never launched any concerted attack on the disenfranchisement of southern blacks. Ironically, as the national Democratic party grew, conservative southern committee chairmen in Congress gained increased strength, which they used to help undercut administrative reorganization and public works spending in the later 1930s and to help abolish the National Resources Planning Board and defeat the Full Employment bill in the 1940s.

Moreover, the conservative Democrats increasingly allied themselves in Congress with conservative Republicans, including many from midwestern farm areas that became increasingly opposed to further New Deal reforms after the mid-1930s. Such opposition developed once richer farmers had benefited from New Deal agricultural subsidies and once the American Farm Bureau Federation gained local administrative control of those subsidies and used its leverage to effect an antireformist alliance between southern planters and richer midwestern farmers. This came at the expense of the urban-liberal wing of the Democratic party, and the increasing Republican loyalties of many farmers after the mid-1930s prevented the development of a more progressive coalition inside the Democratic party between urban workers and midwestern farmers. Such a coalition would have no doubt sustained New Deal public works and facilitated social Keynesianism rather than commercial Keynesianism in the postwar period.

By the time of the Great Society and the War on Poverty in the 1960s, the grip of the congressional conservative coalition was finally relaxed, and there seemed to be new hope for a liberal Democratic

[41] This discussion follows the lines of Weir, "Federal Government and Unemployment," in Weir et al., eds., *Politics of Social Policy in the United States*, 156–62, and Margaret Weir and Theda Skocpol, "State Structures and the Possibilities for 'Keynesian' Responses to the Great Depression in Sweden, Britain, and the United States," in *Bringing the State Back In*, ed. Peter Evans, Dietrich Rueschemeyer, and Theda Skocpol (Cambridge and New York: Cambridge University Press, 1985), 107–63.

party to complete an American version of the full employment welfare state. This was especially true because the civil rights revolution had finally brought most blacks into American democracy, and black opinion placed a high value on governmental efforts to further education and jobs, for many new black migrants to northern cities had not been able to find adequate employment. Organized labor and blacks could come together naturally and easily around employment assurance policies enacted by the federal government.

But once again the internal contradictions of the Democratic party—operating in the congressionally centered and administratively weak U.S. state structure—defeated progressive possibilities.[42] President Johnson, congressional Democrats, and state and local party leaders did not devise the War on Poverty as a self-conscious national full employment assurance strategy, as a way to create a universalistic social alliance including blacks. Instead, thinking in the usual terms of congressional brokering and broadly scattered subsidies to local interests, they decided to add new programs and subsidies for poor and black groups onto established or further subsidies for other locally based interests. Some monies for job training and public service jobs were channeled to black community groups in this way. The intention was to give poor blacks new, special resources, which it was hoped would help poor blacks get ahead in a growing economy and, in the process, add them onto established urban-Democratic coalitions.

But that was not what happened. In practice, economic growth did not prove sufficient to overcome the structural obstacles to employment faced by innercity blacks; yet the channeling of new resources to them in a politically visible way helped trigger conflicts with other Democrats, including established city governments, white ethnic neighborhoods, and even some labor unions. In short, poverty was not overcome, and the northern Democratic party was thrown into turmoil. Soon many white working-class ethnics, as well as previously alienated white southerners, began switching to the Republican party, at least for presidential voting. This trend has continued (with a brief reversal for Jimmy Carter) from Richard Nixon to George Bush and in the 1984 election the Democrats did not get a majority of any white population group other than the Jews. The effect in the 1970s and 1980s has not been only on the presidency either, for even though liberal Democrats

[42] This discussion draws on Weir, "Federal Government and Unemployment," 180–86, and Michael K. Brown, "The Segmented Welfare System: Distributive Conflict and Retrenchment in the United States, 1968–1984," in *Remaking the Welfare State: Retrenchment and Social Policy in America and Europe,* ed. Michael K. Brown (Philadelphia: Temple University Press, 1988), 182–210.

have survived a bit better in Congress, the presence there of avowed nonliberals in both parties has steadily grown—and the possibilities for new uses of federal power have correspondingly diminished.

Just as the upsurge of urban-liberal power during the New Deal helped —once it was channeled into the Democratic party and the U.S. state structure—to spur reactions from the congressional conservative coalition of southern Democrats and Republicans, so in the current period the civil rights revolution and the upsurge of black political mobilization have functioned to unleash the right-wing anti-public-sector movement led and symbolized by Ronald Reagan. It is not coincidental that the policies and programs that were most successfully attacked during the Reagan presidencies were those launched by the Great Society, including the few federal job training and public employment efforts that remained. Nor is it coincidental that Reagan worked hard to debunk the idea that the federal government should be responsible for full employment. Finally, it is not surprising that the Reagan administration did all it could to trim the gains of the civil rights movement and reopen settled struggles between whites and blacks over affirmative action issues. For the Reagan forces understood full well that their ascendancy had grown out of the collapse of a potential broad Democratic coalition in support of enhanced social-welfare interventions by the federal government.[43]

Looking back to what may now be a concluded chapter in modern American political history—the New Deal and postwar era, stretching from the 1930s to the 1970s—I think we can see that a genuinely American full employment welfare state might have been established but wasn't. Much of the reason why such a full employment welfare state was not established lies in the structural obstacles inherent in the U.S. state and political party system, obstacles that I have attempted to analyze here. Yet these state and party structures were also transformed over time by reformers and political leaders. At times those leaders chose political strategies that were not optimal: for example, the strategy in the War on Poverty of attacking poverty in isolation from the economy as a whole and the strategy of mobilizing blacks in particular rather than creating new, broad social alliances that included their needs but ensured greater political support.[44]

For the future, if reformers or Democrats or any other forces in

---

[43] Brown, "Segmented Welfare System," makes this point especially forcefully.

[44] For further elaboration of "universalistic" reform strategies that might work better than the tactics of the War on Poverty, see Theda Skocpol, "Targeting within Universalism: Politically Viable Policies to Combat Poverty in the United States" (Paper Commission for the

American politics get another opportunity to push forward (rather than merely defend) public social provision, they would be well advised not only to respect the structural obstacles of the U.S. polity but also to make better choices within its constraints. Choosing to work for national employment assurance appears likely to remain a potentially popular political choice, although it remains to be seen if any political leadership will soon be forthcoming to devise both the policies and the suitably universalistic political alliances needed to work for this goal. Nevertheless, even if little happens soon, the goal of full employment assurance itself—so clearly articulated in 1935 by the members of the CES—seems unlikely to fade away. For employment assurance accords with longstanding American values, and it would address the distresses of many groups and regions in our presently unsettled national economy. Sooner or later, therefore, a politics of employment assurance—rather than one of welfare—will surely reappear on the American political scene.

"Conference on the Truly Disadvantaged," Northwestern University, October 19–21, 1989, sponsored by the Social Science Research Council and the Center for Urban Affairs and Policy Research, Northwestern University), a version of which appears in chap. 8 below.

CHAPTER EIGHT

Targeting within Universalism: Politically Viable Policies to Combat Poverty in the United States

WHAT TO DO about poverty is, once again, on the public agenda in the United States. Just a few years back, academics and research funders, whipsawed by backlashes against the War on Poverty and the Moynihan report, averted their attention from poverty and other race-related social ills. Then Charles Murray's broadsides against federal social policies in *Losing Ground* provoked outraged critics to enter the fray again; and William Julius Wilson's *The Truly Disadvantaged* revalidated discussion of "the underclass" by progressives as well as conservatives.[1] Now analysts are looking closely and talking frankly about the full range of social problems and policy solutions connected to poverty, including severe inner-city black poverty.

This new interest is good news for citizens who want to strengthen public efforts against poverty. But there are also reasons to worry, and not only because the overall tone of academic and political discourse is much less optimistic than in the 1960s. Recent debates have been imbued with presumptions of a national budget crisis, with cynicism about what government can do, and with extreme pessimism about the intractability of the problems of the inner-city poor. Thus those who want to do more to fight poverty are understandably concerned that their proposals may be stalled or perverted into purely disciplinary measures. Yet they also need to worry about how much the policy prescriptions they are debating recapitulate the flawed presumptions and tactics of the War on Poverty and the Great Society. If supporters of new social policies do find openings in the near future, they need to do better politically than did the antipoverty warriors of the 1960s and early 1970s, whose best intentions were not realized. It is not clear, however, that current debates about poverty and welfare are breaking enough new ground to make politically successful policy innovations likely.

Just as the mainstream debates in the 1960s presumed that hard-core, long-term poverty was largely caused by behavioral problems or deficient skills that could be corrected by special training and community

From *The Urban Underclass*, edited by Christopher Jencks and Paul E. Peterson (Washington, DC: The Brookings Institution, 1991).
[1] Murray (1984); and Wilson (1987).

action programs, the welfare reform consensus of the mid-1980s quickly seized on the idea that the ills of the poor could be cured by mandated work and job training tacked on to existing welfare programs, perhaps supplemented with a year or so of child care and medical coverage for those making the transition from welfare.[2] During the 1960s many liberal professionals focused on rehabilitating young people; today many would accept Lisbeth Schorr's call to expand intensive and comprehensive programs targeted at impoverished families with babies and young children.[3] Similarly, after the War on Poverty got under way, many activists wanted programs to concentrate on helping poor blacks in particular; today one still hears voices such as Roger Wilkins's arguing that, because the black poor are "different," special antipoverty policies should be devised for them alone.[4] Finally, just as advocates for lower-income Americans during the Johnson and first Nixon presidencies argued for directing more benefits and services to all lower-income people, so some redistribution-minded progressives are now making similar proposals for a much larger national safety net without gaping holes.[5]

UNIVERSAL VERSUS TARGETED SOCIAL POLICIES

Along with the small chorus of academic and political voices advocating welfare reforms or new programs and benefits targeted on low-income people (or special sectors of the poor), there are a few voices trying to sing a different tune. Proposing "universalism" rather than targeting, they argue that renewed efforts to deal with the plight of the poor, including the inner-city black poor, ought to be occasions for launching or redesigning U.S. social provision in general. The aim ought to be to ameliorate poverty through broader social programs that include whites along with people of color, and middle-class citizens along with economically disadvantaged Americans.

This position has been forcefully argued by William Wilson in *The Truly Disadvantaged*, a book embodying a paradoxical message that needs to be heard with all of its nuances. The first part of the message has

[2] The mood of this consensus is captured in Kaus (1986).

[3] Schorr (1988).

[4] Wilkins (1989).

[5] Sar A. Levitan and Clifford M. Johnson (1984) suggested cutting back public benefits to the middle class to fund comprehensive job training and public employment programs for the poor. Frances Fox Piven and Richard A. Cloward (1987), p. 99, argued that AFDC, unemployment insurance, and supplemental security income should be merged into a more comprehensive, financially generous, and nationally uniform system of social provision for the poor that would be without bureaucratic hassles. See also Russell (1989).

already been heard: that renewed attention must be given to the multiple pathologies and special problems of the inner-city black underclass, which constitutes about 10 percent of all of the poor.[6] But the second part does not follow simple-mindedly from the first. If vivid facts about severe social problems were all that mattered in shaping policy prescriptions, Wilson's focus on the truly disadvantaged would constitute a call for more finely targeted public policies. Yet he sharply criticizes both racially specific measures to aid blacks and redistributive socioeconomic programs to help lower-income people in general. Racially targeted policies primarily help socially advantaged blacks, he argues, while benefits or services restricted to the poor cannot generate sustained political support: "especially when the national economy is in a period of little growth, no growth, or decline . . . the more the public programs are perceived by members of the wider society as benefiting only certain groups, the less support those programs receive." Following this politically grounded logic, Wilson concludes that the *"hidden agenda is to improve life chances of groups such as the ghetto underclass by emphasizing programs . . . [to] which the more advantaged groups of all races can positively relate."*[7]

Supporters of targeted antipoverty policies have arguments against such universalism. Widespread benefits, it is often said, are expensive, and Americans will not pay taxes to fund them. Furthermore, it is sometimes claimed that universal programs, whether benefits or services, give most of the available resources to those who need them least, either to those already in the middle class or, through the well-known phenomenon of "creaming," to those within the low-income population who are already best prepared to improve themselves. According to the advocates of targeted programs, the social problems now faced by America's most impoverished people, especially female-headed black families in inner cities, can be ameliorated only by highly concentrated and comprehensive benefits and social services devised especially for the poor.[8]

Rarely, however, do advocates of targeted benefits or specially tailored public social services face up to the problem of finding sustained political support for them. Implicitly relying on altruistic appeals to Americans who want to help the disadvantaged, they do not explain why working-class families with incomes just above the poverty line, themselves frequently struggling economically without the aid of health insurance or child care or adequate unemployment benefits, should pay

---

[6] Ellwood (1988).
[7] Wilson (1987), pp. 118, 120.
[8] See Russell (1989), p. 17; Schorr (1988), pp. xxiv–vi; and Wilkins (1989), p. A23.

for programs that go only to people with incomes below the poverty line. Neither do these advocates explain why the American middle and working classes will not simply want to write off troubled inner-city people, or else use repressive agencies—police departments, prisons, and a "war against drugs"—to deal with their threatening behaviors. Some voters feel better about punishing the underclass than about helping it. More broadly, and especially in America, the poor serve as a negative example against which those who "make it on their own" and "earn their own way" can define themselves. Regrettable or not, this attitude is unlikely to change. Such stereotyping of the poor helps to explain why cross-national research on social expenditures has found that universal programs are more sustainable in democracies, even if they are more expensive than policies targeted solely on the poor or other "marginal" groups.[9]

Are we left, then, with a standoff in which advocates of universalism and advocates of targeting can each explain cogently why the other's prescriptions will not adequately help the truly disadvantaged? This standoff certainly exists as long as we remain at the level of logical or highly speculative arguments. Yet three conclusions can be drawn by examining the history of public policies dealing with, or including, poor people in the United States. First, when U.S. antipoverty efforts have featured policies targeted on the poor alone, they have not been politically sustainable, and they have stigmatized and demeaned the poor. Second, some kinds of relatively universal social policies have been politically very successful. Third, room has been made *within* certain universal policy frameworks for extra benefits and services that disproportionately help less privileged people without stigmatizing them. What I shall call "targeting within universalism" has delivered extra benefits and special services to certain poor people throughout the history of modern American social provision, and new versions of it could be devised today to revitalize and redirect U.S. public social provision.

THE TRAVAILS OF TARGETED POLICIES

Without plunging into a detailed discussion of all the government strategies devised in the United States for coping with the poor, I will consider some of the most important initiatives: poorhouses in the nineteenth century, the mothers' pensions launched in the 1910s, and the War on Poverty and associated Great Society reforms of the late 1960s

[9] See Korpi (1980); and Rosenberry (1982). Of course, targeted programs may succeed politically when their beneficiaries are relatively privileged—witness U.S. federal programs such as tax subsidies for private homeowners and parity payments to commercial farmers.

and early 1970s. In each instance, reformers' high hopes of helping poor people were soon dashed against rock-hard political realities.

Poorhouses as a Failed Reform Effort

Poorhouses are the best example of a targeted antipoverty policy in the nineteenth century. Part of a general proliferation of institutions to reform people thought to be defective in a period when the disciplines of the market, wage labor, and political citizenship were being established for the majority, almshouses were intended to "cut the expense of poor relief and deter potential paupers" and at the same time "mitigate the harshness of contemporary poor relief practice by ending the auctioning of the poor to the lowest bidder and stopping the shunting of the poor from town to town regardless of their health or the weather."[10] Almshouses were also expected to improve the character and behavior of the poor: work "would be mandatory for all inmates neither too sick nor too feeble, and both idleness and alcohol would be prohibited. Able-bodied men would be pruned rigorously from the relief rolls; begging would be barred and punished; [and] children would be schooled. . . ."[11] Fueled by all these hopes, the movement for poorhouses peppered them across most of the settled areas of the country (except the rural South) before the Civil War.

But by the 1850s it had become clear that poorhouses were not working as intended and a "preoccupation with order, routine, and cost replaced the founders' concern with the transformation of character and social reform."[12] Intended to cut costs (although in practice it cost more, not less, to maintain people in institutions rather than homes), few poorhouses were adequately funded. They failed to help needy inmates and quickly became prey to corrupt managers who made special deals with merchants and doctors. Appropriate work was often not devised for able-bodied paupers, and the very young, the old, and the insane were simply shut up and often exploited. Furthermore, poorhouses did not always discipline poor people, some of whom learned to come and go as they wished in response to the ebb and flow of outside opportunities.

Before long, poorhouses lost the support of reformers and the public. New movements were launched to abolish all public assistance for the able-bodied and to create more specialized institutions for subgroups such as orphans and the insane. Surviving poorhouses served mainly as

[10] Katz (1986), pp. 22–23.
[11] Ibid., p. 22.
[12] Ibid., p. 25. The following account draws on Katz, chap. 1 and the rest of part 1.

miserable warnings to working people to avoid dependency at all costs. By the turn of the century, poorhouses were principally old-age homes for those unlucky enough to lack resources and family ties. Meanwhile, destitution and dependency proliferated along with industrialism, and the poor, including the able-bodied men who were supposed to have been cured in (or by the example of) almshouses, became more of a problem than ever.

The Marginalization of Pensions for Mothers

Laws allowing local jurisdictions to give benefits to impoverished widowed mothers (and sometimes other caretakers) in charge of dependent children were passed in forty states between 1911 and 1920 and in four more before 1931.[13] The legislation was enthusiastically urged on state legislatures by federations of local clubs whose members were elite and middle-class married women.[14] Local, state, and national associations within the National Congress of Mothers, the General Federation of Women's Clubs, and the Women's Christian Temperance Union argued that all mothers should be honored for their child-nurturing service and, like disabled veteran soldiers, should be adequately and honorably supported by government when breadwinner husbands were not available. Impoverished widowed mothers, the women's associations insisted, should not have to do low-wage labor to survive; and they should not have to give up their children to custodial institutions. Above all, they should not be stigmatized as paupers.

Despite generous intentions and broad popular support, mothers' pensions evolved into one of the most socially demeaning and poorly funded parts of modern U.S. social provision.[15] The pensions were implemented only in certain (predominantly nonrural) jurisdictions, leaving many widowed mothers, including most nonwhites, unable even to apply for benefits. Where these pensions were established, the programs were starved for funds by communities reluctant to spend taxpayers' money on the poor. Consequently, benefit levels were set so low that many clients could not avoid working for wages or taking in male boarders, activities that could open clients up to charges of child neglect or immorality. Social workers, whose organizations had originally opposed mothers' pensions, moved in to become local administrators and caseworkers. Acutely sensitive to possible accusations of political cor-

[13] Children's Bureau (1933), p. 2.
[14] A full account of the role of women's associations in the campaign for mothers' pensions appears in Skocpol (1992), chap. 8.
[15] For an overview of the historical development of mothers' pensions, aid to dependent children, and aid to families with dependent children, see Bell (1965).

ruption and lacking sufficient resources to help more than a few of the needy applicants, they applied eligibility rules and "proper home" investigations with a vengeance. Before long, these conditions turned the pensions into an often cumbersome and demeaning form of public welfare.

When mothers' pensions were federalized as Aid to Dependent Children (ADC) under the Social Security Act of 1935, benefit levels and administrative procedures remained decentralized and the tradition of inadequate funding continued. Indeed, at first, the federal government offered only one-third matching funds to the states. The 1939 amendments to the act increased the federal proportion to one-half but removed from ADC the very "worthy widows" who had originally been the focus of reformers' efforts. Surviving dependents of contributing workers were to be covered by Social Security's Old Age and Survivors' Insurance, leaving poorer caretakers of children—increasingly women without morally approved family histories—to be helped by ADC (which later became Aid to Families with Dependent Children, or AFDC). Nationwide support never burgeoned for this program as it did for old age insurance. Benefits remained low and their distribution geographically uneven. And traditions of surveillance established by social workers became even more intrusive once southerners, blacks, and unmarried mothers began to represent a significant number of clients. Directly contradicting the original sponsors' intentions, mothers' pensions-ADC-AFDC evolved into the core program of what is today pejoratively known as "welfare."

Limits of the "War on Poverty"

Efforts to erase poverty again came to the fore in American politics (indeed, reached an unprecedented visibility and scale) during the administrations of John F. Kennedy, Lyndon Johnson, and Richard Nixon. The nonelderly poor were the visible targets, especially of the widely trumpeted War on Poverty. Once again reformers dreamed of reeducating the poor to take advantage of economic opportunities, especially by reforming juvenile delinquents, giving children a head start and better schools, and offering job training to adults.[16] After the winding down of the War on Poverty, a major role of the Johnson administration's Great Society was to ensure improved access to medical care for the nonelderly poor and the elderly in general. The Nixon administration witnessed large increases in transfers to the poor. Overall, "federal expenditures for cash and in-kind transfers directly targeted to the poor

---

[16] Katz (1986), chap. 9; and Patterson (1981), part 3.

almost tripled from the end of FY 1969 through FY 1974, with most of the increase not in cash assistance, but in programs such as Food Stamps, Medicaid, housing subsidies, and student aid."[17] Aid to Families with Dependent Children was also expanded in these years as states eased eligibility rules in response to changing federal regulations and attempted to make clients eligible for more generous federally subsidized benefits linked to AFDC.[18]

An evaluation of the 1960s and 1970s initiatives against poverty must be mixed. Many people were helped. Elderly Americans, including the elderly poor, benefited enormously from Medicare, increases in Social Security, and the nationalization of residual need-based old-age assistance through the Supplemental Security Income program passed in 1974. Community action programs launched many local black activists into political careers. And "the expansion of cash and in-kind transfers . . . directly benefited substantial numbers of poor women and minorities and their families. The number of female-headed families receiving welfare . . . rose from 635,000 in 1961 (or 29 percent of all such families) to almost 3 million by 1979 (or 50 percent of female-headed families)."[19] Economic expansion between 1965 and 1972 lifted out of poverty perhaps only one-tenth of the 21.3 percent of Americans who were below the poverty line in 1965; government programs lifted more than half of the rest above the poverty line.[20]

But both the service strategies and the transfer strategies of the Kennedy, Johnson, and Nixon years failed to reduce poverty rates much among the nonelderly, and certainly failed to reverse such specifically worrisome trends as the increase in out-of-wedlock births and families sustained only by mothers. Antipoverty warriors can argue that not nearly enough was done or spent to make either services or transfers sufficient to end poverty or to reduce pathologies among the severely disadvantaged.[21] But the antipoverty services and increased expenditures for the nonelderly poor quickly generated political backlashes that ended possibilities for their continuation and improvement. To the degree that antipoverty service efforts were associated with the community action programs that tried to mobilize poor people, especially blacks, these efforts were quickly deemphasized by Johnson, who was chagrined at the anger of local Democratic political leaders, and by Nixon, who was elected through rising discontent with Johnson's domestic and foreign policies and was not about to channel services through urban

---

[17] Brown (1988), p. 193.
[18] Patterson (1981), chap. 11; and Albritton (1979).
[19] Brown (1988), p. 194.
[20] Schwarz (1983), pp. 34–35.
[21] See Schwarz (1983); and Levitan and Taggart (1976).

politicians.[22] In unfavorable political climates, surviving social service programs were also highly vulnerable to charges of corruption.

More significantly, even the broader income transfers emphasized by the Johnson and Nixon administrations backfired politically against lower-income Americans, blacks, and the Democratic party, contributing to Jimmy Carter's retrenchments and then to the rise of Ronald Reagan and of fierce conservative intellectual and political attacks against federal social programs. During the 1970s, public opinion polls recorded that support was decreasing for government efforts to aid minorities and for public social spending, especially on service programs popularly identified with poor blacks.[23] Blacks in general remained staunchly Democratic and in favor of strengthened government social programs. Meanwhile, union members, white urban ethnics, and white southerners moved away from the Democratic party, especially in presidential elections. The perceived position of the party on racial and welfare issues contributed to these defections.[24]

This political situation was rooted in a split between the people who apparently benefited most from the changes in social policy in the 1960s and early 1970s and the people who had to pay higher taxes during the 1970s and into the 1980s. Although many working-class and middle-class families surely gained from increases in social benefits to their elderly relatives, they have not perceived gains to themselves from increased welfare transfers to the poor. Meanwhile, they faced rising financial burdens attributable to higher bites from payroll taxes, the effects of inflation and bracket creep on federal income taxes, and increases in state and local taxes. These tax increases for average workers "occurred in the context of an inflationary economy and thus a steady erosion of real income. Over the 1970s, median real family income declined by 16 percent, while regressive taxes were rising. What developed was a pincers effect on blue-collar and middle-income white-collar workers and their families: declining real income combined with a rising tax burden that appeared to yield no tangible benefits. Little wonder that [such people] began to desert the Democratic party and display hostility toward the welfare programs of the 1960s."[25]

And little wonder that many working-class and middle-class Americans found Ronald Reagan's tax cuts and his generalized attacks on government's social role appealing. Although Reagan's efforts were not as successful as is often supposed, the political and intellectual discourse of the 1980s expressed and reinforced widespread hostility toward big

[22] Patterson (1981), pp. 146–48.
[23] Some poll results are summarized in Brown (1988), p. 198.
[24] Petrocik (1981), pp. 126–32, 139–43.
[25] Brown (1988), p. 198.

government and "throwing money" at poor people. Thus it seems highly unlikely that further redistributive benefits or intensive services targeted on the poor alone can succeed politically. We still live amidst the backlash against the War on Poverty and the Great Society.

SOME SUCCESSES OF CROSS-CLASS SOCIAL POLICIES

If social policies targeted exclusively on the poor have not fared well politically, more universal policies that have spread costs and visibly delivered benefits across classes and races have recurrently flourished. Broad political coalitions have developed to protect and extend these policies, which have also been managed by federal agencies skilled in the arts of public relations and legislative maneuvering. What is more, universal policies have also sustained moral imageries within which specific programs could redistribute income and deliver special services to certain groups of disadvantaged Americans without risking public disaffection. During much of the past century, public education has helped the poor as well as more privileged children at local levels. Yet here I want to focus on federal social policies. Civil War benefits of the late nineteenth and early twentieth centuries, the Sheppard-Towner program for maternity and neonatal health education of 1921–29, and the broadly construed social security system since the 1960s are national or federal-state policies that exemplify what I call targeting within universalism.

Civil War Benefits

Civil War benefits are not often considered a part of U.S. public social provision, but they should be. From the 1870s through the early 1900s, an originally delimited program of military disability and survivors' benefits evolved into a massively expensive de facto system of disability, old-age, and survivors' benefits for all American men who could demonstrate merely minimal service time in the Union armies.[26] The expansion of Civil War pensions, which sopped up from one-fifth to one-third of the federal budget between the 1880s and the 1910s, was fueled by political party competition in late-nineteenth-century patronage democracy and financed by huge "surpluses" from protective tariffs. By 1910 about 29 percent of American men 65 years of age or older (along with 8 percent of elderly women and various younger women, children, and other dependents of deceased men) were receiving old-age pensions not

---

[26] The story is told in Glasson (1918); McMurry (1922); and Sanders (1980).

based on need that were remarkably generous by contemporary international standards.[27]

To be sure, Civil War pensions involved ethnic and regional biases partially correlated with differences in socioeconomic status. The benefits went to native-born northerners and to northern and central Europeans who had immigrated to the North before the 1860s, categories that by the late nineteenth century were disporportionately likely to include farmers, middle-class employees, and skilled workers. Left out of the system were southern whites and most southern blacks, disproportionately farmers and tenants, along with post–Civil War immigrants who tended to be from southern and central Europe and who mostly took unskilled industrial jobs. Nevertheless, the pensions were awarded to many blacks because more than 186,000, some of them freed slaves, had constituted 9 to 10 percent of the Union armies, and they or their survivors were fully eligible. In general, too, the pensions helped many poor whites, including people who had been relatively low-paid farmers and workers and those who had fared better during their working lives but then became impoverished when they lost income and family ties in old age.

Within the overall system of Civil War benefits, moreover, additional aid was available to the poorest veterans and their dependents, especially through the states. Some, such as Massachusetts, offered generous public assistance to needy veterans in their own homes.[28] And starting in 1888 the federal government offered subsidies for state-run veterans' homes, encouraging their establishment in twenty-eight states. By 1910 national and state institutions housed 31,830 Union veterans, about 5 percent of those still living (some served veterans' dependents as well). The men were typically former skilled workers; there were also some former unskilled workers and farmers, but very few from middle-class occupations.[29]

The generous Civil War benefits were unequivocally honorable and were defined in explicit opposition to poor relief. The argument was that they had been *earned*. The 1888 Republican platform urged that benefits "be so enlarged and extended as to provide against the possibility that any man who honorably wore the Federal uniform shall become the inmate of an almshouse, or dependent upon private charity. . . . [I]t would be a public scandal to do less for those whose valorous service preserved the government."[30] Similarly, the Massachusetts stat-

---

[27] The discussion in this and the following paragraph is documented in Skocpol (1992), chap. 2.

[28] Massachusetts Bureau of Statistics (1916), pp. 16, 34.

[29] Cetina (1977), chap. 10.

[30] Johnson (1978), p. 82.

utes concerning aid to veterans and their dependents proclaimed that their purpose was to help worthy persons "who would otherwise be receiving relief under the pauper laws."[31]

Arguments such as these convinced many northern voters and legis-lators. Broad political coalitions, spearheaded by the Grand Army of the Republic and supported by many native-born voters in towns and rural areas across the northern states, campaigned for ever-improved benefits.[32] Mostly these campaigns bore political fruit through the Re-publican party, yet they also gained the support of many northern Dem-ocratic legislators who could not afford to let Republicans outdo them in bidding for votes. That the benefits were bestowed as ostensible re-wards for service also made it easy for individual recipients to take pensions (or public assistance or a place in an asylum) during what was supposedly the preeminent era of "rugged individualism" in American history. As Commissioner of Pensions Green B. Raum explained in 1891, "an old soldier can receive a pension as a recognition of honor-able service with a feeling of pride, while he would turn his back with shame upon an offer of charity."[33]

In sum, the politically viable Civil War benefits not only reached many disabled and elderly Americans, including some of the truly needy, but they did so in ways that bolstered society's esteem for the bene-ficiaries. So popular were these benefits that they eventually reached more than 90 percent of surviving veterans. Despite vociferous attacks against the political corruption that pension expenditures supposedly expressed, the benefits persisted until the generation of men who re-ceived them died out.

Health Education Services for Mothers and Babies

During the early twentieth century, state legislatures established moth-ers' pensions, child labor laws, and protective labor laws for women workers. Congress established the federal Children's Bureau in 1912, and the Federal Act for the Promotion of Welfare and Hygiene of Maternity and Infancy of 1921, better known as the Sheppard-Towner Act.[34] These "maternalist" measures were promoted by political coali-tions that included educated reformers, trade unionists, and geograph-ically widespread associations of elite and middle-class married women, and they were understood as extensions of mother love into the public

---

[31] Massachusetts Bureau of Statistics (1916), p. 30.

[32] Sanders (1980).

[33] Raum (1891), p. 207.

[34] These summary remarks are documented in Skocpol (1992), chaps. 6–9.

sphere. Although all the policies had cross-class backing and univer-salistic justification, some of them, such as mothers' pensions, were fi-nally focused on the poor alone, while others, such as the Children's Bureau and Sheppard-Towner programs, aimed at more broadly de-fined clienteles. The Sheppard-Towner programs expanded rapidly for some years and reached many especially needy people through efforts that never became stigmatized (as mothers' pensions unfortunately did).

The Children's Bureau was established in 1912 to "investigate and report . . . upon all matters pertaining to the welfare of children and child life among all classes of our people."[35] The bureau's chief, Julia Lathrop, mobilized women's associations and reform groups across the nation on behalf of improved birth and infant mortality statistics and public health measures for mothers and children. Working with the women's associations, Lathrop also mobilized broad public support to persuade Congress to enlarge the bureau's budget and increase its per-sonnel.[36] After several years she began organizing similar support for the passage of what eventually became the Sheppard-Towner Act of 1921. Significantly, even though her aim was to reach out to underprivileged mothers (especially in remote rural areas), Lathrop deliberately decided against a narrowly targeted program and arranged for the measures debated in Congress to carry an explanatory clause stressing that "the act is not a charity." If the services of the bill were not open to all, Lathrop believed, they would "degenerate into poor relief."[37]

The Children's Bureau was able to reach large numbers of American mothers through Sheppard-Towner, just as it had done in its previous programs. During seven years of administering the act, the bureau coor-dinated nationwide efforts that distributed 22 million pieces of litera-ture, conducted 183,000 health conferences, established some 3,000 prenatal centers, and visited more than 3 million homes.[38] "Women from every geographic region, social class, and educational background wrote to the bureau as many as 125,000 letters a year," according to Molly Ladd-Taylor, and by 1929 the bureau "estimated that one-half of U.S. babies had benefited from the government's childrearing informa-tion."[39] Yet at the same time, the bureau was also effectively targeting poorly educated white and nonwhite mothers in rural areas for special

---

[35] The text of the enabling act appears in Children's Bureau, *First Annual Report of the Chief* (1914), p. 2.

[36] Parker and Carpenter (1981).

[37] Covotsos (1976), p. 123. Covotsos quotes from a letter by Julia Lathrop to Bleeker Marquette, December 1, 1920, Children's Bureau papers, drawer 408, National Archives, Washington.

[38] Ladd-Taylor (1986), p. 28.

[39] Ibid., p. 2.

help through consultations with public health nurses and clinics, and through conferences sponsored by the act. While allowing wide state-to-state variation in program design, the bureau's leadership prodded all states to improve birth statistics and channel resources toward places where infant and maternal mortality rates were highest.[40] As a result, many state programs did emphasize delivering public health information and services to rural areas and small towns.

Despite its successes in targeting within universalism, the Sheppard-Towner program cannot stand as an unequivocally successful social policy because Congress refused to make the act (briefly extended in 1927) permanent. To be sure, there was never a strong political backlash against it: it remained broadly popular with American women, and most of the elite and middle-class women's associations that had backed the law continued throughout the 1920s to lobby Congress on behalf of its extension. Many states continued Sheppard-Towner programs in new ways after the federal matching funds disappeared. And after a few years the federal program itself was revived through the Social Security Act of 1935. By the late 1920s, however, private physicians wanted to take over prenatal and postnatal health counseling themselves, and their local associations, affiliated with the American Medical Association, helped persuade President Hoover and some congressional leaders to kill the original program in legislative maneuvers.[41]

Sheppard-Towner was vulnerable to cancellation because it had not established a fixed entitlement to benefits, nor had it included a provision for the automatic renewal of yearly appropriations. Thus the broad political support that follows from a universalistic program is not the only explanation for the survival of social policies. Entitlement status or automatically renewable appropriations have also been important. Indeed, the most successful measures—Civil War pensions and social security—have been those that ensured entitlements to broad categories of beneficiaries.

Economic Security for the Elderly

The national contributory social insurance programs chartered by the Social Security Act of 1935 evolved in subsequent decades into a broad and, by international standards, reasonably generous set of income supports and medical services for retired American wage and salary workers and their dependents. Within the inclusive rubric of social secu-

[40] Rothman (1978), pp. 140–41; Costin (1983), p. 136; and Children's Bureau, *Annual Reports*, 1922–29.
[41] Rothman (1978), pp. 142–53.

rity, benefits were gradually redistributed toward poorer elderly people and were larger than they would have received from a mere proportional return on their own payroll taxes collected at their preretirement wage levels. Today Social Security is not only the most politically unassailable part of U.S. public social provision, but also America's most effective antipoverty program.

U.S. social insurance was far from an antipoverty policy in its early years. For the first three decades, the originators and administrators of Social Security concentrated on building mainstream support and extending the scope of the program. They worked out effective relationships with congressional committees and maneuvered to rein in public assistance and to deflect populist demands for noncontributory need-based pensions and conservative attempts to institute universal flat-rate pensions.[42] Even though early beneficiaries reaped windfalls because they had not paid taxes for long, and even though tax increases for social security were repeatedly deferred while benefits were increased, the administrators deliberately portrayed the system as a set of individual "accounts" into which "contributors" paid taxes to build up "earned" benefits. They portrayed Social Security as very different from public assistance, much as Civil War pensions were once contrasted to charity and poor relief. Step by step, new categories of beneficiaries and taxpayers were brought into the contributory insurance system, until by the early 1970s it encompassed more than 90 percent of the labor force.[43] New types of benefits were added to the core of retirement insurance, partially filling the vacuum left by the absence of national health insurance. What was launched as Old Age Insurance (OAI) in 1935 was modified into Old Age and Survivors' Insurance (OASI) in 1939, and further amended to become Old Age, Survivors' and Disability Insurance (OASDI) in 1956. Finally, Medicare was added to the system in 1965.

In a number of ways, social security has always disproportionately favored not the neediest Americans but the stably employed and the middle class: as Martha Derthick has written, "For a long time many elderly people were left out altogether because they had not been in the work force, had not been in the covered portion of it, had not been in long enough to qualify, or were not married to someone who did qualify. Among these were a large number of persons who had to fall back on public assistance."[44] Within the Social Security system, moreover, benefits are pegged to the wage rates at which pensioners have been

[42] Cates (1983).
[43] Achenbaum (1986), p. 59.
[44] Derthick (1979), p. 215.

paid over considerable periods during their working lives. And payroll taxes are regressive because they are set at a flat rate and not collected at all on earnings above a certain ceiling.

Nevertheless, from the start the system gave proportionately higher— although never absolutely higher—retirement benefits to formerly lower-income workers. More important, once Social Security was established as virtually universal for employed Americans, its administrators worked to make benefits higher for everyone, and relatively better for the less privileged, so that benefits could be closer to a sufficient retirement income.[45] Taking advantage of crucial conjunctures in favor of innovations in social policy during the 1960s and early 1970s, Social Security's promoters gained presidential and congressional backing for leaps forward in services and benefits for all the elderly and, at the same time, followed a strategy that Hugh Heclo has called "helping the poor by not talking about them."[46] Amidst the fuss about the War on Poverty and the Great Society, plans for Medicare were brought to fruition, and Social Security administrators began to work for higher retirement benefits. President Nixon and the Republicans did not want to propose less than the Democrats for the elderly, and in 1972 they also saw indexing benefits to inflation as a way to time future increases automatically rather than politically. As for benefit levels, after a small increase under Johnson in 1967, Congress enacted large increases in 1969, 1971, and 1972, so that benefits, adjusted for inflation, rose by 23 percent. More significantly, the proportion of earnings subject to Social Security taxation and replacement rates also jumped. As Martha Derthick has pointed out, "Replacement rates in 1975 were approximately 67 percent for a married man earning average wages and 92 percent for a married man earning the federal minimum wage—up from 50 percent and 67 percent, respectively, a decade earlier, on the eve of the drive for expansion."[47]

After benefits leapt forward for everyone and at the same time increased proportionately more for the lower-wage beneficiaries, Social Security became by far modern America's most effective program for lifting people out of poverty. In general, social insurance does much more than means-tested transfers to raise American families from below to above the officially defined poverty line.[48] This is true even for nonelderly families, who benefit from disability, unemployment, and survivors' insurance.[49] Yet retirement benefits and Medicare are chiefly re-

[45] Achenbaum (1986), pp. 49–60.
[46] Heclo (1986), p. 325.
[47] Derthick (1979), p. 363.
[48] See Weinberg (1985); and Sawhill (1988), especially pp. 1097–1101.
[49] Sawhill (1988), p. 1099.

sponsible for the antipoverty effects of social insurance, which explains why elderly families have benefited disproportionately. Indeed, these programs have shifted the age distribution of poverty in America. According to Gary Burtless, in 1959 "the income poverty rate of the elderly was 35 percent, while the rate for the remainder of the population was only 22 percent. By 1983 the income poverty rate for the elderly had fallen to 14 percent, while for the nonelderly it was more than 15 percent."[50] For elderly Americans who might otherwise be impoverished, the Social Security Administration's practice of targeting within universalism has clearly worked well over the past quarter century.

Indeed, "helping the poor by not talking about them" has not only worked better, at least, for the elderly poor, but has also proved more politically durable than did the War on Poverty and the Great Society's vociferous targeted efforts to help the working-age poor and their children. The gains achieved for Social Security programs during the 1960s and early 1970s proved durable even in the face of Reagan administration onslaughts against social spending. Although public support for welfare declined sharply during the 1970s, some 95 percent or more of people polled continued to agree that "the government spends too little or about the right amount" on the elderly, despite substantial payroll taxes for social security.[51] Talk of a "crisis" in Social Security led to a few adjustments and then died away. When the first Reagan administration discussed cuts in the program, it faced immediate public resistance and soon backed down (except that it continued for a time to use administrative regulations to cut people from the disability rolls). Targeted public assistance programs for low-income people accounted for less than 18 percent of federal social spending (far less than the proportions accounted for by social security and medicare), yet these targeted programs took the brunt of the first Reagan administration's efforts to retrench domestic social expenditures.[52] Hopes of expanding the coverage of impoverished mothers and children suffered, but the elderly clients of social insurance, including those who would otherwise have been poor, preserved their improved economic standing.

There has been, in short, no political backlash against Social Security. Even in a generally conservative period, it has been protected by its broad constituency; and it has continued to be championed by congressional representatives of all partisan and ideological stripes.

---

[50] Burtless (1986), p. 28.
[51] Brown (1988), p. 199.
[52] Palmer and Sawhill (1982), p. 373.

CURRENT POSSIBILITIES FOR TARGETING WITHIN UNIVERSALISM

U.S. history speaks loud and clear to those who would do more now to help the poor through public social policies. Rather than devising new programs narrowly focused on low-income people or the urban poor, and rather than seeking to reform or expand Aid to Families With Dependent Children and other means-tested public assistance programs, policymakers should work toward displacing welfare with new policies that could address the needs of less privileged Americans along with those of the middle class and the stable working class. New policies must speak with a consistent moral voice to all Americans who would be recipients and taxpayers. The policies should reinforce fundamental values such as rewards for work, opportunities for individual betterment, and family and community responsibility for the care of children and other vulnerable people. Even if new measures start small and give significant proportions of their benefits to families who seem less needy than the most desperately poor, advocates for the poor should realize that before long such measures could create new opportunities for more targeted efforts. In contrast, measures that start out small and are narrowly focused may either lose support or (even if popular, such as Head Start) fail to receive the resources they need to meet crying social needs.

To supplement Social Security programs for the elderly, the United States could develop what might be called a family security program available to all children and working-age citizens.[53] The new policies would include child support assurance for all single custodial parents, parental leave and child-care assistance for all working families, job training and relocation assistance for displaced workers and new entrants to the labor market, and universal health benefits.

Child support assurance would establish nationwide guidelines requiring all absent parents (most of whom are fathers) to pay proportions of their wages as child support.[54] As a substitute for the current haphazard system of judicially awarded child support, payments would be automatically fixed and collected through wage withholding, exactly as income and social security taxes now are. Checks to all custodial parents (mostly mothers) would come from the government. They would nearly equal the amounts collected from absent parents, except when the monies were not collected or fell below a minimum benefit needed to raise children, in which case the custodial parent would get the minimum payment from public funds. Such a program would express the nation's interest in helping single custodial parents with the socially crucial work of raising the approximately half of American chil-

[53] I have borrowed a number of ideas from Ellwood (1988).
[54] This proposal is outlined in Garfinkel and Uhr (1984).

dren that are now growing up in such families. The system would address pressing social problems that cut across class and racial lines, since half of all marriages now end in divorce and only half of all divorced mothers receive child support (separated and never-married mothers fare even worse).[55] Because the program "would be sending checks to middle- and upper-income women as well as to disadvantaged ones," there would be "no stigma, no failure, and no isolation under this system."[56] At the same time, an adequate minimum benefit could do much to help needy mothers and, in contrast to welfare payments, would not disappear as soon as the mother went to work.

Although child support assurance could do much to ensure that all children have basic financial support, both dual-parent and single-parent families also need help with the growing challenges of balancing parenting and work outside the home. More and more married women, including mothers of young children, are working outside the home, yet current public policies do remarkably little by international standards to buffer families from the extra stresses of childbirth or adoption or to help them find and finance adequate child care while both parents work.[57] Various policies could address these problems for all families. At a minimum it surely makes sense to move toward paid parental leave for families of newborns or new adoptees, perhaps with legally mandated unpaid leave, including guaranteed reinstatement, as a first step.

Another objective should be to deliver more income through public means to all families that must combine working and parenting, but with larger benefits (proportionately and absolutely) for the neediest families. All families with children could be given larger, refundable tax credits, which would benefit families with two workers and those with full-time homemakers. Or public benefits could be tied much more directly to women's labor force participation by offering refundable tax credits to families that have to purchase child care while a single parent or both parents work.

Help for parents raising children is one part of an overall family security program. The other part must be help for all adults who are looking for jobs. This help would make it easier for families to form and for parents to support their children. And it is consonant with American values because adults are being assisted to help themselves, not put on a permanent public dole. A universally available, federally run labor market system could do several things for displaced workers (including displaced managers and skilled workers as well as unemployed low-wage

[55] Weitzman (1985), p. xvii; and Ellwood (1988), p. 158.
[56] Ellwood (1988), p. 169.
[57] See Kamerman, Kahn, and Kingston (1983), especially pp. 16–22.

workers) and for new entrants to the labor market (including young people, "welfare mothers," and divorced former homemakers). It could identify jobs and areas of the country where new workers are needed. It should provide transitional unemployment benefits and perhaps housing subsidies, if necessary, to help workers and their families relocate. And most important, this system could train or retrain people to help match their skills to available jobs.

As William Wilson and his collaborators have argued, poor job prospects for unskilled young black men are directly linked to low rates of family formation, especially in inner cities.[58] The present welfare system also unnecessarily traps many single mothers into making a stark choice between unskilled paid work at very low wages or welfare benefits that are available only to mothers who do not work.[59] The existing system rarely helps them gain new skills, nor does it urge or help them to relocate, if necessary, to take advantage of decent jobs and housing. A new public labor market system would do all these things, and it would provide help and incentives to low-income, unskilled single mothers within the same broad, nonstigmatized rubric in which aid would be offered to family heads with more education and greater skills. Everyone, moreover, could receive job training and help with job searches in the name of promoting national economic efficiency.

Some analysts believe that a new labor market system should also guarantee public jobs at the minimum wage as a last resort. But this might stigmatize the system as a make-work program, whereas emphasizing training and relocation would make the policies appealing to the working-class and middle-class public. If more jobs are needed in the end than can be generated through private and existing public labor markets, then other kinds of federal and state policies, such as measures to develop infrastructure, might be planned to create new jobs for workers in training. Furthermore, the institution of a higher Earned Income Tax Credit to subsidize low-wage workers might indirectly make more self-supporting jobs available to newly trained workers. Although this is a targeted measure, it qualifies as targeting within universalism because it arranges subsidies through the income tax system in which all workers participate.

Finally, more universally available health benefits are essential if the United States is to improve the efficiency of its labor markets and help working families raise healthy children. The present patchwork system discourages labor mobility and job redefinitions within industries and workplaces because medical insurance for many employees and their

---

[58] Neckerman, Aponte, and Wilson (1988).
[59] Ellwood (1988), pp. 137–42.

dependents is tied to certain professional and unionized jobs, and coverage is not available through other jobs (or through the part-time work that makes sense for many parents). Likewise, the present system rewards welfare recipients (and sometimes people with incomes slightly above a legally defined poverty line) with medical insurance, but leaves many working people, especially low-wage workers, without coverage. This situation discourages recipients from moving off welfare and arouses taxpayer payer resistance to improving the provision of public health care for impoverished families. The present uneven system of publicly provided or tax-subsidized health benefits only for the elderly, the very poor, and the unionized should be replaced either with Canadian-style universal health insurance or with some kind of residual, publicly mandated or contributory publicly funded health benefits.

CONCLUSION

These interrelated proposals for family support and labor market measures that would constitute a family security program for America necessarily raise questions. Could such policies be enacted in the present fiscal climate? If enacted, would they really help truly needy Americans?

The present concern about federal budget deficits is apparently inimical to new social policies that threaten to cost a lot. Some of these policies could save or generate considerable amounts of public money at the same time that they authorized new expenditures.[60] Nevertheless, a family security program of the sort outlined, especially the health insurance and child-care assistance provisions, would require major new budgetary commitments from the federal government. Although public support for addressing social problems, including those of the poor, has recently rebounded, the 1981 Reagan tax cuts did have the effect of shifting congressional debates toward cost cutting, so that many politicians now seem obsessively wary about mentioning tax increases.

Still, the history of the modern Social Security system demonstrates that Americans will accept taxes that they perceive as contributions toward public programs in which there is a direct stake for themselves, their families, and their friends, not just for "the poor." Perhaps the introduction of new programs on a modest scale could be accompanied by a family security payroll tax, collected up to a considerably higher wage base than Social Security taxes are now to avoid some of the worst regressive features. In any event, new universalistic programs and new sources of revenue, to be collected from virtually the entire population,

---

[60] See Garfinkel and Uhr (1980), pp. 120–22; and Ellwood (1988), p. 169. To the extent that they put people to work, labor market policies would also generate new revenues.

not just small subgroups as with the unsuccessful catastrophic illness surcharge, should be discussed together. If this is done, there is reason for optimism about the willingness of Americans to accept new public policies to address family needs that are widely felt.

Of course, proposed innovations do not turn into legislation just because the public might accept them. There have to be articulate political leaders and effective social alliances behind measures if they are to wend their way through the legislative process. Here there is less room for immediate optimism but some hope for action in the next decade. Missing right now are mobilized organizations and broad, legislatively active alliances that include groups other than those advocating help for the poor. Civil rights groups tend to be preoccupied with defending affirmative action or pushing for measures targeted on the nonwhite poor. Similarly, organized feminists and antifeminists are currently engrossed with abortion issues, and their conflict undercuts the cross-class coalitions that might come together in support of new family security measures. Many old-line labor unions are so much on the defensive organizationally and economically that they are preoccupied with issues of labor law, even as emerging unions in feminine social service occupations tend to favor broad social policy agendas. All the same, on a surprisingly bipartisan basis, elected representatives and candidates are now beginning to talk regularly about new child care, parental leave, and health insurance policies, although such talk always goes on for quite some time before particular policies come into being. And business-oriented conservatives may be willing to accept new public social spending, if only to head off regulations that would burden employers with the costs for child care or expanded health coverage.

But can the American poor really be helped by the program I have outlined? Wouldn't this set of policies help principally the middle and working classes, along with the most privileged and least troubled of the poor, leaving behind many of the extremely disadvantaged, disproportionately people of color, who require intensive services to break out of cycles of social pathology and despair? Initially, this might happen. Yet an ever-deepening course of hope and improvement might soon unfold among the poor. Once genuinely new and nonstigmatizing incentives, social supports, and ways of providing job opportunities were solidly in place, the example of a few go-getters who took advantage of new policies and forged better lives for themselves might well propagate among relatives, friends, and neighbors. After the word got out that work really does lead to rewards, a certain amount of the social despair that now pervades the very poor might well begin to dissipate. In a way, this could be the greatest gift that new universalistic family security policies could give to the most disadvantaged among the American poor, for it would facilitate their moral reintegration into the mainstream of national life.

Universalistic policies would also change the attitudes of more privileged Americans, which returns us to the bedrock matter of broad and sustainable political support for antipoverty policies. Just as Social Security has done, new family security policies, once established, would probably nourish broad political alliances prepared to support extensions of benefits and willing to accept redistributions toward the poor at the same time. If and when new public social policies begin to help American families from all social classes and all racial and ethnic groups to meet contingencies of ill health, job loss, and the challenges of balancing paid work and parental responsibilities, then a "kinder and gentler" political nation might actually emerge. With their own values and needs recognized through a revitalized public sector, larger numbers of middle-class American citizens would be prepared to go the extra mile for especially needy minorities. Instead of policies for the disadvantaged alone, targeting within universalism is the prescription for effective and politically sustainable policies to fight poverty in the United States. This is what experience teaches us about prospects for a rebirth of political community.

REFERENCES

Achenbaum, W. Andrew. 1986. *Social Security: Visions and Revisions.* Cambridge University Press.

Albritton, Robert B. 1979. "Social Amelioration through Mass Insurgency? A Reexamination of the Piven and Cloward Thesis." *American Political Science Review* 73 (December), pp. 1003–11.

Bell, Winifred. 1965. *Aid to Dependent Children.* Columbia University Press.

Brown, Michael K. 1988. "The Segmented Welfare System: Distributive Conflict and Retrenchment in the United States, 1968–1984." In *Remaking the Welfare State: Retrenchment and Social Policy in America and Europe,* edited by Michael K. Brown. Temple University Press.

Burtless, Gary. 1986. "Public Spending for the Poor: Trends, Prospects, and Economic Limits." In *Fighting Poverty: What Works and What Doesn't,* edited by Sheldon H. Danziger and Daniel H. Weinberg. Harvard University Press.

Cates, Jerry R. 1983. *Insuring Inequality: Administrative Leadership in Social Security, 1935–54.* University of Michigan Press.

Cetina, Judith Gladys. 1977. "A History of Veterans' Homes in the United States, 1811–1930." Ph.D. dissertation, Case Western Reserve University.

Children's Bureau. 1914. *First Annual Report of the Chief, Children's Bureau to the Secretary of Labor for the Year Ended June 30, 1913.* Department of Labor.

————.1933. *Mothers' Aid, 1931*, publication 220. Department of Labor.

Costin, Lela B. 1983. *Two Sisters for Social Justice: A Biography of Grace and Edith Abbott*. University of Illinois Press.

Covotsos, Louis J. 1976. "Child Welfare and Social Progress: A History of the United States Children's Bureau, 1912–1935." Ph.D. dissertation, University of Chicago.

Derthick, Martha. 1979. *Policymaking for Social Security*. Brookings.

Ellwood, David T. 1988. *Poor Support: Poverty in the American Family*. Basic Books.

Garfinkel, Irwin, and Elizabeth Uhr. 1984. "A New Approach to Child Support." *Public Interest* 74 (Spring), pp. 111–22.

Glasson, William H. 1918. *Federal Military Pensions in the United States*. Oxford University Press.

Heclo, Hugh. 1986. "The Political Foundations of Antipoverty Policy." In *Fighting Poverty: What Works and What Doesn't*, edited by Sheldon H. Danziger and Daniel H. Weinberg. Harvard University Press.

Johnson, Donald Bruce, compiler. 1978. *National Party Platforms*, vol. 1: 1840–1956. Rev. ed. University of Illinois Press.

Kamerman, Sheila B., Alfred J. Kahn, and Paul Kingston. 1983. *Maternity Policies and Working Women*. Columbia University Press.

Katz, Michael B. 1986. *In the Shadow of the Poorhouse: A Social History of Welfare in America*. Basic Books.

Kaus, Mickey. 1986. "The Work Ethic State." *New Republic*, July 7, pp. 22–32.

Korpi, Walter. 1980. "Social Policy and Distributional Conflict in the Capitalist Democracies: A Preliminary Comparative Framework." *West European Politics* 3 (October), pp. 296–316.

Ladd-Taylor, Molly, editor. 1986. *Raising a Baby the Government Way: Mothers' Letters to the Children's Bureau, 1915–1932*. Rutgers University Press.

Levitan, Sar A., and Clifford M. Johnson. 1984. *Beyond the Safety Net: Reviving the Promise of Opportunity in America*. Cambridge, Mass.: Ballinger.

Levitan, Sar A., and Robert Taggart. 1976. *The Promise of Greatness*. Harvard University Press.

McMurry, Donald L. 1922. "The Political Significance of the Pension Question, 1885–1897." *Mississippi Valley Historical Review* 9 (June), pp. 19–36.

Massachusetts Bureau of Statistics. 1916. *Report of a Special Inquiry Relative to Aged and Dependent Persons in Massachusetts, 1915*. Boston: Wright and Potter.

Murray, Charles. 1984. *Losing Ground: American Social Policy, 1950–1980*. Basic Books.

Neckerman, Kathryn, Robert Aponte, and William Julius Wilson. 1988. "Family Structure, Black Unemployment, and American Social Policy." In *The Politics of Social Policy in the United States*, edited by Margaret Weir, Ann Shola Orloff, and Theda Skocpol. Princeton University Press.

Palmer, John L., and Isabel V. Sawhill, editors. 1982. *The Reagan Experiment: An Examination of Economic and Social Policies under the Reagan Administration*. Washington: Urban Institute.

Parker, Jacqueline K., and Edward M. Carpenter. 1981. "Julia Lathrop and the Children's Bureau: The Emergence of an Institution." *Social Service Review* 55 (March), pp. 60–77.

Patterson, James T. 1981. *America's Struggle against Poverty, 1900–1980.* Harvard University Press.

Petrocik, John R. 1981. *Party Coalitions: Realignment and the Decline of the New Deal Party System.* University of Chicago Press.

Piven, Frances Fox, and Richard A. Cloward. 1987. "The Contemporary Relief Debate." In *The Mean Season: The Attack on the Welfare State,* edited by Fred Block and others. Pantheon Books.

Raum, Green B. 1891. "Pensions and Patriotism." *North American Review* 42 (August), pp. 205–14.

Rosenberry, Sara A. 1982. "Social Insurance, Distributive Criteria and the Welfare Backlash: A Comparative Analysis." *British Journal of Political Science* 12 (October), pp. 421–47.

Rothman, Sheila M. 1978. *Woman's Proper Place: A History of Changing Ideals and Practices, 1870 to Present.* Basic Books.

Russell, Louise. 1989. "Proposed: A Comprehensive Health Care System for the Poor." *Brookings Review* 7 (Summer), pp. 13–20.

Sanders, Heywood T. 1980. "Paying for the 'Bloody Shirt': The Politics of Civil War Pensions." In *Political Benefits: Empirical Studies of American Public Programs,* edited by Barry S. Rundquist. Lexington, Mass.: D.C. Heath.

Sawhill, Isabel V. 1988. "Poverty in the U.S.: Why Is It So Persistent?" *Journal of Economic Literature* 26 (September), pp. 1073–1119.

Schorr, Lisbeth B., with Daniel Schorr. 1988. *Within Our Reach: Breaking the Cycle of Disadvantage.* Anchor Press.

Schwartz, John E. 1983. *America's Hidden Success: A Reassessment of Twenty Years of Public Policy.* Norton.

Skocpol, Theda. 1992. *Protecting Soldiers and Mothers: The Political Origins of Social Policy in the United States.* Harvard University Press.

Weinberg, Daniel H. 1985. "Filling the 'Poverty Gap': Multiple Transfer Program Participation." *Journal of Human Resources* 20 (Winter), pp. 64–89.

Weitzman, Lenore J. 1985. *The Divorce Revolution: The Unexpected Social and Economic Consequences for Women and Children in America.* Free Press.

Wilkins, Roger. 1989. "The Black Poor Are Different." *New York Times,* August 22, p. A23.

Wilson, William Julius. 1987. *The Truly Disadvantaged: The Inner City, the Underclass, and Public Policy.* University of Chicago Press.

CHAPTER NINE

Is the Time Finally Ripe? Health Insurance Reforms in the 1990s

RIGHT NOW, in the early 1990s, the time seems ripe for national health care reform. A belief that there are pressing problems about health care access and cost has come together with a sense of *political opportunities* to do something about those problems. This conjuncture of problems and politics is moving the issue of health insurance to the top of the national agenda, and opening a window of opportunity for public policy solutions put forward by experts and policy entrepreneurs who have been lying in wait to change U.S. governmental policies in the health care area. According to political scientist John Kingdon (1984), problems, political opportunities, and proposed solutions must come together before a breakthrough in public policy can occur.

Certainly, we are at a juncture when problems are widely perceived— even by dominant actors in the U.S. health care system and those who, until recently, were quite self-satisfied. Long a strong opponent of reform, the American Medical Association now acknowledges that "our system has its faults," because "over 30 million Americans don't have access to health care" (see AMA 1990; also Todd et al. 1991). Insurance companies are concerned because competition among them is increasingly focused on finding ever-smaller pools of healthier people to insure (Briggs 1992; Jones 1992). Fearing that public resistance to the exclusion of people with preexisting conditions will fuel tough new regulations that further undercut their already tenuous profits, many large insurers are now acknowledging the inevitability of reforms and attempting to influence the terms of new legislation proposed by the Clinton administration. Many employers, too, are willing to join government in a quest for cost containment (Bergthold 1990, 1991; Martin 1993). Large businesses, especially those in unionized industries that already provide employer-sponsored benefits, find their costs rising astronomically and uncontrollably, while small businesses often find it impossible to obtain coverage for their employees at any reasonable cost.

Citizens as well as organized interests are aware of problems. The

Journal of Health Politics, Policy and Law, Vol. 18, No. 3, Fall 1993. Copyright © 1993 by Duke University.

elderly and poor who are in the public parts of the American health-financing system are experiencing increasing squeezes on their access to care, as efforts at cost containment focus disproportionately on the public parts of the system (Ruggie 1992). The regularly employed middle class, too, is becoming anxious about health insurance (Starr 1991). During the postwar period, from the late 1940s through the early 1970s, stably employed wage and salary earners could feel relatively secure about enjoying generous employer-provided and tax-subsidized health benefits for themselves and their dependents (Stevens 1988). But now, as employers try various expedients to cope with rising health care costs, employees are losing certain health benefits, and dependents are sometimes excluded from coverage. Workers are fearful of losing jobs and coverage altogether, or else are wary of changing jobs and ending up with health coverage that doesn't have as generous terms as before. Unionized workers, moreover, are having to devote much of their organizational energy to defending preexisting health benefits for active and retired workers. Industrial profits and productivity gains often flow into covering rising health care costs, rather than into raises in take-home pay or other benefits.

Even outside of the health policy area, experts are arriving at the realization that reforms in many areas of U.S. economic and public policy may hinge on changes that universalize access and bring rising health care costs under some kind of control. One key to promoting efficiency in the economy may lie in part in finding a way to rationalize the health care system. And certainly some of the most intractable problems in other areas of social policy, such as welfare reform, depend very much on finding a way to allow the working poor to gain access to health coverage (cf. Ellwood 1988: 103–4).

At last it has become politically feasible to do something through government about these problems. Until late 1991, experts and politicians took it for granted that it just was not politically feasible to talk about governmental reforms in health care. Then, suddenly, a new sense of political possibility was kicked off by an entirely unexpected "focusing event" (Kingdon 1984: 99–105) in the fall of 1991. After Republican senator John Heinz was tragically killed in a freak aviation accident, a virtually unknown and seemingly unpromising Democratic party candidate, Harris Wofford, won the ensuing special senatorial election that was held in Pennsylvania. Wofford overcame a forty-point deficit in the polls against well-known Republican Richard Thornburgh, who had recently been attorney general under President George Bush. Airing a television commercial that proclaimed "If every criminal in America has the right to a lawyer, then I think every working person should have the right to see a doctor when they're ill," Wofford's come-from-behind campaign featured calls for "national health insurance." His victory, so unexpected by the Washington and media establishment, signaled that access to affordable health care was an issue on the voting public's mind, an issue on which political capital could be gained by politicians willing to propose governmental solutions (Blumenthal 1991; Russakoff 1991).

Subsequently, Democratic presidential candidate Bill Clinton made calls for health care reform one of the centerpieces of his campaign. Clinton's victory over incumbent George Bush—who had seemed certain of reelection just a year before the November 1992 election—has made it a certainty that major health care reforms will be proposed to Congress during 1993.

Overly pessimistic until recently that health insurance was off the agenda, now many experts—perhaps too many—are blithely optimistic that the 1990s will bring fundamental reforms in health care access and financing. In 1992 I took part in a discussion of health care reform during a session of a conference sponsored by the National Academy of Social Insurance. At one point I suggested that there might be some reforms that were not worth supporting in the short run, that it might possibly be better to hold out for certain more fundamental reforms. Henry Aaron, the legendary health care economist, passed me a note that said: "Don't worry, Theda. No matter what happens now, the issue's going to keep coming up until things are finally addressed in a fundamental way." In a certain sense, of course, Aaron is right (see Aaron 1991 for his rationale). But I wonder if there isn't a certain evolutionary functionalism inherent in this way of thinking. It may fail to take a sufficiently hardheaded look at whether political conditions exist (or could come about) that will ensure changes genuinely for the better. Will the right solutions really come together with felt problems and political possibilities during the 1990s?

At this point, I should say what I mean by changes "for the better." As we all know, in any kind of reforms that occur, the specifics are going to matter a great deal, particular details are going to matter. I do not want to address all that. I simply want to point out that if, in the end, the changes don't move things—promptly and irreversibly—in the direction of genuinely including everyone in health care coverage, both preventive and acute health care coverage, I will not define that change as a change for the better. And if the changes don't lead in the direction of creating a broader regulatory framework for cost sharing and cost containment, that will not be a change for the better. Even incremental reforms will have to be evaluated in terms of whether they change the direction of the dynamics of the health care system. Reforms enacted in 1994 are unlikely to be the last word; there will be further rounds of reform throughout the 1990s. Over several stages of change, we need to ensure full inclusion of all Americans in health insurance. And we need to move firmly away from current patterns of cost shifting that fuel inflation and that formally or de facto exclude many people from adequate care and access to relatively equal care. We must move in the direction of creating some kind of overall control—macro control rather than micro control—on the decisions of medical practitioners and patients about costs and benefits.

It is important to realize that John Kingdon's (1984) model about problems, politics, and solutions applies to "near misses" in the political system as well as to actual or effective changes. In other words, it is a model that explains when possible policy changes come up for debate, not whether anything will actually be enacted. What is more, it is not a model that tells us whether things that are enacted actually solve any problems or just make them worse—perhaps leading to reversals of reforms at a later date.

If we look back historically at earlier attempts at health financing reform in the United States, we will see patterns that should worry us in the present conjuncture. Let us take a small historical detour to see what happened in the past to reformers who were absolutely confident that "the time was ripe" for rational and progressive health care reforms. Then we will return to the present, and I will argue that reformers in the 1990s should pay much more attention than most are doing so far to the requisites of political communication with broad, democratic publics.

RATIONAL REFORMERS MEET CONSERVATIVE IDEOLOGUES

Repeatedly during the twentieth century, reformers in the United States have been certain that the time had come to enact broad, publicly financed or regulated health insurance. Such confidence bubbled up especially in the late 1910s and at moments during the 1930s and 1940s. But each time, the hopes of advocates of one or another form of public health insurance were dashed on the shoals of the U.S. political system and against the rocks of fervent conservative opposition to this seemingly logical form of public social provision.

From 1916 through 1920, the American Association for Labor Legislation (AALL) campaigned for public "sickness insurance" to cover American workingmen and their dependents (cf. Numbers 1978; Starr 1982: 237–57; Skocpol 1992: chap. 3). Founded in 1906 and devoted to the use of social science research to promote various kinds of "labor legislation" in the United States, the AALL was a small association of reform-minded professionals, mostly university professors, labor statisticians, and social workers. As dozens of U.S. states enacted regulations requiring businesses to provide industrial accident insurance, the experts of the AALL decided that health insurance would be "the next great step" in the march toward comprehensive social insurance. AALL members believed that there would be inevitable progress toward the enactment of public social insurance in all civilized industrializing nations and the United States would have to be part of this worldwide movement. Reformers in the Progressive Era argued that sickness insurance—to be funded jointly by contributions from business, wage earners, and government tax revenues—would help to prevent poverty among wage earners. Health insurance would also promote economic and social "efficiency," because it would encourage employers, employees, and citizens alike to promote healthful conditions at work and in communities.

To the experts of the AALL, the case for the U.S. states to enact health insurance was so obviously rational and the worldwide course of "social progress" so clearly inevitable that they were hardly prepared for the spread of ideologically impassioned opposition to their legislative proposals. Yet there were plenty of potential opponents. Private insurance companies opposed the death benefits that were to be included in health insurance as designed by the AALL. Business associations such as the National Association of Manufacturers looked askance at the new taxes that health insurance would entail. Private physicians and various state and local units of the American Medical Association worried about the imposition of governmental regulation. And certain labor leaders opposed all forms of public social insurance as an intrusion on union autonomy. As the United States entered World War I, ideologues opposed to health insurance highlighted the bogey of German statism, using opposition to "bureaucracy" as an effective rallying cry for the various forces potentially opposed to health insurance. Health insurance was labeled "un-American." What is more, the increasingly hysterical claims of the enemies of health insurance fell upon the ears of middle-class publics that were already skeptical about governmental efficiency and honesty, not to mention wary of new taxes.

The normally cumbersome operations of U.S. governmental institutions—which required reformers to move proposals, state by state, through two legislative houses, past potential vetoes by governors, and around potential constitutional and judicial obstacles—insured that opponents to health insurance would have plenty of time to build coalitions and many institutional points at which to register opposition (Robertson 1989). By 1920, the AALL-sponsored campaigns for health insurance had been deflected altogether in most U.S. states and defeated in pitched battles in California and New York. The progress that had seemed so inevitable a few years earlier was stopped dead in its tracks; and the AALL itself permanently lost momentum after the nationwide defeat of its all-out campaign for health insurance.

During the 1930s and 1940s, efforts to promote public health insurance—now for middle-class as well as working-class Americans—were pursued by various groups of intellectuals and officials located in and around the various administrations of President Franklin Delano Roosevelt and President Harry Truman (cf. Hirshfield 1970; Poen 1979; Starr 1982: 275–89). At first, reform proposals called for federal incentives for optional state-level health insurance, but during and after World War II reformers' hopes shifted toward a comprehensive, national system of health insurance, modeled on contributory old-age insurance. Echoing the faith of the Progressives of the 1910s, many New Dealers were confident that the United States would inevitably "complete" what the Social Security Act of 1935 had begun, building a comprehensive welfare state that would include national employment assurance, unemployment benefits, and health insurance coverage for all Americans. President Roosevelt never gave full backing to health insurance proposals during the 1930s; and they were left out of the legislation for Social Security because of fears that opposition from the American Medical Association might sink the entire bill if health insurance was included. Nevertheless, the hopes of advocates of national health insurance looked as if they might be realized in the 1940s, particularly when Harry Truman featured this reform in his ultimately victorious bid for reelection in 1948.

Once again, reformist hopes were shattered. Throughout the 1930s and 1940s, all proposals for public health insurance were strenuously opposed by the formidable American Medical Association, which from the 1920s had become truly a peak association of private fee-for-service doctors in thousands of local communities and all the states of the United States. By the 1940s, moreover, private insurance companies had developed an interest in offering health insurance to the middle class. During and right after World War II, major industrial employers were encouraged by wartime controls and provisions of the federal tax code to start offering health insurance as a "fringe benefit" to workers (Stevens 1984, 1988). Thus, not only were industrialists opposed to paying taxes for public health insurance; many of them also became committed to their nascent private systems of health benefits—which had been used as bargaining chips in lieu of higher wages, and which did not seem so costly at that phase of history.

Just as ideological rallying cries against "German statism" brought together potential opponents of workingmen's health insurance during the late 1910s, the various forces ready to weigh in against Truman's plans for national health insurance were brought together in late 1940s by cries of opposition to "communism" and "socialized medicine." The Cold War was emerging, as the United States shifted from its World War II alliance with the beleaguered Russians against the Nazis, toward global superpower rivalry with an imperial Soviet Union. Within the United Slates, witch-hunts were launched against actually or allegedly pro-Communist public officials and labor union leaders. At this conjuncture, it was simple for opponents of national health insurance to label it "socialist," rapidly shifting public opinion away from public financing of health care costs. Reformers who had thought they were furthering a logical extension of the New Deal and Social Security suddenly found themselves in an ideologically uncomfortable position— appearing to support something un-American, even "subversive." To be sure, the newly powerful CIO unions initially preferred to support Truman's plan for national health insurance. But many CIO leaders were themselves victims of anti-Communist crusades. And strong industrial unions were able, when necessary, to fall back on contract bargaining for employer-provided health insurance coverage. From the 1950s through the 1970s, that is exactly what they did, enabling many unionized workers to enjoy very generous health benefits even in the absence of national health insurance (Stevens 1984).

We see, in short, that both in the 1910s and in the 1930s and 1940s, experts and reformers relied upon rational analyses and arguments about how to solve problems of efficiency or access. Reformers were confident that time was on their side, and that public health insurance (of one sort or another) would "inevitably" be enacted in the United States. But each time, not only were there powerful opponents to reform but debates also quickly took a bitterly ideological turn. This tactic was not expected by the rationally minded experts and led to defeats for proposals that might well have gained broad citizen support, had they been more calmly discussed—or effectively dramatized—in the national political process.

ARE REFORMERS READY FOR THE POLITICAL DEBATE OF THE 1990s?

If past battles over health insurance for the United States turned out to be very ideological, leaving the rational reformers mystified and demoralized, it is very possible that this could happen again during the 1990s. Once again, proponents of universal health care coverage may be becoming overly complacent, assuming that rationality and logic will inevitably triumph. Most reformers are placing their faith in technically complicated insider bargaining, overlooking how ideological and politically charged the debates about health care reform are likely once again to become.

From many groups, experts, and politicians, I have gathered statements outlining desirable reforms in U.S. health care access and financing. In the current fashion, I have applied "discursive analysis" to these documents, trying to get a feeling for the audiences that are being addressed. I am interested, in short, in not just what each actor is proposing to do but to whom the actor is talking. More fundamentally, what conceptions of the political process lie behind various proposals? How might changes come about (or be obstructed)? For the most part, I must note, those discussing health care reforms in the early 1990s have remarkably little to say about the civic and governmental processes by which proposals will be adjudicated. One must simply infer who the intended audiences for messages are and how actors think the decision-making process might unfold. What follows are some of my inferences.

Most of today's "rational" reformers in the debates over health care reform are advocates of various schemes that fall under the rubrics of play or pay or managed competition. Supporters of such middle-range, mixed public and private schemes situate themselves in what they feel to be the comfortable center of the spectrum of reform advocates. On the one hand, they want to do much more than merely tinker with the current markets for private insurance; on the other hand, they do not want to go all the way toward universal, government-funded health insurance offering the same basic coverage to all citizens. Middle-range schemes usually aim to build on America's current system of employer-provided health insurance, by requiring and enabling all employers to offer at least basic health insurance to their employees. At the same time, publicly encouraged or subsidized health insurance would be expanded beyond Medicare and Medicaid to include those who are left out of the job-based schemes, as well as those who are dumped from job-based schemes after new regulations on businesses are put into place.

The supporters of middle-range reforms include some very hefty actors in American politics. Along with major unions, a goodly number of major U.S. corporations—such as Xerox, Lockheed, and General Electric—have banded together in the National Leadership Coalition to call for a play-or-pay approach to health care reform (Garland 1991). The Pepper Commission—the U.S. Bipartisan Commission on Comprehensive Health Care, chaired by Senator Jay Rockefeller of West Virginia—called for this approach in its September 1990 report (Pepper Commission 1990; see also Rockefeller 1991; Feder 1992). Building on the Pepper Commission's work, a working group of Democratic party leaders in the Senate—including Senators George Mitchell, Ted Kennedy, Don Riegle, and Jay Rockefeller—then developed a specific legislative proposal incorporating the play-or-pay approach (Peterson 1992). More recently, some politicians and experts have championed "managed competition" approaches that (in some versions) might deemphasize employer-provided health insurance in favor of individual enrollments in plans sponsored by regional health insurance purchasing cooperatives (Starr 1993). During his presidential campaign Bill Clinton at first talked in terms of play or pay ideas (Clinton for President Committee 1992); then he switched to speaking, in very general terms, about managed competition (Clinton and Gore 1992). Since Clinton's inauguration, it has become apparent that some sort of mixed public and private scheme will be worked out for the first round of comprehensive health care reform proposed by his administration.

Advocates of either play or pay or managed competition stress the feasibility of a "pragmatic road toward national health insurance" (Pollack and Torda 1991) or a "healthy compromise" (Starr 1993). Perhaps a single-payer, Canadian-style system of universal coverage for all citizens would be ideal, they acknowledge. But doctors, insurance companies, and employers just will not accept this great a change; and American citizens and politicians will not agree to have all health care costs immediately shifted into the system of taxes and governmental expenditures. Proponents of universal health insurance (such as Marmor and Mashaw 1990; Marmor et al. 1990; Kerrey 1991; and Fein 1992) are presented as unrealistic by advocates of the middle-range schemes. Supporters of the universal approach are requested to "back off" from demanding "too much," so that the "realistic" advocates of play or pay or managed competition can at least get half the loaf in the first stage of reform.

Advocates of middle-range reform plans seem to take it for granted that they will be able to get their approaches enacted through congressional brokering, as quiet bargains among major players in the current system—bargains that would not step too much, just a little bit, on established toes. "Political feasibility" in this context thus refers to an interest group arrangement hammered out in Congress, with special attention to the concerns of established economic interest groups. The question remains, though, whether the political premises that lie behind the thinking of advocates of play or pay or managed competition are really true. Let me highlight some of these premises and raise some questions about them.

One premise that lies behind all middle-range schemes for health care reform is that groups such as small businesses, doctors, and private insurers will accept being hurt just a little in order to be brought into a framework of improved access for all citizens. I wonder whether this is realistic. Advocates of managed competition advocate tough caps on costs for health insurance plans. But won't doctors and insurers anticipate such possibilities and maneuver to keep rigorous cost control mechanisms out of any such legislation? Similarly, most supporters of play or pay envisage that once this sort of system is in place, it will probably evolve toward single-payer, publicly funded national health insurance (cf. Pollack and Torda 1991). Faced with paying either private insurance premiums or taxes, businesses will shift more and more of their workers into the public scheme. (The advocates of play or pay apparently do not worry, as I do, that the residual public medical care program may be so underfunded that it will frighten many middle-class people, who will then fight ferociously against being shifted into it.) But if play-or-pay proponents expect their system to propel a gradual transition toward a single-payer public scheme, how can they imagine that the various interest groups they want to bring into the initial bargain won't notice where matters might end up down the road?

Small businesses know very well that, as soon as they are required to pay for health coverage, their costs will escalate, while any initial public subsidies will probably subside or disappear. Even big business is not united in support of reforms (Garland 1991). Insurance companies certainly realize that, over time, public coverage and regulation will squeeze their profits. Doctors certainly realize that calls for cost controls will increasingly lead (especially in a fragmented multiple-payer system) toward ever more microscopic price controls and second-guessing of their day-to-day decisions. In sum, many of the organized interests that advocates of play or pay or managed competition want to propitiate or bring into the initial bargain can surely envisage exactly what sorts of reform provisions might very quickly lead to outcomes they do not want. Since the legislative bargains are going to be very complex, they can fight to prevent such provisions in the initial legislation, or maneuver to evade or reverse them later.

A second premise of middle-range reform approaches is that Congress can hammer out bargains and that legislative gridlock will soon be overcome. This assumption may seem realistic now that we have a Democratic president in place along with a Democratically controlled Congress. Even so, it overlooks pressures that may be brought against congressional representatives by convinced opponents of any fundamental reforms. Proponents of play or pay or managed competition not only need to bargain with advocates of single-payer schemes; they also need to overcome opponents of any tough government-run reforms. And they must face the fact that after initial reforms are enacted in 1994, powerful interests will be lying in wait to eviscerate the implementation of tough cost controls. There will almost certainly have to be subsequent rounds of legislation, some of which might end up taking place in a changed political context, for example, if the Democrats lose in congressional or presidential elections during the rest of the 1990s.

For congressional leaders and other "realists" who are "settling" for middle-range reform plans at this point, the current debate is very much dominated by the fear of repeating what supposedly happened in the early 1970s (see Peterson 1992). Senator Ted Kennedy and some other Democratic congressional leaders believe that they lost the chance in this earlier period to work out a de facto universal access system, because a compromise failed to occur between Democratic party advocates of incremental change and Democratic party advocates of an ideal national health system. In fact, some observers of the health care reform debates of the 1970s (see Starr 1982: 414) argue that *neither* of these Democratic approaches ever had much of a chance of enactment. The later 1970s was a period of perceived budget stringencies and growing public skepticism about the capacities of government to solve social problems. The presidency of Jimmy Carter was, after all, the precursor to Ronald Reagan's victory in 1980.

But even if the problem during the 1970s represented a failure of Democrats to compromise among themselves on less than a purely comprehensive system of health insurance, worrying about repeating that failing now is a little bit like preparing to refight the last war. People are not taking into account that the political context has changed fundamentally from the 1970s to the 1990s. The concern in the 1990s is much more with cost containment and not simply with spreading social access to health care. Single-payer schemes offer a much more credible promise of simplified, uniform, and effective regulation of medical costs than do play-or-pay schemes and many versions of managed competition. Mixed public and private reform plans propose to retain many payers and fragmented, administratively cumbersome methods of cost accounting. Many possibilities for cost shifting may still remain under these plans; and medical cost inflation is virtually certain to continue. What is more, if supporters of middle-range schemes give in to worries about costs right now and decide to "phase in" full coverage for presently excluded groups of Americans over many years, it is possible that continuing cost increases will lead to later reversals of the promise of full access for everyone to health insurance.

During the last two decades, the context for debates over health insurance reforms has changed both ideologically and in terms of partisan balance. In the 1970s, it may very well have been a question of whether Democrats could come up with a compromise in their own ranks. But now a compromise within Democratic ranks is nowhere near enough to ensure enduring and irreversible changes in the way health care is financed in the United States. Back in the 1970s, "conservatives" were mostly moderate, pragmatic Republicans, who could be counted on to be gentlemanly and reasonable about inside-the-beltway bargains over legislation. Now, however, the conservatives who have the edge in the Republican party and beyond are tough street fighters, hostile to brokering in Washington, D.C., and willing to take emotional, ideologically charged debates to the country as a whole.

This brings us to perhaps the most questionable premise tacitly held by advocates of middle-range reforms. These pragmatic practitioners of insider bargaining seem to assume that ideological battles over public opinion will not prove crucial in the coming rounds of the health insurance debate. There has been little attempt by the advocates of play or pay or managed competition to explain their schemes to the broader citizenry. It is not at all clear that these schemes can be explained very straightforwardly to the American people. Play or pay and managed competition plans are, after all, mind-bogglingly complex, involving adjustments within an already confusing and highly fragmented system of health care financing that involves many, many institutional actors. It is very difficult to come up with simple metaphors that tell the average citizen what the intended changes would do and mean.

Not surprisingly, most of the statements about play or pay or managed competition have so far been directed at business, or the medical profession, or policy experts. Last year, thinking that perhaps the presidential campaign of Bill Clinton might make a stab at a more straightforward message, I asked that campaign to send Clinton's position statements on health care reform. What I received was not reassuring: Clinton's statements as of the spring of 1992 outlined five steps and twelve substeps (Clinton for President Committee 1992). His explanation was very difficult even for someone like me to read through, let alone difficult to incorporate in a speech explaining this approach to the average citizen! Recently, health care reform expert Paul Starr (1993) has written about managed competition as a better middle-range approach than play or pay. Starr writes gracefully, and he presented his views in an article in the *American Prospect* that I am sure was meant to be broadly accessible. But I have read this technically complicated article three times, and I am still not sure exactly what changes managed competition would entail. Nor could I explain them easily to Harvard students, let alone to average citizens.

SPEAKING TO THE CITIZENS OF AMERICA

Contrary to the assumption that health insurance reform will happen through a series of quiet congressional bargains among established players, the debate is already being taken to the citizens of America. During the final year of his presidency, President Bush started sounding the fundamental conservative themes to shape public opinion and to bring together actors around a defensive position. These themes continue to appear regularly in Republican speeches and in ads run in the media by insurance companies, medical groups, and conservative think tanks.

Advocates of both middle-range reforms and single-payer national health insurance have been accused of "socialism," as conservatives ask why we Americans want to move toward governmental "controls" at a time when the rest of the world is moving away from them. Opponents of strong reforms tell us that any attempt to move in the direction of greater public regulation would simply make bureaucracy worse, stifling innovations in health care that save lives and creating rationing and queues for service. "Governmental coercion" is opposed in conservative rhetoric to such ideals as consumer freedom and technological innovations to save lives (see Gradison 1992). Conservative rhetoric is meant to frighten middle-class Americans—especially those who still enjoy relatively good benefits through private insurance—dissuading them from supporting any kind of comprehensive reform. Or if people cannot be dissuaded from accepting initial attempts at comprehensive reform in 1994, such rhetoric is meant to lay the basis for reinterpreting the situation a few years later, when whatever is enacted in 1994 proves not to be successful or socially painless.

In short, during the 1990s, just as in the 1910s and the 1940s, the opponents of any sort of national health insurance have quickly undertaken to create ideological metaphors. They aim to fuel fears of reform among the citizenry and bring together the worries about change of stakeholders in the health economy as it is presently structured. Meanwhile, very little is being done by advocates of fundamental reform to create their own positive ideological metaphors for wide public dissemination.

On the side of those who want reform through an enhanced role for the national or state governments, the problem may be that it would be much easier to explain change in the direction of unified-payer plans of publicly financed health insurance than it is to explain the hoary details of play or pay or managed competition. Both citizens in general and many actors in the present medical care system might find it easier to understand the appeals of an administratively simplified, comprehensive system of health care financing available to every person in America. There may seem to be very little incentive for politicians already in the system—especially representatives in Congress who have to deal constantly with lobbyists for established interests—to declare that they are aiming at such fundamental change as a truly national health insurance system implies. Nevertheless, by not being willing to outline a clear, compelling vision of national health insurance as a desirable end point of reform, the proponents of middle-range reforms in Congress and beyond may actually be undermining their own cause. National health insurance may have to be explained and defended as a desirable goal, before it becomes possible to legitimate lesser reforms that interject greater public control into the health care system. In a climate where conservatives are willing to hammer away against the notion of *any* greater direct governmental involvement in health care, progressive proponents of health care reform may have to face the issue of government's role directly, explaining to the American people why it is not just pragmatic, but actually ideal, to have government increasingly involved in ensuring—and perhaps, in due course, financing—health care for everyone.

Let me close by summarizing some of the straightforward arguments that proponents of single-payer national health insurance can make to the American people about their preferred approach to addressing problems of social access and cost containment.

First and foremost, it is easy to tell people that under national health insurance each individual will have rights as a citizen, rather than through the place he or she happens to be employed. The appeal of equal rights for all citizens can be readily dramatized. Imagine television commercials that feature an unemployed father taking an injured child to the hospital, pulling out the child's "Americare" card, and getting the help that is needed without any complicated forms to fill out.

Proponents of national health insurance can also turn rhetoric about bureaucracy to their advantage, pointing out that the present medical care system has a bewildering variety of rules and paperwork from hundreds of different private insurance companies. The average American citizen knows from experience that the bureaucratic rules and forms are getting more and more complex, as insurance companies increasingly seek to manage and second-guess the care that doctors order. Advocates of play or pay or managed competition cannot easily claim that their approaches would ameliorate this situation; they might well make it worse, especially at first. But supporters of national health insurance can make a credible claim to bureaucratic simplification, arguing that sometimes a greater role for government can actually cut down on rules and regulations. (Parenthetically, doctors might also find this feature of national health insurance quite appealing, for they know that present trends of proliferating insurance regulations are leading to much microregulation of their day-to-day decisions about patient care. Under national health insurance, doctors and hospitals would have to negotiate yearly prices and budgets. But their decisions about individual patients would not be second-guessed by insurance companies.)

Economic efficiency is another goal that could well be furthered by more rather than less comprehensive reform in health insurance. Advertisements and speeches on behalf of single-payer national health insurance could tell Americans how nice it would be to move from job to job without worrying about the loss or diminution of health benefits for themselves or their families. The mobility of the labor force would certainly be enhanced, enabling the United States to compete more effectively in the international marketplace. Many businesses might find it appealing to dump altogether the responsibility of offering expensive health insurance. And single-payer schemes promise to make the capping of health care costs easier, because young and old, the middle-class and the poor, will all be in the same system. Uniform prices can be negotiated and enforced; administrative costs for health insurance will be cut back; and medical care providers will no longer have to deal with uncompensated patients dumped by insurers or other providers.

There are, in short, many advantages to comprehensive rather than incremental governmental reforms of U.S. health care in the 1990s—and these advantages can be easily dramatized to the citizenry as a whole. In my view, today's reform-minded experts need to face the fact that, as in the past, U.S. political battles over health insurance will almost certainly have ideological as well as technical, and emotional as well as rational, dimensions. No matter what happens in the successive elections of the 1990s, it almost certainly will not be possible to rely on purely inside-the-beltway bargains to enact, defend, and build upon truly progressive changes in the American system of access to and financing of health care. Any initial changes will have to be well understood by many Americans, if political support for progress over the 1990s is to be sustained. The access and cost problems of the American health care system will not be solved all at once.

Just as the advocates of Social Security during the New Deal were willing to use compelling metaphors and political rhetoric to explain to the citizenry why it made sense to have new levels of governmental involvement in the provision of old-age security, so will today's advocates of health care reform have to be able to explain their proposals to the American people. Indeed, advocates of health care reforms in the 1990s have more to explain to a skeptical citizenry about why *government* can provide desirable solutions to widely felt problems.

In my opinion, it is easier for supporters of national health insurance to make such a case than it is for advocates of play or pay or managed competition. But whether I am correct about this or not, the challenge of painting a vision of positive changes through government remains for all those who hope that the time finally is ripe to enact full health coverage in the United States. Along with members of Congress who hope to hammer out bargains for reform, health care experts who think about solutions for technical problems need to attend to fundamental processes of political communication. They need to explain to a democratic citizenry where they would like to go and why it is desirable to go there.

If reformers in the 1990s fail to paint an appealing picture of government-sponsored reform, conservatives will—later in the 1990s, if not immediately in 1994—win yet another round in the overly protracted struggle to bring affordable and accessible health care to all Americans. To avoid the fate of progressive health reformers in the past, today's advocates of universal inclusion and socially managed health costs will have to talk with the people of America. Reformers need to engage in a dialogue with citizens, involving them in a process of reform that is certain to happen, not all at once in a back-room bargain, but over many years of adjustment and learning within a democratic polity.

REFERENCES

Aaron, Henry J. 1991. Looking Backward; 2001–1991. The History of the Health Care Financing and Reform Act of 1998. *Brookings Review* 9 (3): 40–45.

AMA (American Medical Association). 1990. *Health Access America: The AMA Proposal to Improve Access to Affordable, Quality Health Care.* Chicago, IL: American Medical Association.

Bergthold, Linda. 1990. *Purchasing Power in Health: Business, the State, and Health Care Politics.* New Brunswick, NJ: Rutgers University Press.

———. 1991. The Fat Kid on the Seesaw: American Business and Health Care Cost Containment, 1970–1990. *Annual Review of Public Health* 12:157–75.

Blumenthal, Sidney. 1991. Populism in Tweeds: The Professor and the Middle Class. *New Republic,* 25 November, pp. 10–15.

Briggs, Philip. 1992. A View from the Insurance Industry. In *Social Insurance Issues for the Nineties* (Proceedings of the Third Conference of the National Academy of Social Insurance), ed. Paul N. Van de Water. Dubuque, IA: Kendall/Hunt.

Clinton, Bill, and Al Gore. 1992. *Putting People First: How We Can All Change America.* New York: Times Books, Random House.

Clinton for President Committee. 1992. *Bill Clinton's American Health Care Plan.* Little Rock, AR: Clinton for President Committee.

Ellwood, David T. 1988. *Poor Support: Poverty in the American Family.* New York: Basic.

Feder, Judith. 1992. The Pepper Commission's Proposals. In *Social Insurance Issues for the Nineties* (Proceedings of the Third Conference of the National Academy of Social Insurance), ed. Paul N. Van de Water. Dubuque, IA: Kendall/Hunt.

Fein, Rashi. 1992. Health Care Reform. *Scientific American* 267 (5): 46–53.

Garland, Susan B. 1991. Already, Big Business' Health Plan Isn't Feeling So Hot. *Business Week,* 18 November, p. 48.

Gradison, Bill. 1992. Statement by the Honorable Bill Gradison before the House Ways and Means Committee, 3 March. (Typescript from the representative's office.)

Hirshfield, Daniel S. 1970. *The Lost Reform*. Cambridge, MA: Harvard University Press.

Jones. Stanley B. 1992. What Is the Future of Private Health Insurance? In *Social Insurance Issues for the Nineties* (Proceedings of the Third Conference of the National Academy of Social Insurance), ed. Paul N. Van de Water. Dubuque, IA; Kendall/ Hunt.

Kerrey, Robert. 1991. Why America Will Adopt Comprehensive Health Care Reform. *American Prospect* 6 (Summer): 81–90.

Kingdon, John W. 1984. *Agendas, Alternatives, and Public Policies*. Boston, MA: Little, Brown.

Marmor, Theodore R., and Jerry L. Mashaw. 1990. Canada's Health Insurance and Ours: The Real Lessons, the Big Choices. *American Prospect* 3 (Fall): 18–29.

Marmor, Theodore R., Jerry L. Mashaw, and Philip L. Harvey. 1990. *America's Misunderstood Welfare State: Persistent Myths, Enduring Realities*. New York: Basic.

Martin, Cathie Jo. 1993. Together Again: Business, Government, and the Quest for Cost Control. *Journal of Health Politics, Policy and Law* 18 (2): 359–93.

Numbers, Ronald L. 1978. *Almost Persuaded: American Physicians and Compulsory Health Insurance, 1912–1920*. Baltimore, MD: Johns Hopkins University Press.

Pepper Commission. 1990. *A Call for Action: Executive Summary*. Washington, DC: U.S. Government Printing Office.

Peterson, Mark A. 1992. Momentum toward Health Care Reform in the U.S. Senate. *Journal of Health Politics, Policy and Law* 17 (3): 553–73.

Poen, Monte M. 1979. *Harry S. Truman versus the Medical Lobby*. Columbia: University of Missouri Press.

Pollack, Ronald, and Phyllis Torda. 1991. The Pragmatic Road toward National Health Insurance. *American Prospect* 6 (Summer): 92–100.

Robertson, David Brian. 1989. The Bias of American Federalism: The Limits of Welfare-State Development in the Progressive Era. *Journal of Policy History* 1 (3): 261–91.

Rockefeller, Jay D., IV. 1991. A Call for Action: The Pepper Commission's Blueprint for Health Care Reform. *Journal of the American Medical Association* 265 (19): 2507–10.

Ruggie, Mary. 1992. The Paradox of Liberal Intervention: Health Policy and the American Welfare State. *American Journal of Sociology* 97 (4): 919–44.

Russakoff, Dale. 1991. How Wofford Rode Health Care to Washington. *Washington Post National Weekly Edition*, 25 November–1 December, pp. 14–15.

Skocpol, Theda. 1992. *Protecting Soldiers and Mothers: The Political Origins of Social Policy in the United States*. Cambridge, MA: Belknap Press, Harvard University Press.

Starr, Paul. 1982. *The Social Transformation of American Medicine.* New York: Basic.

———. 1991. The Middle Class and National Health Reform. *American Prospect* 6 (Summer): 7–12.

———. 1993. Healthy Compromise: Universal Coverage and Managed Competition under a Cap. *American Prospect* 12 (Winter): 44–52.

Stevens, Beth. 1984. In the Shadow of the Welfare State: Corporate and Union Development of Employee Benefits. Ph.D. dissertation, Department of Sociology, Harvard University.

———. 1988. Blurring the Boundaries: How the Federal Government Has Influenced Welfare Benefits in the Private Sector. In *The Politics of Social Policy in the United States,* ed. Margaret Weir, Ann Shola Orloff, and Theda Skocpol. Princeton, NJ: Princeton University Press.

Todd, James S., S. V. Seekins, J. A. Krichbaum, and L. K. Harvey. 1991. Health Access America—Strengthening the U.S. Health Care System. *Journal of the American Medical Association* 265 (19): 2503–6.

CHAPTER TEN

From Social Security to Health Security?

AN "American Health Security Act" is what President Bill Clinton hopes to be able to sign into law in 1994, after Congress has processed the legislative provisions he submitted in the fall of 1993. By its very title, the call for "Health Security" invokes the precedent of the Social Security Act of 1935. And in his 22 September 1993 speech to Congress and the nation, the president spelled out the founding moment for U.S. social provision that he hopes to repeat:

> It's hard to believe that once there was a time—even in this century—when retirement was nearly synonymous with poverty, and older Americans died in our streets. That is unthinkable today because over half a century ago Americans had the courage to change—to create a Social Security system that ensures that no Americans will be forgotten in their later years.
>
> I believe that forty years from now our grandchildren will also find it unthinkable that there was a time in our country when hard-working families lost their homes and savings simply because their child fell ill, or lost their health coverage when they changed jobs. Yet our grandchildren will only find such things unthinkable tomorrow if we have the courage to change today.

Rhetoric aside, Clinton's invocation of parallels across time naturally raises a question that I, as an analyst of U.S. social policy-making, find quite fascinating: What *are* the similarities and differences between the politics of Social Security in the 1930s and the politics of health care reform in the 1990s? And in making this juxtaposition, what can we learn about the prospects for President Clinton's proposed health care reforms?

There certainly are some striking similarities between the campaign for Social Security legislation in the 1930s and the current efforts on behalf of "American Health Security" legislation. At both junctures, dislocations in the U.S. economy and in preexisting arrangements for social provision raised genuine "security" concerns that spread well into the ranks of the broad American middle class. Unemployment and the plight of the elderly were the chief concerns during the Great Depression, whereas losses or reductions of employer-provided health insur-

Journal of Health Politics, Policy and Law, Vol. 19, No. 1, Spring 1994. Copyright © 1994 by Duke University.

ance benefits are worries for many wage- and salary-earning citizens in the hard-pressed U.S. economy of the 1990s.

After 1932 and 1992 alike, newly elected Democratic presidents assembled task forces of government officials and professional experts to work out blueprints for comprehensive reform. The Committee on Economic Security (which drafted the Social Security Act) and President Clinton's Health Security Task Force both operated largely in secret, co-opting certain reformers and their ideas and excluding others from the realm of "feasibility." Both drafting groups, moreover, tried to anticipate the concerns of powerful congressional actors, and sought to build social insurance systems that rely on powerful private economic interests: corporations that would collect payroll taxes in the 1930s, and large insurance companies that would continue to mediate the system of "managed competition" in the Clinton vision of health care reform for the 1990s.

Finally, both President Franklin Roosevelt in the 1930s and President Bill Clinton in the 1990s have used the rhetorical powers of the presidency to appeal to public opinion, promising enhanced long-term "security" to American citizens across all walks of life. Both have tried to arouse a sufficient sense of "crisis" in the public and Congress to override intense opposition to comprehensive, governmentally sponsored change from political conservatives and from many hefty private interest groups.

Yet if there are similarities between the politics of Social Security in the 1930s and the politics of health care reform in the 1990s, there are also important differences. The experts who fashioned the retirement insurance portion of the 1935 legislation—the part that would eventually usurp the label "Social Security"—operated largely outside of public scrutiny and in largely virgin policy territory. Although certain U.S. states had prior public assistance programs and unemployment insurance enactments, there were no state-level contributory retirement insurance programs for the Social Security planners to take into account; and preexisting corporate pension programs had been pretty much destroyed by the ravages of the Depression. The way was relatively clear for the Committee on Economic Security to propose a national, federally administered contributory retirement insurance system. As the Committee on Economic Security proposals made their way through Congress, much of the attention and controversy centered on public assistance and unemployment insurance, rather than on the program that would eventually become "Social Security."

Contrast the situation in U.S. health care by the 1990s, where entrenched private and partial public programs of health care financing and delivery abound. Established stakeholders in the huge and unwieldy

U.S. health care system have many interests to defend. Each stakeholder is acutely aware of every detail of new legislation that may affect it, and many stakeholders have substantial financial and other resources that can be used to influence public opinion. The Clinton reforms must make their way through Congress admidst a constant glare of publicity, evading attempts to mobilize opinion against this or that provision.

The 1990s are also sharply different from the 1930s on pivotal matters of political power and the legitimacy of governmentally sponsored change. During the 1930s, of course, Franklin Roosevelt and the Democrats enjoyed large, indeed growing, electoral majorities, whereas Bill Clinton undertakes health care reform as a president elected by less than a majority of the electorate, and as the titular leader of a shaky Democratic Party. Back in the 1930s, outcries against "government bureaucracy" and "creeping socialism" were not as effective as they usually are in U.S. politics. Amidst the Depression, the American public could no longer believe that business magnates had all the answers, and the New Deal was a time of unusual openness to governmentally sponsored reforms and the expansion of federal power. By contrast the Clinton proposals come at a juncture when government is held in general disrepute. Taxes are not the only issue (opinion polls actually show that a majority of Americans will accept some new taxes as the price of universal health care coverage); more so are the public's worries about governmental effectiveness. Many Americans believe, or are quite ready to be convinced, that governmental "bureaucracies" bungle everything they touch. The Clinton health care plan—devoted as it is to furthering governmentally regulated "managed competition" rather than creating a streamlined single-payer system of universal coverage—is excruciatingly vulnerable to charges of "overregulation" and "bureaucratic aggrandizement." News commentators, not to mention humorists like Art Buchwald, have had a field day with the 1,342-page, 240,000-word Clinton legislative proposal. Representative Dick Armey of Texas has made headway for conservative forces that are really opposed to any fundamental reforms simply by holding up on television a mindbogglingly complex chart of all the "bureaucracies" that would be involved in implementing Clinton-style national health coverage (for the chart, see the editorial pages of the 13 October 1993 *Wall Street Journal*).

By the time the Clinton proposals emerge from Congress, they will very possibly have been stripped of most of the elements of public regulation that are necessary to ensure any modicum of cost containment. More worrisome still is the prospect that rules about comprehensive benefits for everyone will be loosened, or eviscerated in this or that detail, thus allowing many vulnerable groups of Americans to—in effect—be left out of adequate health care insurance in coming years. We could end up with the rhetorical appearance of "health security for everyone" without anything like the federal regulations and funding that would be necessary to ensure the actuality of such universal security.

Comparisons across historical time thus underline various ways in which Clinton's health care proposals are proceeding through Congress under very different political conditions than those that prevailed in 1934 and 1935. Perhaps Bill Clinton will be able to pull off another founding moment for U.S. publicly guaranteed "security," comparable in some ways to what New Deal reformers and Franklin Roosevelt achieved in 1935. Yet there are many things militating against such an accomplishment in the 1990s.

In the final analysis, though, history teaches us still another lesson: watershed legislative moments are only beginnings. In retrospect, we imagine that America's relatively universal social insurance programs for the elderly emerged full-blown in 1935. But actually many political struggles, legislative reforms, and administrative maneuvers intervened between 1935 and Social Security's emergence in the 1960s as America's most effective and popular social program.

It will be the same with whatever happens this year (or next) in health care reform. Hopefully, we will be able to look back from the vantage point of 2010 and say that certain aspirations—for universal coverage and cost containment—were successfully launched in 1994 or 1995. But how it all turns out will depend, not just on what Americans and their leaders do in the early 1990s, but on what they do in the revisitings of "health care reform" that will surely recur for many years to come.

Remaking U.S. Social Policies for the 21st Century

As the turn of a new century approaches, Americans are looking critically at the scope and purposes of their nation's social policies. Signs of fundamental reconsideration cut across partisan and ideological lines, and go beyond particular policy areas. Experts, journalists, advocacy groups, and politicians now repeatedly ask whether "too much" is being done for elderly citizens, while the needs of younger people are insufficiently addressed by existing public programs.

Of course, social policies in the United States have been controversial for quite some time. From the 1960s to the 1980s, matters of poverty, race, and class were at the forefront of discussion. Americans argued about the War on Poverty and the Great Society, and then about the allegedly excessive tax burdens that government was placing upon the hardworking middle class to pay for "welfare handouts" to the undeserving poor. Issues such as these, replete with racial tensions, fueled the rise of conservatism after 1964; and they continue to simmer today. Yet since the middle of the 1980s, the terms of public debate have shifted perceptibly toward matters of generational equity, highlighting the divergent fates of young and old in relation to existing public policies. Many conservatives and liberals agree that fundamental reconstructions may be necessary to achieve generational equity as the nation prepares for the dawn of the next century.

Quite different intellectual and value positions lie behind apparently similar generational concerns, however. Progressive groups may talk about doing more to "help the children of America," but they do not at all have the same criticisms and proposals for reform in mind as conservative groups dedicated to "restoring the American dream for our children and grandchildren." To take two highly visible and appropriate spokespeople, Marian Wright Edelman of the Children's Defense Fund raises quite different sorts of generational concerns than Peter G. Peterson, an investment banker who has been a leading force behind the Concord Coalition, which is principally devoted to dismantling America's universal system of Social Security for the elderly.

The Concord Coalition is nominally bipartisan, co-chaired by two retired U.S. Senators, Republican Warren Rudman and Democrat Paul

Tsongas. Peter G. Peterson elaborated the ideas of the Concord Coalition in his 1993 book *Facing Up: How to Restore the Economy from Crushing Debt and Restore the American Dream.*[1] The book's Foreword is written by Rudman and Tsongas, and its dust jacket declares that its royalties will be donated to the Concord Coalition. As Peterson explains, the Concord Coalition aims to mobilize middle-class public opinion to urge politicians in Washington, D.C., into "doing the right thing" for America's children and our national future by fundamentally revamping existing social policies.

Entitlements for the elderly—especially Social Security, Medicare, and federal pensions—account for much of current federal spending. Peterson holds them responsible for the large federal deficit, and he projects taxes and entitlement spending for decades into the future in dramatic charts that suggest that the nation is certain to "go bankrupt." In sharp contrast to the good fortune enjoyed by people who came of age after the Great Depression and World War II, young adults today are losing out on the American Dream of rising incomes, home ownership, and upward social mobility. Their children—"our grandchildren"—will do even worse, Peterson asserts, suffering under massive tax burdens to pay for entitlements going to overindulged middle-class people, especially the elderly.

The answer to the nation's debt "crisis," according to Peterson and the Concord Coalition, is to drastically cut public spending on "middle-class entitlements." Various specific reforms are proposed, including turning Social Security and Medicare into means-tested programs only for the needy. Resources should be shifted into what Peterson calls "real investments"—that is, privately managed funds. *Facing Up*, in short, invokes the well-being of future generations and offers a grand moral argument on behalf of a call to cut back the public sector in favor of private capital. "More than two centuries ago," Peterson perorates,

> Thomas Jefferson wrote a letter to James Madison in which he warned of the utter inappropriateness in a democracy of a value system that allows the debts of one generation to burden the next. . . . Jefferson would be shocked, saddened, and ashamed to see the $4 trillion noose of national debt we have put around the necks of our progeny—not to mention the trillions more in unfunded federal benefit liabilities we are passing on to future workers. . . . To place the weight of these trillions upon unborn children is to rob them of what Jefferson and the founding fathers promised us: life, liberty, and the pursuit of happiness.[2]

[1] Peter G. Peterson, *Facing Up: How to Rescue the Economy from Crushing Debt and Restore the American Dream* (New York: Simon and Schuster, 1993).

[2] Ibid., pp. 43–44.

A similarly apocalyptic yet substantively quite different vision of America's social crisis and policy options emanates from the Children's Defense Fund (CDF), widely regarded as the nation's leading advocacy group for the young and poor.[3] In its own words, the CDF

> exists to provide a strong and effective voice for all the children of America who cannot vote, lobby, or speak for themselves. We pay particular attention to the needs of poor, minority, and disabled children. Our goal is to educate the nation about the needs of children and encourage productive investment in children before they get sick, drop out of school, suffer family breakdown, or get into trouble.[4]

With support from grants by major national foundations, the CDF was founded between 1968 and 1973 by Marian Wright Edelman, a Civil Rights lawyer, who had worked in Mississippi with the NAACP Legal Defense and Educational Fund, and who had initially come to Washington, D.C., as an advocate for Mississippi's Head Start program. Still under Edelman's leadership, the CDF assembles detailed statistics on social problems and public policies affecting children. It monitors legislative developments in Washington and provides encouragement and information for service professionals and civic activists working on behalf of children in communities across the nation.

Above all, the CDF engages in broad efforts at public education, redefining virtually all problems of poverty and the economy as "children's issues." Edelman eloquently presented the CDF's generational analysis in a 1993 interview for *Psychology Today*:

> We [Americans] have had a decade or so of very painful division by race, by age, and by class, and children were the true victims. Children are now the poorest Americans. Young families of all races suffered an extraordinary decline in earnings—these are the parents of young children, the cradle of nurture for the next generation. We're paying for the results of that.[5]

According to Edelman and the CDF, the "slow progress on children that began in the Sixties, with the establishment of new political and civil rights, didn't last long enough."

> We've obviously had very altered priorities in the last 12 years. . . . Mr. Reagan and Mr. Bush said in effect that it was okay to be selfish and cater to

---

[3] David Walls, *The Activist Almanac: The Concerned Citizens' Guide to the Leading Advocacy Organizations in America* (New York: Fireside, 1993), p. 279.

[4] *The State of America's Children Yearbook 1994*. Washington, D.C.: The Children's Defense Fund, 1994.

[5] "Marian Wright Edelman: An Interview with the Most Concerned Parent in America," *Psychology Today* (July–August 1993), p. 27.

racism. . . . Instead of being considered as national investment priorities, families, children, the poor, and minorities were deemed not important. We had a transfer of resources away from domestic needs—families, job creation, the economy, investing in housing—to the rich.[6]

As if in response to the Concord Coalition, Edelman acknowledges that "we need sensible deficit reduction" to reduce the nation's $4 trillion federal deficit. But "children didn't cause" the fiscal deficit, Edelman argues, adding that "we also have a human deficit. . . . If you don't invest in your people, your children, and your schools, then you're not going to have a productive economy in the future."[7]

GENERATIONAL CRITIQUES IN PERSPECTIVE

Why have generational critiques (of both the varieties we have just samples) recently come to the fore in discussions about the future of U.S. social policies? The answer is not obvious, not to be found simply in fiscal or demographic circumstances.

To be sure, the United States, along with most other Western countries, is going through what Paul Pierson calls "retrenchment politics" in response to economic and fiscal pressures building since the 1970s. Yet the United States stands out compared to European nations—and also in contrast to its Canadian neighbor to the north—for the visibility of arguments over generational equity in its public debates over how to deal with economic and fiscal problems.[8] Ironically, the United States is actually experiencing significantly *less* demographic pressure from governmental programs for the elderly than are many other advanced industrial democratic nations. "Compared to most European nations," Jill Quadagno explains, "the aged in the United States still represent a relatively small proportion of the population, yet no other country has raised the issue of generational equity."[9]

The overall programmatic structure of U.S. social provision, as well as the legacies of previous national political battles about taxes and social programs, help make sense of generational arguments about the future of American public policies. Unresolved struggles from the era of the New Deal and World War II, and especially from the 1960s and

[6] Ibid., pp. 26–27.

[7] Ibid., p. 28.

[8] Paul Pierson and Miriam Smith, "Retrenchment and Generational Conflict: The Shifting Political Fortunes of Programs for the Elderly," forthcoming in *Economic Security, Intergenerational Justice, and the North American Elderly* (Washington, D.C.: The Urban Institute Press, 1994).

[9] Jill Quadagno, "Generational Equity and the Politics of the Welfare State," *Politics and Society* 17(3) (1989), p. 371.

early 1970s and the conservative backlash that followed, inform the generationally oriented political strategies of conservatives and progressives today.

As the essays collected in this book have revealed, the chief features of contemporary U.S. social spending took shape during two watershed periods. New Deal reforms, eventually overlaid by the reforms of the War on Poverty through the early 1970s, culminated in an oddly structured national pattern of social benefits. This pattern features generous and relatively universal programs for the elderly, coexisting with much less generous, means-tested programs for very poor women and children. Groups "in the middle" tend to be left out. Many bifurcations figure in the overall pattern of modern U.S. social spending, including bifurcations by race, gender, and middle class versus poor. A bifurcation by life-course stage—elderly versus young—has also been implicit, ready to come to the fore in public discussions when political conditions became ripe.

Across the Western democratic-capitalist world, the era of the Great Depression through the aftermath of World War II was the formative period for relatively universalist welfare states. Many Western nations launched and brought to maturity combinations of such programs as national health insurance offering basic coverage to all citizens, broad systems of child or family allowances, general old-age pensions, systems of unemployment insurance, and perhaps job training and public employment, covering most wage and salary workers. In the United States, too, liberal reformers within and around the Democratic presidential administrations of Franklin Delano Roosevelt and Harry S Truman battled for these sorts of protections for all citizens or wage earners. For a time it looked as if these American reformers might succeed. The severity of America's economic crisis during the 1930s, coupled with intense expert and public fears about the possible reemergence of mass unemployment after World War II, for a time gave impetus to policy planning for governmentally guaranteed full employment. Certainly, the focus of U.S. social policy debates during the 1930s and 1940s was as much or more on the problems of working-aged men and their families as it was on issues of security for the elderly.

By the time the dust had settled in the 1950s, however, the United States was left with only one relatively universal social program—Social Security's contributory insurance program, structured to protect retired lifelong wage earners and their dependents. Other attempts to institutionalize broad social programs were defeated in the United States. During the 1940s, coalitions of Republicans and southern Democrats dismantled the New Deal's public employment programs, brushed aside proposals for national standards of public assistance, reversed the temporary nationalization of unemployment insurance that occurred during World War II, gutted proposals for governmentally guaranteed full employment, and—last but not least—defeated President Truman's effort to enact national health insurance. The postwar United States was not to have universal social provision, except for retired elderly wage earners.

To be sure, gaps in social protection were temporarily filled for many younger Americans by the GI bill of 1944 and other federal veterans' legislation. Generous educational, health, and mortgage-assistance benefits were guaranteed for privileged cohorts, the veterans and survivors of the many American soldiers who served during World War II and the Korean War. Hardy postwar economic expansion, coupled with the age-cohort–specific social investments promoted by veterans' programs, ensured the "rising fortunes" of many young American adults after the war.[10] Especially well-served were those working- and middle-class whites who entered the labor force, married, and raised children from the late 1940s into the 1960s.

During this same period the Social Security system "matured," incorporating virtually all regular wage and salary earners into its umbrella of disability and retirement protections. Postwar workers enjoyed the promise of a secure retirement following after the upward mobility and economic well-being that many had enjoyed in the U.S. political economy of their prime adulthood years. During childhood, the offspring of these postwar parents also benefited from the security jointly promoted by economic and legislative conditions.

During the 1960s and early 1970s, another series of policy changes happened in the United States, ironically further strengthening the already relatively most generous parts of postwar U.S. social provision. In the aftermath of the Civil Rights revolution, and amidst the economic prosperity of the 1960s, liberal Democrats launched the War on Poverty and the Great Society. The avowed aims were to extend U.S. social benefits and training opportunities to the many poor people and children, including African-Americans, who had not been fully incorporated into the economic growth or social insurance protections of the postwar era. But again, when the dust settled, social programs for the elderly were the biggest winners—by default as well as design.

Certain means-tested benefit programs for the very poor were instituted or expanded in the 1960s and 1970s—programs such as job training, Head Start, Aid to Families with Dependent Children, Food Stamps, and Medicaid. Yet the broadest and costliest new benefit pro-

[10] Katherine S. Newman, *Declining Fortunes: The Withering of the American Dream* (New York: Basic Books, 1993).

grams were Medicare health insurance for the elderly, enacted in 1965, and the indexing of Social Security pensions to inflation, which occurred in 1972. The Social Security Administration and other advocates for the elderly took advantage of the reform ferment of the War on Poverty period to institute long-planned extensions of universal provision for the elderly. Elderly people had crowded the ranks of the poor prior to these reforms of the 1960s and early 1970s.

Since then, Social Security became—and has remained—the nation's most effective antipoverty program, responsible for lifting most elders above the official poverty income level. Middle-class retired wage and salary earners, current and prospective, were also beneficiaries, because Social Security payments are partially pegged to the levels of wages previously earned. As Jill Quadagno explains,

> the 1972 amendments represented a turning point for Social Security, a watershed for U.S. welfare state development. The automatic cost-of-living increases removed benefits from politics and ensured older people that inflation would not erode the value of those benefits. . . . The 1972 amendments . . . solidly incorporated the middle class into the welfare state.[11]

The political staying power of Social Security as a relatively generous and universal social insurance program was vividly demonstrated in the increasingly conservative political era that followed after the Great Society watershed. As essays elsewhere in this volume have detailed, targeted programs for the poor were politically vulnerable after the 1960s. Many middle- and working-class Americans, especially whites, responded to the race riots of the late 1960s and the sobering economic circumstances of the 1970s by turning sour on federal social programs and giving their votes to conservative politicians who promised to cut taxes and trim welfare spending.[12]

In 1980, a very conservative Republican, Ronald Reagan, was elected president, and he immediately set out to enact steep cuts in taxes and federal domestic spending. Perhaps not surprisingly, Reagan and his advisors had more success in persuading Congress to cut taxes than spending. The stage was set for burgeoning federal budget deficits that would, henceforth, make it very difficult to launch costly new federal programs. Reagan and his conservative congressional supporters managed to reduce the rate of growth of means-tested spending. But Social Security enjoyed too much support from middle-class citizens and congressional representatives of both parties to be vulnerable to Reagan's re-

---

[11] Quadagno, "Generational Equity," pp. 355–56.
[12] Thomas Byrne Edsall and Mary D. Edsall, *Chain Reaction: The Impact of Race, Rights, and Taxes on American Politics* (New York: W. W. Norton, 1991).

trenchment politics. The United States emerged from "the Reagan era" with its Social Security benefits still universally structured, and still comparably generous to social programs for the elderly in other nations.

We can understand the generational critiques now being offered by groups such as the Children's Defense Fund and the Concord Coalition in relation to the earlier historical developments just surveyed. New arguments about generational equity make sense given inherited imbalances in U.S. social provision—imbalances more obvious now that the effects of the GI bill have faded into the past, making more apparent than ever the absence of social programs for families in the middle of the age and class structure. Political successes and failures from the 1960s to the 1980s also reverberate through current generational critiques. Although rhetoric has changed, today's progressives and conservatives are carrying on old battles in new terms.

Recall that Marian Wright Edelman launched the Children's Defense Fund between 1968 and 1973 as a Civil Rights activist fresh from the struggles for desegregation and African-American rights in Mississippi, that toughest of Deep South battlegrounds. Obviously Edelman was dismayed as the exhilarating political openings for liberals of the 1960s gave way to racial backlash and increasing conservatism. This happened just as she was establishing herself as a progressive policy researcher and agitator in Washington, D.C. She has made no secret of why she decided to establish a nonprofit research and advocacy organization focusing on children. As she explained in her 1987 book, *Families in Peril: An Agenda for Social Change*:

> CDF came into being in the early 1970s because we recognized that support for whatever was labeled black and poor was shrinking and that new ways had to be found to articulate and respond to the continuing problems of poverty and race, ways that appealed to the self-interest as well as the conscience of the American people.[13]

In addition to talking about a wide array of children's problems, the Children's Defense Fund now features research and policy advocacy about young families, discussing the declining incomes of many young parents.[14] In this way, the CDF tries to move out from its children's focus to discuss the absence of adequate U.S. socioeconomic supports

---

[13] Marian Wright Edelman, *Families in Peril: An Agenda for Social Change* (Cambridge, Mass.: Harvard University Press, 1987), p. ix.

[14] See, e.g., Clifford M. Johnson, Andrew M. Sum, and James D. Weill, *Vanishing Dreams: The Growing Economic Plight of America's Young Families* (Washington, D.C.: Children's Defense Fund, 1988).

for working-aged adults as well as children. Never do Edelman and the CDF directly engage in zero-sum politics by criticizing generous social provision for America's elderly. Mostly, the CDF simply says nothing at all about Social Security, making no comment on its expensive universality. But occasional mentions hint at a mild equity critique: "We moved more than 1.7 million elderly persons out of poverty in the three years following the 1972 revisions to the Social Security Act that indexed senior citizens' benefits to inflation. Surely we can provide families with children equitable treatment."[15] The implication here, of course, is not that less should be done for the elderly; rather that more should be done through government to support working-aged families and their children.

Like Marian Edelman and the CDF, Peter Peterson and the Concord Coalition are also revisiting old battlefields with new tactics, and devising new ways to reach out to the "missing middle" of U.S. social politics—working-aged adults—understood by them as taxpayers rather than as potential beneficiaries of new social programs.

Peterson's *Facing Up* starts with his disarming acknowledgment that he has been a lifelong Republican, but within a few pages he launches into a scathing critique of Ronald Reagan and his policies of the 1980s. Along with other fiscal conservatives and moderate Republicans, Peterson fears the huge federal budget deficits that President Reagan's initiatives helped to create. In this view, Reagan is to be faulted for cutting federal taxes without accomplishing commensurate cuts in the largest domestic social spending programs—especially such "middle-class entitlements" as Social Security, Medicare, veterans' pensions, and mortgage subsidies. For Peterson, the 1972 amendments to Social Security were equally abhorrent. He argues that they put the entire American middle class "on the dole." The elderly in Peterson's portrayal are selfishly robbing their children and grandchildren, and the American Association of Retired Persons is presented as the biggest and most sinister "special interest group" in U.S. politics.[16]

Peterson and the Concord Coalition are taking a new approach to achieving a long-standing objective of U.S. conservatives—making sure that federal social spending is kept to a minimum and is means-tested, targeted only on the most needy. Conservatives understand well that marginal social programs for the poor also are not very politically popular; it is easier to keep them from expanding in a democratic polity. Back in the formative years of the Social Security system, Peterson's

---

[15] Marian Wright Edelman, *The Measure of Our Success: A Letter to My Children and Yours* (Boston, Mass.: Beacon Press, 1992), pp. 85–86.
[16] Peterson, *Facing Up*, p. 82.

conservative forerunners waged a losing struggle to abolish universal social insurance in favor of marginal public spending on the very poor elderly alone.[17] During the presidency of Ronald Reagan, conservatives again became hopeful that "middle-class entitlements" would be restructured. But after briefly raising the possibility of such reforms, President Reagan and his Budget Director, David Stockman, quickly retreated from middle-class programs, and concentrated most of their rhetorical and budgetary fire on means-tested social spending for the poor. Now Peterson and his fiscal conservative allies are taking a quite different approach to what they see as the problem of overly generous federal spending. Instead of appealing to middle-class hostility against blacks and welfare clients, Peterson and the Concord Coalition are appealing to middle-class anxieties and idealism about the national future, and to the interests of working-aged adults as taxpayers.

Leaders of the Concord Coalition are trying to reduce middle-class public support for the Social Security system by arguing that it is really just a set of heavy taxes on working-aged adults to support many non-needy elderly people. Besides, it is suggested, the system is bound to go bankrupt before today's middle-class workers can collect anything, so why should they support it? Concord Coalition critics also argue that if Social Security is cut back into a less expensive means-tested program, money will be saved for programs helping the "truly needy," for federal deficit reduction, and for enhanced private investments that will cause the economy to grow faster. Peterson all but promises that, if only Social Security and other social programs inclusive of the middle class are removed, most middle-class people will be net beneficiaries because renewed national economic growth will create new opportunities for job mobility and private income growth. Like the "supply-side" economists who surrounded President Reagan, the Concord Coalition projects a wonderful future if only the domestic functions of the federal government can be further chopped back in the United States.

POLITICAL POSSIBILITIES FOR THE FUTURE

What is likely to happen to U.S. social policies as America enters the twenty-first century? Will the arguments of the Concord Coalition prevail? Or those of the Children's Defense Fund? Are other strategies possible? Of course the future is now in the making, through public debates and political conflicts whose outcomes are indeterminate. But we can briefly explore some of the alternative possibilities.

[17] Jerry Cates, *Insuring Inequality: Administrative Leadership in Social Security, 1935–54* (Ann Arbor, Mich.: University of Michigan Press, 1983), chap. 3.

Peter Peterson and the Concord Coalition have so far had remarkable success in influencing agendas of public debate. The future viability of federal social spending has been called into question, and universal social programs rendered economically and morally problematic. The greatest successes have been achieved at the level of elite public opinion. Since the mid-1980s, Peterson and others with similar views have published opinion-pieces in such visible and prestigious publications as *The Atlantic Monthly*, *The New York Review of Books*, and *The New Republic*.[18] Moreover, as a condition for winning the last few congressional votes needed to pass federal budget legislation in the summer of 1993, President Bill Clinton promised to set up a "Bipartisan Commission on Entitlement and Tax Reform" charged with making legislative recommendations to the President and Congress. Under the leadership of Senators J. Robert Kerry (Democrat of Nebraska) and Senator John C. Danforth (Republican of Missouri), the Commission started functioning during the spring of 1994. Peter Peterson was appointed to serve on the Commission, and its opening agenda drew heavily from the arguments he made in *Facing Up*.

The campaign now being waged by the Concord Coalition to shape mainstream citizen opinion is more challenging than efforts to influence the ideas of businessmen, politicians, and highbrow editors. All the same, the Coalition enjoys a number of advantages in the political circumstances of the 1990s. Its mass mailings urge citizens to call on President Clinton and congressional representatives to overcome gridlock, to set aside "special interests," and to responsibly address the national interest through balancing the budget by the year 2000. These urgings resonate with arguments made by Ross Perot and his tens of thousands of supporters. They appeal to an American public thoroughly fed up with elected federal officials and skeptical that the federal government can do anything well. Established political parties enjoy few capacities to influence citizen opinion. Thus, much of the initiative in shaping national political debates goes by default to apparently bipartisan groups with resources to use mass mailings and gain access to the media. The Concord Coalition is a preeminent and well-funded example of this sort of opinion-molding politics.

The Concord Coalition's criticisms of universal entitlements are gaining currency just at many adult middle-income and lower-middle-in-

[18] For examples, see: Phillip Longman, "Justice Between Generations," *Atlantic Monthly* (June 1985); Neil Howe and Phillip Longman, "The Next New Deal," *The Atlantic* 269(4) (April 1992): 88–99; Henry Fairlie, "Talkin' Bout My Generation," *The New Republic* (March 28, 1988); id., "An Exchange on Social Security," *The New Republic* (May 18, 1987): 20–23; and Peter G. Peterson, "Entitlement Reform: The Way to Eliminate the Deficit," *The New York Review of Books* (April 7, 1994): 39–47.

come workers do, in fact, feel hard-pressed by the large payroll taxes that are collected for Social Security. The attempt to extend a top-down antitax alliance from attacks on welfare to fundamental restructuring of social insurance for the elderly has its best hope of success if mid-career workers can be persuaded that they have little stake, or else only a negative stake, in the Social Security system—in short, if they see themselves as Peter Peterson portrays them, primarily as burdened taxpayers rather than as beneficiaries.

Still, there are likely to be severe limits to the popularity and legislative viability of the Concord Coalition's message. The huge and resourceful American Association of Retired Persons is not the only probable opponent. Most Americans feel that they have built up a stake in the retirement insurance system, and will profoundly resent politicians who go back on what is popularly understood as a sacred social contract. In addition, mid-career, middle-income working Americans often have elderly parents, in whose economic security, indeed comfort and independence, they have a considerable stake. At one point in *Facing Up*, Peterson argues that the United States needs a new entitlement system that "will encourage us to save more for the future, care more for our children and parents. . . ."[19] How many middle-class women, already overwhelmed with the burdens of combining wage-work and child-rearing, will be enticed by the notion that they should also take added responsibility for their aging parents?

Interestingly, Peterson's book presents a profoundly patriarchal image of how the economy and families work. He lauds his Greek-immigrant father for running a 24-hour-a-day, 365-day-a-year restaurant, while hardly ever appearing at home. Peterson's mother is hardly mentioned, except as someone who lived out her elderly years on income from rental properties bought by the father's savings.[20] Whatever one may think of this portrayal of Peterson's parental family, its gender and economic realities are far indeed from those of the middle-income Americans of today that the Concord Coalition is attempting to mobilize.

As the 1994 Bipartisan Commission gives greater political visibility to the ideas of the Concord Coalition, they are likely to be scrutinized by skeptical experts as well as politically opposed groups. The economic disadvantages of Peter Peterson's ideas will be probed. Would sudden cuts in federal spending really propel national economic growth? What would be the effects on labor markets and wage rates? For example, Peterson recommends delays and cuts in elderly pension benefits that he

[19] Peterson, *Facing Up*, p. 114.
[20] Ibid., p. 52.

agrees would have the effect of forcing more and more elderly people into full- or part-time employment. Yet this would happen even as more and more American wives and mothers need jobs, and even as the federal and state governments are pushing welfare clients into low-wage labor markets. Meanwhile, the U.S. private economy is generating fewer jobs with incomes adequate to sustain either one-parent or two-parent families.[21] Ironically, steep cutbacks in retirement benefits could actually backfire on younger working parents and their children—by creating more competition for jobs and further lowering private wages and fringe benefits that are already under downward pressure.

If the Concord Coalition faces difficulties, what about progressive advocates for "the children of America"? Here, too, the picture is mixed. The Children's Defense Fund has discovered that it can gain considerable hearing from middle-class and business interests as it frames issues of race and poverty in terms of the "need to invest" in American children. But one can wonder how successful the CDF will be in broadening citizen support for social policies that would address the socioeconomic dilemmas of large numbers of working parents. Current CDF publications raise these broader family issues, but there are real limits in what the CDF has, or could, do about them. The CDF has taken only a few steps so far toward reaching out to grass-roots groups of ordinary Americans.

The CDF is *not* a national membership group with direct ties to large numbers of citizens. It does not directly mobilize the parents; rather it speaks "on behalf of" children. It is a Washington, D.C.–based, staffled advocacy organization, very much built around the morally vivid personality of Marian Wright Edelman herself. As a winner of many honorary degrees, a recruit to many boards, and speaker at many functions, Edelman certainly has the attention of U.S. opinion leaders. The CDF has its greatest leverage with liberal congressional representatives and their staffs, and of course with people in the Clinton administration, a number of whom (including First Lady Hillary Rodham Clinton) have been CDF Board members. The CDF also has a real presence with social service professionals and volunteer children's advocates from across the land; two to three thousand of these people attend CDF national conventions each year.

In line with the kinds of influence it is organizationally able to muster, the CDF and its like-minded allies can be credited with concrete legislative victories in the areas of children's health and public funding

---

[21] Sheldon Danziger and Peter Gottschalk, eds., *Uneven Tides: Rising Inequality in America* (New York: Russell Sage Foundation, 1993); and Bureau of the Census, U.S. Department of Commerce, "The Earnings Ladder: Who's at the Bottom? Who's at the Top?" (Statistical Brief SB/94-3) (Washington, D.C.: Government Printing Office, 1994).

for child care services. CDF victories have preserved or incrementally expanded Great Society–era social service programs such as Head Start and Medicaid. Despite the urgency—and often downright grandiosity—of its moral rhetoric, the CDF hews closely to specific legislative agendas inherited from Great Society liberalism, or to the incremental agendas proposed by Democrats in national office.

When it comes to envisioning a fundamental restructuring of U.S. social policies, the Concord Coalition has been much more ambitious than the Children's Defense Fund. The CDF may have achieved more concrete legislative successes (it has been at work much longer). But the Concord Coalition may be doing more to influence Americans' sense of what is problematic and possible in social and economic policymaking for the future. If so, then the Concord Coalition may be morally more successful, despite the undoubted greater ethical legitimacy of an anti-poverty children's crusader such as Marian Wright Edelman.

Let me close by becoming a frank advocate for a certain value position. The limits of progressive children's advocacy as a political strategy underscore the "opening" that still remains in modern American social politics for a broader and democratically rooted approach to issues of family security. According to pollster Celinda Lake, "people are worried that kids' programs are really a cover for a welfare program. While there is some sympathy for welfare kids, there's a lot more sympathy for children's programs when people think they are broad-based."[22] Other pollsters report that Americans want to feel they can do something themselves, in partnership with government, and not just give revenues to existing social programs, monies which many fear will never make their way to children.[23] From the evidence as well as the evidence of history, I conclude that a viable progressive approach to "Family Security" could be devised along the lines that I outlined in chapter 8, at the end of my essay on "Targeting within Universalism" in U.S. social policy.

This strategy for revamping U.S. social provision would extend broad protections from the elderly to working-aged parents as well as their children. The aim would be to bring together new cross-class coalitions focused on social policies to support work and responsible parenthood, rather than emphasizing redistribution only toward the poor—or toward children discussed apart from their parents. A Family Security strategy addresses concerns about generational equity by finding ways

---

[22] As quoted in Paul Taylor, "Plight of Children: Seen but Unheeded: Even Madison Avenue Has Trouble Selling Public on Aiding Poor Youth," *The Washington Post* (July 15, 1991), p. A4.

[23] Ibid.

to do more for people "in the middle," working parents in single- and two-parent households. Among the specific social programs needed are some sort of universal health insurance; employment training and re-training open to American workers at all levels of the employment structure; and policies to support the incomes of single parents and low-income workers. Some of the policy ideas touted by the Concord Coali-tion—particularly reforms in the tax system to help low-income citi-zens—could be incorporated into a progressive Family Security program. And of course many ideas could come from the program of the Chil-dren's Defense Fund.

Yet politically as well as programmatically, the focus should be on involving middle-income working parents more fully in a fair system of contributions and social protections. National taxes and social spending should invest in working families, not just the elderly and social services for children. And a real effort should be made to encourage local educa-tional programs and family-support centers that are run in part by, as well as for, all families in the community.[24]

President Bill Clinton has made some attempts to move in the direc-tion I am advocating. Proposals for universal health insurance, welfare reform, employment training, and tax benefits for working families all express the values of work and responsible parenthood. Such Clinton proposals aim to heal divisions within the Democratic Party that sepa-rate working people from the poor. Clinton administration initiatives aim to extent the universal social protections inherited from the New Deal, extending Social Security rather than repudiating it, as American conservatives remain determined to do.

Certainly, Bill Clinton's presidency has had a very difficult time polit-ically. Some of the reasons have nothing to do with social policy. The President's call for universalism in health care reform, and his touting of work rather than open-ended welfare payments, have been very popu-lar. Yet President Clinton's difficulties in getting even popular social policy ideas through Congress underline that progressives are bound to have a hard time working within the institutions and circumstances of U.S. politics at the close of the twentieth century. As a moderate Demo-crat committed to revitalizing government's capacity to deal with na-tional economic and social problems, Bill Clinton was elected with only a plurality of the popular and electoral vote. He heads (if that is the right word) a Democratic Party that has little unity and hardly any capacity for grass-roots political mobilization. His presidency has had

---

[24] Good ideas along this line appear in Penelope Leach, *Children First: What Our Society Must Do—and Is Not Doing—For Our Children Today* (New York: Alfred A. Knopf, 1994).

to contend with the rock-hard realities of a huge, inherited federal budget deficit in an era when most elected politicians are unwilling to discuss taxes and the public distrusts government and politicians.

In this situation, President Clinton has understandably had a very difficult time in revamping U.S. social policies to offer more support for working families—especially for those "in the middle" between rich and poor. He has, nevertheless, done a good job of highlighting the importance of moving in this direction. Whether or not Clinton loses ground in Congress after 1994, and whether or not he is reelected in 1996, he has already pointed the way toward a promising agenda for U.S. progressive politics and social policy at the dawn of the new century.

In the name of the broadly shared values of work and parental responsibility, all Americans can be asked to contribute as workers, caregivers, and taxpayers. In return, the nation can afford to offer a modicum of economic security and social support to all families, not just in retirement, but throughout their active years of employment and the rearing of "our children." A vision of Family Security along these lines is the only progressive vision that has any chance of social effectiveness and political viability in the foreseeable future.

Index